THE ANNALS OF KENDAL • CORNELIUS NICH

CW0f432734

General Books LLC™, Memphis, USA, 2012.

❧ ❧ ❧ ❧ ❧ ❧ ❧ ❧

PREFACE TO THE SECOND EDITION.

"A Work without a preface (says Sir Francis Drake) would look like a house to which the architect had made no entrance." So that, if I now make a few prefatory observations, and reprint, also, the preface to the first edition, I shall have two entrances to my house; one, connected with the original building, raised thirty years ago, and another (the *posticula),* which is part of the new structure. It sometimes happens (to carry on Drake's simile), when a house is partially pulled down, to be altered and enlarged, that the superadditions mar the unity of the order of architecture, and deform the general appearance. I can only hope that I have avoided this evil, and trust that the edifice will do no dishonour to the town, which abides in my affections, and demands from me every effort and consideration.

Many of the chapters have been rewritten; many facts, previously overlooked, have now been incorporated; and recent events have been recorded, down to the present date. I found, on reflection, several matters, as they appeared in the first edition, susceptible of amendment. I felt especially dissatisfied with the Memoir of John Gotjgh, who was unquestionably one of the most extraordinary men that Kendal, or the North of England, has produced; but my friend, Mr Thomas Gough, has removed this cause of dissatisfaction, and has Drought me and my readers together under obligation by contributing the Biographical Memoir of his father, which will be found in this volume. I am further indebted to him for the classified lists of the productions in Natural History. It is doubly grateful to my feelings to acknowledge these contributions, because, though our pursuits have not always been kindred, Mr. Gough and I laboured long and agreeably together in fields of profitable study.

I scarcely know how, adequately, to acknowledge the valuable assistance received, whilst these pages were passing through the press, from Mr. Alderman John Fisher, and my brother-in-law, Mr. John Hudson. The inscriptions on the Monuments in the Church; the list of Tradesmen's Tokens; and the table of Chronological Events, owe their general accuracy and completeness to the great care bestowed on them by these gentlemen; to the former of whom I am also indebted for reference to several occurrences hitherto unrecorded.

The Meteorological Tables, constructed from observations by Mr. Marshall, will be duly estimated by inquirers in this branch of study. It will be difficult to find another instance of recorded *data,* extending over fifty consecutive years, in this interesting yet infant Science.

Other facts and particulars have been cheerfully supplied by kind friends, who will be content to be included in this general acknowledgment.

An explanation may be required to justify the appearance of the Frontispiece. I should not obtrude on my readers "a counterfeit presentment" of myself, if I had not received from a group of old friends, in Kendal, a complimentaryrequisition, urging that "a portrait of the Author would add to the interest with which the hook would he received;" and desiring, that they might present the portrait and engraving, for the purpose. I was variously associated with the gentlemen alluded to, for twenty years, or more, in the promotion of public works and public institutions, and that circumstance may be regarded as giving value to their proposal. Those who will summon to the mind, feelings, associated with the most active period of their lives, will not misinterpret such an incident. PREFACE

C. N.

Wellfield, Muswell Hill, London, *July,* 1881.

TO THE FIKST EDITION.

The law of custom, says Turner, exacts a preface. It is usually the author's apology for his composition. My apology has, however, been already made and published. I refer to the opinion which so generally prevailed, that a historical account of Kendal was a desideratum, and to the anxiety which has long been manifested for the appearance of such a work. It seems indeed astonishing, that no effort towards a history of Kendal has hitherto been made, and that, in the course of so many years, while the interest was acknowledged with which a topographical description of the town would be welcomed, no one could be found to bring forward the earlier and more estimable records of its history, before time had gathered round them the mantle of obscurity. The origin and infant state of Kendal are, and it may be feared, ever will be, involved in almost impenetrable darkness. There appears only just light enough to show that it possesses the highest claims to commemoration. The site of a station, founded and commanded by the Romans "conquerors of the world;" a town of Saxon institution; the spiritual matron of so many churches, scattered throughout an extensive deanery, over the whole of which, at the introduction of Christianity, she singly diffused "the day-spring from on high;" the seat and capital of a feudal barony of considerable power; the birth-place of royalty; the parent of one of those staple manufactures which eventually contributed to exalt this nation to preeminence. All these, it will hardly be denied, are objects of high interest to the antiquary and the historian; and their importance, as materials of real history, will be found to be fully evinced, although imperfectly elucidated, in the following pages. The facts and incidents, here noted, are, at least, based on genuine records; and I prefer rather to leave them subject to the charge of incoherence, than attempt to fill up by conjectures, vacuities which have been occasioned by the lapse of time.

There is one important feature of this work which I deeply regret should be so imperfectly delineated. I mean that of Kendal Castle. But it has been the singular calamity of that ancient edifice to be almost entirely neglected by all antiquaries and topographers. Speed makes a single, simple allusion to it. Camden contented himself with saying, "The Castle, over against the town, is ready to drop down with age;" and neither of his learned Editors, who, in most instances, added materially to his descriptions, has, in this case, added a single observation. Grose has altogether overlooked it. Lysons did not extend his survey to Westmorland, and has therefore treated the castle at Kendal in the same manner as the other castles in the county. And Dr. Whitaker, who, of all writers, was most eminently qualified to do justice to an illustration of it, came, unfortunately, too late for the search. So that we have no records of its history, except the few fragmentary documents which have been found in the mention of the families by whom it was occupied in the later period of its glory.

Much, undoubtedly, has been lost of the history of Kendal. But I am proud to hope, that (however ill digested the matter may be) I have had access to nearly all that can be available in the present day. It would be very ungrateful not to confess that I have been favoured with many kind and valuable auxiliaries. I have enjoyed the cheering influence of a generous and general encouragement. The first and highest degree of obligation I owe to the Rev. John Hudson, A. M. the Vicar, whose zeal for the success of the work would admit no effort to be withheld calculated to promote it, and whose contributions towards the history of the Church, attach a real value to the chapter dedicated to that subject. The next degree of favour and assistance which I received, was from the late John Thomson, Esq., who offered for my use his manuscripts relating to some of the antiquities of the town. To Mr. Thomas Gough I am obliged for the Catalogue of Plants; and to many kind friends for much valuable information, and for the loan of books—favours which, from their number and diversity, I am thus constrained to embrace in a general acknowledgment. From a con-sideration of these sendees I have, throughout the volume, adopted the use of the plural pronoun. It seems unnecessary to say how much I am indebted to historical books, because, in all instances, to the best of my knowledge, where I have quoted from them, an acknowledgment is made, either by inverted commas in the context, or by references in the notes.

It is improbable, if not impossible, that a work like the present, comprehending treatises on so many different subjects, should be interesting to all; or should be altogether interesting even to any one reader. Such multiform collections must be perused with different feelings, tastes, and sentiments. But I hope that my readers will be candid enough to reflect, that those parts which may seem very unimportant to them, may, perhaps, be the only points of interest to others. Again, I would solicit some lenity, from the consideration that, however easy it may be for one person to discover faults or omissions in what relates to his own studies, it is not so easy for the ordinary faculties of one person to apprehend and illustrate, with accuracy, so many different subjects. This consideration, and the fact that I coidd only apply myself to the performance during those hours which are usually devoted to relaxation and rest, may, I hope, be accepted as an apology for the imperfections with which the work may be chargeable.

It was my original intention to devote one chapter to the manners and customs, obsolete and extant, of the inhabitants. But the quantity of matter on other topics, which, since the announcement of the work presented itself, and the limits of the book, which had been prematurely fixed, conspired to exclude all observations on that subject. I have been constrained, also, from the same necessity, to abridge most of the Biographical Sketches, and other essays in the latter pages of the volume.

C. N.

KIRKBARROW, KENDAL, *April,* 1832.

THE ANNALS OF KENDAL CHAPTER I. GENERAL HISTORY.

To convey a clear and connected outline

of provincial history, from the earliest times, is a task nearly if not quite impossible. The reason of this must be apparent to every one who considers, that for so many centuries the whole land was overspread with the ravages of war, and that most of the relics of topography must have been buried in the general ruin. In a work like this, all that can be done is to collect from the elements of general history the scattered materials of topography; and the reader must be content if, in searching through dark and distant ages, he can catch here and there a glimpse of the deeds of his ancestors, and the scenes which have occurred in or about the place of his nativity. The convulsions of a civilized state usually compose a most interesting part of its history; but the revolutions incident to a barbarous condition are of such a nature that it may be considered fortunate for Letters they are consigned to silence and oblivion. Neglecting, therefore, all tradition, and those fables which are commonly employed to supply the place of history, we shall first briefly consider the state of the inhabitants as it appeared to the Romans on the invasion of this country.

The "aborigines," as Caesar calls the then inhabitants of Britain, were a tribe of the Gauls, who emigrated from the banks of the Eyder and the Elbe, in Germany, and settled in this island five centuries antecedent to the Christian era. The probable conjecture, as Caesar intimates, is, that the interior pnits of Britain, to the north and west, and consequently Westmorland, were peopled by the earliest inhabitants; and the southern parts by those who crossed over from Belgium, in Gaul, for the purpose of invading this island,—all of whom had their names from the tribes they sprang from, Angles, Jutes, and Saxons. A thorough admixture or amalgamation of the Danish and Scandinavian race with the Angles and Saxons had taken effect in the *north* of England, so that Bishop Nicholson, alluding to this admixture, says, "Our borderers to this day speak a leash of languages— (British, Saxon, and Danish) in one; and 'tis hard to determine which of those three nations has

the greatest share in the motley breed." It is indeed hard to say whether, in the Westmorland dialect, and in the names of natural objects about Kendal, more words belong to the Scandinavian dialects than to the Saxon tongue.

The habitations of the ancient Britons were hovels, made of the trunks of trees, rooted in the earth, and interwoven with branches. In these they sheltered during the hours of repose, and by day departed into the fields, or into the forests, for the purpose of hunting. They were divided into many small nations, or tribes; and their governments, although monarchical, were free. Being indeed a military people whose sole property was their arms and their cattle, it was not possible for their princes or chieftains ever to establish a despotic authority over them.

It may not be uninteresting to insert here the description of the Britons, in the northern part of the island, as given by Dion Cassius. "They never cultivate the land; but live on prey, hunting, and the fruits of trees; for they never touch fish, of which they have such prodigious plenty. They live in tents, naked, and without shoes. They fight in chariots, having small fleet horses. They have also infantry, who can run very swiftly, and while they stand are very firm.
Hence the designation "Anglo-Saxon." Letter to Sir W. Dugdale, in Camden's "Britannia" (Gibson's first edit.), p. 81. 'Diodorus Siculue, lib. iv.

Their arms are a shield and a short spear, on the lower part of which is a bell of brass, to terrify the enemy by its sound. They likewise wear daggers. They are accustomed to brave hunger, cold, and all kinds of toil; for they will continue several days up to their chins in water, and bear hunger many days. In the woods they live on bark, and roots of trees. They prepare a certain kind of food for all occasions,—a piece of which, the size of a bean, prevents their feeling hunger or thirst."

Such were the ancient Britons, when Caesar, in his thirst for universal empire, in the year 55 before the Christian era, turned his attention to these shores. After a spirited resistance on the part

of the inhabitants, he landed, as it is supposed, near to Deal; and having obtained advantages, and obliged them to promise hostages for their future obedience, he was constrained by the necessity of his own affairs, and the approach of winter, to withdraw his forces into Gaul. The next summer he landed with a greater force; and though he found a more regular resistance on the part of the Britons, he discomfited them in every action. He advanced into the country; passed the Thames; took, and burnt the capital of Cassivellaunus, one of the petty Princes; and having obliged the inhabitants to make him new submissions, returned with his army into Gaul, and left the authority of the Romans—a mere name and shadow—in the island.

After this, the Britons, during almost a century, enjoyed their liberty unmolested. For it was not till the year 44 after Christ, that the Romans, in the reign of Claudius, began to think seriously of reducing this island. They sent over an army under the command of Aulus Plautius, who gained some victories, and made considerable progress in subduing the inhabitants. He was succeeded by Ostorius Scapula, by whom the southern part of the island was reduced to a province. The Emperor Claudius himself made a journey into Britain, and after a visit to *Camelodunum* (now Colchester) where he received the submission of several British states, he returned to Rome with the title of "Brittanicus."

Suetonius was the successor of Ostorius, in the reign of Nero, and in the 61st year after Christ. He first directed his attention towards *Moma* as is meant in Tacitus, the Isle of Anglesea: the chief seat of the Druids. But though he succeeded in cutting down the groves, and placing garrisons in the towns, he found that the Britons had taken advantage of his ahsence, and were all in arms under Boadicea, Queen of the Iceni. They reduced London to ashes; put the Romans, and all strangers there, without distinction, to the number of 70,000, to the sword; and seemed determined to cut off all prospect of peace, or compromise with the enemy. The military discipline of the Romans, however, at length prevailed, and in a great and decisive battle, fought on the confines of Epping Forest, they defeated the warrior Queen, who, rather than fall into the hands of an enraged victor, put an end to her life by poison. In this battle 80,000 of the Britons are said to have perished.

After an interval, Cerealis received the command from Vespasian; and by his bravery greatly extended the terror of the Roman arms. Julius Frontinus succeeded Cerealis, both in authority and reputation; but the general who finally established the dominion of the Romans in tins island was Julius Agricola, who governed it under the title of Propraetor, in the reigns of Vespasian, Titus, and Domitian.

This great commander formed a regular plan for subduing the island, and rendering the acquisition useful to the contpierors. He carried his victorious arms northwards; and here we have the first mention of the part of the country connected with our present history. According to Ptolemy, the inhabitants of the country between the lofty ridge which now separates Yorkshire from Lancashire and the Bay of Morecambe, were called *Setantii*, or *Segantii;* which district, on the second invasion of the Romans, was included in the more extensive province of the "*Brigantes*"— extending, on the east side, from the Humber to the Tyne, and on the west, from the Mersey to the Eden, and comprehending the five counties of Yorkshire, Durham, Cumberland, Westmorland, and Lancashire. This being the most powerful and populous nation in Britain, during the Roman sway, is most distinguished and celebrated in all the best records of history.

The *Mona* of "Caesar2' is the Isle of Man.

Tacitus informs us, that Agricola "struck a panic into the state of the Brigantes, which was accounted the most numerous of the whole country, by attacking them with great force; and after several, and some of them bloody battles, he reduced great part of Britain by victory, or involved it in war." When

he had alarmed the native inhabitants by his severity, he offered inducements to peace by his clemency. By this conduct many of the states, and amongst the rest the Brigantes, which till then had stood out, gave hostages, and submitted to have a line of garrisons and castles drawn round them. This was the origin of our Roman stations. Cattle being, as we before said, the riches of the ancient Britons, it was their practice to keep their flocks upon the uncultivated grounds which skirted the borders of their respective kingdoms. These were called *"cheangon" "cangii,"* or "*cangani;"* which term *cheangon* signifies "retainers from their condition." Baxter affirms that the Cangii were not a distinct nation, seated in one particular place, but such of the different nations as were employed in pasturage, in feeding the flocks and herds of their respective tribes. "This," he adds, "is the reason that vestiges of their name are to be found in so many different parts of Britain; but cbiefly in those parts which are most fit for pasturage." The inhabitants of this place, therefore, were the *Setantian Cangii,* forming a part of the kingdom of Setantii, who, possessed a portion of Lancashire and the southern part of Westmorland—probably about the same which afterwards formed the Barony of Kendal. The northern part of this county was annexed to Cumberland, and formed the state of the Volant ii. The river now called the *Kent* was anciently written " *Can"* and continued so till after the time of Camden.

ROMAN ROADS AND STATIONS.

The Roman roads and chain of camps by which this country was held in subjection are traced on the following diagram. We are not able in this place to do more than give a general Mr. Whitaker's 'History of Manchester." description of the routes, north, south, and east, from the station at Kendal.

Going northwards or rather *north-west,* the road leaves the station at the *ford* across the Kent helow the foot of Mill Lane, from thence it proceeds hy Stane Bank Green and Boundary Bank to Cunswick Scar and *Raderheath,* thence to Dan Hill and Restane. About High

Restane the road hi-forked, and became two roads, one going by a Borrens Raderheath: 'Ruidra,' the road over the hill.

Danes Hill, where the Danes may have had a Damp, or fought a battle. which lies near the line of Railway, across the *Troutbeck,* over a ford at Troutbeck Bridge, and to the head of Windermere, where the station "Dictis" stood. Here was placed a company of Nervian soldiers—" Prefectus numeri Nerviorum Dictensium Dicti." From *Dictis* the road went up the *caasa* (causeway, in polite phraseology) by Ambleside, forded the Stockgill above the Salutation stables, at Hollicar Ford *(Holy Cairn* ford), mounted the hill by Hollicar Lane and Seathwaite; again recrossed the Stockgill near High Groves, and winding out of the valley by *Woundale* into the head of the vale of *Troutbeck,* where it passed over "the Tongue" and up the steep of High Street and Froswic by a path which still bears its original name of "Scot-raik." The other road from Kendal starting at the junction aforesaid, near High Restane, proceeds by another *Borrens* good lights in a blind road are these names to Ravenscarth,—originally *Rafen-sccer*—along the edge of Hill Bel (ii Baal), and Froswic, to High Street. At the shoulder of High Street, the two roads from Kendal and Ambleside unite, and thence the road proceeds over the table-land of High Street (where we laid bare the Roman pavement in two or three places, a foot beneath the turf that now covers it); along the ridge of Riggendale (Higgendun) and down by Martindale, skirting for some distance, the river Eamont, to *"Brocavum"* Brougham.

Going northwards, from Kendal to Borough Bridge, traces of the road, actual and nominal, are nearly all lost. But there is an undoubted Roman name in Whinfell, viz. *"Borrens,"* which draws our attention in that direction. We incline to the opinion that the road went by the Spital, Laverock Bridge, Mealbank, and Patton *(Path-en,* plural in Saxon "paths," or *Padden,* Teut. "to tread "), to Borrens aforesaid; thence along what is marked as a bridle road in

Hodgson's map of Westmorland, over Whinfell common, and the Hause, to Borough Bridge. From the station "Alaunae," at Borough Bridge, to Kirkby Thor, the road proceeded by Castle How, at Tebay, over Orton Fell, down by Wicker Street (where there are traces of a British town), past Crosby Rafenswath, by Borrens and Caster-rig in King's Meaburn, and across the Eden to the Station "Galacum" at Kirkby Thor. Galacum and Brocavum were united by a road which the present turn-pike road mainly occupies for the whole distance.

Southward, from the Kendal station, the road seems to have gone by Low Barrows Green, and Stainton, (Staneton); there it bifurcated, one branch proceeding by way of Kirkby Lonsdale to Lower Casterton, where it would join the straight road between Borough Bridge and Overborough; the other branch proceeding from Hincaster by *Borwic* (Burgh-wic), where traces of docks were found, and Carnforth (Cairn-ford) to *Longovicum* at Lancaster. The name *Warton*, which is near the line of route, suggests the idea of a battle in that locality. At all events names are our best guides in the absence of actual remains of roads, and for these we have explored the country in vain between Kendal and Lancaster. Many persons may, within their own recollection, recall instances of a country road diverted, and after less than twenty years found the abandoned foundation past all recognition. Why, then, should we wonder at the general oblivion of Roman roads after a lapse of fifteen hundred years? The wonder rather is that any traces of such works are still extant.

We must next endeavour to describe the station itself, and its general arrangements: CONCANGIUM.

This Roman Station stands somewhat more than a mile south of the town. The situation of the camp is held to be decisive evidence of its having been designed by *Agricola*. "When the genius and experience of *Agricola* marked out the line of stations through the country of the western Brigantes, he planted them along the banks of considerable rivers which empty themselves into the *Mare Vergivium,* but in general above the points at which those streams cease to be navigable." The place where Concangium stands is called "Water Crook," from the remarkable bend, or bends, in the river at that spot. It is three miles, or so, above the highest History of Richtnondshire, vol. ii. p. 212.

point at which the Kent could he navigahle, even in the Roman era, when the stream was prohably greater than it now is; for one can hardly imagine the Roman galleys, like salmon, successfully surmounting the *catoditpm* below Force Bridge. The lines of circumvallation are now but faintly marked, so that persons have gone over the ground without recognising them. This, however, will not occur to an antiquary acquainted with Roman castrametation. On the east side, the agger is well defined up to its original angles, and it still maintains a considerable elevation above the outlying ground, as well as the area within. The site of the *pretorian* gateway, which is on this, the east side, is shown by a depression in the agger. The ramparts on the opposite side, (the *decumana),* are much obliterated. Repeated overflowings of the river have washed away the fosse at the north-west angle, and the agriculturist appears to have assisted the river at the south-west angle, so that between those two agencies the ditch and rampart on the western side are dislocated, and.nearly destroyed. The rampart seems to have been constructed entirely of earth without any parapet of wall, for there are no traces of mural foundations, and there are few sandstones, such as were used by the Romans, to be found in any of the farm buildings. This fosse would therefore become an easy prey to the swollen stream, and to the levelling hand of the husbandman. The situation is peculiarly advantageous. If the whole valley of the Kent be sought, no other spot can be found where an encampment could derive such protection from the river. It washes the north side in a parallel line, the west side on a curve, and the north side also by a devious line. Such a tongue of land is not unusual at the con-

fluence of two rivers, (and the Roman architect, under Agricola, appears to have been directed to those situations); but, as far as we know, no other instance can be found of one current flowing in its natural course along three sides of a Roman station. This probably accounts for the absence of those strong walls of defence such as were deemed necessary at "Alaunaa," Borough Bridge, and many other stations. Another circumstance, again, enabled the Roman commander here to dispense with extraordinary field works, viz., the thorough watch and ward which the soldiers had who were planted at the *rnons exploratorium* on Helme. The *Vigila:* on Helme stood facing the pretorian gateway of the station, and commanded, likewise, the approaches on every side, so that any surprise of the garrison seems to have been almost impossible. The station is a parallelogram of unequal sides, measuring 500 feet from east to west, and 380 feet from north to south. It ranks in importance, as a *Castrum Siativum,* and being on the usual plan, the following drawing will represent the design and general arrangements for lodging the troops within:

According to the "Notitia," the soldiers stationed here were a company, or companies, of watchmen. The entry stands thus: *Frafectus numeri vigilum Concangios.* If we are entitled to infer, with the author of "The Roman Antiquities," from Caesar and Suetonius, that a *Prafect* uniformly commanded auxiliary troops, as a *Tribune* commanded legionaries, these watchmen in that case belonged to the *allies* of Rome, and were probably Gauls. What number were here, is left to conjecture. By the absence of the word *cohortis,* which is frequently used in connexion with stations of secondary magnitude, it may be fairly supposed that the garrison here comprised more than one cohort. *Numeri* expresses no particular number. Pliny considers that it signified strictly the muster-roll. By the usual reckoning, a cohort (480 men) required only 21,000 square feet for garrison accommodation, and the area of this station comprised 160,000 square feet, so that fully half a legion of soldiers could be accommodated, besides ample provision for baggage, tents, and camp followers.

What other works and buildings were originally at Water Crook, cannot now be told. Horsley visited the place, and observes, "the *town,* I believe, has chiefly stood between the fort and the river on the west (south south-west) side, for here they still plough up cement and stones." And Dr. Whitaker remarks that "the *city* has contained about fourteen acres." There is no such space as fourteen acres "between the fort and the river on the west side." Both statements, therefore, as to "town" and "city" must be taken with reserve, in the absence of all traces of foundations and of domestic utensils. Horsley states that Mr. Guy, then living here, possessed some Roman coins and seals, and a medal of Faustina; but these are all lost, and no other relics have since been discovered, excepting a hypocaust, some urns, and the pottery works hereafter mentioned.

The hypocaust was noticed by Machell, on a personal visit, and was found, he says, "Underground, being built with bricks or tiles on the inside, fixed one into another, run over with cement half-a-foot thick; and the bottom paved with bricks one foot broad, and three inches thick. In these ruins, too, were reservoirs for water, made with cement, and a semicircular course of vacuities, like ovens, divided by thin bricks."

Some Urns were discovered in the year 1813, under the left bank of the river, where the stream takes another sweep, *south* of the marble mills (opposite to the mills). The river, by its tortuous course, forms a second tongue of land at this spot, and on one part thereof stands a conspicuous knoll, called *Sattury,* of pyramidal shape. When the first edition See *Excreitus,* in Smith's " Greek and Roman Antiquities," p. 500. About the beginning of the eighteenth century.
of this Book went to press, in 1832, the knoll was crowned with a tree; but, in the meantime, this sylvan ornament

has fallen, either to the winds or the woodman's axe. Why the name of *Sattury,* which tradition has so long preserved, was given to it, is uncertain. Mr. West (the historian of Furness) suggests that some altar may have stood there dedicated to Saturn. We incline to the opinion that this plot of ground —from Sattury to the river—was a tumulus, or general burial ground, for the garrison. It would be close by the road from the Station southward, and a sufficient (about the usual) distance from the encampment. The Romans never intermingled the dead with the living. This supposition is supported by the discovery of the Urns before-mentioned at the tip of this tongue of land. One of these Urns was 15 inches deep, and 10 inches in diameter, and contained human ashes; but unfortunately it was broken to pieces in being taken out of the earth. Another Urn 8£ inches deep, and 6 inches diameter at the swell, is still in good preservation, in the care of our friend George Webster, Esq., of Eller How, who, fortunately possessing archaeological tastes, was mainly instrumental in the discovery of these sepulchral remains. The following is a representation of the Urn at Eller How:
It contained human ashes, calcined; together with some iron and charcoal. The presence of iron is singular.

The pottery works (probably the same that Machell alludes to) were discovered about the same time as the Urns just mentioned, but in a very different locality. These were opposite to the Camp, across the river, just at the foot of "Mill Lane," by the edge of the brook before it joins the Kent. There were the remains of a kiln, and several pieces of (new-made?) brick. We lately examined some of these, and caused one (an angle brick) to be deposited in the Museum. It seems to carry evidence, in its structure, of being composed of a loamy alluvium, such as may be seen by the margin of the brook at the spot, having little resemblance to the compact bricks made of pottery clay. Close to the kiln was a pit, with some human skeletons thrown loosely and slovenly into it, covered with the *dibrii* of the kiln. Intelli-

gent persons who examined the skeletons suppose that they had been hastily buried there after the Roman pottery fell into disuse; otherwise, they argue, the bones must have been calcined by their proximity to the kiln. The argument might be carried a point farther; for the human skeletons would have mouldered away before the lapse of fifteen hundred years.

The following descriptions of the Monuments and Altars are from Horsley:— 1. A monument of two freedmen of Publius Bassus inscribed,

Publiiis. Aelius. Publii filius Sergia *(tribu)* Bassus quaestor designntus legionis vicessimie

Valentia victricis vixit annos et

Publius Rivatun liberti et Hero mile legioms sextce vietricia faciendum curarunt

Siquis *in hoc* sepulerum alium mortuum iutulerit inferet fisco. dominorum noatrorum

"This monument, I think, has been erected *by* the care or order of two freedmen of Publius Bassus (one of whose names is lost with a part of the stone), and by a soldier in the sixth legion, part of whose name is also broken off; what remains looks like *Heron,* a name which occurs in another inscription in our collection. (Cumberland, No. LII.) The latter part of the inscription I believe has contained a penalty against any who should presume to deposit another dead person in this sepulchre; obliging them to pay a fine into the Emperor's exchequer. The last line, which is imperfect, should express the fine." 2. "A remarkable altar without inscription. It has a festoon with clusters of grapes above it, on each side, which made me suspect it might be erected to *Bacchiis:* 3. "A small altar within the house. The word *dew* is sufficiently clear and distinct: from which I thought of *Bern Nymphs* with reference to the river. But from a character partly resembling an *m* which follows it, (DEEV) Mr. Ward thinks it is rather for *Minerva. 4.* "A description of Urn, which I found lying in the kitchen garden. It is exactly of the same size and shape with that in Mr. Gilpin's collection at Scaleby. Mr. G.'s is said to have had a cover to it, but I did not hear of any such thing belonging to this at Water Crook. (Vide *Horsley,* fig. XI. p. 192.) 5. "An imperfect statue, designed very probably either for *Silenus* or *Bacchus.* If for the latter, as I rather think, it confirms my conjecture that the altar (2,) was consecrated to this deity. The *corolla* (of which he has given a draught), was, in the memory of an aged person yet living, placed upon the head of the image, though it is now by some unhappy accident broken off, and the rest of the image lost:"—

We conceive both this statue and the altar with festoons of grapes (previously figured in the woodcut and on the frontispiece), belong to *Bacchus,* whose British name was *Heus* or *Ilu,* and his surname *Cadarn,* which last word means "mighty." *Hu, the mighty,* was a popular Deity with the Cymry or Cumry,. whence comes Cumry-land, or Cumberland.

The Monument, Altar, and Statue, figured here, are now placed in the Museum, at Kendal, having been presented by Mr. C. Wilson, the owner of the Water Crook estate.

It remains only to say a few words respecting the name of this Station, and the probable time of its foundation.

With regard to the name, as it is a *Notitia* Station, excluded from Antoninus' Itineraries, there are none of the evidences of sequence and distances, in relation to other Stations, to help its identity. But all reputed Antiquaries concur in holding it to be *Concangium,* excepting, perhaps, Dr. Gale, who for some unexplained reason places *Brovanacis* at Kendal. Camden, at one time, had some doubts about it, but *Gough,* his last editor, speaks decidedly in favour of Concangium. *Stvkeley* and *Ilorsley* were also both of this opinion, and Dr. Whitaker, adding his powerful testimony, fortifies the conclusion. If argument were wanting, there is something in the etymology of the name, which it is surprising none of those learned writers should have noticed. The original name of the river Kent was *Can,* as the old name of the county of Kent is *Cantium. Con* and *Can* are duplicates, signifying "head," or "principal," and the *Cangii* were doubtless the chief pastoral tribe inhabiting the district between the Kentmere hills and the estuary of Morecambe. The name Concangium, then, was given in honour both of the aboriginal inhabitants and the river, to win favour with the people brought under subjection. Such, at least, is in strict accordance with the general policy of Agricola.

With regard to the date or foundation of this Station, it is not possible to define it nearer than to say, that it lies probably between the years A.D. 80 and 90. As Agricola marched northward by the valley of the Lune, in A.D. 79, and continued his operations in Cumberland and Scotland till the year 84, he would have to encounter the Brigantes in their strongholds, lying between the Solway, through the western districts of Cumberland, the shores of Windermere, and the valley of the Kent down to Morecambe Bay, on his return to head-quarters at Chester. That was doubtless the period of the foundation of *Concangium.* By that time the prowess of the Roman levies was known to the native Britons. They had not only swept the Brigantes before them in their upward march, but had driven the Caledonian Picts and Scots headlong to the Grampians, routing the armies of *Oolgacus,* till then held to be invincible. On the other hand, the Brigantes in this neighbourhood were not without their advantages, and might oppose considerable resistance to the invaders. They might, for instance, be strongly posted on *Potter Fell,* on *Cunswick Scar,* on *Castle How Hill* (supposing that to be British), on the *Castle Hill,* and on *Helme.* The conflict, therefore, may have been arduous and prolonged, and we have a right to infer that the Roman commander was not too sure of holding his conquest, by the circumstance of laying hold of the aid of the river in so remarkable a manner, for the protection of his garrison. How long the station remained in the occupation of the Romans may be left to the cogitation of the reader. The situation was warm, sheltered by the hills on the north and north-east; the lands about it were fertile for grain or pasturage; and there seems to be no reason why the Romans. should have departed from Concangium and Castlesteads, till they took their final leave of Britain, in the middle of the fifth century.

Above this station, and nearer to the town, is a place called "Watch Field;" the ancient name of which has evidently been "Wath-Field" or "Ford-Field." For, in the grant to the Church, made by Gilbert, Cth Baron of Kendal, mention is made of "Wath-slack," in tracing the boundaries from Stainbank Green,—" *usque ad viam de Helsington;"* and according to the authority of some persons now living, there is still a public way from the Helsington Road, and a ford across the river, at this very place. Another confirmation of this matter is to be found in the practice of the Romans, who never carried their roads over bridges (unless the rivers were impassable), but by fords. To these fords they paid the strictest attention, and accordingly we always find, at no great distance from them, mounds of earth, thrown up for exploratory stations. Nor can there be mueh doubt but the mound of Dr Burn seems to have adopted the commonly-received name of Watch Field, and assigned it as a Watch to the station without much consideration or research.

C earth in the Vicar Fields has been made for the purpose of watching this ford across the Kent. A similar mound is found at Halton, near Lancaster, where there has been, and still is, a ford across the Lune.

CASTLESTEADS.

About a mile and a half from *Concangium,* on the summit of a high hill called Helm, was the *castrum exploratorium* called *Castle-steads.* It has been a rectangular fort 60 feet by 120, and had two ditches on the south, three on the north, and, on the other sides, was defended by precipices. There is no doubt but this was the exploratory fort in connexion with the station at Water Crook. It is in sight of the beacon on Warton Crag, which communicates with Lancaster. The engraving will afford a better idea of the form of the castrum than can be given by the pen.

In 1806, a gold coin, or medal, of Vespasian was found within the chapelry of Natland, in a lineal direction from Concangium to this castrum exploratorium. It was found some distance below the surface of the earth; and as no remains of works have been discovered between the two Helm is the original of Helmet, a Saxon word, and signifies the crest or apex. There is a round-topped hill in Grasmero called Helm.

Castle-steads, or Castle-steeds, says Richard Gough, is the common name given to the castella on the wall of Hadrian. There were two forts near Corbridge, in Northumberland, called *CostU-ttetdn.— Vide* "Camden's Britannia," p 235. stations, it seems probable that it bad been scattered by one of the soldiers in passing from one place to the other. This coin was purchased by the late Mr. Emanuel Burton, of Kendal, but is now lost. CONEYBEDS.

Another exploratory fort, or encampment, called Coneybeds, is situated on Hay Fell, on the east side of Kendal, in the field immediately above the house called High Park, belonging to Wm. Wilson, Esq. It is nearly on the summit of the hill, and overlooks the vale of Kendal. Before the inclosure in 1814, its vallum and fosse were very perfect, inclosing a bell-shaped area, the upper end of which was 128 feet in breadth, its sides 208, and the southern end, which was semi-circular, 224 feet in diameter. About half "Coneybeds" is thought to signify *high graves.* way down the area, and on its eastern side, were two interior entrenchments, having a sort of bending street between them, and each of them having the southern end semi-circular. The less of the two which adjoined the east vallum was 42 feet on the north, 70 on the east and west sides, and 70 across the south. The other was 64 feet on the east and west sides, and 80 on the north, and across the south. Both of them had pits unequally dispersed (as is represented in the engraving), all of which, except the central one, which was round, were of irregular shape. The remaining part of the great area was

smooth. This encampment overlooked the fort on Helm, and commanded a view of several hills in Lancashire, Cumberland, Westmorland and Yorkshire; of the estuary of the Kent; and, in clear weather, extended even to the mountains above Beaumaris, in Wales. This station was trenched after the inclosure, but nothing was discovered to lead to its history. From its form it must have been made in the latter period of the Roman empire; and probably was a place of temporary retreat for the garrison at Water Crook.

In the time of the plague which desolated the kingdom in 1597-8, provisions were brought to this spot by the country people, and deposited for the inhabitants of Kendal, which was their only intercourse during that destructive period, when, according to the following inscription from a stone in the Church of Penrith, 2,500 of the inhabitants of Kendal were swept away:—

A. D. 1598, *ex gravi peiti qvice regianibus hiece incubuit*
obierunt apud Penrith 2260, Kendal 2500, Richmond
2200, Carlisle 1160. *Poiteri avortite vos el invite.*

CASTLE HOW HILL.

On the western side of the town, on a rocky hill, opposite the Castle, and about the same altitude, is a circular mount of gravel and earth, about 30 feet high from the plane on the top of the rock. The crown of the mount is flat, and has been defended by a breast-work of earth and a narrow ditch. There has also been a ditch diametrically through it, from east to west. Round its base is a deep fosse and high dike, strengthened with two bastions on the east. The whole circumference of the crown is about sixty paces. Dr. Stukeley, in his *"Itinerary?'* calls it Saxon. Horsley observes, that it is very like the exploratory mounts which are to be found in other places near the military ways. But whether it is Roman, and relates to the station at Water Crook, or more modern still, he does not take upon him to determine. If it be reasonable to conclude that it is Roman, this, and the hill opposite, on which the Castle stands, were no

doubt exploratory mounts to guard the Roman way. This hypothesis receives strength from the circumstance of a Roman coin of Marcus Aurelius, which is still preserved in Hutton's Museum, at Keswick, having been, it is said, found within the walls of the Castle. Some persons, however, are of opinion, that the name should be Castle *Law* Hill, and believe that it has been made by the Barons of Kendal. or by one of the Saxon chiefs.

In 1788, being the centenary of the revolution, the inhabitants of Kendal erected, in memory of that event, a stately pillar, or obelisk, on the crown of the mole, bearing the following inscription:— Sacred to Liberty.
This Obelisk waa erected in the year 1788.
In memory of the Revolution in 1688.

In reference to the obelisk, we cannot do better than quote the glowing and nervous language of Mrs. Radcliffe, from her "Tour," in 1795:—" On one of the brows that tower over the town, stands a testimony to the independence of the inhabitants,—an obelisk, dedicated to liberty and to the memory of the Revolution in 1688. At a time when the memory of that Revolution is reviled, and the praises of liberty itself endeavoured to be suppressed by the artifice of imputing to it the crimes of anarchy, it was impossible (alluding to her own patriotic feelings) to omit any act of veneration to the blessings of this event. Being thus led to ascend the hill, we had a view of the country over which it presides: a scene, simple, great and free, as the spirit revered amidst it!"

"Immediately below Castle How Hill (says Pennant) is a spot called *battle-place!'* Why it was so called he has not informed us. We can find no such place now by that name.

GENERAL HISTORY, CONTINUED.

We must now again recur to matters of general history. In the course of the second century the insurrections and inroads of the northern hordes had made such havoc in this territory, that the Emperor Severus repaired to Britain, and established his court at York (Eboracum), the capital of the Brigantes. Advancing from York with a powerful army, he drove the Caledonians within their frontiers, and erected a stone wall within the vallum of Adrian, and very nearly upon the site of that celebrated northern rampart. The loss of the Romans in this expedition was, according to Dion Cassius, 50,000 men, partly by war, and partly by cutting down and draining the mosses. There were eighteen stations on the line of Adrian's wall.

About the year 446-8 the Romans finally abandoned this country; and Britain, now deprived both of the Roman soldiers, and of the flower of her youth, who passed over with them, became an easy prey to the northern invaders, who now appear under the names of Picts and Scots, two powerful and distinct and ferocious tribes, acting in confederacy. War was their sole pursuit, and slaughter their chief delight. They broke through Severus's wall, though fortified and well supplied with the munitions of war; and it is further affirmed sacked and burnt all the towns in the north of England. In this deplorable situation, the inhabitants invited over the Saxons; and thus, with a view to protect themselves against an evil which was apparent, they fell upon another which they had not contemplated. The Saxons peopled several provinces in Germany: one of which, and that which now more especially sent out its inhabitants into Britain, was called *Anglia,* or England, as the venerable Bede and other historians have related. Hence Sir Walter Scott, in his "History of Scotland," says, the *Picts* were so oalled from their habit of staining or painting their bodies; and that they were descendants of the ancient British Caledonians. The *Scots, "* to the great confusion of ancient history," were of Irish origin, who established themselves on the coast of Argyloshire.

"History of Manchester." this country was afterwards, by King Egbert, denominated *England*

The Saxons having driven the Picts and Scots within their own borders, and taken possession of the principal cities, they sent for a further supply of troops from the shores of the German ocean, and evinced a determination to take possession of the country. After numerous battles, fought with various success, the renowned Arthur, animated by the wrongs of the Britons, took the title of King, and became the leader of their wars. In tracing his victories, although we find no mention of Concangium, yet we can discover that he must have passed through Kendal; for the first of his battles was fought at the mouth of a river not far from Chester; the second, third, fourth, and fifth upon another river, called the Douglas, in Lancashire; the sixth upon a river which is called *the Bassos;* and the seventh in " Sylva Caledonis," subsequently called "Inglewood Forest," in Cumberland The river *Bassos* is therefore some river between the Douglas and Inglewood Forest; and we find no river at all similar in name directly upon this line of march except the *Beetha.* The principal branch of this river is called "Pisa" or " Pesa," on which, by that name, the learned historian of Manchester has fixed the sixth victory of Arthur; and it is far from improbable that formerly it retained this name to its junction with the estuary. How far up the stream it bears now the name of Betha, or Beela, we have not been able to ascertain. Hodgson, in his excellent Map of Westmorland, calls it by no other appellation to its source. This river runs by the village of Beetham, in this county; and that Beetham has been the place of a battle appears to be confirmed by the great number of human bones which are found in digging in almost every part in and about the village. It is indeed to be regretted that further search for relics was not made when some of the modern houses were erected, on the south side of the stream, where the bones are chiefly found The Saxons being here again defeated, formed at last in " Sylva Caledonis," or Inglewood Forest, 1 In the *Teutonic* language, *eng* signifies "narrow," or "strait;" therefore *England* seems to describe a neck of land!— *Vide "*Restitution of Decayed Intelligence in Antiquities." whither the Britons, under command of Arthur, pursued and attacked them. In this battle nearly the whole army of the Anglo-Saxons wao cut to pieces.

Within thirteen years, however, of the death of Arthur, the Saxon conquests had so far advanced, that the whole of England was considered as subdued, and was erected into seven sovereign states, under the name of the *Heptarchy.* This part of the country, which during the Roman period had taken its name from the Brigantes, was changed by the Saxons to that of "Northumbria," or Northumberland, the territory to the north of the Humber.

Egbert, having reduced the Saxon heptarchy into a monarchy, and called it England, divided his acquisitions into several portions or shares; and after the preservation of peace, set over each of them a *Comes* to rule them; whence each portion was denominated "comitatus:" a scyre or county—that is to say, "an earldome." So that the kingdom of Northumbria was divided into divers scyres or provinces: 1. The province on the east, from the river Humber to the river Tees, he styled Euryckshire, or Yorkshire.

2. From the Tees to the river Tyne, he called Durohmshyre; being the province of the Bishopric of Durham. 3. From the Tyne to the river Tweed, Northumbria, or the shire of Northumberland. 4. On the west side of the river Solway to the river Duddon, he called Carliershire or Cumberland. 5. The part on the west of Durham and Lancashire, he called Applebyschyre or Westmorland. 6. From the river Duddon to the river Mersey on the south, he called Lancasterschyre.

"Through the whole of the Saxon period," says Turner, "the kingdom of Northumbria was the most perturbed. Usurper murdering usuiper was the pervading incident; and scarcely had the sword of the assassin been cleansed from its horrid pollution, before its point was turned upon its master, and he was carried to the sepulchre which he had just closed upon another." In the ancient Saxon Chronicle, we are told, "History of the Anglo8Saxous," vol. ii. p. 110.

"This year (A. D. 966), Thored, the

son of Gunner, plundered Westmorland. " And again. A.D. 1000: "This year the King Ethelred went into Cumberland, and nearly laid waste the whole of it with his army." We may be assured that the country about Kendal shared largely in the ravages of these unsettled times.

Scarcely had the shout of the victory gained by Harold over the Norwegians, at Fulford, near York, been heard across the island from the Humber to the Mersey, when intelligence was received of the landing of William of Normandy, afterwards called the Conqueror. The English army, under Harold, met the army of the invaders near Hastings, and after a sanguinary battle, which continued through the day (Oct. 14, 1066), William joined in the final conflict, secured the victory, and with it the crown of England.

No sooner was the Norman Conqueror seated on the throne of England than he began to exercise the power of conquest, using his giant's strength with the "tyranny of a giant." To guard against a surprise he caused numerous castles to be erected in the north of England. He placed all the land in the kingdom under the system of feudal tenure, which had been partially introduced under.the Saxon dynasty. These possessions, with very few exceptions, besides the royal demesnes, were divided into baronies, with the reservation of stated services and payments, and were conferred on the most considerable of the Normans. These barons, who held of the Crown, shared out a large portion of their lands to other foreigners, who bore the name of knights or vassals, and who paid their lord the same duty and submission in peace which they themselves owed to their sovereign. The whole kingdom contained about 700 chief tenants, and 60,215 knights' fees. And as none2 of the English were admitted into the first rank, the few who retained their landed possessions were glad to be received under the protection of some powerful Norman baron, though at the cost of an oppressive burden on Ins estate.

If the reader of this book would form for himself any conjecture as to the pop-ulation of Kendal at this time, he must bear in mind that the whole population of England, at the Norman Conquest, is estimated, by the best authorities, at not more than a million and a half or two millions of inhabitants.

The turbulent state of the country, in the succeeding reigns, served so to increase the Norman castles, that, by the latter end of the reign of Stephen, there were the almost incredible number of 1,115 castles in England. Every baron, or leader of a party, had his castle, wherein it is generally supposed he exercised unfeeling tyranny over his vassals, for Matthew Paris styles them " very nests of devils." The barons held their grants on condition that they should perform *castleguard* with a certain number of men. In process of time, these services were commuted for annual rents, sometimes styled *ward penny* and *wayt-fee* but most commonly " castleguard rents," payable at fixed days, under heavy penalties, called *sursises.* The general military tenure of this county was by homage, fealty, and cornage, which last seems to have been peculiar to the border service, or knight service. Cornage was early converted into a pecuniary payment, and *whiterent* was the lord's rent paid in *silver.* There was also another tenure, called *drengage,* peculiar to these parts, which Dr. Bum proves to have been the most servile of all tenures; for by it the tenants were held in "pure villenage," and as common drudges—were bound to the lord as members of the manor, and usually sold with the farm to which they belonged. THE BAEONY.

In tracing the Barony of Kendal, we find the first baron to have been Ivo De Talebois, otherwise Taillebois, otherwise Talboys, of the House of Anjou, who came over with the Conqueror, and who, in virtue of his marriage with Lucy, sister of the two Saxon earls, Edwin and Morcar, seconded by the favour of the Prince, obtained a large portion of the north of Lancashire, and so much of Westmorland as still goes under the designation of the Barony of Kendal. William, the great grandson of Ivo de Talebois, caused him Blount's "Law Dic-tionary." 'Gough's "Additions to Camden."

"History of Westmoreland," p. 21. self to be called "William, de Lancaster, and Baron of Kendal," before the King in Parliament.

In the Kerden's MSS. preserved in the Library at Manchester, the descents of the family are thus given:— 1. John de Talebois= Lucia 5. William de Lancaster 2nd I I

Helwiise_6. Gilbert

T 7. William de Lancaster 3rd.

The Castle at Lancaster, which was built by Roger de Poictou, not only served as a military fortress, but was used also as the baronial residence; and it is very probable that the title of "de Lancaster" was assumed by the 4th Baron, and continued to the 7th, on account of the Barons of Kendal residing sometimes at that place and sometimes at Kendal. Tins, we say, is very probable, because it will appear, in tracing the history of the residents at Kendal castle (through the monuments in the Church), that we cannot go further back than to Helwise, eldest sister and co-heiress of William de Lancaster 3rd. Nor does it appear that the title "de Lancaster" was ever revived in this barony after the Castle of Lancaster was conferred upon Edmund Crouchback, by King Henry III.

From that time the castle at Kendal became the constant residence of the eldest branch of the baronial family, till it at length lapsed to the Crown.

In the time of Gilbert, the sixth baron, the Scots, under This William de Lancaster, by will, bequeathed his body to be buried in the quire of Furnesa Abbey, near to the tomb of his grandfather, William de Lancaster 2nd. And as William de Lancaster 1st was a great benefactor to this Abbey, it is very probable that he also was buried there.

Duncan, Earl of Fife, entered and plundered the town of Kendal, broke open the church, and put all the inhabitants to the sword, sparing neither age nor sex. From that time the inhabitants of these parts may be considered to have been wholly engaged in the border service.

In the time of Robert de Ross, of Kendal Castle, this town must again have been subject to depredations. In the 21st Edward I. Robert de Clifford, Lord of Westmorland (from whom the office and title of high sheriff of the county descended to the Earls of Thanet), was made Keeper or Warden of the Marches, in the north towards Scotland, and in the year 1298 was summoned to attend with his horse and arms at Carlisle. This Robert de Clifford was slain at the battle of Bannockbum, near Stirling, on Sunday, June 24, 1314, when Edward II. commanded in person against the renowned Robert the Bruce. After the defeat which the English sustained in this engagement, the Scots overran the whole north of England, down into Yorkshire, partly from revenge, and partly from a desire of plunder. After which the English borderers rallied again, and made reprisals on the territories of the Scots. We may form no incorrect idea of the merciless havoc committed in these incursions from the borderer's ejaculation in the " Lay of the Last Minstrel:"—

"They burn9d my little lonely tower: It had not been burn'd *for a year or more."*

The Kendal men are very honourably mentioned in a poem descriptive of the battle of "Flodden Field," which is reckoned to possess many historical truths:—

"The left hand wing, with all his route, The lusty Lord Dacres' did lead; With him the bows of Kendal stout With milke-white coats and crosses red. "
»
» «
"There are the bows of Kentdale bold, Who fierce will fight and never flee." Holinshead's " Chronicles," p. 91. Of Dacre Castle, near Penrith.
It seema not improbable that "White Hall" (originally, perhaps, *White Cloth Hall)* has taken its name from the manufacture of this "milk-white cloth.9'
This battle was fought in the 5th Henry VIII. commanded by the Earl of Surrey, on the part of England, against the Scot-

tish King, James IV., in person. The signal victory obtained on this occasion by the English has been attributed by historians chiefly to their "unrivalled skill in the use of the long bow." The corpse of James IV. was found among the slain, pierced with two arrows. Such was the admitted superiority of the English in archery, that the Scotch held it as a proverb that " each archer bore at his belt the lives of twentyfour Scots:" that being the number of arrows with which he was usually supplied.

The following extract from a letter addressed by the Earl of Surrey to Cardinal Wolsey, and dated at Berwick, 27th Sept., 1523, shows a valorous achievement of the Kendal men:

"The next day I sente my said Lord Dacre to a stronghold called *Fernherst,* the lord whereof was his mortal enemy, and with him Sir Arthur Darcey, Sir Marmaduke Constable, with 700 of their men, one cartoute, and dyvers other good peces of ordynaunce for the field. The said Fernherst stode marvellous openly within a greate wood. The said two knights with the moste parte of their men, and Strickland, your grace's servante, with 300 Kendal men, wente into the wood on fote with th' ordynaunce where the said Kendal men were so handled that they proved *hardy men* that *went noo foote back* for theym! And fynally, with long skirmishing and moche difficulty, the house was threwn downe; and above 30 Scottish slayne, and not passing four English men, but above sixty hurt."

Sir Thomas (afterwards Lord) Wharton, of Westmorland, became eminent and high in trust with the King (Henry VIII.), as a most active and vigilant Warden of the Marches. He first signalised himself when deputy Warden of the Marches under Lord Scroop, in the memorable rencontre at Sollom Moss, of which there is scarce a parallel in history. In the 34th Henry VIII. Sir Thomas Wharton called to his aid (by letter of proclamation) the gentlemen and their followers Sir W. Scott's " History of Scotland." within the bounds of the West Marches, subject to the border service, whose numbers show the propor-

tionable value of their respective estates. At that time, among others, were mustered by *Walter Strickland,* of Sizergh, 200 horse, *Sir John Lowther,* 100 horse and 40 foot, *Sir James Leyburne,* of Cunswick, 20 horse, *The son of Sir Jeffrey Middleton,* of Middleton Hall, 20 horse.
Anthony Ducket, of Grayrigg, 20 horse, *Thomas Sanford,* of Askham, 80 horse and 20 foot, *Lancelot Lancaster,* of Barton, 20 horse and 20 foot.
Some idea of the achievements they performed in this kind of warfare may be formed by the following extract from Haine's "State Papers;" the total amount whereof, in one inroad or *forray,* from the 2d July to the 17th November in the same year (1544), is thus computed:—

Towns, towers, stedes, parish churches, &c. cast down and burned 192
Scots slain 403
Prisoners taken 816
Nolt (i.e. horned cattle) taken 10,386
Sheep 12,492
Nags and geldings 1,296
Goats 200
Balls of Corn 890
Insight *(i.e.* household furniture) not reckoned.

The great proportion of archers which Westmorland supplied for the Border Wars is ascertained by an abstract of the musters of horsemen and footmen within Westmorland and Cumberland, taken in September and October, 1584. It appears from this, that of a total, for both counties, amounting to 8,350 men, Westmorland furnished 4,142— of whom 1,400 were "archers furnished," and 1,300 "billmen furnished." Every person from sixteen to sixty years of age was liable to be called at a moment's warning, by proclamation of the Lord Warden of the Marches. In a Commission issued by Queen Elizabeth, to inquire into the Lands, tenements, &c. of the Barony of Kendal, which her Majesty took of the Dowager Marchioness of Northampton in lieu of other lands, it is found, "that the tenants of this barony, from the age of sixteen to sixty, had always been accustomed, and still owe to be, at all times, in their most defensible array, for the wars, ready to serve their prince, on horseback and on foot, at the borders, &c., *on their own proper cost* and charges, being warned thereto by beacon, fire, post or proclamation, and there so to continue during the Lord Warden's pleasure." The beacon hills of Westmorland were Stainmore, Orton Scar, Whinfell, Farlton Knot, and Hardknot. Burn's "History of Westmoreland." CHAPTER II.

ECCLESIASTICAL HISTORY.

In tracing the progress of religion, through the ages already mentioned, it will be our object to compress as much as possible the abundant matter which presents itself, and to select only so much as may appear to form a suitable preface to our account of the Church.

When the Romans invaded this island, they found that the religion of the Druids formed one of the most considerable parts of its government. This appears to have been a most extensive species of superstition. Besides the power which it placed in the hands of the priest, to inflict severe penalties in this life, it is thought to have inculcated the doctrine of the transmigration of souls: and how effectually such a doctrine would tend to render the extent of its authority commensurate with the fears of its votaries, it is quite unnecessary for us to say. In fact, no instance occurs in history where superior knowledge ever attained such an ascendant over ignorance and credulity as is recorded of the Druidical worship of the Gauls and Britons. The chief seat of the Druids was in the isle of Anglesea; and against this place Suetonius Paulinus determined to direct his main operations. The scene of his attack is described, by Tacitus, as one of utter despair. The Roman soldiers, at first struck motionless with the sight of the Druids, at length rushed forward, bearing down all before them, and involving a promiscuous mass of men and women in their own fires. Many fled before the advancing Romans, and took refuge in these northern parts. Hutchinson has an hypothesis, which is very probable, that the fort of Maybrough, or Mayberie, near Penrith, was a temple of the Druids, and that it was fortified by them

to check the pursuit of the Roman armies. There were some circles situate on Potter Fell, near Kendal, which had the appearance of being draidical; and if so, they may with propriety be traced to the same period. They were situated half way up the fell, on a flat plain, which affords the singular advantage of overlooking, without being observed, the whole valley, southwards; fortified in front by a steep sloping breast-work, and backed by a precipice, which rises immediately in the rear. This place might afford both the security of a fortress, and the opportunity of an observatory. About a mile below, at a place called Low Groves, tradition has placed another druidical altar, but of this altar no traces are at present to be found. Low Groves may mean 'wood' or 'graves;' and Potter Feld (Danish) might be "*the Potters Field,* to bury strangers in." *(St. Matthew* xxviL 7.)

So superstitiously attached were the inhabitants of Britain to this species of idolatrous worship, that the Romans, unable to reconcile them to their own laws and institutions, were at last obliged to abolish it by penal statutes; a violence which had never, in any instance, been practised by these tolerating conquerors.

In the year 1702, a brass medal is said to have been discovered in the island of Anglesea, (upon removing the rubbish from the remains of the chief druidical tribunal), which was inscribed in Hebrew, 'This is Jesus Christ the mediator;' and hence some have inferred that Christianity was preached here so early as the first century; and that the possessor of this medal was one of the Christian ministers who had been condemned and sacrificed by the druids. But, however that may be, certain it is, that Christianity had taken root before the arrival of the Saxons: and that it had recommended itself even to the Roman legionaries. The invasion, however, of the Saxon infidels, for a time obscured, if not extinguished, the light of the gospel. For both Gildas and Bede represent that nation, as, above all others, the subverters of the altars, and the enemies of the priesthood. Partially de-

stroyed when the Fell was inclosed, in Nov. 1841.

The words 'groue' and 'grief' (Saxon), *grave,* are synonymous.

Gildas Brit. Ep. 23. Bede, *lib.* i. p. 22.

D

But Providence provided instructors for our ancestors in another quarter. Gregory, surnamed the Great, having had his compassion excited by the sight of some English youths exposed for sale in the streets of Rome, resolved to attempt the conversion of their countrymen, who, he was told, were heathens. Gregory was advanced to the pontifical chair in the year of Christ 590; and in the year 596, he appointed Austin, or Augustin, a monk of the convent of St. Andrew, at Rome, together with several others, to endeavour to bring the inhabitants of Britain to the knowledge and profession of Christianity.

About the year 624, an event happened which paved the way for the further propagation of the gospel amongst our progenitors in the north. This was the marriage of Edwin, king of Northumberland, with Ethelburga, daughter of Ethelbert, king of Kent. She, being a Christian princess, had the free exercise of the Christian religion secured to her and her household; and was accompanied into Northumberland by Paulinus, who had been consecrated a bishop by Justus, archbishop of Canterbury. This prelate, who is justly called the 'northern apostle,' was not only allowed to perform the duties of his sacred functions in the queen's household, but also to preach the gospel to as many as were willing to hear it. Edwin was a stout pagan when he made proposals for marriage to Ethelburga, and succeeded in his suit only by allowing her the free exercise of her own conscience in religious matters, saying "that ought to be no hinderance, and if upon due examination he found the Christian law to be better than his own, he would himself embrace it." But Edwin continued in his idolatry for some time, till lying sick of a dangerous wound, he appealed to Paulinus, and promised that "if Christ, whom they (his wife and the bishop) so much extolled, would give him cure, and victory over his enemies, he would without more ado receive this religion." He recovered his sickness, his enemies fell into his hands, and from that time worshipped he no more his idols. We can believe in the conversion of Edwin without yielding assent to any miraculous cure of his ailment, or any other of the miracles which Bede has recorded. Dr. Hook excuses them as "Canterbury tales," belonging naturally to the credulity of that age. Edwin was baptized by Paulinus in A.D. 627. Northumbria was, at that time, occasionally divided into two provinces, under the names of Deira and Bernicia, of which the former comprehended the whole tract of country interposed between the Tyne, the Mersey, and the Humber. Paulinus commonly followed the court, which resided sometimes in Deira, and sometimes in Bernicia, preaching, and baptising his converts in some neighbouring stream or fountain. " His presence at Dewsbury is attested by a cross, whereon was once an inscription to that effect. At Whalley there are still three crosses, to which tradition has, with one voice, assigned the office of commemorating the same event; and though these last have no inscription now remaining, yet.the obeliscal form, and the ornaments in fretwork, used in common by the Norwegians, Saxons, Danes, and other northern nations, prove their antiquity to be great; probably of the date of Paulinus. The crucifix upon the obelisk, 0 cross, in the churchyard at Penrith, is no doubt a memorial of the same kind, and intended to commemorate the same event, as it is on record that Paulinus founded the church of Kirkoswald. Now, if Paulinus preached both at Whalley and Penrith, he may have passed by the banks of the Kent, although there be now no relics to prove his having preached or planted Christianity here. From Penrith it is probable he turned into Swaledale; for we find it recorded, that in one day he baptized, in the river Swale, no fewer than 10,000." Drayton, the poet, states the number at 10,000 men, besides women and children, in the following lines:—

"For when the Saxons first received the Christian faith,
Paulimu, of old York, the zealous bishop then,
In Swale's abundant stream christen'd ten thousand men,
With women and their babes a number more beside,
Upon one happy day, whereof she boasts with pride."

That the church of Kendal was contemporary with Paulinus is indeed too much for us to assert. For the See the Introduction to Dr. Hook's "Lives of the Archbishops of Canterbury." Bede. Nennius apud, 15 script, p. 117. testimony of Bede (the "candle of the English Church ") is to this effect, "Nondum oratoria vel Baptisteria in ipso exordio nascentis ibi Ecclesite poterant cedificari; attamen in Campodono, ubi tunc villa regia, erat, fecit basilicam. " This, therefore, and the church at York, were probably the only places of worship in the Northumbrian kingdom, contemporary with Paulinus. But the probability is, that all the places where Paulinus preached would be held sacred; that memorials would be erected, and that divine offices would be performed there, from the very first: and if so, the climate would soon admonish the most hardy and zealous congregations, that shelter and comfort are indispensably necessary to undisturbed devotion.

That there was, however, an ancient Saxon church at Kendal, and that it was, in all probability, the only church in what is now called the Deanery of Kendal, will appear a consequence from the following facts. No sooner was the Norman conqueror seated on the throne, than his active mind suggested to him a great national work, which will serve to transmit his name to posterity, with a degree of veneratioa That work was entitled the 'Domesday Booke and though the exact time of taking it is not sufficiently clear, yet the probability is, that it was commenced in the year 1080; and it is evident, from the insertion at the end of the second volume, that it was completed in the year 1086. The devastation made by the conqueror in the

northern counties, rendered it impossible to take an exact survey of some of them; and accordingly we find that the south of Westmorland, and a part of Cumberland, (both of which were included in the West-Riding of Yorkshire), are the only parts surveyed in the counties of Northumberland, Cumberland, Westmorland, and Durham. The parts of Westmorland surveyed are as follows:—

"Middletun, Manzerge, Cherchebi, Lupetun, Prestun, Holme, Bortune, and Hotune:" viz. Middleton, Mansergh, Kirkby (Lonsdale), Lupton, Preston, Holme, Burton, and Hutton, (probably Hutton Roof);

Domesday Booke, that is, " Book of Judgment," *Domm Dei;* because from that, as from the Day of Judgment, "there lyes noe appeale."—*Lamdovme MS.* And then it is added,

"Hioc Laiiuit Torsin pro 12 maneriis. "

Again, amongst the possessions of Tosti, earl of Northumberland, we find "Castertune, Berebrune, and Tiernbi;" that is, Casterton,
Barbon, and Thrimby:

And then follows,
"Omnes hie Villa) pertinent ad Witetun, Tosti Comea habuit."

Again,
"In Stercaland: Cherchebi, Helsingtun, Staintun, Hotun, Fatun:" viz. Kirkby (Kendal), Helsington, Stainton, Hutton, and Pattern.

And then follows,
"Hsec habuit Gilmiohel."

Amongst the lands of Roger of Poictou, we find,
"Biedun, Fareltun, Prestun, Hennecastre, Euresheim, Lefuenes;" viz. Beetbam, Farlton, Preston, Hiucaster, Heversham, and Levena.

In this part of Westmorland, therefore, we may safely conclude, that Kirkby Kendal and Kirkby Lonsdale were the only places in the two vales that had churches, because the distinguished name of 'Cherchebi' is there given to them respectively. There can indeed be no doubt but many of the other places had buildings for worship, either with or without a cemetery, or place of burial; but then, they were all dependent churches; places of worship dependent upon the great Saxon churches at Kendal and Lonsdale. This appears to be confirmed by the circumstance of' Warton' not occurring at all in the Domesday Survey; from which it may fairly be presumed, that the several townships, of which that parish now consists, were immediately dependent upon the church at Kendal. We may date the subdivision of the great Saxon parish of Kendal, into the several parishes of which the Barony now consists, from that era after the conquest when property first begfin to be confirmed and consolidated. Vide "History of Richmondshire," vol. ii. p. 292.

Previously to the Norman Conquest the district of country comprehending the parish of Kendal was within the dominions of Malcolm, king of Scotland.

But though we cannot trace the *date* of the Saxon church, yet we can trace the date of the huilding in its present form, with great precision. The church was given by Ivo de Talebois, before mentioned, to the abbey of St. Mary's at York: which grant, together with a munificent grant by William de Lancaster II., fifth baron of Kendal, was confirmed by Gilbert, son of Roger Fitz-Reinfred, who married Helwise, daughter and heiress of the aforesaid William de Lancaster II. A copy of this confirmatory grant was in the possession of the late Vicar Hudson. It appears from the boundaries therein described, that a considerable addition was then made to the aforesaid grant of William de Lancaster II. This Gilbert, sixth baron of Kendal, had a grant from the crown, in the year 1189, of the whole 'Forest of Westmorland, Kendale, and Furnesse,' and soon afterwards procured a grant for a weekly market at Kendal, on Saturday. He died in the fourth year of Henry III. *i.e.* in the year 1219. Now it is very probable, that at or about the time he made the grant before mentioned, and also exerted his interest for the benefit of the town, he was no less attentive to the structure of the church. And this appears to be confirmed by a discovery which was made in the year 1829; at

which time it was determined to clear the pillars and arches from the repeated coatings of whitewash with which they had been covered, and to restore the whole of the interior to its original state of beauty and grandeur. The workmen employed in this restoration, discovered, in the pillar on the south side of the altar, a recess which had been filled up with stones, and covered with plaster and whitewash. It was formed by a Gothic arch of neat workmanship; and over the point of the arch was an inscription, which by the then vicar was interpreted' Salutis nostrae, anno 1201. ' Now The stone containing the inscription abore alluded to, formed the apex of tho arch of the piscina which was entirely renewed during the restoration of the Church in 1850852. The stone was in consequence ejected from its position, and may now (1861), be seen lying almost uncared for, in the Bellingham the style of the building corresponds, in every respect, with this date; for the Gothic, or Saracenic, architecture was not known in this kingdom till the latter end of the reign of Henry II., and was partially and gradually adopted in the two succeeding reigns of Richard I. and John. In the time of Henry III., Grose says, this style gained a complete footing, "the circular giving way to the *pointed arch,* and the massive column yielding to the *slender* pillar." It is further stated, that many of the old buildings, erected in former ages, were then taken down in order to be rebuilt in the new taste. We may therefore conclude, that the ancient Saxon church, consisting of the centre, and, at least, the two adjoining aisles, was either wholly rebuilt, or enlarged and beautified in the year 1201. The era of.the second aisle, to the south, is indeed uncertain; but that of the north aisle, which is very wide and spacious, belongs to the reign of Henry VIII. The Bellingham chapel, at any rate, in this aisle, is proved by an inscription which was on the tomb of Sir Roger Bellingham, to have been built in the time of Henry VIII. (See Inscriptions in a subsequent page.)

There are some peculiarities which appeared on clearing the pillars, and

which deserve the attention of Antiquaries. One of the massy pillars at the west end of the nave is formed of hewn limestone, but the rest are interlarded with a mixture of red sandstone. The limestone we conceive to have been dug from the place now called "Gillingrove;" the same, most probably, as that described in the grant before recited by " Ccecum illius Blindbeck.' But whence came the red sandstone? It is not in sufficient quantity to warrant the belief that it was quarried for the church. The probability is, then, that it was brought from the ruins of some ancient structure; and the most likely source was the Roman station at Watercrook. H this conjecture be well founded, we may conclude that these stones formed part of the ancient Saxon church, and were brought by the founders of that church

Chapel. With all deference to the architects under whose superintendence the restorations were effected, we take the liberty to say, that this stone is worthy of preservation, and its expulsion was an act of vandalism and desecration. Grose's Antiquities.

from the station at Concangium. In corroboration of this hypothesis, we may quote the opinion of Drake, who says that, when converted to Christianity, "the Saxons defaced, or demolished every Ronian altar, or other votive monument of the Romans, discovered in their time. For their own conveniency, and to eradicate all marks of paganism, they made use of the ruins of Roman buildings in the erection of their churches." The same red sandstone is found in the structure of the castle, as will be mentioned hereafter.

In the ecclesiastical survey, commonly called 'The Taxation of Pope Nicholas,' the church is stated to be divided into two medieties, viz. 'pars Gulielmi et pars Gualteri' This taxation was computed about the year 1291, and the church is there stated to be in the diocese of York.

In 1301, it was appropriated to the Monastery of St. Mary's, at York, and the original is still preserved amongst the archives of the registry there; of which the present Vicar is in possession of a copy.

In 1321, the abbot and convent bound themselves and their successors to find and maintain a chantry in the church, at the altar of St. Mary, for one secular priest, and to allow him *5l.* for the purpose of celebrating mass there.

In the general ecclesiastical survey of Henry VIII. the living is valued at 99?. 5s.; this is one of the highest valuations in the king's books.

In 1553 the following pensions appear to have been paid to those who had been incumbents of Chantries in Kirkby Kendal, *viz.*: £ «. d.

St. Mary's Chantry, to Adam Shepard, incumbent..368

St. Antbonys Chantry, to Robert Base 3 4 4

St. Christopher's Chantry, to John Garret 2 14 7

St. Thomas Becket's Chantry, to Adam Shepard...4 13 4
St. Leonard's, alias le Spittle Chantry, to Jeffrey Bainbridge 440

This agrees, in some respects, with the return of the Commissioners appointed to inquire of colleges, chantries, hos Drake's "Eboracum." vol. i. p. 28. MSS. Ebor.
pitals, and free chapels, in the reigns of Henry VIII. and Edward VI. who certified, that there were in Kendal, *one* stipendiary in the chapel, and *four* other stipendiaries; but they further state, that there was the chantry of our Lady, Becket's chantry, and Trinity guild Probably the last of these was then composed of St. Anthony's, St. Christopher's, and St. Leonard's.

In the ecclesiastical survey before alluded to, the deaneries of Kendal and Lonsdale are united, and form part of the archdeaconry of Richmond, and diocese of York. But upon the consecration of the see of Chester, in 1541, these deaneries were separated, and made part of that bishopricIn 1856, they were annexed to the diocese of *Carlisle,* and now form part of that see. The deanery of Kendal (part of the Archdeaconry of Westmorland) contains the following 38 churches and chapels; to which we have annexed a statement of their re-

spective valuations in the king's books, and have also noted whether they now stand charged, or have been discharged, from the payment of first-fruits and tenths.

£ i. d.
Kendal, Westmorland, Vicarage 92 5 0
St. George, Kendal
Burneeide
Crook
Grayrigg
Helsington
Hugill, or Ings
Kentmere
Natland
Long Sleddale
New Hutton
Old Hutton
Selside
Staveley
Underbarrow
Winster
Beetham, *dis.* Westmorland, Vicarage 13 7 6
Witherslack, do.
Bolton le Sands, *dis.* Lancashire, Vicarage 4 15 0
Overkellet, do.
Bubton, *dis.* Westmorland, Vicarage 15 17 34
Preston Patrick, do.
Bum's "History of Westmoreland."
Those in small capitals are Parish Churches. The others, as they respectively follow, are Chapels of Ease under them, and not in charge.

Grasmere and Windermere were, anciently, only chapelries within the parish of Kendal. But having little or no communication with the mother church, on account of the distance, they have, in length of time, acquired the reputation of distinct parishes. Each of the rectors, however, pays to the Vicar of Kendal, to this day, the annual pension of 13s. *id.* Mortuaries are also paid throughout both parishes, to the Rector and Vicar of Kendal, in equal moieties.

We now proceed to a description of the Church in its present form.

Is a spacious and very striking building, of plain, perpendicular, gothic architecture, dedicated, as appears from the grant of Gilbert, the sixth Baron of Kendal, to the Holy Trinity. It consists

of the nave, (to which there is a Concerning this, many erroneous statements have been published. In the will of Sir Walter de Strickland, knt. it is required, that "a Prist shall synge for me and my ancestors at *St. Katin'i* auter in Kirkby Kendal three years." From this recital, the Editor of the Lonsdale Magazine imagined the church to be dedicated to St. Catherine; whereas, it is probable, that the altar within the Strickland chapel only was dedicated to that saint. In a topographical account THE CHURCH clerestory), chancel, and four side aisles, so that it consists of five open aisles, like the church of St. John Lateran at Rome. The two exterior aisles, north and south, were added to the previous three aisles, as before said, about the beginning of the 16th century. From the capitals of the pillars spring high arches, of the pointed or gothic order, which altogether produce a grand and imposing effect, well calculated to solemnize the ordinances of religion. The length is 140 feet, and the breadth 103 feet, interior measure. The tower is engaged, and stands on four arches; the height from the floor to the point of the eastern arch is 33 feet; from the floor to the point of the northern and southern arches 24 feet; and from the ground to the point of the western window 35 feet. At some former period (the date of which cannot now be ascertained), the tower appears to have been raised; and at that time the ringers, who had previously had their station on the ground, were placed in a belfry, made at the height of fifteen feet.

There appears to have been four altars in the church, dedicated as follows:— 1. The great altar in the chancel, to the honour of the Holy Trinity. 2. The altar on the north side, to St. Mary the Virgin. 3. The altar on the south side, to St. Catharine. 4. The altar in the Parr chapel (now the Vestry).

The piscina was found in a mutilated state, when the church was restored in 1829, as before stated.

The tower is 25 feet wide, and 80 feet high. Till the year 1774, the peal consisted of six bells; but in that year (the sixth having been burst, and not having been quite tunable with the rest), the peal was increased to one of eight. The first, second, third, and sixth were re-cast; and the fourth and fifth of the old set, became the seventh and eighth of the new peal. In the year 1816 the fifth of this peal was cracked, and at that time a subscription was entered into for of Kendal, in the Monthly Magazine, for 1801, the church is inaccurately Raid to be dedicated to St. George. And we have somewhere seen it ascribed to St. Mary. Our authority, however, that it was dedicated to *The Trinity,* must be admitted to be unquestionable.

adding two new bells to the peal. The sum required was soon raised, and the year 1817 was ushered in by the ringers, on the new peal, under the superintendence of Nicholas Wilson, one of the first scientific ringers in the north of England. It is generally allowed that they now constitute one of the most harmonious peals in the kingdom. Perhaps the situation of the church may aid in producing the effect which establishes this opinion. As the wind may direct, the volume of harmony, issuing from the lofty steeple, is borne sweetly on the bosom of the stream to a considerable distance, or is reflected in other directions, with echoing cadences, from the brow of one eminence to another. The weight of the peal is as follows, viz:—

Cwt. qrs. lbs.

Treble 700

Second 6 3 20

Third 804

Fourth 8 1 20

Fifth 9 10

Sixth 10 2 11

Seventh 14015

Eighth 1530

Kinth 19 3 9

Tenor 25 0 15

Total.... 125 0 10

The inscriptions on the bells, according to the present arrangement, are as follows: 1 T. Mkars Of London Fecit 1816,

These Two Treble Bells Were, Purchased, By Subscription, IN COMMEMORATION OP THE GLORIOUS, ACHIEVEMENTS OP LORD Nel'son,

And His, Orace The Duke Op Wellington Who With Devine Assistance Gave Peace To Surrounding Nations AND TO THIS, FAVOURED Isle

We,ll Sing Their Praise, And Join In Glorious Harmony This Noble Peal. 2 T Mears Of London Fecit 1816,

Kendal 29 Oc,, 1816 This Subscription Was Pbomoted By M,, Nich,, Wilson Of, This Town, Who By His Fervent Zeal In The Cause, Assisted By The Vlcar, The Mayor, Aldermen, And Nis Brother Townsmen He Carried Into Effect, The 18,,TM Of June 1816: Beino The Annevebsary Of The Ever Memorable Victory Of Waterloo, That Distroyed An Inveterate, Foe And, Gave To Europe The Blessing Of Peace. 3. On this Bell there is now no inscription. It is very likely the re-casting of a former 3rd bell, which (according to Dr. Burn) contained the following distich:

"Our voices shall with joyful sound Make hills and valleys echo round."

4 Pack & Chapman Of London Fecit 1775

Such Wond'rous Pow'r To Musick's Given.

It Eleates The Soul To Heaven. 5 Whilst Thus We Join In Cheabfull Sound.

May Love & Loyalty Abound

Pack & Chapman Of London Fecit 1774.

6 Ye Ringers All That Prize Your Health 8c Happiness Be Sober Merry Wise & You'll The Same Possess

Pack & Chapman Of London Fecit 1774.

7 In Wedlocks Bands Shall Ye Who Join With Hands Your Hearts Unite So Shall Our Tuneful Tongues Combine To Laud The Nuptial Rite

T Mears Of London Fecit 1816. 8 These Bells Were Beoast From A Peal Of Six To Eight 1774 By The Direction Of Tho. Strickland Tho". Scarbbrick Aldermen.

Bryan Wii.lson Rev". Jn. Willson. MA: W". Strickland Jam. Willson & Hen". Shepherd, A Committee Appointed By The Vestry Of This Parish Tho. Symonds D:D: Vicar

Pack & Chapman Of London Fecit 9 1631 Has Tres Campanas Iam Tota Parscia Sanas

Reddidit Vt Qvarta Est Tertia Qvinta Bimvl THIRD FOVRTH AND FIFT AND ALL MAY TOLL

OTH PARISH CHARGE WITHOVT CONTROLL.

10 ME SONITVS NOL.E MEMOREM TVBiE FACIT 1631

In addition to the aforesaid ten bells, there is a small bell which formerly hung on the roof of the Bellingham Chapel, and which is sometimes called "the parson's bell;' sometimes also, "the tinkler." It was removed during the incumbency of Vicar Robinson about 1804, and placed in the Tower along with the rest, and is now used as the ringing-in bell, after the usual peal is ended, at morning and evening services.

RESTORATION.

The church was closed for nearly two years, from 1850 to 1852, to undergo renovation and repairs, and was re-opened again on the 3rd of June, 1852.

The chancel had been allowed to fall into dilapidation, and all the pillars in that part of the church were out of the perpendicular, varying, according to the report of the architects, from nine to twelve inches. It is, by the way, singular to remark that no vertical settlement had taken place—the arches all retaining their true form, and it is difficult to account for this remarkable deflection of such massy pillars. The Master and Fellows of Trinity College, Cambridge, with a liberality which does them credit, determined upon a thorough restoration of the chancel. For this object they voted a sum of 1,300?., afterwards increased to 1,800/., and they must be looked upon as individually subscribing, for the sum mentioned was not set apart from an accumulated fund for such purposes, but its appropriation was a deduction from their own personal receipts. This act of liberality deserved high praise, and the inhabitants of the town duly appreciated it. The college determined also to put in a new east window, of noble dimensions, with intricate tracery. The chancel roof, low and unsightly, was replaced by one of elaborate design, in harmony with the character of the church. The eastern gable of the chancel was also entirely rebuilt, and the old Vestry taken away. A timber arch was thrown across the central aisle, separating the nave and the chancel, having hammer beams and subsidiary braces, all richly moulded, and the spandrels resting on angel corbels bearing shields and scripture mottoes, filled in with rich tracery.

The townspeople, to whom their venerable edifice is dear, were encouraged by the good example aforesaid to complete the work so well begun. Indeed the necessity for renovation throughout every part of the church, was equally great as in the chancel, and immediate steps were taken in the matter. The entire body of the church was repewed, the seats all of them being open, on a consistent plan, additional accommodation was afforded to the extent of above 300 sittings. The church, it is calculated, will now seat 1,400 persons. The beautiful west window was restored, and the doorway beneath, closed up as an entrance, by the position of the organ in front, was re-opened, and, in fact, rebuilt and enlarged.

From this entrance a very good sight of the interior is obtained. The whole length of the edifice, 140 feet, from west to east, is opened out in one uninterrupted view; and though there is nothing comparable to York Minster, owing to the simplicity of the structure, and the absence of ornamental architecture, yet the effect is very imposing. There is, however, extent, massiveness, and lightness, and the complete and finished appearance of the whole structure, with the beautiful east window, so well placed in regard to position, and so admirably ordered in all its proportions, together with the effect of the rich stained glass window in the Lady's Chapel, produce an effect which those who were used to the dilapidated appearance and interrupted prospect formerly exhibited, could hardly have conceived possible.

The organ gallery erected about 1702, occupied the west end of the nave till 1847, when it was removed, together with the organ which stood upon it, the latter being placed on the floor, almost immediately against the main entrance doors, which were thus for all practical purposes closed up. In 1801, two wings were added to the organ gallery, "for the accommodation of the inhabitants," as if the space of the floor had been insufficient for the requirement of the pews. These galleries were anything but elegant in design, and impeded the fine general view of the structure obtained from the communion rails or chancel.

The handsome new entrance porch was erected at this period, replacing an old porch of which the only tolerable feature was a circular arch of early Norman.

The font was undertaken by the ladies of the town, and private subscriptions enabled them to raise it on a massive pedestal, and pave the floor of the baptistry with encaustic tiles.

The " brasses" previously distributed over the church, were collected at the restoration in 1852, and are now laid altogether in Bellingham Chapel, and a tablet in brass is fixed to the adjacent column, stating that "the aforesaid 'brasses' are precisely the same as they were found at the time;" in witness whereof the names of the officers of the church are recorded, viz.:—

Joseph Watkins Barnes, *Vicar.*
William Chaplin, *Curate.*
Churchwardens.
John Mann, *Church Husband.*
    Edward Bbanthwaite.
Joseph Baruow.
Rainfortii Hodoson.
Thomas Busher.
Thomas Brocklebank.
Joseph Morton.
    Isaac Edmondson.
Robert B. Hunter.
Samuel Compston.
Henry Crago.
Anthony Nicholson.
Christopher Birkett.
    John Washington, *Parish Clerk.*

The appropriation of pews and sittings was determined by ballot, regard being had to the amount of subscription respectively made by persons or families. The whole of the nave, was, however, left free for the use of the poor, and for inmates of 'Sandes's Hospital,' and 'Old Maid's Hospital.' This appropriation, though not, we apprehend, ecclesiastically legal, is as near an approach as could be made to an arrangement satisfactory on the whole. Seats in a church are open to the parishioners generally, and cannot be set aside by the churchwardens, or occupied beyond the service. Usage, however, and convenience have assigned fixed seats to those who stately attend on the sabbath ordinances, and so long as no undue claims are asserted, or rights arrogated which have not existence, we are little disposed to quarrel with anything so apparently equitable and convenient. The seats in the west end gallery, for which a payment was, made, which formed part of the organist's salary, were transferred to the east end of the second aisle from the north.

The first act of restoration is due to the Rev. John Hudson, M.A., vicar, who, as before said, in 1829, cleared away from the pillars and arches the unsightly limewash that covered the ashlar-work and marred their beauty. But the crowning work, in 1850-52, was begun and mainly carried through by the energy of the vicar of that day, the Rev. Joseph Watkins Barnes, M.A. He was a man who united in his character all the requisites for the task—considerable knowledge and taste in ecclesiastical architecture, determined perseverance in his object, and extreme liberality, this last quality having been exercised by him on the occasion to the utmost limits of his benefice.

The opening ceremony took place on Thursday, the 3d of June, 1852, on which occasion the church was crowded throughout. Prayers were read by the Rev. the Vicar, and the sermon was preached by the Bishop of the diocese, from 1 Chron. xxix. 16: "0 Lord our God, all this store that we have prepared to build Thee an House for Thine Holy Name cometh of Thine hand, and is all Thine own."

Stained glass windows were presented by the following persons:—

Great East Window, Hilton Halhead, Liverpool.

The Weat Nave, Jamks Gandy,

Heaves Lodge.

The Alderman's Chapel, Major Alan Chambrb, London.

The West end of North Aisle, G. A. Gelderd, Aikrigg End.

Do. Edward Brown, Bath.

The Baptistry, Executors Op The Late William Robinson.

Bellingham Chapel, Thomas Cooper.

Clerestory windows:— 1. Rev. J. W. Barnes. 9. Mrs. E. L. Barnes. 2. Gerard Gandy. 10. John Fisher. 3. Thomas Taylor. 4. Henry Horne. 5. Cornelius Nicholson. 6. Anthony Garnett & Brothers. 7. Rev. G. F. Weston. 8. Thomas Gocoh and 11. Edward W. Scott. 12. Rain Forth Hodgson. 13. J. G. J. Ireland and Thomas Rickards. 14. Mrs. Thompson Bindloss. 15. Thomas Webster. Samuel WniNtREY. 16. Hilton, Halhead.

The Tower Clock was given by Christopher Gardker.

The Nave was restored at the expense of the Parish by a rate of £440.

The Master and Fellows of Trinity College, Cambridge, rebuilt the Chancel and the Great East Window, at a cost of £1,689 6a. lOrf.

The whole Cost of the Restoration was £6,400.

The Organ.—The original organ was built in 1702, at the time of the erection of the west end "Organ Gallery," previously alluded to. It had only one row of keys, with nine stops. Subsequently a "swell" was added; and again, some time after that, a "choir" was superadded. In 1846, it had become so far dilapidated and unworthy of its position, that an effort was then made to have it reconstructed. A subscription, set on foot for the purpose, soon procured the requisite fund, viz. ci'CiOO. It was rebuilt under the superintendence of Mr. Scarisbrick, the organist, by a firm of organ-builders in Manchester, and is now one of the finest instruments in the north of England. The old stops available were carefully selected and used in the new organ. It consists of the following parts or properties, viz.:— 3 manuals and a pedal8board of 29 notes.

13 stops in the "great" organ.
8 stops in tho " choir" organ.
9 stops in the 9 swell" organ.
3 stops in the "pedal" organ.
5 "coupling" stops.
5 " composition " pedals.
1,900 pipes in the total.

Up to the time of this reconstruction in 1846, the organ had stood in the gallery. It was then placed on the floor at the west end, barring the entrance to the church by the western door! From hence, it was very properly removed, on the restoration of the church in 1852, to the Bellingham Chapel, at the east end.

Mr. Thomas Scarisbrick, the organist, has fulfilled his office with great ability for thirty-nine years, having been appointed The instrument, the Organ, was invented and introduced into the Church of England as early as the time of Theodorus, A.d. 680.—Dr. Hook's "Lives of the Archbishops of Canterbury," vol. i. p. 198.

organist in 1822, at only eighteen years of age, after a competition with several rival candidates.

We now proceed to a description of some of the Monuments in this ancient fabric:—

Parr Chapel.—In the quire of the south aisle, which has a flat wainscot ceiling, with roses at the intersections of the rafters, is a large tombstone, of black marble, without any inscription. It adjoins the wall on the south, and on the north side are the following arms: 1. Those of Parr (two barulets), quartered with Roos (three water bougets, two and one). 2. Brus (vaire, onebar). 3. Fitzhugh (three chevrons interlaced). At the east end, are all the preceding arms quartered, viz. 1 and 4. Parr quartered with Roos (the former without the bordure). 2. Parr quartered with Fitzhugh. 3. Roos quartered with Brus. And encircled by the Garter. It will appear from our records relating to the castle, that these arms give a clue to the history of the residents there. The arms on this tomb are a strong proof (and this has long been a questionable point) that under it he the remains of Sir William Parr, and very probably some of the families of Roos and Brus, as before

mentioned.

Upon the ceiling of this quire, which is somewhat dilapidated, are five escutcheons, four of which form a square, and the fifth occupies the centre. At the north and south angles on the east side are the arms, 2 1. North. Parr quartering Roos.

2. South. Parr quartering Fitzhugh and Roos. Roob quartering Brus.

In the centre, 3. 1 and 4. Parr quartering Green (azure, three stags trippant, or).

2 and 3. Green quartering Maplethorpe (azure, a chevron between three cross crosslots, or; on a chief or; a lion passant, gu).

At the north and south angles, west side, are, i. North. Green quartering Maplethorpe.

5. South. Roos.

3 and 4 refer to a continuation of the family of Sir Thomas Parr, which will be given in our account of the Castle.

"In 1628, *we are informed,* there was the following inscription on a monument in this quire. On a tomb, a man in armour, kneeling; on his breast, two bars, argent, within a bordure, sable (for Parr). On his wife's breast, quarterly, 1 and 4 Green. 2 and 3 Maplethorpe. And about it was written,

"Pray for the soul of Thomas Parr, knight, of king's body, Henry VIII. master of his wardes, and sher who deceased the 11th day of

Nov. in the 9th year of the reign of our said sovereign lord, at London in the Fryers, as his tomb doth record."

In the glass window over it were these arms: quarterly, 1 and 4 Parr, without the bordure, a crescent for difference.

2 and 3 Poos. And over them was inscribed, "Arma Wil. Par militis."

Strickland Chapel.—In the quire of the second aisle, from the south, in a chapel, inclosed by some good screen work, is an ancient monument of grey marble, without inscription, but with the following coat armour: 1. 1 and 8. A fesse dancette, between ten billets (for Deinconrt).

2 and 4. Three escalope, two and one. 2. The same, impaling a saltier, with a

mullet pierced (for Neville).

It would appear, from these quarterings, that this monument records two things: 1. The union of the families of Deincourt and Strickland. 2. The union of Sir Walter Strickland (who died 18th or 19th Henry VIII.) with the daughter of Sir Palph Neville, of Thornton Briggs, in Yorkshire. But whether it was erected on the death of the said Sir Walter, or whether the second quartering was added at that time to the arms previously inscribed on the tomb, we have not been able to discover.

It is somewhat remarkable that, from that time to the year 1656, there are not in this chapel any traces of interments, although twelve generations, at Sizergh, can be distinctly traced in that interval. But in that year, a raised tomb of black marble, resting on four pillars, had been erected, in memory of Walter, son of Sir Thomas Strickland and Jane his wife.

Beneath a marble canopy, is a remarkable figure of this Vide Whitaker's "Richmondshire," p. 327, and our remarks on Sir Thomas Parr's burial8-place, in the account of "The Castle," at a subsequent page.

boy, in alabaster, dressed in a loose gown. The following is a representation of this tomb:—

Around the margin of the tablet is inlaid a border of white marble, containing four lines of English verse, within which is inscribed the following Latin epitaph:—

This Pvre-refined Strvctvre Does Memorize Sacrvm
Spectatifsimje Speratifsimse prolia
Hlc Iacet Gvaltervs Strickland,
Fllivs Natv Maximvs
Thomze Strickland
De Sizergh Militis
& IANCE VXORIS ILLIVS MECSTISStM.tf.
CVM QVATVOR ALMS INFANTVLIS,
EIVSDEM STIRPIS & STEM ATI S;
HlC SEPVLTIS,
trie GUaltcrus;
SlCVTI PRIMOGENITVS, ITA OPTIMIS DOTIBVS
APPRIME CONSPICWS;
EXIMI/E IN DOLIS, INCLYT/E MENTIS
VVLTVS AMABILIS, SVAVlSSIMvE CONVERSATIONIS

SVIS, QVO NEMO CHARIOR,
DOMESTICIS GRATIOR
CVNCTIS ACCEPTIOR

Corpus humo memoriam Seculo, anima Deo

D D D

Obyt Y 20 Ok Septem 1656.

He must have died young, for, in the year 1646, there is an indenture preserved, containing covenants of an intended settlement on the marriage of the said Sir Thomas Strickland with Jane, widow of Sir Christopher Dawney, baronet, and if the marriage took place in that year, the boy here interred could not have been more than about nine years of age, and the marble effigy corresponds well enough with this supposition. The said Sir Thomas was made banneret, in the field, by the king in person, and was knight of the shire in 1661.

Against the east wall is a monument in memory of Mary, wife of Thomas Strickland, and daughter of Simon Scroop, of Danby, Esquire, who died in 1737. This monument bears a shield, with three escalops (the Stricklands' arms) impaled with azure, a bend, or, (the arms of Scroop,) surmounted with the Stricklands' crest, a full-topp'd holly-bush. Motto: "*Sans mat*"

There is also, in this chapel, a neat, plain monument, to the memory of Charles Strickland, of Sizergh, who died in 1770. And of Jarrard Strickland, of Kendal, who died in 1795. Also, of Cecilia, daughter of William Townley, Esq. of Townley, wife of the above-named Charles, and afterwards also of the said Jarrard. She died at Sizergh, in 1814. And, also, of Thomas Strickland Standish, son of the aforesaid Charles and Cecilia, who is buried in Standish Church.

Bellikgham Chapel.—The stately chapel of the Bellinghams of Burneshead, where the organ is now placed, is raised an entire story above the rest of the aisle. In 1850-2, this chapel was entirely re-roofed, and the old elaborate oak ceiling, then much decayed, was replaced with a new one of similar design, in imitation of the rich fret work, and stalactical ornaments of the same period in stone. It is adorned with gilt bosses

containing bugle horns and other bearings, the cognizances of the Bellingham family. Two of the windows in the clerestory were, many years ago, in repairing the roof, barbarously walled up, and it is to be regretted that, at the restoration of the church, they were not again opened out.

In the south east corner of this Chapel, there was formerly a box tomb, which contained several brass plates sunk into the cover of the tomb. The tomb is now removed, but the top flag remains on the level of the floor, and shows where the plates had been; they represented two effigies (a man and a woman), and four escutcheons, one at each corner of the stone. On a separate plate was the following inscription:—

"Here under lyeth Sir Roger Bellingham, Knt. (which of his own proper costs and charges builded the Chapell of our Lady within this church of Kendall), and of Margaret his wife, daur. of Sir Robt. Aske, Knight, and of Elisabeth his wife, daur. to the Lord John Clifford, now created Earl of Cumberland, which Sir Roger died the 18th day of July A.d. 1533, and the s Margaret dyed the day of, A.D. 15, whose souls Jhesu pardon."

This inscription is of great historical importance, as showing that the Bellingham Chapel was built in the time of Henry VIII. and that it was dedicated to the Virgin Mary (" Our Ladye"). So we understand it.

On the north side of this tomb was a freestone panel, which has been carefully inserted in the pillar at the head of the tombstone. It bears the following arms, quartered: 1. A bugle horn, stringed. 2. Three bendlets, and on a canton, a lion rampant. 3. Three bugle horns, stringed, two and one. 1 and 3 are Bellingham, the latter being the Sussex branch. The second is "Burneshead."

There is an ancient helmet, suspended from an iron rod, immediately over this tomb: and, as the seventh in succession, viz. Sir Roger Bellingham, was a *knight banneret,* and was certainly interred here, we conclude, that this helmet either belonged to him, or was suspended in memory of his having received that most honourable distinction, usually conferred by the king on the field of battle. Probably the effigies Hist, of Richmondshire.

'Dr. Burn identifies " Our Ladye's Chapel" with the Alderman's Aisle (see "Westmorland," p. 76), but we think this a mistake.

This helmet, commonly called *"the RebeVs Cap,"* forms the theme of a popular narrative, which, although we doubt its authenticity, it might perhap be considered unpardonable to omit here. In the civil wars of the Commonwealth, there resided in Kendal, Odo Colonel Briggs, a leading magistrate, and an active commander in the Cromwellian army. At that time, also, Robert Philipson, surnamed, from his bold and licentious character, *Robin the Devil,* inhabited the island on Windermere, called Belle Isle, which, with the estate of Calgarth, and some property in Crook, his family possessed for many years. This Col. Briggs besieged Belle Isle for eight or ten days, until the siege of were those of him and his lady; and had the escutcheons been preserved, they would have enabled us to trace the history of the family, and interments, with more precision.

In a pew which formerly adjoined this quire, and which had probably been the ancient family seat of the Bellinghams, was a brass monument representing the effigy of Sir Alan

Carlisle being raised, Mr. Huddleston Philipson, of Crook, hastened from Carlisle, and relieved his brother Robert. The next day, being Sunday, Robin, with a small troop of horse, rode to Kendal, to make reprisals. He stationed his men properly in the avenues, and himself rode directly into the church in search of Briggs, down one aisle and up another. In passing out at one of the upper doors, his head struck against the portal, when his helmet, unclasped by the blow, fell to the ground and was retained. By the confusion into which the congregation were thrown, he was suffered quietly to ride out. As he left the church-yard, however, he was assaulted: his girths were cut, and he himself was unhorsed. His party now returned upon the assailants; and the

major, killing with his own hand the man who had seized him, clapped the saddle upon his horse, and, ungirthed as it was, vaulted into it, and rode full speed through the streets, calling to his men to follow him; and with his party made a safe retreat to his asylum on the lake. The helmet was afterwards hung aloft, as a commemorating badge of sacrilegious temerity. This narrative is still extant in a ballad of the times, entitled " Dick and the Devil," now of course extremely rare. The adventure is celebrated, also, by Scott, in his poem of Rokeby:—

"All eyes upon the gateway hung
When through the gothic arch there sprung
A horseman arm'd, at headlong speed—
Sable his cloak, his plume, his steed.
Fire from the flinty floor was spurned,
The vaults unwonted clang returned!"

Rokeby, Stanza 33, Canto vi.

In Bowness Church there is an epitaph on a slab of stone, referring either to *Robin* or one of his family—not quite certain. It runs as follows:—

"The author's Epitaph upon himself, made in the tyme of his sickness. "A man I was, wormea meate I am, To earth returned from whence I came. Many removes on earth I had, In earth at length my bed is made: A bed which Christ did not disdaine, Although it covld not him retaine. His deadlie foes might plainlie see, Over sin and death his victorie. Here must I rest till Christ shall let me see, His promised Jerusalem and her felicitie. "Veni Domine Jesu veni cito. "Robert Philipson gent, xiiij.' Octobris an. salutis 1631 anno. "iEtatis sua 63 "V Bellingham, in armour. This monument was removed at the restoration of the church, and placed in the north wall, within the quire of the Bellingham family. It bears the following inscription:—

This Alan was grandson of Alan Bellingham, the eighth son of Sir Robert, son of Sir Roger Bellingham, knight banneret, before mentioned. His said grandfather purchased Levens and Helsington, Gaythorne, and Fawcet Forest, and divers lordships in Lancashire and Northumberland He was a

bencher of the Inner Temple, and one of the king's council at York, for the northern parts. In the 13th Eliz. he was knight of the shire for Westmorland. Here are found the following arms: 1. Quarterly, 1 and 4 Bellingham (three bugle horns, stringed, sable).

2 and 3 Burneshead as before. 2. The same arms, impaling quarterly: 1, party, per chevron, sable and ermine, two boars' heads, couped, or (Sandford). 2, three lioncels rampant, argent (English). 3, or, on a chevron, between three mullets, pierced, azure, as many fleurs-delys of the field (Crackenthorpe). *4,* argent, two bars on a canton gules, a lion of England (Lancaster). Motto: " A ins y Test."

The other part of the court armour in this place does not relate to interments, but merely to the transition of the property: viz. from Alan Bellingham to Sir James Graham by purchase; and from his daughter and heiress to Henry Bowes Howard, earl of Berkshire, into whose family she brought, by marriage, the whole of the inheritance, of which we have now given this brief account. The Howard arms are, gules, a bend between six cross crosslets, fitchy argent, with an augmentation in the midst of the bend, on an escutcheon, or, a demi-lion rampant, pierced through the other quarters of mouth with an arrow, within a double tressure, counter flory, gules. The crest on a chapeau gules, turned up ermine, a lion guardant, Ms tail extended,-or, gorged, with a ducal coronet, argent. Supporters: on the dexter side, a lion guardant, or gorged ducally, argent; on the sinister, a lion, argent. Motto: "Non quo sed quomodo."

The Bellingham chapel, since the extinction of the family whose name it bears, is become the property of the parish, at whose expense it is kept in repair.

On a pillar, at the head of the tomb before mentioned, is a small mutilated monument of white marble, inserted in grey freestone, to the memory of Dame Thomasin Thornburgh, wife of Sir William Thornburgh, of Selside, knight, During her widowhood she kept a book of accounts of her receipts, expenses, and disbursements, whence, in an account "of the holle years waigea of her servants at Selsatt" (now Selside), it appears, that she had *nine* male servants, whose united annual wages amounted only to 10?. *Is. id.*; and and daughter of Sir Robert Bellingham, of Burneshead, knight (the last of the family at that place), son of Sir Roger Bellingham, knight banneret, before mentioned Upon the monument are the following six coats, quarterly, being the arms borne by the Thornburghs:— 1. Ermin, a frette and chief, gules. (Thornburgh.) 2. Argent, two bars on a canton, gules, a cross flory of the first.

(Broughton.) 3. Argent, two bars, and a canton gules, over all a bend, argent. (Copcland.) 4. Sable, a frette, argent. (Harrington.) 5. Argent, three bugle horns, sabled, stringed gules. (Bellingham.) 6. Argent, three bendlets, gules, on a canton of the second, a lion rampant of the first. (Burneshead.)

The inscription is as follows:—

On Earth Three Score A Tene Years Spent

Or Nighetherabowts This Lyffe Changed

Dame Thomasin Thornbvrgh Hence Went

Heavenlye Ioyes To Ioye Expected

Wiffe To Sir William Thornbvrgh Knyght

Whylst On Earth He Was Remaynyng

Sir Robert Bellingham Gentle Knyght

Hir Father Was Wyth Whom Ending She Desired Sepvlted To Be

As Here Hir Corps, Hir Hope Serving Vnder Lyeth As Yove Maye See

Hir Spirit Wyth The Blessed Being

The Eleventhe Of Avgvst She Expired

A Yeare Of Christ On Thowsand Fyve Hvndreth Ei6htie Too

This World She Left (thereof Not Loth)

Almightie God Hir Sowle Receeve

To Hevenly Blis She Hvmblye Craved.

It is remarkable that, in a church of such great antiquity, there are so few monuments remaining in memory of the vicars. After the dissolution of monasteries, the rectory, with the advowson of the vicarage, was granted to Trinity College, in the University of Cambridge, by Queen Mary, in the first year of her reign, that is in the year 1553. Dr. Burn thinks it did not come immediately into the possession of the college, for that an indenture is preserved amongst *eight* female servants, whose united wages make no more than 4?. 8. *Sd.*! This document bears date 1579.— Vide Burn's "Westmorland," p. 119.

Lord Lyttleton's evidences, at Hagley, bearing date the 15th year of James I. 1617, stating, that Thomas Lyttleton was then possessed, in right of his wife, among other estates, of the advowson of the church of Kirkby-Kendal. But it appears that this statement must have been founded on some lease granted by the abbot and convent of St. Mary's, at York, before the dissolution; for, in 1562, we find, that Ambrose Hetherington was presented by the master and fellows of Trinity College, to the vicarage of Kirkby-Kendal; and, in the following year, the vicarage house and premises were surveyed, by order of the college. We have taken some pains to trace the succession of vicars, and we believe the annexed list to be as correct as can be made out, from the documents now existing:— 1. Alan de Esyngwald. 2. 1301. William de Madestan.; 3. 1312. Roger de Kirkeby. 4. Thomas Qreenwode. 6. 1366. Thomas de Leynesbury. 6. 1432. Richard Garedale. 7. 1439. John Bryan. 8. 1495. William, Abbot of St. Mary's, York. 9. Thomas Maynes. 10. 1550. James Pilkington. 11. 1551. Nicholas Ashton. 12. 1562. Ambrose Hetherington, D.D. buried July 13th, 1591. 13. 1591. Samuel Heron, resigned. 14. 1592. Ravlph Tirer, B.D. died June 4th, 1627. 15. 1627. Francis Gardener, B.D. 16. 1640. Henry Hall, B.D. 17. 1656. John Strickland. 18. 1658. William Brownsword. 19. 1672. Michael Stanford, MA. died March 2d, 1682. 20. 1683. Thomas Murgatroyd, M.A buried April 17th, 1699. 21. W99. William Crosby, M.A. died December 7th, 1733, aged 69. 22. 1734. Richard Cuthbert, M.A. died November 7th, 1744, aged 48. 23. 1745. Thomas Symonds, M.A. D.D. in 1773, died Feb. 16th, 1789, aged 79. 24. 1789. Henry Robinson, M.A died Feb. 25th, 1806, aged 58. 25. 1806. Matthew Murfltt, M. A. died Nov. 7th, 1814, aged 50. 26. 1815. John Hudson, M.A. died Oct. 31st, 1843, aged 70 27. 1844. Joseph Watkins Barnes, M.A. died May 15th, 1858, aged 51. 28. 1858. John Cooper, M.A. *He* was never connected with 'Trinity,' as we are informed; but W&b Fellow of 'Christ's' at his presentation. Of the above, there are only memorials of nine, viz. 1, Ralph Tyrer. 2, William Crosby. 3, Michael Stanford. 4, Richard Cuthbert. 5, Thomas Symonds. 6, Henry Eobinson. 7, Matthew Murfitt. 8, John Hudson. 9, Joseph Watkins Barnes. The following are copies:— 1. On a brass plate within the communion rails:

Herevnder Lyeth Y» Body Of M" Ravlph

Tirer Late Vicar Of Kendall Batchler Of Divinity, Who Dyed The 4тм Day Of Ivne, An: Dni: 1627.

London bredd me, Westminster fedd me

Cambridge sped me, my Sister wed me,

Study taught me, Liuing sought me,

Learning brought me, Kendall caught me,

Labour pressed me, sicknes distressed me,

Death oppressed me, & graue possessed me,

God first gave me, Christ did saue me

Earth did crave me, & hcauen would haue me.

2. Also, within the communion rails, on a brass plate: H. s. E.

Willielmus Crosby, A.M.

DUNELMENSIS

Collegij S. S. Trinitatis Cantabrig.

Ab: Anno 1690

Socius.

HUJUS ECCLESLE AB ANNO 1690 VICARIUS

Obijt Septimo Die Decembris

This vicar, a man of exemplary morals, has the merit of having put a stop to the revolting practice of burying the dead without coffins.

3. On a marble monument against the

north wall, removed from over the old vestry door: Hie in proximo situs eft Michael Stanford.

Erat ornamentum literarum et decus,
Veritatis cultor eximius,
Fidei propugnator strenuus,
Ecclcfue Anglicans Hookerus alter
Et Fanaticorum malleus.
Et Quicquid Vel Cupiunt Vel Debent Esse Viri
Is ADEO, omni laude major,
Coelo maturus,
Suum ad triumphum evectus eft,
Quinto Nonas Martij
iSalutis Reparata;) Mdclxxxii".
.Etatis Suse Xlviii".
AnimarumhicCurx) x ".
Hoc
WlLLIELMUS RAWLINSON
de Gilthwaite=Rigge Armiger
Summus EI Amicus
In memoriam
Posuit.

4. On a flat stone in the church-yard at the east end of the church: Here lies buried

The Rev. Richard Cuthbert, A.m.
Vicar of Kirkby-Kendale:
In whose Character
The Christian, the Scholar, and the Gentleman,
Rendered each other more illustrious,
His Zeal was happily tempered with Knowledge and Moderation,
His public Labours and private Conduct Agreed to demonstrate the integrity of his Life.
Stranger! suspect not this Epitaph of Flattery;
His Praises are more fully inscribed on the Hearts of all who Knew Him
And His Master's Presence will reward and perfect his Virtues,
By a more intimate Converse with the great Exemplar.
Ob. Nov. 7. A.D. 1744. /Etat 48. Cur. huj. Par. II.
Here also lietli
Dorothy his Daughter aged *1.*
Richard his Son aged 6.

5. On a marble monument against the north wall, formerly8 placed in the alderman's aisle: Sacred to the Memory of

The Rev. Thomas Symonds D.d.

who died the 16 '. Day of February 1789:
having been 45 Years Vicar of this Parish,
"Forgive The Wish
That Wou'd Have Kept Thee Here.'
Reader, whoe'er Thou art,
expect not the florid Epitaph,
the Modefty of him whom it fhould perpetuate forbad:
He only wifh'd to be remember'd
by the Virtuous few,
with whom he lived Refpected and died lamented.

6. A plain flat stone on the south side of the church-yard, near the private door to the Vicarage, marks the grave of the Eev. Henry Kobinson, vicar, bearing the following initials and date:

H. R.
1806.

7. On a small monument against the wall of the north aisle, removed from the Bellingham Chapel:

To the Memory of THE REVEREND MATTHEW MURFITT A.M.
Vicar of Kendal and formerly Fellow of Trinity College,
Cambridge,
who died Nov9. 7. 1814 Aged 50 Years.
He was a pious, learned and eloquent Divine:
A sincere friend, a kind husband,
, and in every relation of Life
a most worthy man. 8. On a marble monument against the south wall near the vestry: TO THE MEMORY OF
The Rev". JOHN HUDSON M.A.
VICAR OF THIS PARISH FOR 28 YEARS,
AND LATE FELLOW AND TDTOR
OF TRINITY COLLEGE CAMBRIDGE;
WHO DIED OCTOBER *3197,* 1843,
AGED 70 YEARS.
HE WAS ESTEEMED FOR HIS
SINCERE AFFECTION, HIS SOUND JUDGMENT, AND STERLING TALENT.
HIS MERITS AS TUTOR WERE ACKNOWLEDGED
BY A MEMORIAL GIFT
FROM HIS GRATEFUL PUPILS.
HOW HE APPROVED HIMSELF AS VICAR
IS ATTESTED BY THIS MONUMENT,
ERECTED BY
AFFECTIONATE MEMBERS OF HIS FLOCK.
9. At the Cemetery, Kendal, is a monu-

mental tomb, of mediteval design, to the next vicar, the Rev. J. W. Barnes, with the following inscription, in old English characters:

"Here rests the body of the Rev. Joseph Watkins Barnes, M.A. for fourteen years Vicar of Kirkby-Kendal, and formerly Fellow of Trinity College, Cambridge, who departed this life May 15, 1858, in his 52d year."

The following suggestions as to the symbols on the tomb may be interesting. Within the trefoil of the right gable are the cup and paten, indicating the clergyman's office. As the heart, the seat of affections, is on the left side, so on that side of the monument the initials I.H.S. are inscribed, symbolizing trust in Christ. At the head is the emblem of the Trinity, showing the assent of the understanding to the truth of Revelation; and at the foot the Bible, God's written word—" A lamp to our feet and a guide unto our path."

Out of the many remaining neat and elegant monuments which adorn this church, we shall only select a few, beginning with the next, in point of antiquity, to those of the three ancient families before mentioned, and proceeding in the order of time.

At the east end of the south, or Parr's, aisle, lie the remains of Sir Augustine Nicolls, knight, one of the Justices of the Court of Common Pleas, who, sitting as judge of assize in this town (the assizes being held here at that time, on account of some differences between Francis, Earl of Cumberland, the then sheriff, and the town of Appleby), died August 3, 1616, in the 57th year of his age. His monument unfortunately fell down, and was broken; and when Mr. Hudson became vicar of Kendal, the fragments were deposited in a box kept in the vestry. He restored it as well as the mutilated stale of the fragments would permit. The following is the inscription (the letters here in italics being supplied from the Fax ton monument):— f ONE OF THE CARDINALL VERTVES IS HIS NAME
THE FOVRE TO FEWE TO COMPREHEND HIS FAME
TO THE MOST RELLIGIOVS *ATSV*

RENOWNED MEMORIE OF

S» AVGVSTINE NICOLLS KNIGHT LATE OF FAXTON IN

NORTHAMPTOSHEIRE (HEERE BVRIED) WHO WAS SECOND

SONNE OF THOMAS NICOLLS OF THE SAME COVNTYE

HE WAS STVDENT OF Y« LAWES IN THE MIDDLE

TEMPLE LONDON, BECAME READER THEREIN Y9 LAST

YEARE OF QVEENE ELIZABETH, OF WHOM HE RECEA

VED HIS WRITT OF SERIEANT ATT THE LA WE THE

MICHAELMAS TEARME IMMEDIATLV FOLLOWINGE.

AFTERWARDS S&R/EANT TO PRINCE HENRYE OF

FAMOVS MEMORIE AND THE QVEENE HIS MOTHER

THEN ONE OF HIS MAKES JUSTICES OF HIS COVRT OF

COMMON PLEASE AND KEEPER OF YE CREATE SEALE

TO YB MOST 1LI.VSTR10VS AND MIGHTYE PRINCE

CHARLES WHO HAVINGE LBOVRED IN Y« HIGHE

AND PAINFVLL CALLINGE OF A MOST REVERENDE AND

IVST IVDQE FOR THE SPACE OF FOVRE YEARES

FELL NDER THE HEAVIE BVRTHEN OF IT (HEERE ATT

KENDALL) SITTINGS THEN 1VSTICE OF ASSIZE AND

COMMINGE TO GIVE IVDGMENT VPON OTHERS BY

HIS COMFORTABLE AND CHRISTIAN DE-PARTVRE

RECEAVD. WEE A88VREDLYE BELEEVE HIS IVDGME?

WITH MERCYE8 IN THE YEURF OF OV» LORD. 1616

THE 9 3, DAY OF AVGVST IN THE 14m. YEARE OF

THE RAIGNE OF OVR SOVERAIGNE LORD KINGE IAMES, AND THE 57TM.

YEAJfF OF HIS AGE.

WEAKE MVSE THAT WOVLDST DISCI-PHERE OVT SVCH IOYE8

THAT NOW ARE ENDLESSE BY FAST FADINGE TOYES

It is said that ho died iu the "Judge's Lodgings," at what was the head iun of the town, "Fox's Inn," so called. It stood in the yard next to the Commercial Inn yard, south.

» This word has evidently been ' YEARES' originally.

There is a cenotaph in Faxton church, Northamptonshire, inscribed with this same chief epitaph. The verse here superadded, beginning, "He whom no Bribes," is omitted at Faxton, and the epitaph at Faxton contains a verse which is not here.

The arms are very perfect, and are: sable, three pheons, ar. with a crescent for difference. Crest, a wolf's head erased, sable.

In the chancel, lie the remains of the Right Eeverend Robert Dawson, bishop of Clonfert, in Ireland; who, in the time of the Irish rebellion, returned with much difficulty to his native country, and died at his father's house, in Kendal. Over his grave is this epitaph, on a brass plate.

HIC IACET REVERENDVS IN CHRISTO PATER ROBERTVS DAWSON EPISCOPVS 2 CLONEFERTENSIS ET DVCENSIS HIBER NICVS QVI 2OBIIT DIE DECIMA TERTIA 6 AP RILIS 1643.

Over the porch door is a very handsome marble monument, to the memory of Thomas Sandes, founder of the hospital and the school, now known by the name of Sandes's Hospital. The inscription is as follows: Heus Peripatetice.

Sifte, difce, et (si pofsis) imitare.

En pulchrum, tibi virtutis, Specimen, Eximium, ingenij et laboris, exemplar.

Humana, quicquid valuit, solertia;

Quicquid magnum, Iaudabile, utile,

Honefta, potuit afsequi, vel efficere, in-duftria,

Illud totum, optime valuit, afsequutus eft, effecit,

PrudentiS, Charitate, diligentii summa;

Illud nempe,

(Quem nec mirari licet, nec satis dolere)

Egregius induftria; Fautor,

Singularis Literarum Patronus,

Pauperum perpetuus Pater,

THOMAS SANDES, Qui, annis satiatus, Cselomaturus,

(Charifsimae Conjugi heu! breve nimis superftes)

Hinc abijt,

Vicefimo secundo die Augufti,

Annof Salutis humanael Mdclxxxi.

(/Etatis Sua;) Lxxv.

Abijt (inquam) non obijt, nequit enim mori,

Dum sit hominibus virtus, aut, virtuti hiftoria.

At-at!

Sileat periturum marmor:

Omni dum marmore Perennius,

Et vel Memphitica, diuturnius, Pyra-mide,

Ipfe, sibi monumentum, struxit,

Gerontocomium.

On a brass plate on the floor of Bellingham chapel, formerly on the fourth pillar in the second aisle from the south: TO THE MEM OR Y

OF THE

Most Religious, and Orthodox Christian The most Loyall Subject, and most ancient 6-

Serviceable Member of this Corporation, wherof

He was once Alderman, and thrice, MA-JOR:

WILLIAM GVYof Water8Crook Gentleman Who dyed the twenty fifth day of December

Had Loyalty been Life, Brave Gvy thou'dst Than Stood Kendall's Everlasting Alderman Nay could the joynte vnitcd force of All That's good or verfous over death prevaile Thy life's pure thrc'd noe Time or Fate could fever And thou'dst still Liv'd to pray; KING live for Ever But thou art gone: A proof such Vertue is Too Good for Earth, And oiuly fit for Blifs, And blifsfull Seats: Where, If blefst Spirits doe Conceme themselves with any thing below. Thy pruy'r's the same, Thou still do'st Supplicate, For Charles his Life For England's Church, &- Stat Whirst to Thy just Eternal Memory Envy and Malice must in this Agree / None better Lov'd, or Serv'd, his Prince then Thee 9

On a brass plate on the floor of Bellingham chapel, which, before the restoration of the church, in 1850-2, was on the floor of the north aisle, towards the east end of the same:

Here Vnder Lyeth The Body Of Alice

The Wife Of Roger Bateman Of Ovld Hvtton Clothier. Davghter Of Richard Garthwait Of Garssdale Yeamon Who Dyed The 2jtm Day Of March 1637 Being

Aged *L6* Yeares 5 Monthes & Od Dayes And Left Issve 3 Davghters Agnes, Margaret And Elizabeth.

Shall we entruft a graue with fuch a gueft,
Or thus confine her to a marble cheft
Who though the Indies met in one fmale roome
TV are fhort in treafure of this pretious tombe,
Well borne, & bred, brought vp in feare & care
Marriage which makes vp women, made her rare
Matron & maide with all choyfe virtues grac'st
Loueing & lou'd of all, a foule fo chaft,
NE're rigg'd for heauen, with whome more dare
Venture their flates with her in blliffe to f hare
She liueing virtues pattern, the poores releife
Her huf bands cheifeft Ioy, now dead his greife.

On a brass plate, on the floor of Bellingham chapel,-which, before the restoration, was placed opposite the present pulpit: 21gh to this Pillar lyes y« Body of MTM FRANCES Strickland late Wife to
M IOHN STRICKLAND of
Strickland & Daughter to EDWARD BACKHOUSE
of MORLAND Efq;
g *I* Born *I* 1690) Marry'd We Iune *I* 1708
W (Bury'd) (1725
Emblem of Temporal Good I The Day that gave
Her Birth and Marr'age, saw Her in the Grave
Wing'd with its native Love her Soul toot flight
To Boundlefs Regions of Eternal Light
Of Bleafe Hall? (See a subsequent page.)

In the east end of the north aisle, lie the remains of Sir Thomas Braithwaite, knight, and on a brass plate in the

Bellingham chapel is the following inscription:
Here Lieth The Body Ok s Thomas BRAITHWAITE KNIGHT LATE OF BURNESHEAD: WHO DIED THE J4 DAY OF MAY ANNO DOMINI J683 ET,TATIS SIL LXVL
This Sir Thomas was one of the sons of Richard Brathwaite, author of "Drunken Barnaby," by his first wife, Frances, daughter of James Lawson.

Against a square pillar, at the west end of the church, is the following inscription, written on parchment, and framed with a narrow oak frame (formerly suspended from a nail in the pulpit pillar): M. s.
Viri vere Generofi
PJurimisque nominibus defideratiflimi Georcij Sedgwick.
Qui,
Omnibus cultioris humanitatis dotibus, abunde ornatus
Honorabili D. *T.* Philippo
Comiti Penbrochienfi,
Celeberima; deinde illius Vidua:
Amanuenfls fibi Locum meruit:
Cujus Familia, (qua nemo Famulus non floruit)
Annis pariter atque opibus auctus (monente munificentitfima Domini
Partis foeliciter fruendis, Sedem
Senectuti fuse comparare)
Fundum, huic Municipio vicinum, emit dictum Collinfeild.
Vbi plus tribus Lustris
Singulari in pauperes charitatc,
Amicitia in proximos,
Erga omnes benevolentia
Notis omnibus charus et amabilis vixit,
Nec paucioribus flebilis obijt
Decimo Die Iunij (Salutis Humanae l Mdclxxxv. Anno _..,
I. Atatis *lux*) LXvii.

At the west end of the church, is the following inscription, on canvas, in a black wooden frame, and in black characters on a gold ground: Here lyes Frances late Wife, of Jacob Dawfon Gent, who departed this life 19,,.
Iune 1700: in y" *IS'*. year of her age.
Who by a Free, *&* Chearfull refignation

of herfelfe
(even in the midst of this worlds affluence)'
has left us juft grounds to hope fhe is now happy.

In the east end of the north aisle, and against the north wall, is a white marble monument, to the memory of John Leyburne, of Cunswick, the last of an ancient and very considerable family in this county. The inscription on the monument is as follows!
To the Memory of
Iohn Leyburne late of
Cunfwick Esq: who died y 9
of Decem: 1737: Aged 69.
In whom that Ancient, Loyall
& Religious Family is now extinct
Whofe Example this Infcription
Recommends to Pofterity,
For under this Stone lies the
Remains of a most Affectionate
Hufband, a Charitable Neiglu bour, and
a Kind Mafter.
In Dealings Just, In Words
Sincere, Was humble in Prof=
perity, Heroickly refign'd in
Adverfity, Whofe unaffected
Devotion, Strict Sobriety, &

This epitaph has given rise to a witticism, used sometimes as a toast on particular occasions of festivity, *viz. "May we all live at Jamb Dawaon2s wife died."*

Unwearied practice of Chriftian Duties, is worthy ye Imitation of All. He had two Sons, who died in their Infancy fo hath left no Iffue to inherit his *Virtues* And that the Memory of them may not perifh with y Name
Lucy his wife hath Plac'd this Monument, as a Memorial
of her Love and Efteem.
Aliferemini Miferemini met,
Saltern vos Amici met I Iob 19 .

On the top of this monument are the arms of Leyburne: (az. three lioncels, rampant, three, two and one; argent, langued and membred, gules), quartered with Dalston, Lucy, his wife, being the heiress of Dalston, (argent, a chevron between three blackbirds' heads, sa. bills, or.)

On a marble slab, in Parr's chapel, now the vestry, against the east wall:

Here Lyes

Iohn Archer Efq. Doctor of Phyfick and

One of his Majeftie's juftices of the Peace for the County of Weftmorland who Departed this Life on the fourth of December 1735.

He was a worthy Man, a skilfull Phyfician, an impartial Majeftrate, and an Amiable Friend.

His mind was Generous, his Temper Sweet his Underftanding Extenfive: In Nature

Compafsionate, in Virtue Severe.

He adom'd the Reafonable Being with the

Dignity of Morality, the True Chriftian with the Sanctity of Religion.

He was a Delight to his Acquaintance, an Honour to his Profefsion, and a Happinefs to his

Country.

Dear and Defirable is the Memory of Doctor

Archer; Cruel and Lamentable is the Lofs of him; Every Eye Overflows with Tears, every

Breaft is fill'd with Sorrow, and every Houfe is become the Houfe of Mourning.

Near the door of the Strickland Chapel lie the remains of Mr. West, the learned author of the "Antiquities of Furness," &c. He was particularly honoured with the friendship of the late Mrs. Strickland, and died at Sizergh, on the 10th July, 1779, aged 62. It is remarkable that no lettered stone should have been erected to perpetuate his memory.

In the east end of the north aisle, and against the north wall, is the monument of Judge Wilson, with the following inscription, written by the late Richard Watson, D.D., bishop of Llandaff: In Memory of Sir JOHN WILSON, Knt.

One of his Majefty's Juftices of the Court of Common Pleas,

Bom at the Howe, in Applethwaite, 6'. of Auguft 1741,

Died at Kendal, 18! of October, 1793:

He did not owe his Promotion to the Weight of great Connexions,

which he never courted; nor to the Influence of political

Parties, which he never joined; but to his profefsional Merit,

and the unfolicited Patronage of the Lord Chancellor Thurlow,

who, in recommending to his Majefty so profound a Lawyer,

and so good a Man,

realized the Hopes and Expectations of the whole Bar,

gratified the general Wifhes of the Country,

and did Honour to his own Difcemment and Integrity.

In the south aisle, near the S.W. entrance, is a handsome monument of black marble, containing the following tribute to the genius of Romney: To the Memory of

UEORGE ROMNEY ESQUIRE,

The Celebrated Painter;

who died at Kendal, the 15. Nov, 1802, in the 68. year of his age, and was interred at Dalton the place of his birth.

So long as Genius and Talents shall be respected his Fame will live.

In the Aldermen's aisle is a handsome monument, to the memory of the late Judge Chambre, bearing the arms of the Chambres, with the following inscription: IN MEMORY OF

SIR ALAN CHAMBRE KN.

LATE ONE OF HIS MAJESTYS JUSTICES

OF THE COURT OF COMMON PLEAS

AT WESTMINSTER

OB XX SEPT MDCCCXXIII

iET, LxxxIIL

At the north-west comer of the church is placed a monument, with martial emblems, of white marble, dedicated to the memory of "12 officers, 15 sergeants, 18 corporals, and 364 private soldiers, all of the 55th (Westmorland) regiment of Toot, who died of disease, exposure, and fatigue, during the war with Russia, in Turkey and the Crimea, in the years 1854 and 1855." This monument, along with other similar ones, in different churches in the country, will stand as a record of disgrace to the Government Commissariat, by whose improvidence so many valuable Lives were lost.

The Communion Plate belonging to the church was stolen, about the year 1778, during the incumbency of Dr. Sy-

monds. It consisted of three silver flagons, two silver cups (gilt), two silver salvers, and one or two smaller cups of silver. This plate (of which no traces could ever be discovered), was soon afterwards partially replaced.

The fabric of the church is now sustained by voluntary contributions—the question involving the principle of the levying of church rates having been negatived at Easter, 1859, on a hotly-contested division of the parish.

The church-yard was closed for burials in 1855. Till the year 1822, it was exposed to injuries from the children in the town, to whom it was a common play-ground. But in that year, by the exertions of the vicar, aided by the churchwardens, and the public spirited gentlemen 6f the town (who raised a subscription for the purpose), it was enclosed with iron palisades, and is now the peaceful and unprofaned receptacle of the dead. The tombstones and inscriptions are here numerous, and many so entirely decayed as to be illegible. The oldest of those now remaining legible, is on the south side, not far from the west door leading to the old vicarage; the inscription on which was some years ago renewed, on a brass plate, and is as follows: This

Monument is the

First erected in this Church Yard,

and is

TO THE MEMORY OF

ANTHONY YEATES, OF HOOD RIDING in OLD HUTTON,

Who died the 21" July 1733 Aged 72;

also of

AGNES his WIDOW,

Who died the 15 '. Dec'. 1758 Aged 81;

also of

ANTHONY their Son,

Who died the 28 t Oct,'. 1775 Aged 75;

and

MARY his WIDOW,

Who died the 19! March 1787 Aged 85.

On a marble tablet, against the south wall of the churchyard, near the private door of the old Vicarage: IN THE EARTH BENEATH ARE DEPOSITED,

IN A PIOUS CONFIDENCE IN THE MERCY OF GOD

THE REMAINS OF,
CATHARINE ROBINSON; WIFE OF THE
REV. HENRY ROBINSON
VICAR OF THIS PARISH:
OF WHOSE UNSPEAKABLE SORROW AND
REGRET
THIS SILENT MARBLE IS A MEMORIAL.
SHE DIED MARCH XIX. MDCCXCIX.
AGED XxxVIIL
HE DIED FEBRUARY xxV. MDCCCV1.
AGED LVIIL
ALSO THE REMAINS OF THE
REV. HENRY ROBINSON THEIR OLDEST
SON,
VICAR OF OTLEY IN THE COUNTY OF
YORK,
WHO DIED XIV OF AUGUST MDCCCXXXIV
AGED XLII YEARS.

The present vicar of the church is the Rev. John Cooper, M.A., late fellow and tutor of Trinity College, Cambridge. He "read himself in" on Sunday morning, August 15, 1858, introducing and concluding the reading of the Thirty-nine Articles with some appropriate remarks.

The *earliest* entry of burial in the register of the parish church at Kendal (but which is evidently a copy of some older document now lost) is that of

"The wife of John Hodgson. May V. die 1555." The *Jirst original* entry is under the heading

"1569. The Booke of chnsens, I,myalls, and weddygs, a" 1509."
Funera.
"Kobartus Fyssher. 7. die Aprilis."
The *last* entry is as follows:—

"James Capstick, Market Place, Sep. 9, 1855. 7 months. J. W. Barnes, Vicar. "

The registers having been continued uninterruptedly (with slight exceptions) over a period of just three hundred years.

CEREMONIAL OF THE INDUCTION OF VICARS.
The following form or ceremonial of induction is usual in all parishes, and is always observed at Kendal Church:— A deputation of the churchwardens having assembled in the porch of the church, await the arrival of the vicar, whom having received, they proceed to present with the key of the church, with which he immediately opens the door, entering the church and taking possession thereof by locking himself *in* and the others *out.* He then ascends to the belfry and tolls one of the bells for a short time, then coming down and opening the door he admits the "lock-outs," upon which they all adjourn to the vestry, where the deed of his induction having been subscribed by the vicar, and attested by the signatures of those present, the ceremony concludes.

THE CEMETERY.
The cemetery for the townships of Kendal, Kirkland, and Nethergraveship, is situated in Park and Castle Lands, in the township of Kendal, and consists of two portions of ground, separated by a township road. The plot on the north side of the road, nearly six acres, is consecrated, and set apart for members of the Established Church. The other plot, two acres and a half, on the south side, is appropriated to the use of dissenters. Neat lodges and chapels form the two (opposite) entrances, and suitable shrubs, with meandering walks, diversify the grounds. The corner-stone of the chapel connected with the Established Church was laid by John Hudson, Esq. , on the 28th November, 1854. The first burial took place on the 14th September, 1855, being that of Miss Louisa J. Percival, aged 47 years.

About half an acre on the west side of the consecrated ground is appropriated to the use of the Roman Catholics.

The cemetery was consecrated on the 23d August, 1854.

Subjoined is the number of burials that took place during the last year (1860), viz.:

In Consecrated ground 149
Unoonsecrated ground 22
Total....... 171
In the previous year (1859) 223

St. Thomas' Church.
The growth of the town, at the north end, which took place in the interval between the years 1820 and 1835, called for increased church accommodation in that locality— farthest removed from the parish church; and a subscription, munificently headed by Mrs. Thomasin Richardson, widow, for i?l,000, soon realised a sufficient fund for a new church, which was built in 1837, and dedicated to St. Thomas. It ignores the traditional custom of the middle ages in placing what was called "the altar window," to the east; the tower front, in tins case, being to the east, and the chancel, with its communion window, facing the west. It is designed in the "old English," or lanceolated, style, and the proportions are well sustained. The tower, surmounted by pinnacles and crockets, rises to a height of ninety-five feet, the vestibules being on either flank of the tower. The windows are the usual triple and double lancet windows of the period of "the order." The interior consists of a nave, seventy-five feet long by forty-five feet in breadth, opening upon the chancel, twenty-four feet by fifteen feet, The.seat accommodation is equal to about 850 sittings, of which 500 are free. It cost only about 3,000?. Alderman Geo. Webster architect. The present incumbent is the Rev. J. A. Latrobe, M.A., Honorary Canon of Carlisle, who was appointed in 1839. It has an ecclesiastical district, within defined boundaries.

A handsome parsonage house, for the perpetual use of the incumbent of St. Thomas's, was erected in 1854, on elevated ground immediately above the church, with funds raised by subscription chiefly through the exertions of Mr. Latrobe. The cost, including land, was 1,*001.*

St. George's Church. This church (like St. Thomas's) is a "district" church. It stands on what was a piece of waste ground, that extended from Stramongatc bridge to "Stock beck." The ground was generally raised four feet or more, to escape the overflowing waters of the Kent. The erection commenced in 1839, and the church was consecrated on the 17th June, 1841. The endowment was transferred from (old) St. George's Chapel, and the funds for the erection were procured by subscriptions from the inhabitants, augmented by a grant from the Church Building Fund. The church is 118 feet long, by 64 feet wide. The style of architecture is what is called "the lanceolated," or early English (of the 13th century), the simplicity of this order being considered best adapted to the native material, the Kendal fell limestone. The west gable is flanked by two octagonal towers, thirteen feet in diameter, which rise to a height of 100 feet, and give striking effect to the building, as seen from any point of view on the south-west or the north-west. The interior consists of nave and chancel, with a spacious vestibule opening on the nave. Galleries extend along the north and south sides and the west end The accommodation is equal to about 1,300 sittings, of which 900 are free and unappropriated. The cost of the church was about 4,500?. *Architect,* Alderman George Webster.

A neat parsonage house, for the incumbent, was erected at the head of Castle Street, in 1849, at a cost of 850?. raised by public subscription.

The organ— a fine instrument—cost £460. RELIGIOUS HOUSES.

At the head of Capper Lane (a corruption of Chapel Lane), there was formerly a chapel, the dedication of which we have not been able to discover. Dr. Burn says, it stood near "Well-Sike," but it is our opinion that it stood at the head of Capper Lane. A quantity of human bones, and a skeleton, nearly entire, were dug up, in making the foundation of the house belonging to Mr. J. Swainson, at the comer of the field called " Little Roods." This field we conceive to have been the cemetery of the chapel. A brass coin, supposed to be a Saxon coin, but so defaced that the legend was unintelligible, was some years ago found near the head of "Capper," on the north side. The chapel, in this place, may have been of Saxon foundation.

Anchorite House.—On the west side of Kirkland, is a house called Anchorite House, which, as the name implies, has been formerly the sequestered abode of an anchorite, or religious recluse. Tradition reports, that it was originally a small hut, the shape of a bee-hive; and the narrow road which conducted to it made two circles round the house: and the fences of this road concealed the dwelling from the gaze of passengers. Before the house is a fine spring of

clear, pure water, called "Anchorite Well," which supplies the principal part of Kirkland—

"Wherein the Hermit dewly wont to say
His holy things each morn and eventide;
Thereby a crystall streame did gently play,
Which from a sacred fountaine welled forth alway."
Spenser.

The present dwelling was erected about ninety years ago, by the late John Shaw, Esq., one of the magistrates lor the county of Westmorland, and also for the borough of Kendal.

All Hallows' Chapel stood at the head of the lane which still bears that name, opposite to the Black Swan All Hallows is synonymous with *All Saints.* For an interesting account of the origin of this designation and of the Festival, see Seymour's "Survey of London," lib. i. p. 284.

Inn, at the lower side of the field called *Chapel Close.* (Vide Speed's Plan, letter Q.) Dr. Burn obviously refers to this place, as "a chapel at the head of the Bank, upon an hill called Chapel Hill, now demolished: and an house erected upon the site thereof, where the arms of Roos are very apparent in the front." The chapel is reported to have been taken down (we cannot ascertain how long ago), for the purpose of widening the road. The arms of Roos are now nowhere observable.

Not far from this place, and adjoining the said Chapel Close, on the north side, is an isolated cemetery called *The Sepulchre,* where some of the *Society of Friends* have been buried.

St. Anne's Chapel, Dockwra Hall.— " There was another chapel, called ' St. Anne's Chapel,' which is supposed to have been situate near Dockwra Hall; and at this place there was a house in Mr. Machell's time, which, from the form of the windows, and the fabric thereof, seemed to have been this same chapel." So far from Dr. Burn. If the reader will refer to Speed's Plan, prefixed to this volume, he will find it very prominently placed; representing a spacious fabric, with lofty tower, and ap-

parently enclosed by a high wall, like the manor-houses of the border counties. It stood on the site of an out-house, in a field between the Union Buildings and Horncop. Dockwra Hall was formerly the seat of a family of its own name. We find, from an inquisition taken at Kendal, in the 49th Edward III. on the death of Johan, wife of John de Coupland (who, for his services in the battle of Durham, had the moiety of the manor of Kendal, afterwards called the "Richmond Fee," granted to him by the crown, it having become escheated for want of heirs of the de Lindsayes), that Robert de Docura was one of the jurors on that occasion; and that (doubtless the same) " Robert de Docura held of the said Johan de Coupland, divers tenements in Kirkeby-Kendale, by fealty, and the service of *2s.* a year, as of her manor of2 Kirkeby." There is an epitaph in the church of Lilley, in Herefordshire, to the memory of Thomas Dockwra, the elder, Esq., lord of Puckeridge, and "descendant of the ancient family of Dockwras, of Dockwra Hall, in Kendal, nephew and heir unto the right honourable Sir Thomas Dockwra, lord grand prior of the knights of St. John of Jerusalem." The chapel spoken of by Burn was probably an oratory within the house, and might be dedicated to St. Anne.

St. Leonard's Hospital.—The place called 'Spital, the common contraction of hospital, is about a mile from the town, on the road to Grayrigg and Appleby. It is now a good farm-house, connected with a farm-of 300 acres, belonging to the Earl of Lonsdale. The hospital, of monachal times, stood close upon the site of the present farm-house, and by the side of what was, we believe, originally the Roman road from *Concangium* (Water Crook) to *Alauna* (Borough Bridge). Like most of the hospitals for lepers, it was dedicated to St. Leonard, and was hence called "St. Leonard's Hospital." Unfortunately there is hardly a scrap of positive history to be found of this place, and yet there are circumstances of great interest connected with it. This hospital appears to have been not a dependency, but a relation of the Priory of Coningshead; for William de Lancaster, who was fourth Baron of Kendal, gave the advowson of this hospital to the Canons regular of St. Augustine, about the end of the twelfth century. The same benefactor founded Conishead Priory, first as a hospital, giving it also to the Canons of Augustine, and that was some time afterwards erected into a priory. At the end of the fourteenth century, this establishment at Kendal came to Sir William del Parr, and at the dissolution of the smaller houses, it was granted to Alan Bellingham and Alan Wilson, Esqs., and was valued then at *lll 4s. 3d.* per year. But it languished for some time after this, struggling. for existence, as is proved by the following entry, made in the reign of Edward VI:

"Hospitium S'ci Leonardi prope villam de Kirkby-de-Kendale, nuper monasterio de Conyshead, pertinent val. *il.* 13j. *id."* "Beauties of England and Wales," p. 194.

The loss of C?. 10s. per annum in so short period (reckoning the value of money at that day) shows how spoliation was at work. Looking at the vast possessions of the early Barons of Kendal, and their great liberality in other cases, it can hardly be doubted that this hospital, lying under the shadow of their castle home, would in the first instance be richly endowed and protected. It had a double office of charity to fulfil, namely, to lodge and feed the decrepit, indigent, and lepers; and to relieve the poor wayfaring passengers, who daily called for "prog and prayers" on their journey to and from Kendal. The endowment, therefore, would include a grant of lands for growing oats, for pasturing cows and sheep, so that bread, cheese, milk and butter, might be raised on the spot, whilst 'Spital Woods, which probably extended even as far as "Shaw End" (the end of the wood), might supply "fire-elding" for the house, and "pannage for the hogs." One of the fields belonging still to the 'Spital estate, situated on the west side of Far Cross Bank, bears the name of *Vineyard,* which suggests the idea that the monks "lived under their own vines,"

and drank the juice of the grape. In Beezon Fields, behind "Castle Dairy," there was a fish-pond, where fish had been stored ready for the cook. This pond has been gradually filled up; but there may still be seen a depression in Beezon Fields, which is very likely the site of the fish-pond.

Hospitals like this, comprised, in their household, a master and a certain number of "brethren," with a chaplain, and license to celebrate divine offices. In our account of the church, we mention the Chantry of St. Leonard, alias "le Spittle," "with a yearly revenue for the maintenance of a priest.". It appears to us probable that this chantry was not connected with the church so long as the hospital existed, but belonged to the priest or chaplain " daily celebrating " within the chapel of the hospital. After the destruction of the hospital, the chantry and revenues attached to it might be transferred to the parish church, and no doubt were so.

In the summer of 1836, as workmen were sinking the foundations of the present farm-house, they dug up a quantity of human bones, and fragments of sculls, apparently belonging to six or eight corpses. They were found at irregular distances, and at various depths in the earth—two of the corpses within six inches of the surface, the rest from two to three feet deep. There were no signs or traces of a coffin with the bones, or near them, and no vestiges of vegetable earth beneath. A slab of red sandstone conglomerate (such as is to be seen in the bed of the " Mint") was found at the same time, with a kind of rude cross upon it; but this is more likely to have been a relic of the hospital than a tombstone. The absence of coffins, the irregular assemblage of bones, the limited number of sculls, and the fact of drainage works having been since carried on over the whole area of this place, without discovering other corpses, all tend to the belief that there was no cemetery here, and that these remains belonged to persons slain in some encounter on the spot, and indiscriminately buried in the hurry of the fray. We have the clear probability of such an

occurrence in what is variously called "The Northern Rebellion," the "*Aske* Rebellion," and "Pilgrimage of Grace," in 1536-37, temp. Henry VIII. The Abbot of Furness and the Prior of Conishead were directly implicated by Henry as *participes criminis,* in this rebellion, with *Askes* party; and an anonymous witness, in answer to an inquiry instituted by the king, declares as follows:—

"I say I wrott the sayd Letter to th Prior of Cartmelle (or Conishead) at the request of one *Collenes,* bayliffe of Kendal, at whose only mocon requeste and interpellation I wrott the same Letter," &c. (*Baines History of Lancashire).*

Here we have Collenes, *the* bailiff (the Lord's bailiff, or bailiff of the castle estate?) in treasonable correspondence with the Prior of Conishead; and the king commanded that all suspected persons were to await his Majesty's pleasure *in prison!*

Now, there is a circumstance of local and domestic character not to be overlooked here. Kendal Castle, at the period alluded to, was one of the residences of Katherine Parr; and her husband, at the time, (her second husband) was Lord Latimer. Latimer is ranked among the leaders of this insurrection, and, although there is no reason for identifying Katheriue with her husband's bigoted or rebellious conduct, (rather the contrary), it is quite probable that, through the marriage, he would claim to have local connexion with Kendal, and influence with that part of the population who were, in this movement, defending the monasteries, and resisting the introduction of the Form of Common Prayer. Froude says, it was about the 12th of February, 1537, that a rabble from Kendal, Richmond, Appleby, Penrith, &c., collected under one of the Musgraves, about 8,000 in number, and attacked Carlisle. They were beaten, and driven back by Clifford's troops, which contained " a sprinkling of the professional thieves of the Border." What is called "wholesome severity" could alone restore order. *Martial law* was proclaimed in Westmorland; Cumberland, &c. Henry said, "The further you shall wade in the investigation of those persons that call themselves 'religious,' the more you shall detest them. Our pleasure is, that you cause execution to be done upon a good number of the inhabitants of *every town,* village, and hamlet, that have offended,—better that these traitors should perish than a slender punishment should not be a warning to others. Finally, as these troubles have ensued by the monks and canons, you shall cause all them that be in anywise faulty *to be tied up* without ceremony." This order "to tie up"—this "wholesome severity"—was observed strictly; and seventy-four persons, laity and clergy, were hanged in various places in Westmorland and Cumberland!" I find," says Froude, "among the records an entry, that "the bodies were cut down and buried by certain women."

Here, then, we venture to think, is the required explanation of time and circumstance, when the persons whose bones were discovered in 1836, met their fate, and were thrown beneath the sod "unhouselled, unanointed, unanealed."

We now proceed to a description of the Castle, and some of those ancient manor-houses and mansions which were the residences of the families whose names are recorded in the monumental memorials in the church; together with such of the ancient customs and ceremonies as demand notice.

Froude's "History of England," vol. iii. pp. 200—203. THE CASTLE

Is situated on Castle-hill, a verdant knoll, of oval shape, composed of rounded stones, and gravel. It commands an extensive view to the north and south-west. In the near ground is the town, with here and there a stately poplar waving o'er its azure roofs. About the valley the numerous hills are clothed with wood, or smile in verdure, amid a range of fertile inclosures, through which, in gleams of real beauty, the waters of the river serpentize from their native hills in the north, down the shining tract of country, till they become lost in the estuary which unites them with the ocean. In the distance are magnificent mountains, towering high, which, adding to the beautiful, the sub-

lime, and picturesque, constitute an elegant and striking landscape.

Here stood the noble Castle, whose remains are scarcely now sufficient to tell how vast it was.

"Where the great lord inhabited: now grass,
Thin grass, and king-cups grow within the path."

It is much to be regretted that we cannot establish the date of this Castle. There is, however, very little doubt, that it was raised altogether, or in part, by one of the earliest barons of Kendal. And if in part only by one of the first barons, the completion of it must be assigned to those who lived in the twelfth, or in the earlier part of the thirteenth century. Mr. Hallam has acquiesced in the opinion of Dr. Whitaker and Mr. King, that a circular tower, as a keep, was commonly the first structure of ancient castles. To the lower chambers of this keep there was no admission of light or air except through long narrow loop-holes, and an aperture in the roof. In course of time, the barons wht owned these castles began to covet a more comfortable dwelling. The keep was either much enlarged, or altogether relinquished as a place of residence, except in a time of siege; while more convenient apartments were sometimes erected in the tower of entrance, Coleridge.

Vide " State of Europe during the Middle Ages," vol. iii. p. 416. Author of the Essays on Ancient Castles, in the " Arehaeologia." over the great gateway, which led to the inner ballium or courtyard.

The circular tower (not seen in our partial view of the present state of the ruins) is the most entire part and has evidently been the strongest: but the precise time when it was erected, and whether the rest of the building be coeval with it, must, we fear, for ever remain in obscurity. All that we can say on this point is, that the order of architecture and the arrangement of the apartments carry a pointed resemblance to some other castles which have been referred to the time of the Conqueror.

The material employed in its construction, has been principally the blue

"silurian" rock of the neighbouring hills, with some freestone for the doors, windows, and quoins; and the mode of building has been the same as was generally adopted in castles erected immediately after the Conquest. The outsides of the wall were first laid with stones as regularly as their shape would admit; the insides filled up with the like materials, mixed with a great quantity of fluid mortar, which was called by the workmen *grout work.*

The freestone before mentioned is chiefly the old red conglomerate which strikes across the valley, underlying the limestone, but there are also to be found in the building, blocks of white or yellow sandstone, and where these latter have come from is a mystery to us. The "old red" is seen abundantly in the bed of the "Mint" and the "Sprint," and has lately been unveiled nearer to the Castle. It was found close to Netherbridge, and shown to cross the river there, dipping into the Castle-hill. It is quite possible, therefore, that it may have been quarried for the Castle, or even for a prior work, in the depression now or formerly occupied by "Willow-wand Tarn," on the south-east side of the Castle-hill.

The first historical mention of the Castle that we have been able to discover, is in the time of Gilbert Fitz-Reinfred, who married, in the 1st Richard I. (1189), Helwise, daughter and Cockermouth Castle for a particular instance. A method of building before that used by the Romans. heiress of William de Lancaster the second. He ohtained from king John a continuation of the honour of Lancaster, and executed the office of sheriff of Lancaster from the 7th to the 17th of that reign. Gilbert was unfaithful to his patron, and joined the rebellious barons; but William, his son (usually called William de Lancaster the third), having been taken prisoner, Gilbert accepted the king's terms to pay for his ransom, and that of Ralph Deincourt and Lambert de Brus, his esquires, twelve thousand marks, and to find hostages for his own and their future fidelity; besides which, he was compelled to deliver into the king's hands his *cas-*

tle of Kendal, &c. It is probable that in the reign of Henry III. the castle and manor were restored to the immediate successor of Gilbert, viz. his son, William de Lancaster the third, for we find that he was placed in his father's trust as keeper of the honour of Lancaster, the grant of which bears date 25th Henry III. He died childless, and his great estates descended to Peter le Brus, by Helwise, his older sister, and William de Lyndesay, by Alice, his second sister. A partition of the estates than took place, when Peter "obtained the castle and manor of Kendal as his principal seat." Alice's portion was what is called the Richmond Fee.

By an inquisition taken on the death of Peter le Brus, son of the aforesaid Peter, and the second who succeeded to a moiety of the barony of Kendal, called the Marquis Fee, we find that the said Peter died in the 7th Edward L (1279), seised "of a moiety of the manor of Kirkeby-in-Kendale, and as parcel thereof, of *the castle,* with the parks, vivaries within the parks, and herbage therein of the yearly value of ten marks, &c." This inquisition also finds, that the said Peter le Brus died without any heir of his body; and that Margaret, Agnes, Lucy and Laderine, were his sisters and coheirs. The Castle, "with all in Kendal that had been Peter's, and whatsoever belonged to Peter in demesnes, villenages, rents and services of *free men and others,"* fell to the share of his eldest sister, Margaret le Bras, who was married "History of Richmondshire," vol. ii. p. 291.

"History of Westmorland," p. 41.

to Robert de Ross (or, as it was most commonly written, Roos). The said Robert de Ross and Margaret his wife had a son William, who had a son William, who had a son Thomas de Ross (died 1391), whose daughter and heir Elizabeth was married to William del Parr, knight, by which the Castle, the advowson of the hospital of St. Leonard, and the fourth part of the manor of Kirkby-in-Kendal were conveyed into this family. We will trace briefly the genealogy of the Parrs from this time to their extinction. The jurors, on the inquisition of William del Parr,

knight (who survived his wife, and died 6th Henry TV. 1405), find that John Parr, knt., was his son and heir. This John did not long survive his father, for the inquisition afterJiis death bears date 9th Henry IV. He was succeeded by his son, Thomas Parr, knight, who, in the 6th Henry VI. appears, by an inquisition of knights' fees, to have held one-fourth part of the manor of Kirkby-in-Kendal, by the service of the fourth part of one knight's fee. He died in the 4th Edward IV. (1464), leaving two sons, William and John. Sir William Parr, knight, heir of Sir Thomas, married Elizabeth, one of the three sisters and coheirs of Henry, Lord Fitzhugh (whose arms appear on the third shield of Parr's monument, and also in the quarterings at the east end of the same, as described in our account of the church). He was made knight of the garter by king Edward IV.; and was knight of the shire for Westmorland in the 6th, and again in the 12th of that reign. He appears to have been living in the 22d Edward IV. but in what year he died we have not found. He had two sons, Thomas, the elder, and a younger son, Sir William Parr, of Horton, in Northamptonshire. He was younger son of Robert, Lord Roos, by bis wife Isabel, daughter of the king of Scots. There is an effigy of him in *Eastwick* Church.

It is this Sir William Parr whom we suppose to be interred beneath the altar tomb, at the south-east corner of Kendal church. For the arms thereon are encircled with the garter.

'He died in 1548, and was buried at Horton, where, says Pennant, there is a remarkable monument of him, in alabaster, recumbent, with his lady by his side. He left two daughters only, married into the families of Tressam and Lane. His relation called him to court, but his age forbade him the pleasures, and his own reservedness the freedom of that place; before which he preferred the pious, peaceable, and hospitable way of the country, where popularity affected him more than he affected it,— no man being more The eldest son, Sir Thomas Parr, knight, succeeded his father. He was master of the wards, and

comptroller to Henry VIII. He married Maude, daughter and coheir of Sir Thomas Green, by whom he had issue one son and two daughters, viz. William Parr, afterwards Marquis of Northampton, Katherine, last wife of King Henry VIII. (of both of whom we shall hereafter give biographical memoirs), and Anne, married to. William Herbert, earl of Pembroke, concerning whom we have been unable to find any interesting particulars.

Sir Thomas Parr, knight, father of qtieen Katherine, &c., by his will, dated November 7th, the 9th of Henry VIII. , bequeathed his body to lie in Blackfriars' church, London, "if he chanced to die within twenty miles thereof." All his manors, lands and tenements, he left to his wife Maude during her life. He willed his daughters, Katherine and Anne, to have 800*l.* between them, as marriage portions, except they proved to be his heirs or his son's heirs, and then they should not. He willed his son William to have his great chain, worth 140?., which the "king's grace" gave him. And 100 marks to be bestowed upon the chantry of Kendal. This will was proved in the year 1517. By an inquisition, after his death, of his lands in Westmorland, the jiirors find that he was seised of the manor of Kendale, with 1,000 acres of pasture, and 400?. rent, together with the appurtenances in Hutton-Hay, Strickland, Hugill, Greenrigge, Ullerthorne, and Kirkby-inKendal.

The instruction in the aforesaid will, that his body was to lie in Blackfriars' church "if he chanced to die within twenty miles thereof," appears to be the only foundation for the statement made by Dr. Burn, and quoted by Miss Agnes Strickland, that he, Sir Thomas, "was evidently not buried in Kendal church, but in Blackfriars' church, in London. " There seems to be no evidence for any *positive* statement on either side. The church alluded to in London is the beloved by the vulgar—no man less iti love with them. It being his observation, rather than his countryman, Sir Edward Montague's saying,—'that if you do the common sort of people nineteen courtesies together, yet you may lose their love," if you go but over the stile before them.'—Lloyd's "State Worthies," date 1670.

" History of Westmorland," p. 75, and "Life of Katherine Parr," p. 179. parish church of Blackfriars, St. Anne's, which originally belonged, says *Stowe* to the "Friar Preachers of London, where Parliaments often sat, and Noble Personages were there harbored." We have taken some pains in the investigation of this matter. There is no tomb, nor any monumental record of the burial of Sir Thomas Parr, in the church or churchyard of Blackfriars. The parish register there is necessarily silent as to the fact, for it dates back no further than 1562, (and where is there a perfect, continuous register that goes beyond this?) The probability as to the place of burial turns upon the circumstance whether Sir Thomas "deceased at London," which words are attributed to an inscription that was at one time, *according to tradition,* in Kendal church. But *tradition* also says that the large tomb in the Parr chapel, without inscription, belongs to Sir Thomas. So here is an even balance of evidence. It may perhaps be contended, that as his wife, Maud, subsequently bequeathed her body to rest in Blackfriars, that favours the supposition of Sir Thomas being buried there. And with suppositions on both sides, the matter must rest for the present.

Dame Maud Parr, widow of the above-named Sir Thomas, by her will, dated May 20th, 21st Henry VIII., bequeathed her body to be buried in Blackfriars' church. In this will she mentioned her son and heir, William Parr; also her daughter Anne, and Katherine Borough, her daughter, and Sir William Parr, her brother, and Thomas Pickering, Esq. her cousin—steward of her house. Her will was proved December 14, 1531.

In giving the family history of the Scroops, of Bolton, Dr. Whitaker has published a long and interesting correspondence between Lady Parr, Lord Dacre, and Lord Scroop, relating to an agreement for the marriage of the son and heir of Lord Scroop with Katherine (destined afterwards to a higher station), eldest daughter of the said Lady Parr. — Lord Dacre was perhaps chosen as negotiator in the treaty, on account of his relationship with both families, being father of Lady Scroop, and cousin of Dame Parr; but it would seem, *"Survey of London,"* hook 3, p. 691.

See Epitaphs in the Church, *ante,* p. 52. from this correspondence, that he would fain have taken undue advantage of his "righte well-beloved" cousin's anxiety to effect the union, and thereby secure to his grandson a greater portion of her inheritance than either she considered reasonable, or, as she tells him, was consistent with "the customs of the countre." This character will be found evidenced in the following letters, which are too full of interest to admit of curtailment: 1.—*A Letter from Maud, Lady Parr, to , Lord Daere.*

Most honorable and my very good lord, I hertly reco'mend me vnto you. Where it pleasid you att your last beyng here to take payn in the mater in consideracion of marriage between the Lord Scrap's son and my doughtor Kateryne, for the whiche I hertly thank you; at which time I thought the matter in good furtherance. Howe bee yt, I perceyve that my seid Lord Scrop is nott aggreable to that consideracion, as more playnly may appere vnto you by certeyn articles sent to me from my seyd lord, the coppy of which articles I send you herein inclosyd. My lord's pleasour is to have a full answere from me before La'mas next comyng, wherefore it may please you to bee so good to have this matter in yo remembraunce, for I perceyve well this matter is not lyke to take effecte except it be by yo helpe. The joyntour is lytle, for xi m'res whiche I *wall nott passe,* and my seyd lord wyll nott repay after marriage hadd, and cc marcs must nedys be repayd yf my doughter Kateryne dys before the age of xvi yeres, or ells I shuld breke Master Parr's wyll, whiche I shold be lothe to doo; and ther can be no p'fyto marriage vntill my lord's son com to the age of xiiii, and my doughter to the age of xii, before whiche tyme if the marriage shuld take none effect, or be dissolved, either by deth, wardshipp, disagrement, or otherwyse, whiche may bee before thatt tyme, notwithstondinge marriage solemnysed, repayment must nedes be hadd of the hole, or ells I myght fortune to pay my money for nothinge. As for the daye of payment, I am content with the first day, and the resydue of his days of payment bee too shortt for me. Qladd I wold be to have the mater goe forthe yf itt myght be convenyently; yff it please you to call to remembrsumce the co'icaciou before yow at Greenewiche was that I shold paye att yo desyre xi c marcs, whereof c marcs in hand, and every yere after c marcs, which is as muche as I may spare, as yow knowe; and for thatt my doughto' is to have c marcs joyntour, whereof l marcs I to have for her fynding vntill they warre able to lye together, & then they to have the hole c marcs, & repayment to be hadd yf the marriage took nott effecte. My lord, itt may please you to take so muche payne as to helpe to conclude this matter yf it woll bee; and yff you see any default on my partt I shall be ordred as ye shall deme good, as knoweth Jh'u, who preserve your good lordshipp. Wrytten at the Rye the xiiii. day off July. My lord, it may please your lordship to gyff credence to this berer.

Your cousyn,

Maud Parrs. *To the Right Honorable and my iingular good lord, my Lord Daeree, this bee delivered. 2.—Articles for thep'te of Henry, Lord Scrop of Bolton, for Mariage between the Son and Heyre apparent of the laid Lord Scrop, and Kateryne Parre, Doughtor of Dame Maude, Lady Parre.*

Fyret, the seid Lord Scrop is content for xi marcs of money to gyffe a xl' ffoefment, whereof x to be taken yerely for the ffynding of the seid Kateryne Parr, daughter to the seid Dame Maude Parre, and the residue of the seid ffeoffement to enter to y when the seid Lord Scrop's son & heire shalbe come to the age of xviii yeres, and after the death of the seid Lord Scrop to make the fieofement furth c marcs.

Item. Yf the Lady Parre wyll pay xii marcs in money the ffeofment to be c' after the deth of the seid Lord Scrop, so that the hole fieofement remayne in the seid lord2s hands to his seid son & heire come to the age of xviii yeres.

Item. Of the aforeseid xi marcs vi' marcs to be payed att the synyng of the indentures of covenante, & v" marcs to be payed in the ii yeres nexte following, by even porcions. And yf the seid Lady Parre wylle paye xii marcs, vi marcs to be payed at the synyng of the indentures of covenante, & vi marcs to be payed in the 2 yeres nexte followyng by even pore'cms.

Item. The seid Lord Scrop wyll *not agree to repay no money* after the marriage to be solempnyzed & executed, ne to enter into no covenante by especyaltye for the governaunce of the children duryng the nonage of them.

3.—*Lord Dacre's Answer to the above Letter and Articles.*

T Madame, in right hartie maner I reco'mend me vnto you, and by thande of yo' servant, berer hereof, I have receved yo writing, dated at Rye the 14th daye of this instant moneth of July, and to me delivered yesternight, to gidres w' copie of certein articles to youe sent fro my Lord Scrope touching the marriage to be had betwene his son and your doughter Katheryne, by the contents whereof I doo perceyve ye think that the seid mater in communicac'on of mariage, which ye thought had beene in good furtheraunce, is like to go bak, bereason that my said Lord Scrope is not agreable to suche co'municacion as was had of the same at my last being v' youe, for even so and many causes specified in yo said l're and articles at length. Cousin, sens my dep'ture from you I assure you I was not two nights to giddres at myne owne house, bereason whereof I had never leisour to labour in thes matres. And I do think, seing my Lord Scrope cannot be contente w' the communicac'ons that was had at my last being w' you, whiche was thought reasonable to me, and as I perceve semblably to his couneell, that this matter cannot be brought to no p'f cte end w'out mutuall communicacion to be had w' my said lord, aither by my self, my son, or my brother. Wherfore, as sone as conveniently any of us may be

spared this matter shal be laboured, trusting veryly that I shall bringe it to a good pointe, and as I shal do therein ye shal be advertised at length. I have promise of my said lord, and of my doughter, his wif, that they shal not marie their son w'out my consent, which they shall not have to no p'son but vnto youe; and undoubtedly my said lord must uecles have some money, *and he has nothing to make it of but onely the marriage of his said son,* wherefore my full counsaill is, that ye be not over hasty, but Biiffre, and fyually ye shalbe well assured that I shall doo in this mattre, or in any other that is or may bu aither pleasure, profitte, or suyrtie, to you or my said cousin, yo daughter, that lieth in my power. *At Newcastcll, the penult Daye of Julii, A", xvo //. VIII. I.*

Right honorable and my singular good lord, I recommend me unto you: I have receyved your l9re dated at Newcastell the penult day of July, and by the same I perceye your pleasure, aud also what payn ye intend to take in the matter betwene my Lord Scrope and me, for the whiche I hartely thank you. The Lord Scrope seid to a servant of myne that he wold uo longer drive tyme in that matter with mo, but ho would be at large, aud take his best advantage as with the lord treasurer, whiehe had made moc'ons to be in communicac'on with him. Therefore it may please you at your couvenyent leysour to have this matter in your remembrauiice, and thus I am alweys bold to put yo lordship to perns aud busines, which I pray God I may some p'te defray, which shuld not be failed if it lyuth in my poure, be the grace of Jh'u, who preserve your good lordship. Wrettyn at Esthamsteed, this axij daie of August.

Your

Maud Parre. *To the Right Honorable and my syngler ijoud lord, my Lord JJaere. 5.*
No Address. Apparently from his Mother to Lord Serope
My lord and son, I reco9mende me unto you in right hartio manner, aud by thande of your servant, bringer hereof yesterday, I received your writing dated the x daye of this instant moneth, I oud-

erstanding therby that for suche communications as has been had and moved betwene my Lady I'arr and yowo by your counsells concerning the marriage of your sonne and myn according to the teno thereof, ye have now sent w your servant, this said bringer, the articles of the same, wherein ye desire that ye may knowe my aunswer in writing; and, further, that ye wold be sorry for any suche consideracions that any long drife were made therein, as further your said writing purporteth. My lorde, your son and hcire, is the gretest jewell that ye can have, seeing that he must present your owne p'son after your deth, vnto whorne I pray God len long yeares. And yf ye be disposyd to marie him, or he be com to full age, when he may have som hym self, I cannot see, w'out that ye wold marry him to one heire of land, whiche wolbe ryght costly, that ye can mary hym to so good a stok as my Lady Parr, for divers considerations, first, is remembring the wisdome of my seid lady, and the god wise stok of the Grenes whereof she is comen, and also of the wise stok of the Pars of Kendale, for al whiche men doo looke when they do mary their child, to the wisedomo of the blood of that they do marry w'. I speke not of the possibilitie of my Lady Parr's daughter, who has but one child betwene her, and viiic marcs land to inherit thereof. Such possybilities doth oftyntymes fall, and I speke it because of the possibilitie that befelle vnto myselfe by my mariage, aud therefor, in myn opinion, the same is to be regarded. My lord, to declare vnto you trewely, I assure you your copie of articles conteyning your demands, which ye have now sent, and my ladi's demaunds, is so far in sundre, that in manner it is vnpossible that ever ye shall agree in that behalf; wherefore, if ye can be content to go groundlye to work, and go to a short conclusion, I think it best that ye goo after the co'mon course of mariage, that is to sey, to geve c marcs joy nt' for the payment of xi marcs, that is to sey, ii-ii or v marcs to be peyed at the making vp of the covenante, and c yerely, vnto suche tyme as the som be fvlly ron, the one child to be in the kepinge of my seid lady; and if it fortune the said p'sons one or other of them to die befoer carnall copulation had betwixt them, or before thage of consentment, then the som receyved to be repayed at suche dayes and after suche forme as it was delivered, w'out new mariage may be had w' the yong child, for I think it is not convenient nor prouffitable that c marcs should go out yerely of your land to so yong a p'son as my said lady eldest doghter, if it fortune, as God defend, that y said son and myne die. And thus, my lord, I assure you thys is theffecte of my opynyons; and if ye can thus be content, the matter shall shortly take effect. Also, I think it good, but I wold not have it comprised in the covenante, that during the tyme of 3 yeres, by whiche tyme my seid son and yours woll com to consentment, that he shold be with my said lady if she kepe her wedowhede, and ye to fynd hym clothiug, and a servant to adwate vpon him, and she to find hym mete and drink, for I assure you he mought lerne w her as well as yn any place that I kuowe, as well norture, as Frenche and other languuage, whiche me semes were a comodious thinge for hym.

No Signature.
At Morpeth the xvii day of December A"
XV-H. VHJ. 6.

Right honorabull and my syngler good lord, I hertly reco'mend me vnto you, thankyng you of your manyffold paynes takyn between my Lord Scropp & me, and concernyng the same I have receyved your lettres, and my Lord Scropp's also, and right well p'ceyve the contents of the same; wherein I have takyn advice of my Lord of London, and dyvers other of my husband's ffriends St myn, who thinke thatt my seid Lord Scropp's offer, as well concernynge the joynter as the repament off my money, *is so littill & so farr from the customs of the countre, and his demand is so greatt ifc so large off me, with the shortt payment!, that my seyd ffrends woll in no wyse thatt I shall medic with the seyd barganc after my seid Lord Scropp's offer ik demand.*

My lord, seynge this matter hathe beyn so longe in co'itac'on, I am ryght

sorie on my p2tie it can nott take effecte, for in good faith hotherto I never had co'icac'on for no maryage to herr, for thatt I wold haue beyn so gladd shuld havo goon forward as this, or ells I wold not have made so large offers for the forderaunce of the same as I have. My lord, I beseche you to be good lord vnto my cousin, the berer, in suche cause as he hath to do in y p'ties, that the rather through your good helpe he may obteyn his right of suche thinges as his father gave hym in his bequest, the whyche shalbe hard for him to obteyn w'out your favor. And thus the Holy Goost preserve your good lordship to his pleasure.

Your

Maud Parbe. *From the Court at Greenwiche, this xr Daye of Marche. To the Right Honourabell my Lord of Dacrts thys be delyvered.*

The praise herein recorded of Dame Maud Parr may be fairly esteemed her due; and the "wisdome of the seid lady" overcoming her natural inclination, determined that she "shuld in no wise medle with the said bargane."—This negociation took place in the loth Henry VIII. , when, if our date of her birth be correct, Katherine was eleven years of age.

William Parr succeeded his father, Sir Thomas. He was thrice married,— first, to Anne, daughter and heir of Henry Bourchier, earl of Essex (a family of high antiquity, and having immense possessions in the county of Essex); secondly, to Elizabeth, daughter of George Brook, Lord Cobham; and thirdly, to Helena, daughter of Wolfangus Suavenderg, a Swede, who survived him. In the 30th Henry VIII. he was created Lord Parr and Ross, of Kendal; and in the 35th, Baron Hart, of Northamptonshire. In the latter year he was also created Earl of Essex, in right of his wife Anne. And, finally, in the 1st Edward VI. he was made Marquis of Northampton; and from hence that part of the barony which he held received the name of the Marquis Fee. On the 18th of August, 1553, he was condemned as a traitor for espousing the cause of Lady Jane Grey. However, he was soon afterwards restored in blood,

but not immediately to his estates. These, it appears, were given up to him by favour of Queen Elizabeth. He died in the 13th Elizabeth, being the last of the family.— In his steward's accounts is the following item: "In money paid to the abby and convent of St. Mary's, York, for the tithes of corn and hay of all the demesne lands of the castle of Kendal, called Myntesfeet, Gallobar, Kirkefield, and 20 acres of inclosure at Stanecross, lying contiguous 44s. 8d. as allowed in account of preceding years."

This brings us to the conclusion of all that we find important to be said respecting the family; and now we are conducted, by the order of time, to the remaining history of the Castle. Dr. Burn has committed an error in calling her Helen. He seems not to have been aware that the Marquis was more than once married; and so has confounded the name of his last wife with the first. Morant's " History of Essex." The date of the Castle's decay, or destruction, may fairly be taken from the attainder of the Marquis of Northampton. And as only nineteen years—viz. from 1553 to 1572—intervened between that event and the time when it is proved to have been in ruins, the most plausible conclusion seems, that it was dismantled or thrown down in the Marquis's unsuccessful engagements against the crown in favour of Lady Jane Grey. The queen (Katherine) and the marquis are both generally represented to have been born here, the former in, or about, 1513; and suppose we even date the decline of the Castle from this period, it requires extraordinary credulity to believe, that, in fifty-nine years, it could, from mere desuetude and gradual decay, have sunk into a state of complete dilapidation.—A report long prevailed, and (perhaps for want of a published history) was long credited, that it was blown down by Oliver Cromwell from off Castle How Hill; and hence some have been led to believe that the mount was at *that time* purposely constructed for the demolition of the Castle. This notion scarcely admits of serious consideration. The following extract will show, beyond doubt, that the Castle was in ruins *almost an entire century before the time of the Protectorate/*

By a survey of the Marquis Fee, made by order of the dowager Marchioness of Northampton (who had dower assigned to her by letters patent of Queen Elizabeth), in July, 1572, we find the Castle thus minutely described:—

"The Castle of Kendal is situate on the knowl of an hill, within the park there, and on the east side of the town, with a fair and beautiful prospect. The out walls are embattled 40 feet square; and within the same no building left, saving only to the north side is situate the front of the gate-house, the hall, with an ascent of stairs to the same, with a buttery and pantry at the end thereof; one great chamber and two or three lesser chambers, and rooms of ease adjoining the same; being all in decay, both in glass and slate, and in all other reparations needful. Under the hall are two or three small rooms of cellars. In the south side is situate a dove cot in good repair. The yearly rent of the demesne, and one-fourth part of the toll (of Kendal), 64£ 14s. Yearly rent of the tenants at will in Newbiggin, in Kendal, 4?. 3s. Yearly rent of the burgage lands there, *101* 5s. *6d.* Fourth part of the fishing of Kent, *11. 2s. 4d."*

Not long after this, Queen Elizabeth made an exchange with the Marchioness for the Marquis Fee, giving her other lands in lieu thereof. And in the 23d Elizabeth the said queen granted "a part of the demesne lands belonging to the castle, by the name of the park of Kendal, with divers edifices, buildings, lands, tenements, and other premises to the same appertaining," to Ambrose, Earl of Warwick, to hold in soccage, as of the manor of East Greenwich. What became of the Castle, and other demesne park-lands, we have not found, until the reign of Charles II., when they appear to have been in the hands of Sir Francis Anderton, of Lostock, in the county of Lancaster, baronet. His son and heir, Sir Charles Anderton, settled them to the use of himself, for life, remainder to his first and other sons, in tail male. Lawrence, one of the younger sons, succeeded, after many difficulties, to the estate, and sold it in 1723, to John Huggins, Esq. The said John Huggins dying in 1735, the same descended to his brother and heir, William Huggins, who devised it to his two sons-in-law, Sir Thomas Gatehouse, knight, and the Rev. Dr. James Musgrave, who sold the property in 1765, to the late Thomas Holme and James Dowker, of Kendal, and Benjamin Hall, of Newton, in Cartmel, Esquires. These gentlemen after selling part of the lands, divided the remainder amongst themselves, and2 the Castle falling to the share of James Dowker, Esq., came eventually to Mrs. Thomasin Richardson, his daughter. And at the death of Mrs. Richardson it was bought by Mr. Alderman Thompson, formerly M.P. for Westmorland, and is now held by his executors.

When Gray (the poet) visited it, in 1769, he says, " almost the whole inclosure-wall remains, with four towers, two square and two round, but their upper parts and embattlemcnts are demolished: it is of rough stone and cement, without any ornament or arms, round, inclosing a court of the ike form, and surrounded by a moat; nor ever could it have been larger than it is, for there are no traces of out-works." To this Mr. West replied (1779), "had Mr. Gray ascended from the end of Stramongate Bridge to the castle, which was the only way to it when in its glory, and is the easiest at present, he would have observed a square area that had been fortified with a deep moat, and connected with the castle by a drawbridge, where was probably the base-court." The stones are now entirely removed, and the ground levelled, "and laughing Ceres reassumes the land." Dr. Whitaker inclines to the opinion that it had no out-works.

The castle has suffered little injury, and undergone little alteration in our time, excepting in the two following instances.—In 1813, the foundations were strengthened, and the walls repaired; and the banks of the fosse on the western side were planted with the trees which are now beginning to conceal too much of the ruins. In 1824, a ponderous mass of the wall, which many years before had detached itself from the north front, and stood, like an inverted cone, on the site of the drawbridge, was, by a brisk wind in January, blown down, and shattered into fragments. Its dimensions were 12 by 22 yards.

It is impossible for a contemplative mind to survey these time-worn ruins of ancient magnificence, without being inspired with some of the melancholy reflections which Hutcheson has so finely pourtrayed in his survey of a similar fortress: "How fluctuating are the affairs of man! how changeable are all sublunary things! These towers submit to the destroying hand of time! How are thy honours wasted, and thy pride brought low! Authority and rule are rent from thy hands, and thy conquering banners are delivered up to the darkness of oblivion. Thy chambers are no longer the abode of security! Where the jocund guests laughed over the sparkling bowl, adders now hiss, and owls sing the strains of melancholy to the midnight moonshine that sleeps upon thy mouldering battlements!"

There are two appurtenances of this ancient castle to notice, viz. the Castle Mills, and the Castle Dairy.

Castle Mills are situated on the west side of the castle, not far from the river; and on a stream of water which is turned H from the main-course of the river, by a wear or dam. These mills appear to have been erected for the purpose of grinding corn for the castle: and there is still the remains of an arch, which probably formed part of the ancient structure. AVe conclude that the tithes of these mills formed au 'item' in the ancient endowment of the church: for in the general ecclesiastical survey of Henry VIII. they are stated to amount to *15s. 8d.* (" Decim molend. Castell vis. viiidl ")

This property belonged to the Corporation until the year 18.53, when it was purchased by Messrs. J. J. and W. Wilson, for the sum of 5000?. (See the Article on Manufactures in a future page.)

Stands on the north-west side of

Wildman Street, about fifty yards from Stramongate Bridge. It appears, from the name, to have been the milk farm belonging to the castle. In the house, there appears to have been a chapel, which was, most probably, appropriated to the husbandmen and menial servants under the potent barons, in the plenitude of their power. Dr. Burn says, "there was a chapel at It might also be placed hero for the purpose of administering divine con. eolation to the pilgrims who were about to undertake the perilous journey over Shap fella; just, " as in former times, divine service was performed in the oratory upon Chapel island, near Ulverstone, to persons crossing the sands."—West2s Antiquities of Furness, p. 15.

the east end of Straniongate Bridge, called All Hallows' Chapel." But this appears to have heen a mistake, for Speed's Plan shows, that All Hallows' Chapel stood at the head of the lane which hears its name. The reference in Burn's History is evidently to the chapel at Castle Dahy. The following description of this place is from "Notes and Queries":—

On a stone outside, on a shield or eseutscheon, are incised the letters "A. o.," of an ancient fashion, a cord with sundry knots being intertwined, anil the date, 1564:—for Anthony Garnett, then proprietor.

On the upper bevelled stonework of a window to the extreme left are incised "QVJ Vadit Plane—Vadit Sane A.o." This same idea is rendered into English on coeval glass in Worlingworth Church, Suffolk, " heyt wulke plainly —walketh sauely." Entering what is now the kitchen, but which is only a portion of the original apartment partitioned off, the clavey, or mantelshelf, extends the whole breadth of the house, and is formed of oak in curved panels, the moulding battlemented, with which the opposite end, now forming part of the entrance passage, corresponds.

In the south window of the same is a quarrel (No. 1.) with, "1567—Omnia Vanitas—A.o.," with interlaced cord, " Viendra Le Iovr," a skull. Another (No. 2.) with a fleur de lis, within a tasteful border, in cinque cento style, surmounted by a crown; both executed in yellow stain.

In a bedroom up stairs, is a massive carved-oak bedstead, the head-board of which has upon it, carved in bold relief on the top triangular panel, the centre-piece gone, first row below-dexter, a mask with horns, after the Roman antique; middle, a scroll, with "omnia batlttas," a shield, having "a.o." conjoined by a fanciful knotted cord, a scroll with " VlwOTa U four," and skull; sinister, mask in cinque cento style: lower row, three lions' masks in as many panels.

On a buffett or ambry, upper part, "Oia: Vanitas: Honor: a central piece missing Divicie: Potestas;" lower part, " Anno Dni 1562." On each side "A.o.," as before. The bedstead above named is of the same date, as the carving on both, in certain parts, coincides.

In the window, on a quarrel (No. 1.), "A.o," and the date " 1565." (No. 2.) Au oak tree erased, argent, fructed or; on its branches an eagle and child of the second. No. 3. as No. 1. in the room below No. 4., an oak tree erased; on its branches an eagle and child or, the face proper.

On oak bosses on the ceiling; that next the window has a shield of four quarterings: 1st, two fesses engrailed, on the upper one a mullet pierced, Parr; 2nd, three chevronels in fess braced, Fitzhugh: 3rd, three water bougets, two and one, Ross; 4th, apparently three rabbits, two and one,.... On another, farther from the window, a second shield of four quarterings; first and fourth a fess diincette between nine billets, four and five, Deincourt; second and third three cockle shells, Strickland.

Some years ago, in an old oak chest, in this house, were discovered, a Missal, a MS. Genealogy of some of the Saxon kings, and two sets of Beechen Roundels. The genealogy One set of the Roundels, and the Missal, are in the possession of Mrs. Braithwaite, widow of Garnett Braithwaito, Esq., of Plumtree Hall.

is well written, on vellum, and illuminated. It extends from Adelwald, the 19th king of Northunibria, in the heptarchy (759), to Edward II., surnamed "the Martyr." The Missal is in very good condition, excepting that it wants the title-page, and unfortunately the date. The Roundels may perhaps require some explanation; being, as we conceive, very scarce and little understood. The name is descriptive both of their shape and substance; for they are made of beechen wood, planed thin, and are circular, about five inches in diameter. A set consists of twelve, having distinct borders, six of either, uniform. In the centre is represented an animal, existent or fanciful, and inscribed with a maxim or motto in rhyme: 1.

The representation of a skull, and below it the following quatrain.

"A wyfe yt maryethe husbandes thre
Was neuer wyshed thereto by me;
I wolde my wyfe sholde rather dye,
Then for my death to wepe and cry."
2.

A leopard, as anciently represented in the arms of England. (').

"And he that reades thys verse ener uowe,
May hape to haue a lourynge sowe
Whose louckes are lyked (') nothynge so bail
As ys hyr tounge to make hym made."
3.

A white greyhound collared, () the collar bezante.

"If that a batcheler thou be,
Kepe thee so sty 11; be rulede by mce,
Lest that repentaunce all to latt
Hewarde thee wyth a brocken patte."
4.

A red fox.

2 I shrowo hys harte that maryed mee;
My wyfe and I canne neuer agree;
A knauyshe quene by Jys I sweare,
The goodman's bretche shee thynke3 to woare."

(') A leopard is the correct heraldic term for the English lion, as here drawn, lean, gaunt, and savage-looking, with tail and tongue well developed; a very different animal from that depicted now-a-days. () Libeiiccl, or like to. *Tounge,* in tho fourth line, has reference to that rubicund member of the royal beast aa depicted in the original. () This was one of the supporters of Henry VIII's anus. 5. A red squirrel.

'-Thys woman may haue husbands fyve,

Hutt neuer whyll sheo ys alyve;

Yett doth shee hoppe (') so well to spede;

Geue up thy hopp, yt shall not nede."

8. A red camel.

"Aake thou thy wyfe yf shee oann tell

Whether thou in maryage hast spede well;

And lett hyr speake as she dothe knowe,

For zx pounde she wyll saye no."

7. A white elephant.

"Thou aret the hapeste man alyue,

For euery thynge doth make the thryue;

Yett maye thy wyfe thy master be,

Wherefore tacke thryft and all for mee."

8.

A white panther spotted.

"If thou be younge then marye nott yeat;

If thou be olde thou hast more wytte;

For young menes wyues wyll nott be taught,

And old menes wyues be good for noughte."

9.

A white talbot.

"Take upp thy fortune wythe good happ, ()

Wythe ryches thou doste fyll thy lappe,

Yett lese weare better for thy store,

Thy queytnes yn shal be the more."

10 A golden leopard or spotted panther.

"Rescue thy hape () as fortune sendeth,

For god yt ys that fortune lendeth;

Wherefor yf thou a shrowe () hast goott,

Thynke wyth thy selfe yt ys thy lott."

11.

A hare.

"Thou mayst be poore, & what for yt f

Hou yf thou hadeste nether cappe nore hatt?

Yett may thy mynde so queyt be,

What thou mayst wyn as muche as thre. "

0) *Hoppe* and *Hopp* a play of words with reference to the habits of this mercurial little animal.

( ) Hap and Hape, " *luck."* Example: "A fox had the *hap* to fall into the walk of a lion."—*L'Estrange.* (In Johnson.) () " A shrew has got." Spiteful and indignant, like the shrew field-mouse. —(See *Brockettt " Glotsary.")*

I-'.

A white unicorn.

"Thou hast a throwe to thy good man,

Parhapes auunthryft () so what than;

Kepe hym as lounge as he cann lyue,

And at hys ende hys passpot geue."

These roundels are said to be of the time of Henry VIII. The letters are similar to those of his day, in half printing, half running hand; the initials at the beginning of each line being in red, and what are termed Lombardic. The roundels seem to have been used in games of chance. In No. 12, *throwe* alludes to the use of dice, and similar allusions appear in other places. Mr. Thoresby considers that they were "played in the manner of cards." It is supposed (says he) that the Nuns of Arthington extracted at once edification and amusement from them.

This house is now the property of Mrs. Garnett Braithwaite.

SIZERGH HALL

Is a tine old fortified building, and a fair specimen of the manor-house, of first respectability and importance. It is one of those which, having continued to be the residence of one family for a series of years, has never fallen into decay. As such we shall give a more particular account of it.

It stands about three miles south of Kendal, in a pleasant park; and the towers command an interesting and extensive prospect to the north and southeast, of fertile fields and thriving plantations, bounded by an horizon of majestic hills.

The etymology of this name carries the appellation back to the earliest cultivation of the land. The first syllable is from the Saxon *sic,* "a furrow," from which comes our word (') " A spendthrift." () "Lombardic" is distinguished by long heads and tails; and is so called because it was introduced by the Lombards, in 569; who were the original bankers, or money dealers in England,—whence comes " Lombard Street," in London.

() Thnresby's Ducatus Leodinensis, p. 182. syke; and the last syllable (connected in meaning) from the Saxon *ergh,* or the Suio-Gothic *arf,* signifying "ploughed land."

The house is nearly of the usual form, consisting of a centre and two wings. The great tower or peel, at the southeast corner, sixty feet in height, remains entire. This tower dates from the time of Henry VII. and contains, still, a few of the original windows of that date.

It is the strongest part of the building, and must have been designed as a place of refuge or defence. In the corners of this tower are closets for watchmen, with apertures obliquely made in the wall, so that no weapon or missile could enter the apartment beyond. It is embattled, and contains embrasures. The centre, containing the old Hall, was perhaps first altered in the time of Elizabeth, and was further unfortunately modernized and subdivided about the year 1770, still remaining unfinished. Its original form (says Dr. Whitaker) is described thus: The room extended to both fronts, having been nearly a square of forty feet. The principal entrance was at the east corner on the north side, and on the same side were two deep embayed windows; and opposite, in the situation of the present front door, was a vast fireplace with a moulded stone arch. In the lower wing, which is very ancient, but not embattled, are a modern breakfast-room and a dining-room, wainscotted with oak, in ancient panel-work. In the upper stories of the great tower, is the Chapel, plain, and modern. Also, the To the change of architecture introduced in the reign of Edward III. succeeded the castellated houses of the fifteenth century. The regular quadrangular houses, not castellated, were sometimes built during the same age, and under Henry VII. became universal in the superior style of domestic architecture. Of these, the dwelling-house usually took up one side of the enclosure, or court-yard, and the remaining three contained the offices, stables, and farm-buildings, with walls of communication.—Hallam's "State of Europe during the Middle Ages," p. 419.

In the 10th Henry VI., pope Eugenius IV. granted to Sir Thomas de Stirkland (the eighth in descent) and Mabel, his wife, license for a domestic chapel and portable altar; which bull is yet extant, with the seal of lead very fair, about the breadth, and somewhat more than double the thickness of an English half-crown; with a cross on one side, and underneath EUGENIUS P. P. IIII. On the reverse, two faces of venerable old men, and, above, the letters SPAS E.—" History of Westmorland." drawing-room, finely wainscotted with oak, which opens to the north front of the tower. And, opposite, on the same floor, the principal bed-room, now called queen Katherine Parrs.

This room seems to have been so named, from a supposition that queen Katherine retired to reside here "after the king's death." This conjecture is not sufficiently discountenanced by Dr. Burn, who merely says "it perhaps may be true, but if it were se, the queen could not reside here long; for she married again so soon after the king's death, that had she then proved pregnant, it was said that it would be doubtful to what husband the child should belong, and she died the year following." That the queen may, at some early part of her time, have lodged temporarily at Sizergh we can hardly doubt, from the intimacy that subsisted between her family and the Stricklands; but it is highly improbable that ever she visited it after the death of her royal consort. The king died in London, in January, 1547. The queen departed this life in September, 1548, at Sudeley, in Gloucestershire. During the short interval between these events, her attention must have been engrossed, first with the funeral ceremony of the late king, then with the hasty and unfortunate celebration of her marriage with lord Seymour, and from that moment, as it is represented, to her dissolution, with the consequent "accumulation of griefs, which her constitution sunk under." We know, moreover, that during the months of her brief widowhood, after the death of the king, she lived at "her fine jointure house, at Chelsea, on the Thames." And after her marriage with Seymour, she lived part of the time at Hanworth (one of the manors belonging to her dower), and after that, till her death, at Sudeley Castle. So it is next to impossible that the queen lived or even

visited Sizergh "after the king's death. " Another error occurs in the appropriation of this room, from the belief that the arms of England and France, which are carved in oak, and placed over the fire-place, are designed to commemorate queen Katherine. See Agnes Strickland's "Life of Katherine Parr," pp. 257 4 271. It in said, that those arms were put up by queen Katherine Parr, widow of King Henry VIII.—" History of Westmorland," p. 103.

Whereas, they are really those of queen Elizabeth, with the red dragoii and lion as supporters, and as a motto, 'vivat regina, 1569.' Katherine, as queen, bore for her arms, quarterly, six pieces, and the quarterings were ensigned with a. royal crown, with a K. and P. for Katherine Parr. This room is hung round with gobelin tapestry of exquisite beauty. In the vestibule, also, are hung, three pieces of tapestry, illustrating the story of Anthony and Cleopatra.

It appears, from some notes written by the late Mrs. Strickland, at Sizergh, that Walter de Strickland, the 13th in the pedigree,' put up' many of the wainscots and carvings in the drawing-room and other parts, and built the wing on the south-west side, chiefly, as it is said, for his military purposes. The time of this gentleman, and the dates in several parts of the work attributed to him, agree precisely with this statement. In the wing alluded to is the date 1558, the 1st of Elizabeth, and this Walter died in the 11th of that reign.

The oak wainscotting of this house is very fine, and is nearly all of one period, viz. from Henry VIII. to Elizabeth, inclusive. There is indeed a remnant of the old cane-work pattern in the library; but all the rest is part of a general plan for fitting up the whole house in the same elaborate and expensive manner, about the beginning of queen Elizabeth's reign. The finest specimen of veneering in wood, is in a room called the Inlaid Room, in which the panels of the wainscot-work of the bed, are, with wonderful labour, variegated with holly and fossil oak; all perfectly undecayed, and in colour unfaded as new. The cornice of this bed is surmounted with a

shield, bearing the arms of Strickland quartering Deincourt, elegantly carved in oak. Date 1568.

In the breakfast-room, amongst others of less consequence, is a portrait of Mary, queen of Scots, and in the dining-room are portraits of admiral Strickland and Thomas Strickland, bishop of Namur. Also, portraits of king James II. and his queen; Charles II.; Prince Charles, the Pretender, and his lady; and of lady Blount. In the same dining-room, over the chimney-piece, on a shield, quarterly, are the following arms; Strickland quartering Deincourt, Neville (with a mullet), and azure, a cross botony, or (for Ward); supporters, a stag collared and chained, and a bull with a mullet on his breast.

In the windows of the hall, are the arms of Deincourt quartering Strickland, Roos, and Parr; these two last are thus accounted for; Katherine, the wife of John de Roos, was daughter of Sir Thomas Strickland, which John de Roos died young. His widow Katherine assigned over to her said father the wardship and marriage of her daughter Elizabeth, which Elizabeth was afterwards married to William del Parr, knight. There are also in the windows of the hall the arms of Deincourt, quartering Strickland, Roos, and Parr. Also, Strickland quartering, or, three fleur de lys, sable (for Beetham); and argent, a chief indented, azure (for Burton).

In various apartments are these arms: quarterly, 1, Strickland, 2, Deincourt, 3, Neville, 4, Ward quartering Tempest and D'Arcy. Quarterly, Strickland and Deincourt, impaling quarterly, Neville and Ward. Quarterly, 1, a fesse between three crescents, 2, on a cross, five leopards' heads, cabashed, 3, a chevron between three roses, 4, three bars wavy, raided, 5, a cross moline, 6, a bend, engrailed flory and counter flory, impaling quarterly Tempest, and D'Arcy, differenced by a martlet.

The whole of this mansion is well worthy the attention of the artist, who studies to imitate ancient models.

On the ancient monument in the church, as has been already mentioned, appear the arms of Deincourt, quartered with those of Strickland; and in our account of the Castle, it is further mentioned, that when Gilbert, 4th baron of Kendal, sided with the rebellious barons in the time of king John, he paid for the ransom of his son and Ralph Deincourt and others, 12,000 marks; and also gave hostages for his future fidelity. Amongst these hostages we find the daughter of Ealph Deincourt, and the son and heir of Walter de Strickland. With respect to Walter de Strickland, it is clear that he resided at Strickland Hall, in the parish of Morland; for he had a license to keep a chaplain in his family at Strickland, about the beginning of the reign of Henry III. on his giving juratory caution that his chaplain should not injure, in its revenues, the mother church of Morland. Reg. Wethernl.

In the 23d Henry III. (1239), we find that Robert de Stirkland, knight, by deed, dated at his manor of Great Stirkland, on the eve of St. John the Baptist, granted to William, his son, and Elizabeth, daughter of Ralph Deincourt, knight, on their marriage, his whole manor of Great Stirkland, with the services of free tenants there, together with the appurtenances, to hold to them and the heirs of their bodies; remainder to his own right heirs. This Robert we conceive to have been the son of Walter, and the same who was delivered to king John as a hostage, and if so, the daughter of Ralph Deincourt must have been very young when given as a hostage, for the date of the aforesaid deed is twenty-three years subsequent to the date at which the hostages were given. But however that may be, we have now traced the union of the families whose arms appear on the monument mentioned in our account of the Church. And we may conclude, without fear of error (what has never yet been intimated in any account of Sizergh) that the Stricklands, at that time, removed to Sizergh, and that Sizergh was the residence of the Deincourts, and came to the Stricklands by marriage with the heiress of that family. For the Deincourt arms are in the chief place on the ancient monument before referred to; and

we can trace a succession of the Stricklands, at Sizergh, from the time of the said marriage to the present. In what year Sir William Strickland died we have not found, but in the 35th Edward I., his son, Sir Walter de Strickland, had a grant from the king of free warren in 'all his demesne lands in Helsington and Heversham, and all other his lands jn the county of Westmorland,' for his good services in the parts of Scotland; consequently Sir William must have died in or before the year 1307.

Dr. Burn has carefully, and at great length, illustrated the history of this family at Sizergh, from Walter de Strickland, knight, in the time of king John, to Thomas the grandfather of the present representative, W. C. Strickland, Esq., being twenty-one generations. The plan of this work does not admit of our giving the whole pedigree; but we shall set down the particulars of the family from the time where they are discontinued in the History of Westmorland.

21. Thomas Strickland. He was twice married. First, to Anastasia Lawson, eldest daughter of Sir John Lawson, baronet, of Brough Hall, Yorkshire; and, secondly, to Kathe rine Gerrard, daughter of Sir Robert Gerrard, of Garswood, in Lancashire. By his first wife he had issue—1. Charles Standish (on whom devolved the Standish estates). 2. Thomas. 3. 4. Anastasia and Elizabeth; both died young. 5. Monica; married to Sir John Gerrard, baronet, of Garswood New Hall, Lancashire. 22. Thomas Strickland, born the 7th September, 1792. He married, in 1824, Mademoiselle Ida de Finguerlin Bischengen, youngest daughter of the baron de Finguerlin Bischengen. They had issue, two sons, namely, Walter Charles, the eldest, who now resides at Sizergh, and Henry Charles, the younger, a Lieutenant in the army, who died at Barbadoes in 1852.

The name was spelled Stirkland, or Styrkland, until the time of Walter, the 9th in descent at Sizergh, who lived in the reign of Henry VI. It is derived from *stirk-land* (in Morland),—"pasture ground for the young cattle called *stirks.*

"

Mere antiquity is not all that the Strickland family can boast. What is far greater praise remains to be said, that they have for so many ages been eminently serviceable to the state. In the border sen8ice, especially, and in the civil wars during the commonwealth, the name of Strickland stands conspicuously—ever in defence of the legitimate rights of the crown and the best interests of the community. At the battle of Edgehill, October, 1C42, Sir Thomas Strickland (16,) was created banneret, by king Charles in person. The same Sir Thomas was privy purse to king Charles II. And there still exists, at Sizergh, the badge of that office, which is a square purse of rich crimson silk velvet, having on it the royal arms, with the initials C. R in gold embroidery.

From Edward II. to the time of the Restoration, they served The ancient title of "knight banneret" was generally given as the reward of military merit, and conferred by the king in person on the field of battle, and under tho royal banner. The knight banneret (so created) took precedence of baronets and knights of the bath, and ranked next after barons.— MS. Notes at Sizergh. in parliament seventeen times as knights of the shire for Westmorland. CUNSWICK HALL.

This ancient hall stands in a sheltered situation, below Underbarrow and Cuswiek Scar, and is literally buried in a plantation of stately and venerable trees. So that if there bu as much truth as ingenuity in the opinion of Lucas, that "the maintenance of old wood about a family mansion was a signal to the country that plenty and economy together reigned within," Cunswick Hall, in the day of its pride and power, must have been the very residence of 'plenty and economy.' The house is fast falling into a. state of dilapidation, and has lost almost every feature of its original dignity. In the interior there was, a few years ago, one piece of furniture of ancient carved oak, date 1647. Over a double-arched gateway, leading to the court, is a stone, bearing the royal arms, quartering England and France.

The first of the family who long possessed Cunswick, of whom we have found mention, is Roger de Leyburne. Fuller says, "the first Leyburne, or Leburn, that I find, was Roger de Leyburne, who married Idonea, the younger daughter of Robert, last lord Vipont." But this is somewhat incorrectly stated; for the 'lord Vipont,' to whom he refers, was Robert de Veteripont, to whom king John granted considerable possessions both in Westmorland and Cumberland. This Robert de Veteripont had two daughters, Isabella (not Sybil, as Fuller states), and Idonea; who being very young at the time of their father's death, were committed by the king, as their ward, to the custody of Roger de Clifford, of Clifford Castle, in Herefordshire, and Roger de Leyburne, of the county of Kent. These custodians married the said two (laughters to their two sons and heirs, Roger de Clifford and Roger de Leyburne. After the death of Idonea, without issue, the whole of the Veteripont inheritance, including the shrievalty of the county, became vested in the heirs of Isabella, by Roger de Clifford, Dr. Burn records only fifteen instances of their having served in parliament. We have found two more among the family records.

and so afterwards, by marriage, to the Tuftons, present Earls of Tbanet. William de Lancaster, baron of Kendal, in the reign of Henry III., granted Skelsmergh to Robert de Leyburne; but what relation this Robert was of Roger de Leyburne, before mentioned, we have not found. This family represented the county of Westmorland in 1305, 1314, 1404, 1410, 1422, and 1541. But when, and who was the first that resided at Cunswick, it is impossible to say. The last of the family, John Leyburne, having engaged in the rebellion in 1715, this estate became forfeited, and was purchased of the crown by Thomas Crowle, gentleman; after the death of whose son, George, it was purchased by Sir James Lowther, and now belongs to the Earl of Lonsdale.

About a quarter of a mile on the N.E. side of the hall, on the Cunswick estate, are distinctly visible, the remains of a camp, consisting of five mounds of earth, four of which formed a square, standing two and two, in juxta-positiou; the fifth is about 35 yards from the rest, on a little eminence, and would seem to have been designed as an advanced post, or observatory. It is situated on a low piece of ground, as it were in a shallow basin, and is quite unobservable till closely approached. The dimensions of the mounds are from 15 to 20 yards long, by from 6 to 8 yards wide. The enclosure has been defended on two sides, by a strong wall, about a yard thick, now level with the ground. This wall would mark out an area of near an acre of land, having the encampment in its centre. We can do little more than conjecture the time to which it may be referred. The probability is that it was a Danish Camp. It is not very far from Dan Hill (Dane's Hill), mentioned at p. 6.

BUENESIDE HALL.

Burneside, or, as it was formerly called Burneshead Hall, is situate about two miles north of Kendal. It stands on a tongue of laud formed by the junction of the Kent and the Sprint. As it is on the side, and not at the head of the burn, we cannot reconcile the ancient orthography of the name with the situation of the hall. It is proved, however, hy all writings and monumental inscriptions, that it was spelled Burneshead during the residence of the families of Eurneshead and Bellingham, and down to the time of the Braithwaites. It seems to have conferred its name on the first possessor (unless indeed it may be presumed to he Saxon), as, after the Conquest, grantees invariably took the name their lands were called by. Of the family 'de Burneshead,' we have only been able to find the last, viz. Gilbert de Burneshead, who, in the 11th of Edward L purchased Lanibrigg of Thomas de Chenaye. He had an only daughter and heiress, Margaret, who was married to Richard Bellingham, of Bellingham, in Tindalc, in the county of Northumberland. The Bellinghams thus came to Burneshead in the reign of Edward II. and continued in possession of the manor for some time. The arms on the tomb in the church, clearly refer to this marriage, and we conclude, that whenever that tomb was erected, it was intended principally to be in memory of Richard de Bellingham and the heiress of Gilbert de Burneshead.

Sir Henry Bellingham, of Burneshead, was attainted in the time of king Edward IV. for having sided with the house of Lancaster in the then civil wars; and all his lands were granted to William and John, sons of Sir Thomas Parr, knight, of Kendal Castle. The last of the Bellinghams who resided at this place, viz. Sir Robert Bellingham, sold it to Sir Thomas Clifford, and, according to Sir Daniel Fleming's papers, Sir Thomas sold it to one Fitzwilliaui, who again sold it to Machell, of Kendal. Machell sold it to Robert Braithwaite, of Ambleside, and this brought the family of Braith Dr. Whitaker.-See page 55. This family resided at old *Bratkay,* and the circumstance forms another probable instance of persons being named after property. *Braithwaite* was very likely the original name of the estate; composed of *bra,* q. *brae,* a sloping bank, and *thwaite,* (Sax.) land cleared of wood. There is a house or hamlet near Hawkshead, which is still called Braithwaite, in full: and the learned antiquary of Ful ness says, that in that part of the county, in the time of Henry VIII. there were living Geo. Braithwait, bailiff, and 18 tenants of the same name. There is, also, a village two miles from Keswick which retains the name of "Braithwaite!" waite to Burneshead. These Braithwaites were of a very ancient and honourable family: ancestors of the Brathwaites, of Warcop, of whom Richard, alias " Dapper Dick," author of Drunken Barnaby, &c., was a member. Thomas Brathwaite, who lived temp. Elizabeth, made a rare and valuable collection of gold, silver, and brass coins and medals, mostly Roman, which, in 1674, were presented by one of the family to the University of Oxford. Most of these coins were found in the ruins of the Roman station, at Ambleside. The arms of Brathwaite are, gules, on a chevron argent, three cross crosslets, fitchy sable.

Richard Brathwaite sold the estate of Burneside to Mr. Thomas Shepherd, from whom it descended to his son Thomas, commonly called Justice Shepherd. This gentleman sold the Hall, and part of the demesne and corn tithe, to Christopher Wilson, of Bardsea, Esq. who settled the same upon his daughter Sarah, on her marriage with John Gale, Esq. of Whitehaven. The present possessor is Stephen Brunskill, Esq. of Lambrigg Foot.

In Machell's" survey, in 1692, the hall is described as consisting of a court, with a lodge and battlements, through which was an ascent to the hall. Before the court was a large pond, on each side of the passage to the gate; and in either pond a little island, with a tree planted in it; and in the windows of the gallery and the dining-room were the Brathwaites' arms, with impaliugs of the several families to which they were related.

The hall, although it bears certain evidence of having been a strong and spacious fabric, is now, by frequent mutations, become uninteresting to the antiquary. The great tower, 15 yards by 10, has crumbled away nearly to the basement story, This Mr. Shepherd was born at Natland, and was esteemed one of the most active and useful magistrates of his time. He was chairman of the bench, for which he was, in every essential, eminently qualified. He was, besides, a clever wit, a polished gentleman, and a benevolent and worthy character. He died in 1762, in the house now occupied by the Misses Brumwell, in Stricklandgate.

Thomas Machell, of the ancient family at Crackenthorpe Hall. He made a collection of materials relating to the history and antiquities of this county, of which Bp. Gibson and Dr. Buru both made use. which is slated over, and converted into a shippon. The hall, or centre, has been long modernized, and adapted to the conveniences of the farmers who inhabit this part. None of the arms mentioned in Machell's survey are left. The arched gateway, which is very strong, alone stands firm and unmoved; and if left unmolested, will yet outlive many generations. COLLIN FIELD

Stands pleasantly situated on an eminence, about half a mile from the southern extremity of the town, commanding an eastern prospect. It may have received its name from its situation, *collin* being probably a corruption of *collis*—a hilly (high) place. A degree of peculiarity is attached to this house, in consequence of its having been the occasional domicile of that distinguished lady, Anne, Countess of Pembroke. In Whitaker's " History of Craven" (p. 321), it is stated "that, from Skipton Castle into 1Westmorland, the Countess pursued the direct way by Settle, Kirkby Lonsdale, Kendal &c., to Brougham." So that, if the evidence which remains in the furniture of the house be deemed insufficient to support the assertion that the Countess lodged at Collin Field, this additional circumstance, we conceive, will be satisfactory. In the then bad state of the roads, and comparatively slow operations of travelling, the Countess would be unable to accomplish the distance (seventy miles) between Skipton and Brougham, or the reverse, in one day; and as this is the only house between these places which can furnish her peculiar traces, it seems fair to conclude that she made it her halfway house, and lodged here with her favourite ex-secretary, on her journeys either way.

Collin Field possesses every feature of the manor-house of lesser magnitude. It forms three sides of a quadrangle, the fourth having been secured by a strong wall, where was the entrance. In cases of assault, during the border *raids,* the inhabitants, having brought in the cattle, were shut up within the walls. A good supply of water, which is still found under the floor of the first kitchen, would help to sustain a long siege. There are no criteria of architecture about the building by which we can ascertain its precise date. Mr. George Sedgwick, secretary to the Countess of Pembroke, bought it about the year 1660, and speaks of it as a house at that time. And we should say, that, if not the original structure, all else that remains to be admired must certainly be attributed to him. He who counted his mistress so ex-

emplary in all things, could hardly fail to be inspired with her love for repairing and beautifying her residences. Mr. Sedgwick, in a memoir of the Countess, says, "When she came down into the north, in 1649 (where she continued till her death, in 1675, a year or two in Yorkshire, and a year or two in Westmorland), she found five of her castles, viz. Skipton, Appleby, Brough, Brougham, and Pendragon, thrown down in the late unhappy wars. She immediately resolved to repair them, notwithstanding the malignancy of the times. All these buildings and repairs could not be computed at less than £40,000, as she made appear by the yearly books of her accounts. A great estate God had blessed her with, and given her withal a noble heart, and an open and liberal hand, to do good generally to all. In what castle soever she lived, every Monday morning, she caused ten ahillinsrs to be distributed among twenty poor householders of that place; beside the daily alms which she gave at her gate to all that came. All groceries, spices, stuffs, and the like, which she used in her house, all wines, malt, hay, corn, and straw for her stables, she bought of neighbours and tenants near the place of her then residence, paying always ready money when they came for it. Seldom had she anything from London, being desirous the country might receive benefit by her. She wore, in her latter days, very plain and mean apparel. A petticoat and waistcoat of black serge (q. Kendal manufacture?) was her constant wear, nor could any persuade her to wear others!"

This distinguished lady, of whom Dr. Donne said, "that she knew well how to discourse of all things, from predestination to slea eilk," employed Dodsworth to compile her family histories, which comprised three large folio volumes, some of which, with the diaries she herself regularly kept, are yet extant in Appleby Castle. We think no apology will be required for our inserting the following interesting description of this remarkable lady, in her own words:—

"I was very happy in my first constitution, both in my mind and body, both for internal and external endowments. For never was there a child more equally resembling both father and mother than myself. Mine eyes were black, like my father's, and the form and aspect of them quick and lively, like my mother's. The hair of my head was brown, and very thick, and so long that it reached to the calf of my leg, when I stood upright, with a peak of hair on my forehead, and a dimple in my chin. Like my father, full-cheeked; and round-faced, like my mother; and an exquisite shape of body, resembling my father. Now, when I caused these memorials of myself to be written, I have passed the sixty-third year of my age; and, though J say it, the perfections of my mind are much above those of my body."

From Mr. Sedgwick's memoirs of Ms own life (quoted at length by Dr. Burn), we select the following passages, pertaining to Collin Field:—

"After eighteen years' service with this good lady, she began to mind me of myself, and my future well-being in the world; often repeating to me a verse of Mr. Samuel Daniel, the famous poet and historiographer, who had been her instructor in her childhood and youth,

'To have some silly home I do desire.
Loth still to warm me by another's fire.
'

She further declared her noble intention to me, that when I met with some small habitation, she would give me 200?. towards the purchase, which she punctually performed.

"Within awhile God directed me to Collin Field, a small estate held under Queen Katherine, as part of her jointure, by a moderate rate and fine, convenient for the church and market; freed from all assizes and sessions; where by God's blessing I enjoy a quiet and retired life to my contentment; having oftentimes the society of several of my worthy friends and neighbours from the town of Kendal, having lived here above 14 years at the writing hereof, 1682."

Over the porch, at the entrance door, is a stone bearing this inscription:

Kvnc mea mox hvivs sed postea uescio cvivs, 1663.

a.

I. M.

This stone is supposed to have been brought from Brougham Castle.

On the hall door is a large wooden lock, which the Countess of Pembroke sent here, with her portrait; as she did to all places which she was in the habit of visiting. She herself kept the master-key, and could thereby make these places her refuge in times of need.

The principal apartments of present attraction are on the second floor, some of which contain the best specimens of the Elizabethan windows in this part of the country. One of these rooms is furnished with antique chairs, and several paintings of first-rate excellence; viz., portraits of Admiral Strickland and Bishop Strickland, copies of those at Sizergh; and unfinished sketches of the Passions, by Romney, presented by the artist to Mr. Yeates. In this room, also, is the portrait of the Countess, taken in 1650, and one of Allan Pricket, Esq. , Recorder of Kendal, who resided at Natland Hall. In one of the lodging rooms is a fragment of an oak carved bedstead, called the "Countess' bedstead." It bears no date, but contains the initials "A. P."

After the death of Mr. Sedgwick, Collin Field became the residence of the Chambre's family. Here Walter Chambre, Esq., father of Sir Alan (of Abbot Hall), was born. About 100 years ago, John Yeates, father of Anthony Yeates, Esq., of Kirkland, purchased Collin Field estate of Mr. George Sedgwick, nephew to the above named Mr. Sedgwick, who sold it in consequence of removing to Appleby. It came by will from Anthony Yeates, to Michaelson Yeates, Esq., the present owner.

The primitive order of this house has fortunately been saved from martyrdom, by coming into the possession of the Yeates' family; and it rejoices us, that, amid the ruins of time, and the desolating hand of selfishness, there are still to be found persons with taste, judgment, and liberality inspired, to preserve some of the memorials of antiquity.

BLEASE HALL.

Blease Hall, now a farm house, is situated in the township of Old Hutton, about four miles from Kendal, on the Kirkby Lonsdale (upper) road. It has been for many years in the possession of the Wilson family, of Highgate, Kendal, and is now the property of Richard Wilson, Esq., of Lancaster. There is at present nothing remarkable about the Hall, except one large room, beautifully wainscotted in oak, which has originally been very splendid, formed in square panels, with mouldings placed diamond-wise. The whole is divided at intervals by carved pilasters with caps and bases, and surmounted by a frieze and cornice, reaching to within about two and a half feet from the ceiling; this space of two and a half feet being in part an elaborate piece of stucco work. The wainscotting at present only extends along three sides of the room—the other portion having been removed when the side wall was rebuilt some years ago— at which time, it is thought, the curious old dagger (now in the Museum at Kendal) and several ancient coins, were discovered behind the wainscotting.

The mantel-piece in this room is also of oak, and very handsome, though sadly dilapidated like the rest: it is supported on two large oaken figures, richly carved, and the frieze is divided into compartments by four "graven images," the caps of which are also ornamented with figure heads above them; there is an oak panel of inlaid workmanship, (now loose) in the room, which has originally occupied the centre compartment of the mantel-piece. Another loose panel, also of oak, contains the date of "1644," and over one of the doorways are the initial letters "H. B." which, as well as the date, are incised, and filled in with a black substance.

The room is of ample proportions, apparently about twentyfour feet long, by eighteen feet wide and twelve feet high. The ceiling is in stucco, and divided by two beams into three compartments, the centre one of which is of very ornate workmanship in the style of the period, while the other two are at present quite plain, the ornamental work having unfortunately been destroyed during the repairs of the ceiling.

The initials "H. B." are no doubt those of Henry Bateman, who resided here, and who is said to have been a carrier to and from London and York with pack-horses, extensive stabling for which were upon the premises at Blease Hall, almost within living memory. The gang of pack-horses, with the bells tinkling at their necks, on a Sunday evening at Oxenholme, was always sure to be met by a goodly number of sightseers from Kendal and miles around, of all ages and of both sexes, in their holiday attire.

There are three brasses in Kendal Church to the memory of different members of the Bateman family; one of which, that to Alice, wife of Koger Bateman, will be found copied Abridged from a paper by Mr. Aid. John Fisher, in the "Kendal Mercury." at page G8. Her "choyse virtues" are set forth in such strong light, there is no hiding them under a bushel.

GILLTHWATTERIGO.

The name Gillthwaiterigg is composed of three Scandinavian words, *gill,* 'water,' *thwaite,* 'land cleared of wood,' and *rigg,* 'a hillock;' a hill, 'essarted,' near the brook. The mansion on the estate took this topographical and descriptive name. The present house is only a fraction of its original, and has been curtailed, altered, and modernized, at different times. It was in the Elizabethan order, with stone mullion windows, a gable roof, and contained a curious winding stone staircase. It was not embattled, nor surrounded by a courtyard, and comes therefore more within the category of mansion than manor-house.

By an old grant, still extant, it appears that Gillthwaiterigg belonged to the Parrs "of Kendal Castle." In the latter part of the reign of Henry VIII. it was sold to Thomas Duckett, and by one of the Ducketts, was sold, about the year lfi60, to William Rawlinson, then of Gray's Inn. This William Rawlinson is the man who put up the monument in Kendal Church to Vicar Stanford, and who describes himself, in that epitaph, as of "Gillthwaite Rigge." He purchased the estate, as we are informed, "with his first earnings at the bar." He was probably attracted by local feelings and associations, for we find that he had received his education in Kendal, and here also the early part of his professional training, being, in all probability, articled to an attorney in this town. His parents, at the time, were resident at Graythwaite, on the banks of Windermere; and it is worthy of notice, that both Graythwaite and Gillthwaiterigg have remained in the same family ever since. His father, Captain William Rawlinson, was an old parliamentary officer, and had fought both at Marston Moor and Ribble Bridge. William, now under consideration, was second son of the Captain. He was born 1640; was made sergeant-at-law early in his professional career; and on the accession of William and Mary, See tbc Church Epitaphs, p. 12.

in 1688-9, was appointed one of the Lords Commissioners of the Great Seal of England, on which occasion he was knighted. That high office he held till March 1693, when he retired from his professional dignities into private life, enjoying his *otium cum dignitate* for ten years, as he died at Hendon, in Middlesex, in 1703. He devised Gillthwaiterigg to the eldest son of his eldest hrother, passing by his own two daughters, for the purpose, no doubt, of keeping the name connected with the estate. And if so, his intentions have been so far fulfilled. Of the two daughters, the eldest was married to one of the sons of Sir John Lowther, of Lowther, Baronet, for her first husband The other daughter was married to the Right Hon. John Aislabie, of Studley, Yorkshire. Gillthwaiterigg now belongs to John Job Rawlinson, Esq., barrister-at-law. HELSPELL HALL,

Lies nestling under the shadow of Helsfell Nab.' It was once a place of considerable importance, and belonged to one of the Philipsons. But time and circumstance have shorn it of its glory. The only remains of the original building are some good mullion windows, now walled up. The general foundations, however, may be traced, upon strict investigation, and the extent of the building thus partially ascertained.

Some years ago, a bronze cross, two feet in length, was dug up among the ruins, with a small crucifix attached to it, which was thought to be of gold. It is probable, from this circumstance and analogous instances, that there was an oratory and altar within the Hall.

His arms still remain, in painted glass, in the Oriel window of Gray's Inn Hall. Nab: neb: nape. Prom *cncep* (Saxon), "a peak," or "prominence." CHAPTER III.

ANCIENT STATE OF THE TOWN.

It would be absurd to assume any knowledge, or to hazard any conjectures, respecting the precise antiquity of the present town. It is evident that its founders conceived the situation more favourable than that which the Romans had adopted for their station at Watercrook. Protection was, perhaps, the chief consideration of the first architects, and the hills on either side, Castle Hill and Kendal Fell, would readily suggest to them the advantages of the situation. Dr. Whitaker, speaking of Kendal, calls it a Saxon town. This inference is satisfactorily obtained from the appellation *Kirkby,* signifying church town, and so applied in "Doomesday," in the time of the Conqueror. By this faint ray of light, we perceive a few rude habitations, built of wattels, straw and mud, through the vista of nearly eight hundred years. The fact of the *Doomesday Survey* not extending to these northern parts, deprives us of the opportunity of knowing what was the extent of the town in the time of the Conqueror (1066). Dr. Whitaker, has, however, suggested an ingenious method of estimating at least the number of *streets* at the conquest. He says whatever streets do not bear the name of *gate* (which is Saxon) were not then in being. By this rule, Kendal is, at the time alluded to, restricted to four streets, viz., Soutergate, Stricklandgate, Stramongate, and Wildmangate; but we have no right to fancy them as equal to their present extent, either in length or breadth. The *principal* towns were then only like our present villages; and the very circumstance of four streets, with Saxon names, tells very *Kirkby* implies that the place to which it refers was the only *Church town* within the valley.—" History Of Richmondshirk." honourably for the ancient character of Kendal. From this time, a total eclipse occurs, till we find the town suddenly emerging into enviable distinction, by the light of royal favour, in the beginning of the fourteenth century.' Camden and Speed, the cotemporary fathers of English antiquity and topography, in the sixteenth century, have furnished us with few remarks on Kendal; and these writers very indistinctly defined the magnitude and importance of the towns which it was the office of their pens to illustrate. Speed, however, although he is lamentably deficient in his text, has shown adequately, by the Plan appended to his work, the state of Kendal at that time (1614). To supply the want of verbal description, we have reprinted this Plan; and it will be seen thereby that Kendal was then become a place of comparative significance.

The houses and streets were built without any regard to uniformity. Every front house had, and still very generally retains, its proportionate width of ground, diverging at right angles, and terminating, on the one hand, at the Kent, and on the other, at the declivity of the Fell Side. The ground, or croft, as it is called, thus attached to each dwelling, must have been originally designed for the purposes of manufactures. Most of the houses were fronted with large, cumbersome galleries, and the shop-windows—many of which were opened only on the market days,— were without glass, so that the town generally wore a gloomy appearance. These galleries continued till an advanced period of the last century. An aged friend of ours has heard his father relate, that he could walk "dry shod" under the roof of a gallery from New Biggin to Stricklandgate end!

We find also, that, in the beginning of the last century, the town was very ill paved. The author of "A Fortnight's Ramble to the Lakes," describing Kendal about the time alluded to, says:—

"The tenter-grounds on the sides of the little hills resemble the growth of the vine orchards in Spain; and from having The historian of Leeds makes it a boast that that town had three *gatet* at the time of the Conquest.
Vide " History of the Woollen Mauufactures," in a subsequent page. much and many coloured cloths upon them, I should hope that trade flourishes. I would wish to say something in praise of the town, but *it is too ill-paved to mind anything but your feet !*"
Mr. Gray, in 1769, complains of the irregularity of tie houses. In his journal, addressed to Dr. Wharton, he says, "Excepting these (the lines of the two principal streets), all the houses seem as if they had been dancing *a country dance, and were out;* there they stand, back to back, corner to corner, some up hill, some down, without intent or meaning. "

We are fortunately able to describe some of the irregularities and obstructions in the streets to which Mr. Gray refers. And we must be allowed to observe, that some of them were perhaps, not quite without "meaning." NEW BIGGIN.
New Biggin (New Building) stood in the middle of Soutergate, now Highgate *vide* Speed's Plan). It extended thirty yards in length, and was nine and a half yards broad. On the east side the passage was wide enough for wheeled carriages; on the other, the width was only sufficient for foot passengers. This style of building, standing midway in the main street, was common to many ancient towns. There was a similar one in Newcastle, one in Carlisle, and there is still one at Holborn Bars, in London. The building in question was mostly of wood, two stories high; the upper floor supported by twenty-nine strong beams, without joists, which projected beyond the basement story, and supported a gallery (originally). On the west side there were some small dwellings, and one large room called the "Cordwainers' Hall," belonging to the Cordwainers, the last company of *free-men* in the town. It is supposed to have been built about 1500. In 1572 it was held by the Marchioness of Northampton, as parcel of the Marquis fee, and the yearly rent *at that time* paid by tenants at will, appears, from a survey then made, to have been £± 2s. 0d. (See account of "The Castle," ante p. 96.) In 1803, the Earl of Lonsdale and Lady Andover were the chief proprietors of the New Biggin, and they made a donation to the town of their respective interests, for the purpose of having it removed, and the ground laid open to the street, which was accordingly done at that time.

It is matter of regret that no sketch or plan of this building was made before its destruction. Mr. John Richardson, architect (now living), has produced a drawing from memory, executed in 1845, which is believed to be generally correct, and we here present a fac-simile wood-engraving of the said drawing.

It does not succeed, so well as could be wished, in showing what part of the building was "fair to the street," and what was *set back* under a piazza or penthouse. Four of the shops in the front exhibited by the drawing retired within a penthouse, supported by wooden pillars. These shops had windows *without glass,* and with wooden shutters. The other two windows, next the butcher's stall, were glazed. The probability is, that this last named shop had been *renovated* many years subsequent to the erection of the building, when that front was brought forward, and the expensive luxury of glass introduced. One can imagine the sensation that would be produced in the town by such an innovation! It is not exactly certain when glass came into use for shop windows in provincial towns. Bede says, glass windows were first introduced into England towards the close of the seventh century. But, for many centuries after that, the use of window glass was confined to buildings for religious purposes; and we know, from later authors, that, down to the end of the fifteenth century, none but the wealthy indulged in glass windows, for private houses of the first class. The shop in question may have been the very first in the town distinguished by glass windows, and if so, the reader has presented to him, in the view of New Biggin, what he may regard as the most fashionable and frequented part of Kendal about the year 1700.

The picturesque building seen in the open street, north of the New Biggin, will be recollected by most of our readers. That penthouse front was removed in 1828, and replaced by the present bookseller's and jeweller's shops. These were *then* the modern fashion, and, if compared again with most recent examples of plate glass, &c., will show the progress of improvement in the street architecture. The building with 6quare-topped entry belongs not to the past: it is the Horse and Rainbow public-house, almost as it now stands.

BUTCHEES' EOWS,

The Butchers' Rows were open stalls, or benches, ranged along the opposite sides of the street, which was then called "Soutergate" (Highgate), from about the Pump Inn, down to the "New Biggin." One of these stalls will be seen in our drawing of the " New Biggin." They continued till about the year 1782, when the Old Shambles (opposite the Commercial Inn) were built. Whilst the "Butchers' Eows" remained in the main street, as above described, the barbarous custom of bull-baiting prevailed in Kendal. On the 5th of November especially, bull-baiting took place, and the butchers rarely ventured to slaughter a bull unless it had been publicly baited. If any one did so, he had to pay the customary penalty of hanging a sign board out with "bullbeef" on it, or burning candles or a lighted lantern over it, and keeping the lights burning so long *as* any unbaited beef remained on hand unsold! This practice continued in Kendal until about 1790, when it lapsed on the suppression of bull-baiting. The Bull Ring was placed on the High Beast Banks, about the centre of the green. This Eing was applied to another barbarous custom, fortunately now a matter of history. Taking hold of and shaking the bull ring, was tantamount to throwing down the gauntlet as a general challenge to fight, and was not unfrequently done by pugnacious fellowes, on fairs, and market days.

The *New Shambles,* between Finkle Street and the Marketplace, were built in 1804.

There appears to have been some fear, by the authorities of the town, within a century after the "New Biggin" was "sett vpp," that the "lyke or worse (obstructions in the streets) shovld hereafter ensewe," and accordingly the following mandate, in the shape of "An Order for building within this Boroughe" was issued:— *An order for Buyldinge* uWn *this Boroughe.* 5 Decembr The Alderman and Burgesses off this Boroughe off Kirkbie1577 kendall at this pnte present not onelye seinge and throughlie pceyvinge perceiving by sundrye Examples the manyfest hurto and Inconvenyence alredye come to this Boroughe by the great streitninge off the Markett places within the Same, By reason Chefflye off Dyvers howses, shoppes, Taverns, grecis, stayres, & buyldinge heartoafore beinge sufferide to bee sett vpp, made, *k* fframyd by sund rye psonns persons wV'in the Same, But also dowbtinge that the lyke or worse heareafter should ensewe & be attemptyd & doone by others to the ffurther piudice prejudice theroff, Iff spedie remodie, foresight, and redresse should not (in tyme) be had i pvided provided therin— Therfore it is nowe Ordeyned & Constituted by the Alderman & the xij head Burgesses off the same Boroughe at this tyme beinge, That no maner off person or persons whatsover ffrome hencfurthe shall or may Improve, Incroche, stopp, streytten, or take vpp any ffrout roweme or ground to buyld vpon in any parte, place, circuyto, or precincte off the Markett place within this Boroughe off Kirkbiekendall withowte the speciall apoyn*tem.* & asslgnem'. off the Alderman & Burgesses off the Same, or the more pte part off them, ffrome tyme to tyme beinge, vpon payne to losse & fforfeitte to the Chamber off this Boroughe... xx (yff it be done in any parte or place where any m'keth market is kepte), And iff it be done in any other part or place win this borugh owte off the Markett places wher m'kethe market is not kepte Then.. x'. 8 Decembr 1577 Provided Neverthelesse yff any suche buyldinge,

Incrochem'. or Noysaunce hearafter be made Jfc sett vpp, or to be made & sett vpp in any parte or place w'in this Boroughe, That then it shalbe at the pleasure off the Alderman and Burgesses, or the more pte of them ffor the tyme beinge, The Same to pull Dowen or stay at their Discrocons, (The fforfeytonr off the payns aforesayd or either off them in anywise notw'. stand).

The word *Grecis,* we believe, is intended to apply to the stairs of those Galleries by which most of the houses in Kendal were fronted (as before stated). They were flights of stone stairs. The building was constructed of rails of oak timber very rudely "sett vpp, made, & fframyd," and firmly bound together by strong wooden pegs or treenels. The word "grecis," or "grees," is probably Norman French; as the modern French word "*Gris"* means a paving, or flag stone. "Grees," then, in this case, might be the lowest or projecting stair of "the flight." Halliwell in his dictionary of Archaic and Provincial Words, quotes the following illustrations of its use— "A *grese* there was of steppes fiftene."

"Up at a *grese* echo hym lade,
To chambir scho hym broght."

WHITE LION INN.

The clump of buildings, of which the White Lion forms the centre, may be regarded as a frontier specimen, which separates the past generation from the present; and, desiring to perpetuate its picturesque out-lines, we here present a drawing of it as it now stands.

There is no doubt that the first floor of the *front* of this house was one of the open galleries mentioned before, at p. 121; aud the tinman's (" Gardiner's") shop, which is now beneath a penthouse, was under the gallery. Hudson, the botanist, was born in this house *vide* Biographical Memoir); but whether the alteration, which enclosed the gallery, was made before or since the time of his birth, we cannot say. The latest specimens of the true galleried fronts, were the *Elephant* public-house, below the White Lion, and the *pot-shop* on the opposite side of this street (taken down in 1822). Many persons still living may also recollect the half-disguised gallery next to the Foot-ball public-house, in the market-place, where there formerly was a watchmaker's shop. We regret our inability to reproduce all those vestiges of "decayed intelligences." CROSS HOUSES.

The Cross House, in Stricklandgate, was the house where Mr. Noble lived and died. In Stramongate, a building on the site of the house now occupied by Edward Crewdsou, Esq. And, in Highgate, the house belonging to Mr. Miles Thompson, occupied by Joseph Swainson, Esq. On the front of the house opposite to this last, there was a stone, within living memory, with the arms of Roos engraved thereon. These Cross Houses may have been purposely protruded into the street, either for the celebration of some ceremony in monastic or catholic times (as the Roman Catholics still halt their funerals opposite them), or have been erections where tolls were taken; or, again, stations where watch and ward were kept in troublesome times.

There seem, from the names still attached to the places, to have been three crosses erected at nearly equal distances from the town, viz., one at *Stone Cross Barn,* on the road to Millthrop; another at *Cross House Close,* on the road to Burneside; and a third at *Far Cross Bank,* on the road to Appleby.

THE TOWN'S CROSS,

Or Market Cross, stood opposite the Covered Market, and was an obstruction in the street. There still remains a remnant of it in a stone at the corner, vulgarly called "*cold* stone," where the charters and so forth were usually proclaimed. Cold stone is a corruption of "*call stone;*" an appendage common to most ancient towns, where all public matters were "called" prior to the "institution" of belman.

The Maypole

Was another incumbrance, but indispensable, according to the custom of our forefathers. It stood in Kirkland, opposite the house of the late Thomas Reveley, Esq., and was suffered to remain till within eighty years ago. In the time of our good Queen Katherine, who may fairly be supposed to have partaken of the amusements, countenanced by her royal consort, the original festivity of maying and morris-dancing would be here celebrated, by the annual ceremony of "maying" when, immediately after sunrise, on the 1st of May, processions, entering the town at various inlets, streamed through the streets, with music of horns and flutes; boys with their May-gads, and girls with their "brats" full of flowers,—young and old alike joining in merry laughter, and song, and the customary chorus, "We have brought the summer home." When the above-named ceremonies became less fashionable, the May Pole was made the rendezvous of all the milkmaids in the neighbourhood, who came and Vide Hone's " Every Day Book." Willowwands twined with cowslips.—*Sir Bulwer Lytton't "*Harold." The semblance of those times continued up to the present century in the assemblage of young people in the Vicar's Fields, on Easter Tuesday. After spending the afternoon there, they returned in procession through the streets, " *threading grandy needles.*" paraded round it on Easter Mondays. On other occasions of rejoicing, afterwards, such for instance, as terminating an apprenticeship, and the like, it became customary for young men to go and dance around it.

In those times, as we are informed, there were some elegant buildings in the town, which, although they might not add to its uniformity, would, at least, preserve it from an appearance of poverty: BLACK HALL, (so called, perhaps, in contradistinction to White Hall), in Stricklandgate, was a fine old mansion. It was, for many centuries, the residence of an ancient and distinguished family of the name of Wilson. Thomas Wilson, of this family, married, in 1577, Mary, sister to Sir Richard Fletcher, of Cockermouth. He (Thomas) had a brother, Henry, who lived here, and was the first Alderman, and chief magistrate of this borough, under the charter of Queen Elizabeth, in 1575. George, son of the aforesaid Thomas, married Alice, daughter of Sir Thomas Brathwaite, of Burneside Hall, and granddaughter of Richard Brathwaite, alias *Dapper Dick.* This George had a son and successor, George Wilson, born at Black Hall, who, also, had a son George, and he again had a son George. These three gentlemen successively inhabited chambers, in Symond's Inn, for upwards of 150 years, and were eminently distinguished lawyers. The last of this family was Mary, lady of the late Sir Hugh Inglis, Baronet of Milton Bryant, Bedfordshire.

BROWNSWORD HOUSE, (lately the Pack Horse Inn) opposite to Black Hall, was likewise an elegant residence, and belonged to a family of the name of Alderman Wilson presented to the corporation of Kendal two splendid silver cups, or flagons, inscribed—" Presented by Henry Wilson, first Alderman of Kendal, to the Corporation of that town." These cups, together with some other plate, were, many years ago, exchanged for a set of candlesticks. This Alderman Wilson had a son, Henry, who resided mostly in London. He devised a legacy for sending three poor boys to the metropolis, and binding them apprentices there; but, by some mischance, it appears, this legacy was never appropriated.

Brownsword, one of whom was Mayor of this borough in 1695. King James I. lodged one night in this house, in passing between London and Edinburgh. This was possibly on the occasion of his going to London, on his accession, in August, 1617. There was a fine oak bedstead in the house, much carved, called " the king's bed." WHITE HALL (abbreviated, as we conjecture, from White Cloth Hall) was another stately mansion. It stood upon the site of the present Town Hall, and was the residence of the Robinsons, afterwards of Rokeby Park. The front projected with two wings: the windows were stone mullioned; and the staircase was of stone—spacious and circular. The ground which now forms New Street, was a garden, attached to the hall.

RESTRICTION OF NUMBERS AT WEDDING DINNERS.—1575.

The "Boke off Recorde" of the Corporation of Kendal, from which we have elsewhere quoted, contains regulations respecting bridals, drinkings at churchings, &c. The following is the order relating to " Bryddalles: "—

Brydalles the

Nomberes Itm it is Orderyd and Constitutycl by the Alderman and (Secundo die Burgesses, w" the ffull advise and assennte aforesayd, that ffebruarij 1575/ no pson or psonns off what estate or oallinge so ever he, she, or they bee off, whiche either be nowe dwellinge or w heareafter shalbe dwellinge orresydentew'Mn this Boroughe or Librties hearoff, shall, after the foresayd sevynth daye off ffebruarij nexte comynge, provyde, prepair, or make or cause or suffer to be provided, prepayred, or made at or win his, hers, or their howse or howses, or at or in any other howse or place win this Boroughe or librties hearoff beinge, Any Bryddall Dynner or weddinge dynner off or ffor any pson or psonns nowe or hearafter beinge and Dwellinge win this Boroughe or librties hearoff, and marryinge & weddinge as is aforesayd in the Sames, above the Nomber off *Twentye iltune s* off towen ffolks in all as is aforesaid Vpon payne to fforfeite & lesse to the vse off the Chamber off this Boroughe for everye suche faulte xx».

Part of this bed is now preserved, among other relics of antiquity, at Ivy Cottage, in Rydal.

'A"meass" was four persons, so the number fora " Bryddalle Dynner," was

K limited TRADESMEN'S TOKENS.

Up to the 17th century, there was no regular currency authorized hy the State, but that of silver, and occasionally a little gold. The smallest coin in use was a silver penny, which after a time became divided, by shears, into halfpence, and farthings (a *"half"* and a *"fourth-ing"*). These pieces were so small that they were constantly liable to be lost; still the State failed to provide a larger coin of less valuable metal. Hence the trading community were driven to the necessity of devising a substitute of their own. In some places tokens of lead were cast, which continued to be issued up to the year 1613. Prior to this, tokens of stamped leather, issued by private traders, were in circulation.

Then followed brass and copper tokens, which, by the time of Charles II., were issued without restriction, and without "patent." These small coins contributed materially to the benefit and convenience of trade. They were coined by incorporations of cities and boroughs, by guild companies, and by tradespeople and victuallers, at pleasure. Every community, tradesman, or tradeswoman, that issued this useful kind of specie, was obliged to take it again, when brought to them, and, where many sorts were current, a tradesman kept a sorting box, into the partitions of which he put the money of the respective coiners, and at proper times, when he had a competent quantity of any one person's money, he sent it to him, and got it exchanged for silver. These coins had most of them the peculiar devices of the community or profession of their coiners. The following is a complete descriptive catalogue, with engravings, of the whole series of the Kendal tokens, which are at present known to have been issued either by individual tradesmen of limited to eighty persons! For a "Wyffe's Kyrkeing," the limit was " three measses of ffolkes," or twelve persons. One cannot imagine a reason for these restrictive Bye-Laws, without reference to the indulgence of dissipating habits.

From this term has probably arisen the provincial term *bran,* which we frequently hear given, not only to the copper coinage, but also to wealth generally. For instance, it is usual to say, in speaking of a man possessed of property, "he is worth a deal o' brass." the town and neighbourhood, or by any of the "Twelve Severall Companyes" of incorporated freemen, or fraternities of traders which were formerly associated, constituted, and recognised, within this borough.

The catalogue is composed of nine varieties, arranged in the order of their respective dates, extending, it will be seen, over an interval of thirteen years—viz., from 1656 to 1669— Hadwen's Token (No. 9) being the only one which is not dated.

Obrerse—"thom. Sandes. Of"—In the field, A teasel and a wool-hook. *Reverse*—"kendaix. 1656"— „ A wool-comb.

In Mr. Boyne'a collection. Thomas Sandee, who was Mayor of Kendal in 1647-8, made a fortune as a dealer in "Kendal Cottons," and resided in the front house of the "Elephant" yard, (now the Elephant inn, which was rebuilt about thirty years ago,) using the back premises as his warehouses. He founded, in 1670, " Sandes' Hnspital. " (See subsequent page.) *Obv.*—"mercers' Company In Kendai."—In the field, The arms of the Mercers' Company.

Rev.—The arms of the Corporation of Kendal, with " 16 " and "57" on each side of the shield respectively, and "Kk" above the same.

The token is a neat one, farthing size, and is in Mr. Boyne's collection. In *Snelling* it is engraved without the Kk above the shield: probably a variety. The original dies, much worn, were found in 1803, among the ruins of the "New Biggin," where the cordwainers had their hall, and are now in the Natural History Societj 's museum.

Obv.—"outer. PLAT. Of "—In the field, Three Maltese crosses. *Rev.*—" Kirkbt = KENDALL "— „ The date "1659," with three stars of five points above and three below.

Oliver Plat was a gentleman of considerable property, both in Kendal and the neighbourhood, and lived on his own estate at Summer How, in Skelsmergh. The property, in Kendal, known as the Kainbow Inn, belonged to him; and an oak table and oak panel, bearing the inscription (boldly carved), "O.P. E P. 1638," were discovered when the house was rebuilt, about twenty-five years ago. He was a Roman Catholic; hence the Maltese crosses.

No. 4.

Obr. -" EDMOND. Adlinoton "—In the field, The arms of the Dyers' Company. *fov.*—"in. Kendall: 1659 "— „ The initials ". A.

E: I"

The dyers, as elsewhere shown, seem.formerly to have been associated corporately with the shearmen. The "shearmen-dyers" are mentioned in the poetical account of the guild procession in 1759 (printed at page 139). The compliment paid in this effusion to Kendal industry, we cannot omit twice quoting:—

"Thus English wool, by shearmen-dyers wrought,
Equals the finest silks from India brought."

Edmond Adlington was "sworn" as a shearman-dyer in the year 1649, and followed that business in 1655 and 1657, as evidenced in the corporation books. The family came originally from Yealand in Lancashire, and carried on the above business there, and also at Kendal, simultaneously. They were quakers, and tradition says that Edmond was a man of immense bulk, weighing upwards of twenty-four stones, and that his wife was of little inferior weight, being upwards of twenty-two stones. He retired, and died probably at his native place, at a great age. Nicolson and Burn (History of Westmorland, p. 536), in recording some of the eccentricities of the early quakers, as described by Francis Higginson, vicar of Kirkby Stephen, a clerical pamphleteer against the sect, in the time of Cromwell, say:—"Some of them stood (oddly draped) upon the market cross, on the market days, preaching from thence to the people. There is no doubt that persecution drove the Quakers to excesses bordering upon martyrdom, which a gentler treatment would have prevented,—excesses for which the oppressors and not the victims must be held responsible.

Obv.—"company. Ok. Shearmen "—In the field, A pair of croppers shears. *Rev.* —"in. Kendall. 1666 "— ,, The shearman's teasel brush or frame ,,.
Mr. Boyne, whose collection comprises this token (which is also engraved in *Snelling),* observes that, to those who are unacquainted with the woollen manufacture, a description of the use of the two articles represented on the token may not be uninteresting, as they are now almost entirely disused, the great improvement in machinery, which does the work better and cheaper, having superseded them. The large shears were

used by the croppers to cut all the long hairs off the cloth; and unless great care and precision were used, there was danger of cutting the cloth, so that none but experienced workmen were employed, and they earned great wages. During the Luddite riots in the West Hiding of Yorkshire, in 1812, many of these artisans were implicated, some of them having been thrown out of employment by the improvements in manufacture, and many by their intemperate habits. The long hairs are now removed by a spiral steel blade fixed on a revolving cylinder, which gives a fine, even *nap* to the cloth. The hand *teasel* brush, which appears on the reverse of the token, was used for brushing the cloth—a brush being held in each hand—an operation which is now also done by machinery, the *teasels* being placed in a long narrow iron frame, which is worked by steam-power. The vegetable *teasel (Dipaacus fullonum),* we may add, continues to be used—no artificial brush having yet been found to answer the purpose better than the natural one. The Bodleian collection contains this token; and Mr. Alderman J. Fisher has the die for the reverse.

There were formerly twelve free companies in Kendal. The following list of them is taken from the "Boke off Recordo:"—1. Chapmen, Marchannts, & Salters; 2. Mareors and Drapers, Lynnen & Wollen; 3. Shearmen, Fullers, Dyers, & Websters; 4. Taylers, Imbrodyrers, & Whilters; 5. Cordyners, Coblers, & Curryerrs; 6. Tanners, Sadlers, & Girdlers; 7. Inholders, and Alehowsekepers, & Typlers; 8. Butchers and Fisshers; 9. Cardmakers and Wyerdrawers; 10. Surgons, Scryvyners, Barbors, Glovers, Skynners, Parchement, and Poyntemakers; 11. Siuythes, Iron & Hardwaremen, Armerers, Cutlers, Bowycrs, Fletchers, Spuryers, Potters, Fanners, Plumbers, Tynkers, Pewterers, & Metallers; 12. Carpenters, Joyners, Masons, Wallers, Sclaters, Thatchers, Glasiers, Paynters, Pleysterers, Dawbera, Pavers, Myllers, & Cowpers. These incorporated companies gradually became extinct, the last of them (the cordyners or cordwainers) be-

ing "broken up" in 1800, in consequence of one Robert Moser refusing, most properly, to recognise any legal power in the company to impose a Cue upon persons, not being freemen, commencing business within the borough.

No.).
Obi:—"THOMAS. WILSON8."—In the field, The arms of the Corporation of Kendal.
"KIHK *Iiev.* —" THOMAS. WABde. OF "— ,, LAND . 1666."

In the Bodleian Library. Bequeathed to it in a cabinet of tradesmen' tokens by Browne Willis, the celebrated antiquary, who died in 1760. Whether Messrs. Wilson and Warde were partners in trade, or merely joint8 issuers of the token, we cannot say; but instances of joint8issue by neighbours in trade are not unfrequent. This token was not known of till the year 1844.

Kirkland, being out of the Mayor's liberty, was much resorted to by tradesmen not free of the corporation. The arms are here engraved as they appear on the token in the Bodleian—the fourth quarter appearing more like reversed drops (or guttes as the heralds call them) than spiudles; but we can only regard the difference as a blunder of the die engraver.

Ole.—" Iames Cocke Ivnior ""—In the field, A game cock.
"nis *licv.*—"OF KENDALL 1667 "— ,, HALFE PENNY
» r

This is in Mr. Boyue's collection. Mr. Cock, who is supposed to have been a manufacturer, was Mayor of Kendal in 168182. He was "sworn" a member of the Mercers' Company in 1655. His residence was in "The Park;" and the property now occupied by Mr. R. Hudson, druggist, in the "Butcher's Row," belonged to his family. There was a figure of a cock in stained glass in one of the windows. This token is in the Bodleian Library.

Obv. — "nic: Howlandson. Of. Ouavhio "—In the field, A pair of scales and a spade or malt-shovel.
"nis *Rev.*—"IN. KENDALL. PARISH. 16G9"—,, HALF PENY
... »

Richard Rowlandson was a fell-monger and woolstapler, and lived on his own estate at Lambert Ash, Grayrigg, where he eaiTied on his business. He had branch establishments at Kendal, Kirkby-Stephen, and Kirkby-Lonsdale. It is stated that he walked to London and back on business three times, and that he was there in the time of the Great Plague in 1665. This token obtained but a small circulation in consequence of the Act of Parliament which suppressed the issue of this description of copper currency. The Bodleian contains a specimen.

(Hie.—" Iohn HABWEN. "—In the field, A cone resembling a sugar-loaf.

" B *Rev.—*" IN Kendall "— „ The initials, I *F.* ll

This token is of copper, the rest being of brass. It was found in Kirkland in 1853. See List of Mayors in the eighteenth century for Hadwens. VISITS OF THE REBELS IN 1715 AND 1745.

"On the fifth of November, 1715, about 1,600 Scotch and Northumberland rebels came and lodged one night in this town, where they proclaimed the Pretender, and so took their route by Kirkby-Lonsdale and Lancaster, to Preston, in Lancashire, where they were suppressed by the king's troops. It will add to the honour of this borough to say, that not one townsman joined the rebellious crew. But, on the other hand, the present Mayor, Thomas Scarisbriek, Esq., was in a particular manner serviceable to bis king and country upon this occasion, in hazarding himself to gain a perfect account of the strength and design of the rebels. This account he transmitted to the commanding officers of the king's troops at Warrington, Liverpool, &c., with so much speed, as gave them notice to prepare for the attack, which, by that means, happened to be at Preston three or four days sooner than they could possibly have had an express by way of London, which loss of time must have given the enemy an opportunity to have penetrated further into the kingdom." 17845.—The rebel army, under the command of Prince Charles Edward Stuart "the Pretender," reached Kendal, in its progress south-

wards, on the evening of the 22nd of November, and halted over the 24th, on which day (Sunday) the principal officers, with three ladies, one of whom was the lady Ogylvie, attended divine service in the church. The service was performed by Mr. Crackenthorp, master of the grammar school; Dr. Symonds, the vicar, having quitted the town through fear. At that time it was customary for the poor people to stand in "beggarly array" at the church door, with the sexton and other subordinate officers of the church, who held pewter plates for alms. The rebel officers, after having ascertained the object of the charity, gave liberally, some gold and others silver.

By the time the Pretender and his adherents reached Derby, the Eoyabst army, under the command of the Duke of Cumberland, had become strongly reinforced, and were marching to meet the enemy; so that the rebels thought it prudent to beat a retreat. About ten o'clock of the forenoon, on the 13th of December, a hundred horse, of the Duke of Perth's establishment, reached Kendal. The country people being at market, mobbed the rear of this troop, and as they were turning down the Fish Market, one of the rebels was

'Wharton9s Chrouolngy.

killi2d by a musket-shot wantonly fired out of a window, whereupon the town's people closed in, and took two other soldiers prisoners. The fire was now returned upon the inhabitants by the rebels, when John Slack, a respectable farmer, was killed on the spot, and Richard Pindar, a shoemaker, and an ostler (whose name we have not ascertained), were seriously wounded. After this, the people dispersed, and suffered the troops to proceed on to Shap. In the evening of the same day, the main body entered the town, and hearing that one of the hussars was slain, they breathed indignant revenge. The cess and public money were demanded, under the severest military execution. It was with the greatest difficulty that the magistrates could pacify the chiefs, by representing that the inhabitants of the town were innocent, and, that in a public mar-

ket it was impossible to detect and punish the offenders. At length their wrath was somewhat appeased; and the contributions were abated to (our living author says) *1501.* As they were departing out of the town, their rear rank plundered some houses, and robbed several people of their shoes, one of whom was John Askew, a shearman, who had his shoes taken off Ids feet. Such was the distress occasioned to the poor by these ravages that the trustees of the Town's charities were induced to depart from the instructions of Benefactors, and apply the funds at their disposal to the emergencies of the moment: for instance, the managers of Prissoe's charity gave the yearly rental of their two fields, 6?. 10s., and their "own allowance" of *ten shillings,* and 30s. out of "accumulations," altogether *Hi.* 10s. , for the relief of the pillaged sufferers. The proverb says, "it is easy to be charitable with other people's money;" but Prissoe's Trustees went beyond the proverb, and actually gave "their own allowance," as they took care to record duly, the magnificent sum of ten shillings! The Pretender slept in the house formerly occupied by Miss Thomson, in Strickland First edition of " The Annals." They were not like an old townsman and cotemporary of ours, on whom we called to solicit a subscription for the dispensary, when he said, "No! you print the subscriptions, and I don2t like *my* charities to be advertised; and what I give privately, that is *nothing In nobody."* The last clause of the sentence was known to be literally true. gate, where, also, he held a levee. On the succeeding night, the same bed he had slept in was occupied by the Duke of Cumberland, then in close pursuit of the rebels. Having inquired where Prince Charles had slept, he desired to rest on the same couch. The next day witnessed the defeat of the Scotch at Clifton Dykes, near Lowther. THE GUILD.

Formerly this town had its Guild processions, at intervals of 21 years, as was the custom of most manufacturing towns. The last Guild celebrated here, was on the 4th, 5th, and 6th of June,

17o9, and was carried to such an extravagant height of splendour, that, it was said, many of the tradesmen were nearly ruined by the expenses, and the festival has consequently ever since been discontinued. It will be interesting to know in wbat manner the procession was conducted; and we have met with a curious sample of poetry, published on the occasion, which conveys this information in more pleasing and faithful terms than we could employ: Arise, bright Sol, parent of light and day,

Dispel the clouds, thy brightest beams display,

To gild the scene the muse intends to paint,

And ev'ry hero justly represent.

Ingenious Hermes, god of arts and gain,

Propitious smile, and aid my humble strain;

Give me, 'tis thine to give, a tuneful tongue:

Arts are the subjects of the poet's song.

Kendal, long famed for trade and useful arts,

Sends forth her skilful sons with joyful hearts,

Cloathod with the product of their native land,

Wrought with the labour of each artist's hand.

In order ranked, they march with solemn pace,

With music, flags, and every martial grace.

WOOLCOMBERS.

See Jason first the advent'rous prince appear,

A chief well skill'd in arms, untaught to fear,

There were of old time among our ancestors, certain companies of confreries of men called *Glides,* first instituted for exercise of feates of arms, though after they were of other professions,—and these were called Gildbrethren; and for shortness of speech *a Gild.* The word "gild" in itself signifyeth *free* .md *houn-tifM.*— Verstegan.

Who the wide swelling ocean ventured o'er,

To fetch the golden fleece from Colchian shore.

A shepherd too and his fair shepherdess,

In all the gaiety of rural dress.

With mitred prelate, reverend for his age,

His steed on either side led by a page;

Precede the Combers, deck'd with softest wool,

Refined by passing thro' the pointed tool.

TAYLORM.

See our first parents next in order go, Adam and Eve, who first taught men to sew, Cloath'd with green leaves to hide their nakedness, Nor knew, nor wanted they a finished dress. But Taylors follow who've improv'd tho art, And cut and suit the cloth to ev'ry part. They cloathe the rich, the poor, the young, the old, And screen our bodies from the pinching cold. Their honour2d brother, Hawkwood too, appears, With his brave aid-de-camp and grenadiers, Who could not only shape but also fight, The favourite of a king, a martial knight.

SHEARMEN-DYERS.

In solemn pomp the warlike Edward shines, His arts more useful than the Indian mines; He taught the haughty Qaul his arms to dread, And trade among his happy Britons spread. Our Kendal shar'd tho prudent monarch2s care, And feels the favour both in peace and war. With him the joyful Shearmen-dyers come, Whose sole dependance is upon the loom; The Weavers find employment for them both, These give a colour, those refine the cloth. Stuff from the Weavers, yet unfit to wear, Of home-spun wool, thoy tenter, dress and shear, And make it like the finest cloth appear. The Dyers stain it beautiful to view, With crimson, scarlet, never-fading blue; Thus English wool, by Shearmen-Dyers wrought, Equals the finest silks from India brought.

WEAVERS. Minerva next appears, a warlike maid,

The fam'd inventress of the weaving trade;

And poor Arachni5, who as poets tell,

Was made a spider but for weaving well.

Their train the sons of art, a num'rous band,

Who guide the shuttle with a nimble hand,

Most neatly dress'd with labour all their own:

A prettier sight in Kendal never known.

SHOEMAKERS. Lo! Crispianus comes, of royal race,

A youth adorn2d with ev'ry princely grace;

An honour to the gentle craft, and still Of equal fame iu military skill.

Next Crispin, prince of Shoemakers, appears,

Attended by six stately grenadiers;

With him his lovely spouse, a princess born,

Fair Ursula, more beauteous than the morn.

To these succeed the brothers of the trade,

With each a splendid sash and gilt cockade.

IRONMONGERS AND METTLEMEN.

Next march the Smiths, inuiM to toil in fire. Without whose aid all arts must soon expire; The god of fire, great Vulcan, leads them on, Arm'd at all points, and glitt'ring like the sun. Not like the limping god whom poets feign In bands of wedlock join2d to beauty's queen; But like the god of war prepared to charge, So broad his shoulders, and his limbs so large. His band all men of metal, brisk and gay, Their dress bedeck'd with steel as bright as day; Or those that melt the iron from the ore, Or forge the anchor for the sounding shore; Or with the hammer beat the ductil gold, Or various forms of shining silver mold.

TANNERS.

Next march the Tanners, fam'd in days of yore For tanning hides for shields which heroes bore. Who has not heard of Ajax's sevenfold shield, Which nor to sword nor missive spear would yield, And wont as much admire, as much adore, The Tanner as the Chief the buckler wore?

BUILDERS.

The glorious Builders next salute our eyes, By whom aspiring domes and temples rise; Our splendid palaces, our ample squares, Our stately bridges, castles, all are theirs. Our Merchant vessels, all our ships of war, Are model'd, wrought and finished by their care. Britannia's glorious guard! To them we owe Whatever praises Britons can bestow.

CLOVERS AND SKINNERH.

Skiuners aud Glovers who with nicest care, Provide white kid for the new-married pair,

Or nicely stitch the lemon-coloured glve,

For hand of bean to go to see his love.

Before them see the Conqueror, William, ride,

Led by a page in buff, on either side.

MERCERS.

The Mercers next appear, a goodly train,

For whom our hardy Sailors plough the main;

Fraught with the labour of our artist's hands,

Thro' hottest climes they roam to distant lands.

From whence they bring the richest treasure here.

To pay us well, for what we well can spare.

Those bring whate'er may please the nicest eye,

Or the most luscious palate satisfy:

These bring the kind preservatives of health:

These are the government's and people's wealth.

MAYOR, ALDERMEN, AND OTHER GENTLEMEN.

See, last, the sword of justice and the mace

Are born before the Mayor with solemn grace;

Twelve Aldermen his courtly train compose,

Who, dressed in decent state, the grand procession close.

These are the guardians of our liberty,

The representatives of majesty;

Who keep the peace and execute the law,

Reward the good and keep the bad in awe.

Long may they rule, and each offender bring

To punishment and shame. God Have The King.

The known number of persons who took part in the procession were, Wool-combers, 100; Taylors, 150; Shearmen-dyers, 80; Weavers, 300; Shoe-makers, 100; Ironmongers and Mettlemen, 80; Tanners, 60; Builders, 100; Glovers and Skinners, 70; Mercers, &c., not numbered. Strangers were allowed to join if they requested, and were furnished with sashes and cockades, "provided they had given a fortnight's notice." It is probable that these "strangers" were persons not free of the *guild,* or in other words, not free of any of the trade companies. This seems to us more like the meaning of the word "strangers," than having reference to persons coming from other neighbouring towns.

POSTAL COMMUNICATION.

Up to the close of the last century, the postal communication was infrequent and snail-paced. About 1780 to 1790, one John Jennings, landlord of the Unicorn public-house, at Kendal, carried the letters between Kendal and Lancaster, by a horse and cart, John going to Lancaster on one day, and returning to Kendal on the next, which was thought to be a great achievement compared with "former times." The only intermediate post-office was at Burton. Country people got their letters when they had occasion to visit the towns named, by calling for them at the post-office, sometimes once a week, sometimes once a month.

The Unicora stood on the ground which is now occupied by the Odd Fellows' Hall. CHAPTER IV. MODERN STATE OF THE TOWN.

The town of Kendal is often compared with Bath, in its natural situation. The comparison is true in this respect, viz. that in each case part of the town is built in terraces, against a "fell side." Bath, certainly, has the advantage in art, the houses being more elegant and commanding: but Kendal has the advantage in nature, having hills of striking outline on both sides of the valley, with a brotherhood of still grander mountains at the head, whilst the bright waters of the Kent meander below, in sinuous lines of silver, around the bases of numerous hillocks:— 'It flows through the valleys So beauteous and free:

The land's crystal chalice,

From mountain to sea!"

The Castle hill, with the old Castle crowning its summit, is a fine object, to which Bath cannot furnish a parallel. This hill, together with Aikrigg hill, north of it, and many similar ones, as far as Crooklands, south of it, are so many *medial moraines,* composed of what geologists call boulder drift, due either to the action of diluvial currents, before the floods were "gathered together into a heap," or else to the action of glaciers, under a temperature of perpetual congelation. Either theory, the diluvial or the glacial, may have its advocate, but tins is not the place to discuss theories.

"Benson Knot," on the east side, is 1,098 feet, and "Kendal Fell," on the west, is 650 feet above the level of the sea

It is enough to.say, that the gravel and boulders composing these moraines have in part, at least, been drifted from great distances, and been rounded by ice, or water, or both. Few situations present such a variety of geological features. On the west side of the town, is a wall of mountain limestone (Kendal Fell), full of characteristic fossils: on the east side (Hay Fell), a rather higher wall of silurian, with older forms of life, in less abundance; whilst the waters of the river interpose to separate the two strata and their inhabitants, as if by the law of "natural frontiers." And further, several bands of a totally different intermediate rock, an "old red sandstone conglomerate," stretch across the valley as though the opposite walls of rock before mentioned required rafters of different structure to hold them in their places. These rafters of "old red" exhibit, on their surface, proofs of abrasion, and the occurrence of primeval storms, which probably swept away the overlying limestone, and determined the course of the valley. In some places, the thick beds of limestone are inter-laminated with thin beds of sandstone. These various strata, it is almost needless to say, yield diversified products. The limestone produces building materials, fertilizing compost for the land, and beautiful marble. The silurian rocks produce water for domestic uses, free from excess of lime; and advantage is duly taken by the inhabitants of these favourable conditions.

The name of Kirkby-Candale, taking its ancient orthography, is of very clear derivation. Kirkby is of Saxon origin. *Can,* or *con* (used variously), is the primitive British and Roman appellation, afterwards continued by the Saxons. (See Concangium, p. l(i.) The whole is thus explained. *Kirk* (church), *by,* or *bye* (a dwelling or village), *can* (head, or principal), *dale* (valley). Signifying, therefore, Church town, or in its infancy, Church village, in the chief valley of the river. Or, the word *can* may have been applied to the river and not to the valley, as there are three streams from the northern hills of which *can* is the head or principal. By this A list of the Fossils, Plants. &c., will be found at the end of the book.

"Bye Laws " are hence derived. The *Town's Laics,* as inferior to General (Statute) Laws. Mr. Whitaker, and Dr. Whitaker. adaptation, the meaning will be, *Church town, siiuated on the banks of the principal river in the valley.* Camden, who, it must be remembered, wrote in Latin, calls it *Candale.* His editor, Bishop Gibson, in his additions, writes it *Kendale.* We may therefore pronounce the latter to be the English translation of the former. The adjunct Kirkby is now almost generally discontinued, and we shall therefore not employ it further in this work.

The river Kent rises out of High Street (the Roman street), above Kentmere, and running by Staveley, Burneside, Kendal, Sedgwick, and Levens, falls into an estuary of the bay of Morecambe.

Kendal is the largest and most important town, though not the metropolis, of the county of Westmorland. It stands 188 feet above the level of the sea, in lat. 54. 15' K, and long. 2 52' W., 260 miles from London.

It consists of two main streets, in continuity, from north to south, from which all the other streets, lanes, alleys, crofts, &c. branch off at right angles. The streets generally carry their explanation in their names, some of which we shall attempt to elucidate: *Highgate* (the principal street from the south), is so called from its situation, being the highest street or *gate* (Sax.) in the town. This street had first been named *Sowtergate* (the *south-ex* street), and is so designated in the first "Boke off2 Eecorde," in 1575.

Stricklandgate (continuation of the main street), from the ancient family of Strickland, or one of the adjacent townships called Strickland. *Finkle-street* (branching N.E.) is derived from the Scandinavian *vinkel,* which signifies *an elbow,* a name that has frequently been given to a minor street or way, taking a crooked direction from a principal one. And certainly this street makes an angle resembling the arm in the human body. There was an ancient well in Finkle-street,—a draw-well, with axletree and bucket; and we find by an "order," in 1594, There is a Finkle-street in Richmond, in Sedbergh, in Carlisle, and in Newcastle, all of which are places of antiquity.

L that "twoe sworne men" were " yearelie appointed to see the same Well clensed & mainteined," with powers to enforce a fine of *2d.* for every offence, to be levied "of the master or dame's goods," offending against the order.

Stramongate, or as it was formerly spelled *Stramondgate,* is a continuation of Finkle-street, expanding in its descent to the river, and terminating at the bridge on which it confers its name. It is said to be called after a person of the name of Straman; and Speed has put it Straman's gate. But what seems to us a more probable derivation is, that as after heavy rains the lower part of the street became frequently inundated, and the road which conducts by the southwest bank was raised by an embankment or *mound,* to defend it from the violence of the waters; so the street obtained the name of *stream-mound-gate.* Or, it might be suggested simply by the *stream* running *on* the *gate. Long Pool* (the former appellation of the streets now called Wildman Street and Gandy Street) had also, it is probable, its name from the same liability to be flooded as Stramongate. *Wildman Street* was "Wildman Gate," in Speed's time. *Gandy Street* is named after the builder of the houses in that street. *All Hallows' Lane,* crossing Highgate in an oblique direction with New Street, received its name from the chapel which stood at its head, dedicated to "All Hallows." *Captain French Lane* is said to be called after a gentleman of the name of French, who purchased, and perhaps rebuilt most of it after the time of Speed's publication, as in his Plan it is called *Rotten Howe. Stukely* says, this name, Botten Row, "relates to panegyres (general assemblies) or fairs." But another derivation gives it as *"Routine Row"* because the procession of "the Church" (the Host) was taken by that *route.* Something may be said in this case in favour of each, but we prefer the latter derivation. This Rotten Row would be the *route* by which corpses were taken from Sowter-gate to the (old) cemetery at Kirkbarrow. *Cross Bank* received its name from one of the Cross Houses which stood here. *Kirkland* is so called from being situated on the land of the Church. It is a distinct township, divided from Kendal by a brook called Blindbeck. *Blindbeck* has its name either from the obscurity of its source,—its feeders being lost in the fissures of the limestone rocks in Gillingrove; or from the British word *blaen,* signifying a point, extremity, or end: *the town-end beck. New Street* obviously asserts its own signification. It is also sometimes called Lowther Street, from the family name of the Lord Lieutenant of the county. *Union Buildings* are so named from having been erected by a society of tradesmen *uniied* for that purpose.

STREET IMPROVEMENTS.

Little alteration appears to have been made in the streets and buildings from the time of Speed's publication, and perhaps long before that, till 1782, when *New Street* was erected. Some of the yards, indeed, may have become enlarged, and others curtailed, at the frequent exchanges of property; but public improvements were slowly manifested This town (as has before been intimated) suffered much from its exposure to the inroads of the Scotch, and from the ravaging plague in 1598; and, it was two centuries before it completely recovered the effects of these visitations. The next considerable improvement, in point of time, to the building of New Street, was in 1803, by removing New Biggin, and throwing open the main street. After which, alterations gradually, but still somewhat slowly, occurred, until the spirit of improvement fully manifested itself in 1818 and 1819. The date of the new town may, we conceive, truly be placed here, at the time of the opening of the Lancaster and Kendal Canal. This event gave On Friday, the 18th of June, 1819—the anniversary of Waterloo—the Lancaster and Kendal Canal was opened by a grand aquatic procession. The Mayor and Corporation, having proceeded to the Canal Basin, preceded by music and flags, entered a fine barge equipped for the occasion, which, with some smaller boats, sailed down the canal, to meet a numerous party of gentlemen from Lancaster. The parties joined at Crooklands, whence they an impulse to the public spirit of the inhabitants, and formed the commencement of a new era in the history of Kendal. It discovered new channels of commerce—it brought that necessary commodity of manufactures, coal, at a cheaper rate; and by adding facilities (which had long been desiderated) to the exportation of our produce, caused an increase of wealth, and an increase of the working population; and thus contributed, at once, all the means of commercial prosperity and public accommodation. We shall enumerate a few of the street improvements and additions which immediately follow this event:

The old *Miller's Close Bridge,* which had stood since 1743, and was very narrow, and ill adapted to be the general medium of intercourse with the canal, was now thrown down, and wholly rebuilt on a wider scale. The large warehouses, and other buildings at the canal harbour, were all erected at this time; Kent Lane (which before was very steep, and so narrow that two carts could scarcely pass) was thrown open, and the ascent considerably diminished; Long Pool was widened; Gandy Street erected; Kent Terrace and Castle Cres-

cent were built shortly after. The *Union Building Society* commenced operations about this time; and indeed on every side, numerous habitations were superadded to the town. The National School reared its imposing front over the heads of the other buildings; and in a very short time, the town assumed a new and modern appearance,—so very different that any person having been absent a few years, could scarcely have identified it. In 1822, the principal entrances to the proceeded in company towards Kendal. There were in all sixteen boats, ornamented with flags of various devices, and containing three excellent bands of music. Along the whole line every eminence was Crowded with spectators, who were highly delighted with the novelty and splendour of the scene. As the procession approached the town it was greeted by the firing of cannon, placed on the Castle Hill on one side of the valley, and in Chapel Close on the other. It was a gratifying and interesting spectacle. A greater number of persons had seldom, if ever, been seen congregated together in Kendal. The packets, &c. arrived in the Basin about four o'clock, when the company disembarked, and went in procession through the streets to the Town Hall, where a sumptuous dinner was provided, of which 120 persons partook. John Pearson, Esq., Mayor, in the chair. A ball at the King's Arms, in the evening, concluded the festivities of the occasion.

town were widened, and the obstructions at Blindbeck Bridge, and afterwards at Nether Bridge, were removed. To this must be added, that due attention was given to the condition of the streets; which are in good state of repair.

The terrace, of most commanding exterior, on.the east side of the town, is "Kent Terrace." It is built on what was formerly called Thorney Hills, from the abundance of thorns, long ago uprooted. The houses have the advantage of a fine sweep of the Kent immediately in front, and a good view of the town at a little distance beyond, crowned by Kendal Fell. "Castle Crescent" is an extension of this terrace northwards, formed of

houses with less pretensions, but uniformly neat. The Terrace was built in 1824, and the Crescent followed some years afterwards.

"Cliff-side Terrace " occupies the slope of Kendal Fell, on the west side of the town, and commands extensive views to the north-east. It was built in the years 1851 to 1853.

The front houses in the streets are generally three stories high, and the back cottages two. They are built of limestone, found in great abundance on Kendal Fell, close at hand. Some are faced with this stone, hewn smooth; others are roughcasted with lime and sand; these are every two or three years new coated with lime-wash, which gives them a neat and clean appearance.

There are few public buildings, properly so called, in Kendal; and these have been erected chiefly, either by subscriptions of the tradesmen, or by the benefactions of private individuals.

THE OLD MOOT HALL
Stands at the S.W. corner of the Market-place. It is a plain building for the purposes to which it was applied. It consisted of a court-loft, with ante-room for retiring juries, &c., which being separated by partition slides, might be thrown together as necessity required. It is surmounted with a square tower, which contains a clock. The first moot hall, which stood on the site of the present building, was erected in 1592. The present erection was made in 1759, and has gradually fallen into dilapidation and disuse. It was sold by auction on the 12th April, 1859, for 280?., to Mr. Job Bintley, Surveyor, when the Courts of Session were removed to the Whitehall (now Town Hall). The public clock, proj ecting from the tower, still remains, and we say, with regard to it, *esto perpetua.* THE HOUSE OF CORRECTION.

This commodious and well built prison-house stands on the site of an ancient " house of correction," which, in 1776, is thus minutely described in the State of Prisons, published about that time, by Howard the philanthropist:

"Only *one* room for men and women, 18ft. by 13ft., with *one* window, about 2ft. square; no chimney; no court; no water; no sewer. The keeper has a garden; salary, *6l. 10s.*; no fees. The town prisoners are allowed sixpence a day; the country prisoners four-pence.

"Jan. 23,.... Prisoners 3—two men and a woman.

Sep. 18,.... ,, 0—Deserter *one"*

Again, in three years afterwards, 1779, Mr. Howard visited it, and makes the following minute:

"May 11,.... Prisoners 0."

The "one room," above described, comprised the whole building; which served to accommodate the keeper, his family, and the prisoners, who all lived together. It was an ill-built house (now past all remembrance), with a *thatched roof,* and must consequently have been a very insecure and inconvenient prison-house. Over the door was a stone, inscribed with the following distich:

"If people woulde be goode and live in feare
The Juatices woulde never send them here."

The present structure presents a striking contrast to the one above described, in magnitude, and in every requisite It is worthy of note, that at this latter visit, there was not one prisoner in the county Bridewell, at Appli-by.

for a prison. It occupies an area of 2,000 yards, fenced by a thick wall. in some places 14 yards high. There are 53 night cells, about 6ft. by 8ft., fitted up with clean beds, and an ample supply of warm clothing. These are distributed through nine spacious yards or wards, with day rooms, cooking rooms, &c., plentifully supplied with water, which is conveyed into recipient cisterns, in different parts of the buildings, above and below, by the action of a forcing pump. The surplus water, &c, is carried off by a common sewer. On the second story, are seven debtors' rooms, having three beds in each room, comfortably furnished, and well ventilated. The yards and apartments for the different sexes are perfectly distinct and disunited. The cleanliness and regularity of the prison are admirable throughout; and the attention paid to the bodily comforts of the prisoners is also highly creditable

to the benevolent feelings of the governor.

The building has grown to its present dimensions by erections at different periods since the year 1817, and is estimated to have cost 5,500i *Governor:* Mr. Christopher Fawcett.

Salary, 100?. per annum; one half of which is paid by the borough, and the other by the county.

Officiating Chaplain: Rev. H. N. Collier

NEW TOWN HALL.

The Town Hall stands in the centre of the town, and is the most commanding of the street edifices. The front, though only thirty-seven feet in width, is effective, consisting of a rusticated basement for the principal entrance, which is surmounted by a balcony fronted with Ionic columns and pilasters of fine freestone. The length of the building, stretching down New Street, is 148 feet; but the longitudinal effect is inarred by the narrowness of this street. This building was originally called "Whitehall," being erected in the year 1827, by a joint-stock association, in shares of 55/. each, the then Corporation ranking among the shareholders. The several apartments, consisting of news-room, ball-room, billiard-room, card-room, lecture-room, shops, and offices, were rented out to pay interest on the amount of capital invested, which was 6,000t But as in course of time new halls sprang up elsewhere for lectures and public meetings, whilst the taste for county balls declined, the yearly income of this building fell off until the shareholders were reduced to infinitesimal dividends. Meanwhile, the Old Town-hall (at the entrance to the market-place), where the Council were wont to meet, and the Quarter Sessions were held, became dilapidated and insecure, suggesting the desirability of a change in the Hall of Justice. In 1858 negotiations were set on foot between the authorities and the shareholders of the Whitehall Buildings, when this property was sold, and formally transferred to the Corporation for the sum of 2,2507. The ball-room, retiring-rooms, &c. were then converted into the Court of Quarter

Sessions; part of the basement was formed into lock-ups, with different cells; and other changes were made with money borrowed by the Coiporation on mortgage. The County agreed to pay for the accommodation of county business, 507. per annum for the Court of Quarter Sessions, and 10?. additional for the cells, making 60?. per annum gross rental. The alterations above indicated being effected, the New Town Hall was formally inaugurated by a public dinner, given by the Mayor, John Wakefield, Esq., in September, 1859. This gentleman has liberally offered to place a public clock in the front of the building at his own cost; and a suitable tower to contain it has been designed by Geo. Webster, Esq., the original architect of the building.

THE BANKS.

There are two banks, both situated in Highgate; one a private bank, belonging to Messrs. Wakefield, Crewdson, & Co. , the other a joint-stock establishment, called "The Bank of Westmorland." The first banking establishments in the town were two, popularly denominated "Wakefield's Bank," situated in Stricklandgate, and "the Kendal Bank," begun by Messrs. Maude, Wilson, & Crewdson, in Highgate. These opened together on the 1st of January, 1788, and continued separately in operation until the 1st of January, 1840, when the partners, Wakefields of one house, and Crewdsons of the other, united or amalgamated, and "the Kendal Bank," in Highgate, was continued under the existing firm of Wakefield, Crewdson, & Co.

The Bank of Westmorland started in February, 1833, in New Street, until the present handsome house was erected in 1835. It is a prominent building of the Grecian order of architecture, built of the mountain limestone; from designs by Mr. Alderman George Webster. The Doric pilasters of the facade carry an entablature on which is represented a lion couchant (emblem of strength), life size.

Both banks issue *5l.* and KM. notes. The provincial notes of *l.* were withdrawn from circulation in 1826.

The "Kendal Bank" (Messrs. Wakefield, Crewdson, & Co.) has three branch establishments, one at Ambleside, one at Kirkby-Stephen, and one at Sedbergh.

BANK FOR SAVINGS.

The Bank for Savings was established in 1816, on the principle of Dr. Duncan. No maximum was at first specified for deposits, and the interest was fixed at 4 per cent, per annum for 12. 6d., or any multiple of that sum. In the following year, the first act of parliament was passed relating to banks for savings, and this institution was conducted under the powers of that and subsequent acts, till the 3d February, 1829, when the trustees and managers resolved to place it on an independent foundation, giving their own personal security for the amount of the deposits. From the great facilities afforded for receiving and paying small sums, the bank has gradually increased its operations, till it has about 3,000 depositors, the sums at whose credit vary from Is. to 30?., and the interest allowed is now SI. 6s. 8d. per cent, per annum. The directors are twentyfour in number, one of whom, in monthly rotation, superintends the transactions of the bank. The officers are, an Honorary Secretary (being one of the Directors), an Actuary, and an Auditor. The balance is struck on the 30th June, yearly.

THE RAILWAYS.

The inhabitants of Kendal were among the earliest of the dwellers in provincial towns, at the first projection of Railways, to perceive the advantages of the most improved mode of internal communication; notwithstanding which, it required great exertions, several years, indeed, of continued exertions, to bring railways to and through Kendal. Many country towns not merely stood aloof from the general movement, but organized the stoutest opposition to such "perilous schemes." All kinds of evils were predicted of the coming railway system. Horses would be thrown out of work, and disappear I turnpike-roads, and cross-country roads would be covered with grass! vegetation would perish from clouds of smoke and steam! butter, and eggs, and poultry would rise

to the top price of the metropolitan markets (as if that were a calamity to the community), and many other "evils" would set in with the advent of railways. Only very few, however, of the inhabitants of Kendal joined in this prophetic clamour, and those other towns where it most prevailed soon afterwards bitterly repented of their folly. That physical configuration of the country around Kendal, which, like Hogarth's "line of beauty," is so pleasing to the lovers of natural scenery, presented serious obstacles to the efforts of railway engineers, and also deterred capitalists at a distance from investing in the enterprise. Local subscriptions were insufficient for the work It was therefore necessary for the promoters to supplicate the assistance of the established railway companies in the south, whose interests would be Worcester, Wolverhampton, Windsor, and several towns first opposed railways, and not long afterwards subscribed their money hi condonation of their orrura.

promoted by the extension of their lines northwards. The appeals to the local community were made by calling public meetings; by the publication of letters and articles in the newspapers, by pamphlets, and other means; pointing out the advantages which might be expected to result from the introduction of railways to the manufacturing establishments of the town. These efforts were begun in 1836, and were not relaxed, at least by some few of the most ardent advocates of the system, until the accomplishment of the scheme in 1844. The first public meeting was held on the 19th December, 1837, at the Town Hall, Kendal, Wm. Gelderd, Esq., the Mayor, in the chair, when a numerous committee was formally constituted. The established railway companies in the south, between Lancaster and London, after repeated applications made to them, at length agreed to subscribe among them 500,000/. towards 1,200,000?., fixed upon as the nominal capital of the "Lancaster" and Carlisle Railway Company. " The remaining part of the capital, 700,000?., was obtained by persevering canvass in the district; and the Act of

Parliament, authorizing the railway from Lancaster to Carlisle, vid Kendal, was obtained in May, 1844. The first general meeting of the Company, duly constituted, was held in the Town Hall, Kendal, on the 28th June, 1844, when the following were elected as the first local directors of the board, viz.: Henry Cecil (Col.) Lowther; Edward Williams Hassell; John Wakefield; Henry Howard; Geo. Head Head; John Dixon; H. D. Maclean; and Cornelius Nicholson.

But the direct north and south, or Lancaster and Carlisle Railway, could not, from the nature of the ground, be made to approach nearer to the town than the slopes of Benson Knot, along which the line runs. Some further scheme therefore became necessary, and another company was formed, by the original promoters of the before-mentioned undertaking, entitled the "Kendal and Windermere Railway Company," whose object was to unite the town of Kendal with the main line at Oxenholme, and extend the communication to the " The London and Glasgow Railway. The interests of Kendal considered."—By Cornelius Nicholson. 8yo. Nov. 1837.

banks of Windermere. The capital of this company was 125,000?. It was opposed by a few of the residents in the lake district. The objectors memorialised the Board of Trade, and met with the following rebuke by the Railway Commissioners, in their report to Parliament: "We are precluded from taking into consideration the feelings of individuals who are privately interested. But we must state, that an argument which goes to deprive the artisan of the offered means of changing his narrow abode, his crowded streets, his unwholesome toil, for the fresh air, and the healthful holiday, which sends him back to his work refreshed and invigorated, simply that some individuals may retain to themselves the exclusive enjoyment of scenes which should be open alike to all, appears to us to be an argument wholly untenable."

The following were the first directors, constituted by a clause in the Act of Parliament, viz.: Edward Wilson; John Gandy; George Braithwaite Crewdson; James Bryans; John Hewetson Wilson; John Jowitt Wilson; William Whitwell; and Cornelius Nicholson. The Act received the Royal assent on the 30th June, 1845.

The Railway was opened from Lancaster to Kendal on the 21st of September, 1846, which was made a holiday and day of general rejoicing. An entertainment was furnished forth in the large room of the Whitehall Buildings (now the Town Hall), presided over by the Mayor, who was a director and projector of both companies. In the year 1859, the two railways were leased to the London and North-Western Railway Company, and are now held and worked by that company.

The new Railway station in Kendal was built in the present year (1861).

THE THEATRE.

The Theatre is a tradition of the past. The first theatre that we can make out with certainty, was a building in the Market-place, approached by a flight of steps which led to the dwelling over part of the Foot Ball Inn, and the adjoining premises, mentioned at p. 126. In 1777, when the histrionic art was encouraged in Kendal, that building was deemed inconveniently small; and a large theatre, on the plan of the metropolitan theatres, was erected in the Wool Pack Yard. About the beginning of the present century, the drama began to decline in Kendal, and fell so rapidly into disesteem, that, by the year 1823, the proprietor of the theatre was glad to let it for another purpose, and it was converted into a Meeting-house for the Presbyterians.

THE COVERED MARKET.

Where the covered market now stands, was a chapel of ease (under the parish church), built in 1754, and taken down in 1855, having stood one day in excess of 100 years, from the date of its consecration. It was dedicated to St. George, and therefore called "St. George's Chapel." The west end, facing Stricklandgate, presented a basement of shops, with wine vaults beneath, and the east end formed an avenue which served for part of the market, the chapel being,

in that part, upheld by pillars of masonry. The shops and wine vaults were the property of the corporation; the patronage of the chapel was vested in the Vicar of Kendal for the time being; and the lords of the manor had the right of holding a market in the area. All these parties consenting, the chapel was removed, and a public subscription set on foot to raise funds for erecting a commodious covered market on the vacated ground, to supply the want of protection from the weather, which had long been experienced by the vendors of butter, eggs, poultry, and vegetables, most of whom were females; for (shame to say it) the limited area under the old chapel had been weekly occupied by the corn dealers and millers, whilst the butter-women were exposed to the pluvial elements. The necessary funds having been raised, the foundation stone of the building was laid, with.great ceremony, on the 21st day of July, 1855, by the Mayor, John Whitwell, Esq., "in the hope that with the blessing of the Almighty on the industry of the people and upon the productions and fruits of the earth, the building now commenced may tend to the advancement of this ancient town, and to the accommodation and prosperity of its inhabitants, and of the neighbourhood." The building cost about 700?. *Architects,* Messrs. Thompson and Webster. *Builders,* Alderman John Fisher, carpenter, and Robert Shaw, mason.

GAS AND WATEE WOBKS.

The conjoint management of gas and water works has been recognised in various places. The two operations, supplying products to the same premises, and same consumers, are entirely compatible with the charges of one establishment. Kendal was first lighted with gas on the 25th July, 1825, supplied by the works of a joint-stock company, entitled, the "Kendal Gas-Light and Coke Company." But when, in 1846, the most active men of the town resolved upon securing, what had long been considered desirable, an ample supply of water from the Silurian rocks, for all the habitable houses, it was deemed expedient to buy up the old gas company, and merge

it in a new company to be called the "Kendal Union Gas and Water Company." The capital of this company was fixed at 30,000?., and the shares of the old concern were merged in the new company, being entitled to rank as preference shares, carrying per cent, per annum dividend, with an option to convert the same into ordinary shares, up to the 1st of January, 1851. This option was never exercised, and has now, of course, become extinct. The Act of Parliament met with a show of opposition (whether genuine or simulated, we cannot say), by the landowner most interested; but was, nevertheless, passed, and received the royal assent on the 26th June, 1846. The following were the first directors, as appointed by the Act, viz.:—Cornelius Nicholson, Thompson Bindloss, John Ireland, William Longmire, John Hudson, John Thompson the younger, John Gandy, John Whitwell, John Jowitt Wilson, George Braithwaite Crewdson, and Samuel Marshall. The Extract of the inscription on vellum, deposited beneath the foundation tone.

The water had been submitted to popular analysis, and we took a phial of it to London, and induced the members of the Parliamentary Committee to taste and admire it. company has been highly prosperous, and the public much benefited by its operations. Last year's rental was—for Gas, 2,300?.; water, 1.000?. = 3,300?., The quantity of gas registered for the year at the station meter, was 12,500,000 cubic feet; and the price charged to the consumers is 5s. per 1,000 cubic feet. The number of public lamps lighted is 132. THE OLD VICARAGE HOUSE.

By a survey of the Vicarage, taken in 1563 (which is in Latin), we find some curious particulars respecting the Vicarage House, of which we here present a translation:—

"The Vicar of Kirkby-Kendal holds there, in right of his vicarage, the principal mansion belonging to the said vicarage, consisting of a hall, parlour, bedchambers, kitchen, pantry,— with other apartments for servants; built of stone, and *covered with slates;* with one barn, one stable, one court, one flower-garden, orchard, and kitchen-garden; with a field adjoining, containing by estimation one acre; situated between the church-yard of Kendal aforesaid on the north side, and Nether Bridge on the south side; the common street called Kirk Lane on the west side, and the river Kent on the east side."

This proves the great antiquity of the house. The mansion above described, was enlarged by a drawing-room, erected during the incumbency of Dr. Symonds. The dining-room was enlarged, the hall and staircase altered, and many alterations and improvements made at the commencement of Mr. Robinson's incumbency, in 1789. When Mr. Hudson took possession, the windows in the two wings (which had been contracted) were opened to their former size; and a convenient room, for a library, was added to the building. The north wing of the house was taken down in 1860, by the present vicar, Mr. Cooper, when he built for himself the new Vicarage House, and the building now under consideration was abandoned as a residence for the vicar.

It is proved by the above survey, that the period when the "field adjoining," or the major part of it, was converted into tan-yards, was subsequent to the year 1563; and from other documents it appears that this was done about the year 1700.

Although an improvement was made in the revenues hy the erection of tan-yards, yet some of our readers, still living, will recollect the nuisance at one of the principal entrances to the town. In 1826 the tan-yards were removed, and the ground again laid to the Vicarage Court. A new carriage road was made from the south, which conducts through an avenue of lime, birch, elm trees, and acacias, diversified with shrubs in great variety and abundance. At the entrance to the grounds stands a lodge, in conformity with the classical taste manifested throughout the improvement

We shall readily be forgiven, if we express a wish, that the vicarage premises had extended to the ancient boundary of Nether Bridge, as in former years, or that the trustees had at once

converted the space into an improvement of the entrance to the town.

Several years ago, a colony of rooks established themselves in the lofty and venerable lime trees that throw their umbrageous shadow over the west side of the mansion.

NEW VICARAGE HOUSE.

The vicar's residence is a handsome building, in the Elizabethan order, beautifully situated on part of the glebe lands, called "the Vicar's Fields." It was erected in 1859-60, by the present vicar, the Eev. John Cooper, from designs by Messrs. Bowman and Crowther, Manchester. When the trees and shrubs, recently planted, have reached maturity, the house and grounds will be a considerable ornament to the southern suburb of the town. Close behind the house, on the west, stands one of the round hillocks which we believe to be factitious, belonging to an early age, either Roman or Saxon. It commands extensive views, north, south, and east.

ABBOT HALL.

On the north side of the church, and within the boundary of the grant of Gilbert, sixth baron of Kendal, was a house called Abbot Hall. This must have belonged to the abbey of St. Mary's, and, we conclude, was either the residence of the abbot (the eighth in our catalogue of the vicars of Kendal), and afterwards an occasional residence of succeeding abbots, or else it was a place where they held their courts. Whether the property was sold, together with the greater part of the aforesaid grant, at the dissolution of monasteries, or how it became private property, we have not been able to ascertain. Tradition reports that it stood about the place where the stables and coach-houses are now erected. The present mansion, which retains the name of Abbot Hall, was built in 1759, by Colonel George Wilson, of Dallam Tower, at an expense (says Dr. Bum) of 8,000/!. It belongs to William Wilson, Esq., of High Park, whose father purchased it of Sir Alan Chambre, in 1801. It is now the residence of Edmund Harrison, Esq., J. P.

DISSENTING PLACES OF WORSHIP.

It is generally considered that there are

a greater number of different denominations of professing Christians in Kendal than in almost any other town of equal population. The Meeting-house that tradition reports as possessing the highest antiquity, was on the Fell Side—a house that has, within living memory, been a dwelling, and is now occupied by Mr. John Carradus. Here the Presbyterians assembled for Divine worship; and we are informed, that at one time that sect were exercising their offices of holiness in the upper story, whilst a body of Seceders from the Society of Friends were occupying the lower story of the same house, for a similar purpose. The dissidents from the Friends reverted again to the Society of Friends; but it was agreed that they, and their posterity, should be buried in *the Sepulchre,* on the Fell Side (mentioned at p. 79).

As is represented to have been the case with a place called Abbot Hall, similarly situated, near the church of Kirkby Lonsdale, which belonged to the same abbey.—Vide " History Of Westmorland," p. 247. *Colonel Walk,* which conducts from the church to the town, by the west bank of the Kent, is said to have taken its name from this gentleman, by his constant habit of walking there.

M

We will place the Religious Societies in the order of time. The following are the dates of their introduction, respectively:—

Roman Catholics
Friends 1645
Unitarians (originally Presbyterians) 1687
Inghamites 1745
Scotch Presbyterians 1763
Independents 1772
Wesleyan Methodists 1784
Primitive Methodists 1822
Christian Brethren 1837
Zion Chapel Congregation.... 1843

ROMAN CATHOLIC CHURCH.

The present Church, erected in 1839, stands on ground which has probably been dedicated to the services of the Roman Catholic body since the time of the Reformation. The Church, replaced by the present one, was built in 1793; but before that time, we only know from tradition, that preceding Roman Catholic chapels stood on the same spot. The existing Church has an imposing appearance, making due allowance for the confined space allotted to it, and perhaps exhibits, on that account, the skill and taste of the architect, George Webster, Esq., more than any other of his numerous public buildings. The river front, with its centre gable and angle buttresses, surmounted by crocheted spires, is exceedingly striking. Within a canopied niche, there is a spirited piece of sculpture, representing St. George and the Dragon. The Church is dedicated to the Holy Trinity and St. George. The present priest is the Rev. James Gibson, who succeeded, in 1857, the Rev. Thomas Wilkinson. This latter gentleman died at the advanced age of ninety-four, and had officiated here for sixty-five years! He was one of the last students of the Douay College, was a man of great learning, and most conciliatory disposition.

There is a Roman Catholic Chapel, also, at Dodding Green, a rural retreat on the banks of the Mint.

Friends' Meeting-house.

The Meeting-house belonging to the Society of Friends, or Quakers, stands in Stramongate, on the site of an ancient meeting-house, which was taken down in the year 1815. On the door of the old building was discovered the date, 1688, and as it is probable that the Society was introduced into the town by George Fox, about 1645, it seems fair to conclude that the building had been erected in the year of the date before mentioned. It was found to have been built with clay instead of lime, a practice common in ancient architecture for most buildings, excepting castles and places of defence. In a volume of testimonies, concerning "the Ministers of the Society of Friends," we find a testimony from the monthly meeting of Kendal, written on the death of William Williamson, a preacher, which is recorded to have taken place on the 21st of the Ninth month, 1743. From this testimony, it is proved that the burying-ground was at that time attached to the Meeting-house; for it is

stated that the said minister was interred "in the Friends' burying-ground, at Kendal, on the 24th of the same month. "

The present Meeting-house was erected in 1816. It is an excellent building, and will contain about 1,200 persons. The facing stones are all inlaid with putty, as being superior to lime mortar.

The Society has decreased considerably in numbers within the last twenty years.

Unitarian Chapel.

The Unitarian Chapel stands at the east side of the Marketplace, in quiet seclusion, approached by an arched gateway, which is connected with the parsonage-house, occupied by the resident minister. The Chapel was built in 1720, from funds raised by voluntary subscriptions, added to the absolute sale The appellation " Quakers," was given to this society, at its outset, in the time of Fox, in consequence of that champion having so fiercely defended himself and his cause before two justices at Nottingham, that he absolutely made them *"quake,"* or tremble before him.

of a number of seats, which continue to be freehold (private) property. But the congregation dates still farther hack, there being a register of births connected with it in 1687. In 1699, the Rev. Samuel Audland was minister, to whom succeeded Dr. Caleb Rotherham, in 1710. Under Ms ministry it was that the congregation outgrew their then chapel accommodation, and necessitated the present building. In June, 1752, Dr. Caleb Rotherham died at Hexham, and, in 1756, his place was taken by his fourth son, Caleb, during whose ministry the parsonage-house was built, viz. in 1777. In 1796, Rev. Caleb Rotherham died, and was succeeded by Rev. John Harrison; and on the death of Mr. Harrison, in 1833, the pastoral charge fell to Rev. Edward Hawkes, who is therefore in the twenty-ninth year of his ministry. Edward Holme, M.D., an eminent practitioner in Manchester, who was a native of Kendal, and a lineal descendant of one of the founders of this Chapel, bequeathed at his death, in

1847, the sum of one thousand pounds, the interest of which is to be paid for ever, in aid of the salary of the minister. The Chapel will accommodate upwards of 200 hearers. INGHAMITE Chapel.

This congregation was among the earliest formed of the Society to which it belongs, by the founder, Benjamin Ingham, from whom the sect derives its denomination. The original Meeting-house of the congregation stood on the site of the present Chapel, and was called "Pear-Tree Meeting," because of a large pear-tree that stood near it, which was blown down in November, 1821. The first regular pastor was Thomas Rowlandson, chosen in 1762. He died in 1797, and was followed, in succession, by Christopher Batty, William Wilson,;ind John Huck, the last of whom died in 1845. Robert Dent and Thomas Levens were ordained elders in 1830, and the service is now conducted by one or both of those Dr. Rotherham conducted, for many years, an academy here, principally with a view to qualify his pupils for the ministerial office. The "Monthly Repository " contains a list of fifty-six divinity students, some of whom were eminent scholars and preachers, educated at this academy. gentlemen. The Society are Calvinistic in doctrine, and take the New Testament alone for their guide, both in faith and practice. The chapel is maintained on the "voluntary principle," the sittings being free for all who choose to occupy them. The burying-ground was closed in 1855. In it repose the ashes of Banks, better known as Philosopher Banks, author of a popular "Essay on Mills," and other writings, who died in 1806. The present chapel was built in 1844, and will accommodate about 250 persons. SCOTCH UNITED PRESBYTERIAN CHAPEL.

The body of Presbyterians has undergone several changes and vicissitudes since its introduction into Kendal. Within the period of its existence here, it has thrown off, from its sides, two different denominations, the " Independents" and the congregation of "Zion Chapel;" and in its corporate capacity it has united successively with the 'Burger" and "Relief" churches of Scotland, and on this account is now styled the United Presbyterian Church. The first chapel of this community was built on the Beast Banks, where the burial ground may yet be seen, though closed in 1855, by order of the Health of Towns' Act. In this chapel the Rev. James MQuhae was ordained by the presbytery of Edinburgh in 1764. This gentleman seceded, on principles of Church government, in 1772, and became an *Independent,* taking with him several of the congregation, and the sum of 100?., being part of the value of the property. The next minister was Rev. Thomas Simpson, ordained in 1774. The chapel, now "Hill House," was finally sold, and the proceeds formed the nucleus of a sum which, by subscriptions, was raised to 1,000?. With this fund, the theatre in the Wool Pack Yard was purchased, and converted into a chapel in 1824, and so continues. Rev. Alexander Marshall, ordained in 1825, was the first minister at this place. He was succeeded, at his death, in 1828, by Rev, Robert Wilson, D.D. In 1834, the Rev. Henry Calder From the Greek word *TptafMrtpos,* signifying " elder," or senior.

wood took charge of the flock. After him, Rev. John Guthrie, ordained in 1840. Mr. Guthrie, for sentiments declared to be contrary to the tenets of the Church, was removed by the Synod, in 1843, and he took away with him the worshippers, who thence set up Zion Chapel. Next, came Rev. John Inglis, in 1845, who resigned in 1858, and was followed by the present minister, the Rev. Hugh Grey Wallace. The chapel will accommodate about 450 persons.

INDEPENDENT CHAPEL.

This body issued from the Presbyterians in Kendal, as stated at p. 165. The appellation " Independent," appertains to the position of the minister, who is not subordinate to a presbytery, and also to the Church, which is independent of other assemblies. This Society was established in 1772, and met for some years in a building which had been the theatre, on the north side of the Market-place, next to the Football public-house.

The present Chapel, in New Street, was built in 1782. It is a handsome stone building, and contains sittings for about 400 persons. The ministers, successively, have been the Revs. Luke Collins, James Kay, Thomas Gritton, Robert McLean, William Colfax, John Jefferson, and lastly, the Rev. David Jones (resigned whilst these pages are in the press).

WESLEYAN METHODIST CHAPEL.

The Wesleyan Methodists were introduced into Kendal in the year 1784. The first preachers, by leave of the Mayor, addressed the people in the open Market-place. Soon after that time a Society was organized, who assembled for regular worship in the old theatre, in the Market-place; from which place, a short time afterwards, they removed to a large room in The Fold, in Stricklandgate, and there continued till the present Meeting-house, at the north end of Stricklandgate, This gentleman went out to Caffraria, Cape Colony, as a missionary, in 1838, and has highly distinguished himself there in the cause of Christianity, and in matters of civil government.

The " Independents" arose, in the time of Elizabeth, from among men who counted the practices of the Established Clergy too much like those of the Roman Catholics. was erected in 1808. There is a burying-ground attached to the Chapel, which is now closed. The Chapel will accommodate 700 persons.

PRIMITIVE METHODIST CHAPEL.

The Primitive Methodists were introduced into Kendal in 1822. They preached in the open air, on the waste grounds in the suburbs of the town, for about twelve months, when, having formed a Society, the present Chapel was, in 1823, erected for their use. It stands at the foot of Castle Street, and contains 250 sittings.

CHRISTIAN BRETHREN.

The Christian Brethren, formerly called " Plymouth Brethren," emanated chiefly from the Society of Friends in Kendal. They first assembled in regular congregation about 1837, in one of the public rooms of the Whitehall (now Town Hall) buildings; and, growing gradually

in numbers and influence, they built, in 1858, the present Chapel in Stramongate, which will seat upwards of 300 persons. The distinctive principle of this community, in Church government, is their rejection of formal office-bearers. Their tenets are Calvinistic.

ZION CHAPEL.

The congregation at this Chapel has no distinctive religious appellation. They issued out of the Presbyterians (as stated at p. 166); but they are more like the Independents in principles of Church government. In the " weightier matters of the gospel" they are strictly evangelical. The Chapel, situated in the New Inn yard, Highgate, was built and opened in 1844. It will seat about 600 persons. Present minister, the Rev. William Taylor.

We must next introduce short notices of the local military bodies which have arisen in the present century on national emergencies. The Volunteers of 1803 came forth on occasion of Napoleon I. gathering his armies on the heights of Boulogne, with the object of throwing them upon the shores of England; and the Rifle Volunteers of 1859 sprang from unusual military and naval preparations in France, at the time, by Napoleon III.

KENDAL AND LONSDALE VOLUNTEERS. 1803.

When Napoleon I. threatened the invasion of England, Government passed an Act, granting certain allowances to those Volunteer and Yeomanry corps, throughout the United Kingdom, who were willing to associate for the defence of their country. This Act was passed on the 27th July, 1803, and such was the alacrity with which the loyalty and patriotism of the inhabitants of Kendal and the neighbourhood prompted them to assemble, that on the 19th of the following month a meeting of the lieutenancy was held at Boroughbridge, to make preliminary arrangements; and on the 15th of the next month, September, upwards of 1,000 men, together with officers, were on parade at Kendal, for the purpose of being enrolled and sworn in! Such was the alacrity thus displayed, that when on examination it was found there were more than the requisite number of men, and it seemed desirable to dispense with some who were over and some under an eligible age, no means of persuasion less than a bribe could induce such persons to withdraw from the service!

The Kendal and Lonsdale Volunteers consisted of fourteen companies, of 70 men each, with officers complete. The first regular return of the corps was made on the 1st of December, 1803.

Participating in the patriotic feeling of the time, the Hon. Mrs. Howard, of Levens, bestowed a distinguishing mark of her approbation of the corps, by presenting them with a pair of colours, which she accompanied with the following letter:—

"To Lieutenant-Colonel Maude.

"Sib,

"When I understood that it would be agreeable to the Volunteers of Kendal and its neighbourhood, to receive their colours from one of the family of Levens, it increased my regret at the necessity I was under of leaving the country before the regiment was complete, and that I could not have the honour of delivering them in person. The period for their delivery is probably now arrived; I have therefore to request that you will accept them by the only manner I have now the opportunity of offering them. No words of mine are necessary to give energy to the exertions of those gallant men who have voluntarily come forward in defence of their country.—Animated with a spirit of loyalty to their King, with the love of Liberty and the Constitution, they will, I am persuaded, to a man, esteem death preferable to the tyranny of a merciless invader.

"I am, Sir,

"Your obedient, humble servant,

"frances Howard." "Elford, Dec. 26, 1803.

On Monday, January 16, 1804, the Volunteers had a grand field-day at Kendal, when they received their colours.

The regiment continued to be assembled once every year for training and exercise, sometimes at Kendal, and on two or three occasions at Penrith, until the establishment of the local militia.

It deserves to be recorded, in honour of the corps, and in testimony of the estimation in which they held their commanding officer, Colonel Maude, that, in 1806, they presented him with a service of plate, consisting of a magnificent tureen and four salver dishes of massy silver, which cost 250 guineas, together with a beautiful sabre, and a brace of pistols.

LOCAL MILITIA. 1809.

The Volunteer regiment gave way to the establishment of the regular Kendal and Lonsdale Local Militia, in 1809. The first Return of this regiment was made at Kendal, by Lieutenant-Colonel Maude, on the 9th of June, 1809, and consisted of the following:—

Two lieutenant-colonels, one major, eight captains, seven lieutenants, six ensigns, six staff officers, thirty-two sergeants, thirty corporals, fifteen drummers, and 650 rank and file.

In 1816, the Kendal staff assembled, and marched in procession to the church, when and where the colours were deposited which still hang suspended over the north aisle of this venerable structure. There, also, are hung the flags of the Westmorland, or 55th, regiment.

VOLUNTEER RIFLE CORPS. 1859.

A corps of Volunteers, armed with the rifle gun, and hence called "Rifle Volunteers," was established in December, 1859. It originated in unison with a general volunteer movement of the day, the country having suddenly awoke to a consciousness of its defenceless condition, which had been oracularly declared by the Duke of Wellington a few years previously. This corps consists of two companies, each of them between 70 and 80 rank and file. It is called the "Third Westmorland Volunteer Rifle Corps." The preliminary expenses, accoutrements, &c., were paid from a fund raised by public subscription, since which it has been chiefly selfsupported. The first officers of the corps were: 1st company, Captain Commandant, William Wilson, High Park; Lieut. G. W. Ireland (manufacturer); Ensign, Daniel

Harrison (solicitor). 2nd company: Captain, John Whitwell (carpet manufacturer); Lieut. Harry Arnold (solicitor); Ensign, Cartmell Harrison, Singleton Park (solicitor).

THE CORPORATION.

The Charter of Incorporation was first granted to Kendal by Queen Elizabeth, in the 18th year of her reign (1575). The government of the town was, by this Charter, vested in twelve burgesses, out of which number one was annually elected and appointed to officiate as chief magistrate, one recorder, and twenty-four assistants. Speed says, "Kendal is a place of very civill and orderly government, the which is managed by an Alderman, chosen every yeare out of his twelve brethren, who are all distinguished and notified from the rest by the wearing of purple garments!"

The Charter of Elizabeth remained in operation and effect until the 11th of Charles I. (1636), when a further The seal is made of silver, and is one and a half inch in diameter. The device is a view of the town at the time: with the flag flying from the church tower, and signs of life, in smoke, rising from the chimneys.

Charter was obtained, confirming the former and granting more ample privileges, the substance of which is as follows:—

"That in the town of Kirkby-in-Kendale there shall be a body politic and corporate, consisting of one mayor, twelve aldermen, and twenty chief or capital burgesses of the borough of Kirkby-in-Kendale; to have a common seal; with power to take lands not exceeding 100l. a year.

"The mayor to be chosen out of the number of aldermen, on Monday next before Michaelmas day yearly, by the mayor and aldermen, or the major part of them (of whom the mayor to be one), to continue for one whole year, and from thence until another be chosen and sworn.

"The aldermen to be chosen by the mayor and aldermen, or the major part of them, to continue during life, or until amoval from the office for reasonable cause.

"The capital burgesses to be chosen by the mayor and aldermen, or the major part of them (of whom the mayor to be one), to continue in the office during their good behaviour.

"One man learned in the laws to be recorder or seneschal; to be chosen by the mayor and aldermen, to execute the office during their pleasure.

"They shall also appoint a clerk of the recognizances (or town clerk); and a sword bearer, and two sergeants at mace.

"The mayor shall be clerk of the market; and the mayor and senior alderman shall be coroners for the said borough.

"If the mayor die within the year, or be lawfully amoved from his office, another shall be chosen for the residue of the year. And no mayor shall serve again till after four years from the expiration of his office.

"If an alderman live out of the borough, another shall be chosen.

"There shall be two fairs yearly; one on the eve, day, and morrow of the feast of St. Mark; the other on the eve, day, and morrow of the feast of St. Simon and Jude.

"On Thursday from three weeks to three weeks, the mayor, recorder (or deputy recorder), and two senior aldermen, or three of them (whereof the mayor, recorder, or deputy recorder in the absence of the recorder, shall be two), shall hold a court of record, and view of frankpledge, and shall have cognizance of pleas of matters arising within the borough, amounting to any sum not exceeding *201. "*And they shall have power to make by-laws, for the good rule and government of all officers, artificers, burgesses, inhabitants, and resiants in the same borough, so as they be reasonable, and not contrary to the laws of the land.

"And the mayor, aldermen, and burgesses, may appoint searchers and inspectors of woollen cloth and cottons, and impose fines for offences in the manufacturing thereof.

"And no petty chapman or artificer, not free of the borough, shall, except in open fair or market on the market day, put to sale any wares or merchandizes (except victuals), without licence of the mayor and aldermen under their seals.

"The mayor, recorder, and two senior aldermen, shall be justices of the peace; and they, or any three of them (whereof the mayor and recorder shall be two), may hold sessions, and hear and determine offences; except treason, murder, felony, or any other matter touching the loss of life or limb, in which they shall not proceed without the king's special command. And the justices of the county shall not intromit, unless in defect of the justices of the borough.

"Provided, that nothing herein shall derogate from the right of the hereditary high sheriff of the county, with respect to any goods or chattels of felons and fugitives, waifs, deodands, estrays, views of frankpledge, tourns, and county court, or execution of process.

"And provided, that the mayor, recorder, aldermen, and town clerk, shall not be put or impanelled in any jury at the assizes; and the sheriff shall not impanel them, nor shall they forfeit any issues for not appearing."

With respect to this last clause, the regulations as they stand at present by law for serving upon juries, being made by acts of parliament subsequent to these charters, without any saving of such-like exemptions; this privilege by charter, if ever it was legally in force, seemeth now to be vanished and gone.

A seal, of which the following is *afac simile,* representing the portrait of King Charles L, appears to have been obtained with this Charter:

These two Charters were surrendered to the crown, amongst other charters in many other parts of the kingdom, in the latter end of the reign of King Charles II.

In praying for a renewal of the Charter, about the year 1683, the Body Corporate and inhabitants of the town took the opportunity of soliciting additional privileges and benefits, and to this end they addressed a letter to Sir George Jeffreys, then lord chief justice, another to Francis, lord Guilford, lord keeper of the great seal, and a third to Sir Christopher Musgrave, one of the knights of the shire for Westmorland, that as each of these distinguished persons had honoured the corporation by having become members thereof, so they hoped for the favour of their intercession. The matters which they desired might be humbly offered to his Majesty's consideration were these:— 1. "That his majesty would be graciously pleased to grant us his royal charter *ih novo,* humbly submitting to whatever alterations his majesty in his great wisdom shall think fit to make therein.

2. "We enjoy the tolls of the market here, which we hold by lease from the crown, under the yearly rent of 15?. We have all along managed the said tolls to the best advantage we could, and yet never made above 17?. *per annum* "History of Westmorland," p. 68. These letters are all printed in Burn's "History of Westmorland," page 69. of them. So that the yearly profit will not answer the charge of renewing our lease (as we ought to do) once in ten years. Wherefore if his majesty would be pleased to grant us the said toll in fee farm, under the said yearly rent of *151.,* it would be a great ease to the corporation, and not prejudicial (we think) to his majesty's interest. 3. "These tolls have been anciently, almost time out of mind, received by us; yet of raw hides and apples no toll was ever taken here, in regard (aa we conceive) that heretofore they were not worth the taking notice of. But now the trade in leather and fruit being grown very considerable, if by our charter, or otherwise, such power were given us as might justify our taking toll thereof, it would be a benefit to the corporation, and no less so to his majesty, nor burden to the people, but what they are liable to in other markets.

4. "There is adjoining to the town a parcel of waste ground, called *Dob Freer,* which is all the common of pasture that is belonging to the town, and is no more than a hill full of rocks and stones. The fee and soil thereof doth belong to the crown, but is of little or no advantage to his majesty, neither is it worth to the town above *51. per annum,* but might be of greater uso and benefit to us, if his majesty were pleased to grant us the

soil and inheritance thereof. 5. "We repair and uphold two large bridges, and the half part of a third bridge, at our own proper costs and charges, which is a burden too heavy for us to bear. But if, in consideration thereof, his majesty would be graciously pleased to grant us a thorough-toll of one penny or halfpenny only, for each pack of goods passing into or out of the town, it would be some ease and benefit to us; and is no more than what Carlisle enjoys in a much greater measure throughout the whole county of Cumberland, for all sorts of goods and chattels passing into or out of the said county.

"These are the things we humbly offer, and if it might not be thought too great presumption in us, we would humbly pray in aid the right honourable the lord keeper of the great seal of England, and the lord chief justice of England; who as they have done us the honour of being made members of our corporation, so we hope will do us the favour of interceding with his majesty on our behalf, whilst we shall desire nothing which may be thought in the least prejudicial to his majesty's interest, or which he cannot willingly and easily grant us, but shall thankfully acquiesce in his majesty's good will and pleasure, whatsoever it shall be."

The common designated "Dob Freer," as aforesaid, was, we believe, the whole unenclosed portion of Kendal Fell, at the use of the public at the time. *Freah* is a Saxon word from which we obtain "free," "freeman," "freedom," &c., and signifies " a liberty," or common right. The prefix *Dob* may be from the Celtic "Dubh," signifying water, and might refer to springs of water on the *freah* lands at the date of designation.,.

A new Charter was obtained, and on its being brought from London was ushered in with much solemnity. On the 26th of December, 1684, the town clerk, Mr. Richard Rowlandson, who brought the Charter, was met at Burton by a large number of horsemen from Kendal. And, at the extremity of the town liberty he was met by the mayor, the aldermen, burgesses, and many gentlemen out of the country; where the mayor, kneeling

and bareheaded, received the Charter; from whence it was conveyed to the Town Hall, many hundreds of the people huzzaing at the first delivery thereof, and all the way through the town, the mayor and aldermen being in their robes, with maces, sword, trumpets, music, bells ringing, and other rejoicings. After the Charter was read, the mayor began the king's health at the cross, commonly called "cold stone;" and then treated the gentlemen handsomely at his own house.

This new Charter of King Charles II. does not grant any of the particulars above petitioned for, but is copied for the most part verbatim from that of King Charles L. with a few alterations and additions, viz.

That the mayor shall be chosen by the mayor, aldermen, and capital burgesses;—that on a vacancy of the mayoralty within the year, one of the two senior aldermen shall serve during the remainder of the year;—that they shall hold pleas for any matter arising within the borough for any sum not exceeding *4:01.* ;—and that the deputy recorder shall be a justice of the peace (and may act as such in the absence of the recorder). With a clause, as in all the new charters of those times, of reservation to the crown of a power to displace and remove the mayor, recorder, aldermen, or any other corporation officers at pleasure.

LIST OF FORMER RECORDERS OF KENDAL: 1575. Robert Briggs, Esq. (first recorder), removed 1576. 1576. Thomas Braithwaite, Esq., of Ambleside, died 1610/

1610. William Garnett, Esq., sworn 21st August.

1636. Sir John Lowther, Baronet (nominated in the Charter). 1648. Thomas Braithwaite, Esq., of Ambleside, sworn 30th March. 1673. Alan Prickett, Esq. , of Natland Hall. 1678. Thomas Lamplugh, Esq. 1685. Thomas Dalston, Esq. , sworn 2nd September. 1691. Roger Moore, Esq. 1695. Alan Chambre, Esq. , resigned. 1699. John Harrison, Esq., sworn Feb. 29, 1699—1700.;

1715. Alan Chambre, Esq. (2nd time), resigned.

1738. Walter Chambre, Esq. (son of the last named).

1752. Richard Crowle, Esq.

1757. Roger Wilson, Esq.

1766. Thomas Fenwick, Esq.

1777. Myles Harrison, Esq., died Feb. 16, 1797, aged 82. 1797. Richard Howard, Esq., of Levens Hall, Westmorland, and Castle Rising, Norfolk. Died in 1818.

1818. Fletcher Raiueock, Esq., of Liverpool, sworn Dec. 21

(last Recorder of Kendal).

The Council appointed under the Corporation Reform Act, in 1835-6, not having deemed it necessary to make application to the king in council to have a Recorder for this borough, in conformity with a discretionary clause in the said Act to that effect, the office of Recorder, as well as the right of holding a separate Court of Quarter Sessions for Kendal, consequently ceased.

The Charter of Charles II. continued in force until the sixth year of King William IV., when the Municipal Corporations Reform Act passed the Legislature, and received the Royal assent on Wednesday, the 9th of September, 1835. The Corporation, by this Act, still retained its style and title of the Mayor, Aldermen, and Burgesses of the Borough of Kirkby-in-Kendal, in the County of Westmorland, and Was directed to consist of one mayor, six aldermen, and eighteen councillors—the mayor to be chosen from the Council annually on the 9th November. According to the new Act, the town was divided into three Wards, viz., the East, West, and North Wards, the burgesses being entitled to elect six councillors for each Ward.

These elections accordingly took place on Saturday, the 26th of December, 1835, and the result was officially declared by the old mayor (Mr. Swainson) on the 28th of the same, the polling places being in the Town Hall and the Whitehall Lecture-room. The eighteen coimcillors thus elected met for the first time on Thursday, the 31st of December, 1835, in the Town Hall, and proceeded to the election of six aldermen, five of whom were taken from their own body; the vacancies thus caused in the Council were not filled up until the 1st of November following, when five additional councillors were

N elected to supply them, besides the six to succeed those who retired at that time as directed by the Act. On Friday, the 1st January, 1836, the aldermen and "councillors met in the Town Hall, and elected for mayor, John Richards (afterwards Yeates), Esq., of Kirkland.

On the 31st of August, 1848, the Health of Towns Act passed the Legislature, and on the 19th of July, 1849, the General Board of Health in London made a provisional order for applying the same to Kendal, and on the 1st of August following, this order (together with several others) was confirmed and made law by Act of Parliament. On Tuesday, the 21st of August, 1849, a meeting of the Council was held, and a committee, consisting of the whole body, appointed to consider the provisions of the Act; and the first meeting of the Council. as a Local Board of Health, took place accordingly in the Moot Hall, on Tuesday, the 4th of September, 1849. The Municipal Corporations Reform Act of William IV. with this addition, continues in force and practice within this borough.

CORPORATION OF KENDAL, IN 1861.

The Mayor—William Henry Wakefield, banker, Prizett.

J. J. Wilson.
Wm. Longmire.
Aldermen.
Samuel Whinerey.
John Wakefield.
W. H. Wakefield.
John Fisher.
(The Aldermen are elected for six years.)

COUNCILLORS.

NORTH WARD. EAST WARD. WEST WARD.

Thomas Taylor. James Bousfield. Miles Thompson.
Wm. Wilson. Charles Wilkinson. Thomas Simpson.
Jas. Edmondson. G. F. Braithwaite. Henry Cragg.
J. Baker Barrow. George Jackson. Samuel Compston.

Thomas Head. Samuel Gawith. Samuel Rhodes.
James Busher. James Thompson. Thomas Busher.
(The Councillors are elected for three years.)
Town Clerk—Thomas Harrison, Singleton Park, Kendal.
Borough Treasurer—John Mann.
The following "cut" represents the Arms of the Corporation, engraved on a silver tankard in the possession of that body. Date, 1629. The emblems are three teasels and three wool hooks.

LAW COUKTS. QUARTER SESSIONS OF THE BOROUGH.

These were formerly held before the Mayor, Recorder, or Deputy Recorder, and two Senior Aldermen, Justices of the Peace, in each of the following weeks, namely:—the first whole week after March 31, the first whole week after June 24, the first whole week after October 11, and the first whole week after December 28. At the passing of the Municipal Corporations Act (5 & 6 Will IV. c. 76) this Court was abolished, no petition for a "separate Court" of Quarter Sessions for the borough being presented.

QUARTER SESSIONS OP THE COUNTY.

Until the year 1830, the Sessions for the Kendal and Lonsdale Wards were held at Kendal, by adjournment from Appleby, four times a year, namely, on the Friday in each of the abovenamed weeks; but in the year before mentioned it was agreed and ordered by the Magistrates, that the Sessions for the whole 6County should be held alternately at Appleby and Kendal, twice at each place during the year, except at the Epiphany, when they are holden at Appleby on the Monday, and adjourned to Kendal on the Friday following. None but Counsel are allowed to appear in cases before this Court. Those who usually attend, at this date, are John MOubrey, John Holker, Robert Scott, Edward Dawson, and John Henry Fawcett.

Wool is my Bread COURT OF RECORD.

Until the year 1835, the Mayor, Deputy Recorder, and two senior Aldermen, or three of them, held on every third

Thursday a Court of Record, and View of Frankpledge, wherein they had cognizance of pleas of matters, arising within the borough, not exceeding 40/., according to the jurisdiction granted by the Charter of Incorporation. For many years, however, it had fallen into disuse; and at the passing of the Municipal Corporations Reform Act, this Court was practically abolished.

COURT LEET.

The Court Leet was held on the Monday after Michaelmasday in each year, under the jurisdiction granted by the Charter to the Corporation of the Borough, for the appointment of constables and other public officers of the town, before the Recorder or Deputy Recorder, as Steward of the Leet. The Municipal Corporations Reform Act finally abolished this Court, but for many years previous to that Act it had fallen into disuse.

THE COURT OF CONSCIENCE.

The Court of Conscience, otherwise Court of Requests, or, as it was commonly called, "Wapentake Court," was established by Act of Parliament, in the 4th George III. (1764). It extended throughout the whole parish of Kendal, for the recovery of debts under 40s., which were not to be sued for in any other Court; but its jurisdiction did not extend to rent, nor to any contract relating to a freehold, nor to any matter cognizable by the Ecclesiastical Courts or the Justices of the Peace. At the passing of the Act 9 & 10 Vict. cap. 95, establishing the County Courts or courts for the recovery of small debts, this Court was abolished.

THE COUNTY COURT.

The Act establishing this Court received the Royal assent on the 28th day of August, 1846, and the first Court at Kendal was held in the Town Hall, on the 6th May, 1847, before T. H. Ingham, Esq., Judge. Present Judge, T. H. Ingham, Esq. of Marton House, Skipton.

THE PETTY SESSIONS.

The Petty Sessions for the Borough are held hy the Borough Magistrates, at the Town Hall, in Kendal, on Monday and Friday in each week, and for the County on every alternate Saturday, before the

Justices of the Peace for the County.

KIRKLAND COURT.

The Honourable Mary Howard, as Lady of the manor of Kirkland (being part of the Lumley Fee), holds a Customary Court twice in each year, viz.—on the last Thursday in October, and on the Thursday in Easter week, and a Court Leet on the last Thursday in October. The Customary Court consists of the Steward or Deputy Steward, and customary tenants of the manor, at which all transfers of customary estates are recorded, and admittances granted, and all forfeitures and other acts prejudicial to the interests of the lord presented. There is also incident to the manor a Court Baron, at which the freehold tenants of the manor alone are suitors and judges, and of which the Steward of the Manor is a constituent part. It has jurisdiction in all personal actions (with one or two exceptions) where the debt or damages is under 40s., also of all pleas of land within the manor. The Court Baron, however, has not been held for many years.

KENDAL FELL TRUST, AND MANAGEMENT OF THE POOR.

What is called the Kendal Fell Trust, so combines, historically, the management of the town, in paving, lighting, cleansing, &c., with the management of the poor, that the two subjects cannot be treated separately. This Trust acquired its powers under an Act of Parliament, passed in the 7th Geo. IIL (17b7), which is entitled, An Act for enclosing waste ground, in the borough and township, "for the benefit of the poor, and for enlightening and cleansing the streets of the said town," &c. It may be sufficient to give the following summary of the Act:—

"whereas there is a common or tract of waste ground, called *Kendal Fell,* lying within the burgh and township, by estimation 158 acres or thereabouts, (which is at present of very little advantage)—it is enacted, that the same shall be inclosed, improved, and divided, in such ways as the trustees, or any seven or more of them shall think most expedient and beneficial (excepting the High and Low Tenterfells, which shall not be ploughed up, but reserved for the use of the shearmen and manufacturers 'whole and entire'; and the Bowling Fell, which shall be left open for the inhabitants to walk upon). The profits, from time to time arising therefrom, to be applied for and towards the relief, maintenance, and employment of the poor of the township of Kendal, and for erecting or purchasing proper buildings and edifices for that purpose, and furnishing such buildings. Provided always, that the lands so inclosed and improved shall be subject to be rated and taxed to all parliamentary, parochial and other taxes, and be liable to the payment of the lords' rents (13s. *id.* to the earl of Lonsdale, for the Richmond and Marquis Fee, and 6s. *8d.* to the Hon. Fulke Greville Howard, for the Lumley Fee, yearly), together with the tithes. And the trustees are hereby empowered to make such rules and regulations for the better governing and employing the poor as shall appear to them necessary or expedient, to all which rules the churchwardens, overseers, and other persons to whom the same may relate, are to conform themselves; provided, that such rules and regulations are not repugnant to the law of this realm.

"And it is also enacted by the authority of the said Act, that the trustees, or seven of them, shall and may, at a public meeting assembled once in the year or oftcner if they think fit, agree or contract with one or more fit person or persons for the cleansing and keeping clean all the streets, alleys, &c. within the burgh; and such person so contracted with, shall, on every Monday and Friday, in every week, well and effectually sweep or cause to be swept and cleansed in a proper manner, all the streets, lanes, alleys, open passages, and other places within the said town or burgh, and remove all the soil there found or swept up; on pain that the contractor, for every neglect or default, shall forfeit the sum of twenty shillings.

"And it is also further enacted, by the authority aforesaid, that the trustees may order such a convenient and sufficient number of glass lamps to be erected in the town, and in such manner as they shall think fit, and also, may contract with any person or persons for enlightening, cleansing, and repairing such lamps, for such time as they shall think fit. And for defraying the expense of cleansing and enlightening the streets, the trustees have power to appoint two assessors, to make and settle a general rate, in the same proportion as the poor rates, not to exceed in the whole, the sum of six pence in the pound in any one year; and to nominate and appoint so many persons as they shall think proper to collect the said rate, every such person so appointed, being subject to a penalty of *5l.* on refusal; provided nevertheless, that no person shall be compelled to serve the said office of collector oftener than once in ten years.

"The trustees for carrying this Act into execution shall consist of the mayor for the time being, and twelve inhabitants of the burgh, who are owners of property of the yearly value of *10l.,* and rated and assessed to that amount; and that an election of three new trustees shall take place yearly, in the room of the three who have served four years, in rotation, from time to time, on the third of May, or within six days after, as appointed, of which time the Mayor is required to give notice in writing, which shall be fixed on the door of the Moothall seven days before such election. The Mayor, if present, shall preside at all meetings of the trustees; and in case of the absence of the Mayor then some other magistrate for the burgh shall preside.

"And it is further enacted, by the authority aforesaid, in ratification of an order of assize and rule of the court of Chancery, that the lands called Park and Castle Lands, and the tenements built thereon, shall be held to be within the township of Kendal, and shall be subject to pay one-tenth part of the rates and assessments to be raised for the support and maintenance of the poor of the said township."

The management of the poor continued under the operation of this Act until the passing of the Poor Law Union Act, in 1834; and the management of the lighting, cleansing, &c., formerly done under its provisions, now devolves upon the Local Board of Health. The Act of George III. contains no provision for selling any of the lands, or for granting building leases; and there having recently sprang up a desire to extend the limits of the town, and increase the number of dwelling-houses, with a conviction, at the same time, that the Kendal Fell Lands presented the most eligible plots of ground for this purpose, an Act was obtained in the 24th and 25th Victoria, 1861, which continues the powers of the Trust under the authority of the former Act, gives a power to grant leases for building not exceeding a term of 99 years, power, also, to sell lands for a sum in gross, to make roads, and improve the approaches to the lands, &c., provided that certain lands are thereby "set apart and appropriated for the use of the inhabitants for recreation ground, and for the purpose of drying clothes;" and provided, also, that "no part of the lands now forming the Serpentine Walks (nearly 18 acres) shall be sold, or leased, or exchanged under the provisions of this Act, but the same shall for ever remain appropriated for purposes of public recreation." The Trustees are to apply the rents, fees, and other ordinary sources of annual income, in aid of the poor rate for the township of Kendal. These provisions will release some of the most convenient sites for dwelling-houses; and if the trade of the town nourishes, and the population increases, as we trust may be the case, advantage will surely be taken of these provisions, and new suburbs will spring up in extended streets, or numerous villas.

TRUSTEES OP KENDAL FELL LANDS, IN 1861:

The Mayor.
W. Wilson, manufacturer.
Thomas Simpson.
John Hudson.
John Whitwell.
Thomas Harrison.
William Wakefield.
Cleric—Francis Webster, solicitor.
Superintendent of Lands—H. Hoggarth, land-surveyor, Finkle-street.

As regards the management of the poor, it is more than probable that, previously to the Act of George III., the business had not been conducted on any systematic plan. According to tradition, the first workhouse was on the Fell-side, and the paupers had their weekly pittances doled out, in the overseer's

O. A. Gelderd.
Samuel Rhodes.
John Ireland.
John Jowitt Wilson.
J. G. J. Ireland.
James Bousfield.

office (also placed in that quarter of the town), on the Sunday afternoons. Subsequently to this, the in-door paupers were lodged at Castle Park, whence they were removed to the present Workhouse at the time of its erection.

The present Workhouse was erected two years after the passing of this Act, viz. in 1769; but no interest sufficient to secure a proper regulation of the affairs of this establishment appears to have been manifested by any of the officers, or other inhabitants of the town, until the year 1800. A general examination of the beds, bedding, and clothes of the paupers in the Workhouse was then fully entered upon, and every necessary regulation made for their additional cleanliness and comfort; distinct rooms were appropriated for the accommodation of the sick, and a proper nurse provided to attend to their necessities; a more distinct separation of the different classes of the inmates was adopted; a knitting school was set on foot, and a school for the instruction of children in the first rudiments of education; the committee were appointed to visit the house in rotation, to inspect the different departments. Indeed, the foundation of an excellent system of management was laid by that committee, in justice to whose exertions the least that we can do is to record their names, for the veneration of all who may be compelled to seek an asylum in this Workhouse.

Committee for the year 1800:—

William Dilworth Crewdson.
Timothy Crosthwaite.
William Berry.
James Sinkinson.

Edward Ireland.
James Savage.
William Fisher.
Anthony Sharp.
Nathan Robinson.
Richard Clementson.

By a progressive improvement, until the year 1803, a regular code of laws for the government of the Workhouse, drawn up by W. D. Crewdson, Esq., was adopted by the trustees of the Kendal Fell Inclosure Act. The introduction of these rules, conveying a summary view of the responsible duties of the churchwardens and overseers, is too valuable to be omitted here:— *"To the Churchwardens and Overseers:* "In presenting the following rules to you, and requiring your attention thereto, we have had in view many of the judicious regulations which are upon your minutes, and the great improvement that has been made under the management of the two last committees.

"We wish to give permanency to plans which appear likely to prove so advantageous to the community, and have therefore Bo arranged these rules, that they may be carried into effect with little comparative trouble. By having frequent reference to them in your collective capacity, you will be enabled to point out the particular duties of those who come before you; and when things are out of order, your visitors will be able knowingly to require the delinquents to perform all that is expected from them.

"We also wish you to be well assured, that without a due attention on your part to the economy and government of the Workhouse, no contrivance of structure, nor any rules, can secure it from being the abode of wickedness, disease, and misery.

"Your most important duties are comprehensive, yet clear: they are, to reform the dissolute, to arouse the idle, to punish the refractory, to be in the place of fathers to the orphan, husbands to the widow, and to smooth the path of declining age, warning such as have lived careless of to morrow to make their peace with God. These are not the labours of a day, a week, or a year;

they are subjects for constant exertion, and cannot be accomplished otherwise than by a steady personal attendance. In these important stations dependence ought never to be wholly placed on servants; for with the very best intention, they are liable to be blinded by passion or swayed by prejudice until they punish the innocent and let the guilty go free. To those who are truly conscientious it will afford satisfaction to have the active superintendence and assistance of the committee; whenever the reverse is observed, things are assuredly going wrong, and you ought to double your diligence.

"The necessity for keeping up your weekly meetings at the house is sufficiently obvious. Without this attendance all the regulations you may endeavour to establish will be of little avail. Every law presupposes an attention to its execution, and here you have the executive power concentred. By these frequent meetings, your servants are all kept in their proper places, their hands are strengthened in the prosecution of their duty, and their weaknesses or failures are pointed out before they become injurious.

"The Act by which we are constituted confers some advantages on you peculiar to itself: when misdemeanors are committed you have only to acquaint two of the trustees, and the aggressors are brought to speedy punishment.

"The duties of the committee are general, those of the visitors are particular, and more interesting.

"They should visit the house at least three times in the week, varying their days, to furnish all who want with proper clothing, to see that cleanliness is universally maintained (for which purpose they should look into every room of the house, and visit every part of the premises), to attend to the complaints of the poor, and when they cannot redress them, inform the committee, to see that all the officers do their duty, and in short, to know that all the rules are strictly fulfilled.

"You who are appointed to this office ought conscientiously to attend to its duties, for upou you lies the weight of the order of the house. If the young are dissolute, profane, and immoral, if the middle-aged are encouraging their juniors in the paths of vice, and pursuing, as far as they are able, the same wayward track, and if the old and infirm are miserably existing in this world without any kind adviser to assist in pointing the way to a better, all these lie at your door. If the honest and industrious poor who are driven hither by calamities which in the perpetual vicissitude of human affairs may fall upon any of our heads, are necessitated to herd with the debauched and the licentious, and their children with the profligate and profane, what are you to expect from such a mixture? That the increase of depression, of misery, of vice, and of sin must be multiplied by the number you receive into the house. On you it rests to have a proper division kept between the dissolute and idle, and the well-behaved and orderly poor; restraining those, so that, at least, their measure of iniquity may not be increased; and encouraging these, so as to return them to society again, with spirits as little broken, by requiring and receiving this parochial aid, as circumstances will permit.

"Thus, under the Supreme Director, you may be the means of effecting unlooked-for reformation: you will increase the happiness and contribute to the prosperity of hundreds of your fellow men, you will retire from your office with the blessings of the unfortunate, and the inestimable reward of a good conscience."

The Poor Law Union (under the Act of 1834) was brought into operation here on the 15th July, 1836, and fifty-eight townships were incorporated into "the Kendal Union." No great change, however, took place in the management of the poor in the workhouses until the j'ear 1849, when the manufacture of "harden" (a coarse kind of sacking), which had been earned on profitably within the Workhouse since the year 1800, was disconthmed. A new classification of the paupers was made about the time afore-mentioned, by order of the Poor Law Board in London, and consists of the following Regulations or Bye Laws, which are strictly observed, viz.:— BYE LAWS.

Kendal, July Ulh, 1849.

"kendal Union.

"kendal Workhouse. "That not more than 335 poor persons, at one and the same time, shall be msintained in the Kendal Workhouse; and also, that no poor person, who shall not belong to one of the following classes, shall be maintained in the said Workhouse, viz. :—

Class 1. Able-bodied men, and youths above the age of 15 years.

„ 2. Boys above the age of 7 years, and under that of 15.

„ 3. Girls above the age of 7 years, and under that of 15.

„ 4. Children under 7 years of age, excepting such infants

as may be too young to leave their mothers, at the

Milnthorpe Workhouse.

"Milnthorpe Workhouse. "That not more than 300 poor persons, at one and the same time, shall be maintained in the Milnthorpe Workhouse; and also, that no poor person, who shall not belong to one of the following classes, shall be maintained in the said Workhouse, viz.:—

Class 1. Men infirm through age or any other cause.

„ 2. Women infirm through age or any other cause.

„ 3. Able-bodied women, with their infant children, except such of the latter class as are of good character and are required for servants in the Kendal Workhouse.

THE WORKHOUSE Is a large, uniform building, two stories high, occupying three sides of a quadrangle, the fourth, which is the entrance, being open to the street. It contains, for the purposes of the paupers, one large general dining-room, kitchens, store-rooms, sick-rooms, &c. on the first floor; and on the second floor thirty-five well-ventilated lodging-rooms, which contain eighty-nine good beds, supplied with sufficient comfortable clothing, and capable of accommodating two hundred persons; together with suitable apartments appropriated to the use of the governor and his family. In the yard behind the Workhouse stands a commodious Schoolroom for Boys, and the contiguous building, which was formerly the harden manufactory, is, the lower part of it, appropriated as a play-ground, and the upper part is used for dormitories. What was formerly the Fever Ward is now occupied partly as a schoolroom for girls, and partly as girls' dormitories, with apartments for the schoolmistress. A productive garden is attached to the Workhouse, cultivated by the labour of the inmates.

The present chief officers of the Poor Law Union are— *Chairman of the Board:* James Cropper, Esq.

Clerk: Mr. John Mann..

Present Number of Paupers in the Workhouse.. 160

Weekly average of In-door Paupers, for the year, 1861.. 141

Total expenditure of the Kendal Workhouse, for)

Maintenance of Paupers, and establishment charges, 2,355/.

for the year, 1861

Nett Cost of Maintenance and Clothing of the Paupers, per head, per week 6 *Governor and Governess of the Workhouse:* JOHN AND Elizabeth Jackson.

PUBLIC SCHOOLS.

We shall now present some account of the Public Schools in the town, giving several particulars of their history, and the number of pupils under daily instruction, respectively.

FREE GRAMMAR SCHOOL.

On the north side of the churchyard stands the Free Grammar School, which is a commodious and suitable building, with a dwelling attached to it for the master. It was founded in the year 1525, by Adam Pennyngton, of Boston, in Lincolnshire, who devised 10?. a year for the term of ninety-eight years, to be paid as "a stipend or waidge" for the finding of *a priest,* being an able schoolmaster, to teach a free school in the town of Kendal, to be paid out of certain lands in the county of Lincoln. King Edward VI., in the second year of his reign (1548), granted 10?. to the school, being the perpetuation of Pen-

nyngton's endowment; and the king's commissioners, under letters patent, appointed that Adam Shephard (then Incumbent of St. Mary's chantry, in the parish church) should enjoy the situation of schoolmaster; which grant was confirmed by a decree of the baron of the Exchequer, in the 4th and 5th Philip and Mary. In 1588, the ground on which the School-house stands, together with "one house standing thereon," was granted by Miles Philipson. It was parcel of the grounds belonging to Abbot Hall.

If this was the first duly constructed School-house (and it most likely was), there had been great delay and difficulty in providing it. Adam Pennyngton's endowment dates in 1525. The public subscription list was open, as is proved by Bernard Gilpin's letter, in 1582, and yet the ground was not conveyed till 1588. Either, therefore, the projected building languished; six years at least, for want of funds, or the school was built before the land on which it stands was legally conveyed—a supposition not very likely. We know, from the report of King Edward VI.'s commissioners, that the Grammar School " had been kept iu Kirkby-Kendal long before" the date of that report, 1548. But between 1548 and 1582, the schoolmaster's wage (not paid without interruptions) was only 10?. per annum. No mention is made of a school-house at this time. It is the time when infant Protestantism was passing through the fires of falling Popery. Adam Shephard, the schoolmaster, was a displaced curate of the parish church. He might teach the scholars in his dwelling-house—-perhaps the "one house" alluded to in Miles Philipson's grant of land—or in the aisle of the church (as is, even now, done in some of the poor districts in Roman Catholic countries). From all. which we conclude, that the present School-house wasnot erected till after the year 1588.

By a decree of the Court of Exchequer, 24th Elizabeth (upon a petition being presented by the inhabitants—the vicar concurring in preferring the suit), the revenue of the school was augmented by two several stipends of 4?. 12s.

10d., which had been allowed to curates serving in the parish, and the joint amount, viz. *9l. 5s. 8d.,* is now paid out of the revenues of the county, by the Receiver-General. The sum of 19?. 8s. is also paid to the trustees out of the Chamber of Kendal, which arises from certain burgage rents, conveyed to trustees in the 12th James L for the benefit of the school, and the interest of several donations, which have from time to time been made to the school, but of which no traces can now be found.

The indenture of the 12th James I. gives the appointment of a master, upon that foundation, to the Corporation. But it does not appear from any documents now preserved, in whom the appointment is vested upon the old foundation. As the Vicar, however, was instrumental in getting the salaries of the two curates transferred to the school, there can be no question but that he was always a party in the appointment of a master, on that foundation. And in practice, he still continues to act, on occasions of vacancy, in conjunction with the Corporation.

The following donations (extracted from the "Boke off Recorde ") appear to have been made at the time of building The Table of Chronological Events gives the date of building 1591-2. the school, and were chiefly for the building (between 1582 and 1588?):— *£ i. d.*

Nicholas Bateman, born in Underbarrow 6 13 4

Thomas Wilson, D.D., dean of Worcester, bor n in

Patton. 10 0 0 *Bernard Gilpin,* professor of divinity, and parson of Houghton, Durham, born in Kentmere.... 10 0 0

Agnes Robinson, widow, for an usher 5 0 0

Edward Swainson, of Kendal, tanner 10 0 0

Margaret Eskrigge, widow of Charles Eskrigge, of

Kendal 10 0 0

Robert Bindloss, Esq., born in Helsington (towards the exhibition) 10 0 0

Katherine Lound, of London, widow, born in

Whynfell 1000

Hugh Hyndlaye, of London, draper 10 0 0

Robert Sadler, of London, merchant, born in

Kendal '. 10 0 0

John Robinson, of London, born in Kirkland... 10 0 0

Robert Jackson, of London, silkman, born in Kendal. 10 0 0

Thomas Wilson, professor of divinity, bor n in

Orayrigg 100O

Richard Fox, of Kendal, shearman 10 0

The wifo of John Wharton 0 13 *4*

The Chamber gave, in consideration of the purchasing of the ground for the school-house 6 0 0

The Aldermen and Burgesses also subscribed, individually, in various sums 12 16 8

And the following sums were given by the inhabitants in the different streets, viz.:—

Sowtergate (now Highgate) 4 8 2

Stricklandgate 731

Marketstead 1110

Stramongate 5 1 10

Making a total of.... £159 18 3

But, in addition to the aforesaid money subscriptions, and others, perhaps, there were also donations "in kind;" for it appears that Ambrose Earl, and the Countess of Warwick, gave towards the building "six fair oke tymber trees," and that, amongst the inhabitants, some gave balks of timber and planks, and others contributed by leading stones! Part of the above subscription fund was laid out in the purchase of burgage rents, which are entered, in the corporation books, from the oldest dates to the present time, under the designation of "Usher lands," and *61.,* their rent, is regularly paid to the schoolmaster. Dr. Airey left 40?. in 1617, the interest to he given to the schoolmaster. George Fleming, in 1627, gave 20s. yearly, towards augmenting the salary of the master and usher. In 1680, Mr. Jackson gave to the school 100?. These form the endowments of the school. The master receives for his stipend as follows:—
From the receiver-general, *171.* 16s. *4d.*

; from the corporation, as master's salary, *91.* 8s.; as usher's, *81.* ; as interest on 40?., *21;* total, 37?. 4s. *4d.* Children's payments in last year (1860), 81?.
EXHIBITIONS: TO OXFORD. 1. *Forty Shillingi* yearly to poor scholars going from the Burgh of Kendal to Queen's College, Oxford; given by Mr. George Fleming, in 1627, to be paid by the Mayor and Aldermen, and charged upon two closes of land lying in the *Lawnd,* near Kendal, now in the possession of the Corporation. 2. *The Interest of* 100?., given in 1631, by Henry Park, Alderman, to the Alderman of Kendal and brethren, on trust, to be paid for four years to a poor scholar going from Kendal School to the University of Oxford (without specifying aoy College). The scholar to be born within the parishes of Kendal, Millom (in Cumberland), and Heversham; the preference being given, first, to those born within the town of Kendal; next, to those born within the parish of Kendal; next, within Millom; and last, within Heversham. 3. *The Interest of* 40?., given by Mr. Christopher Jopson, to be bestowed upon a poor scholar going from Kendal to the same College. 4. *The Interest of* 20?. , given by Mr. John Smith, to be bestowed upon a poor scholar going from this School to Queen's College, Oxford. The Annual amount of the above four Exhibitions is payable by the Corporation of Kendal, who have the appointment of the respective scholars.
5. *Three of 51. a year each,* given by Mr. Henry Wilson, of Underley, and arising ont of the Fareton Tithes, to poor scholars going from this School to Queen's College, Oxford. (These exhibitions are for seven years: the Fellows and Provost of Queen's having the appointment.) 6. Mr. Thomas Sandes, of Kendal, certified to the then Provost of Queen2s College, Oxford, by letter dated September 8, 1679, the following clause in his will:—
"Item, I give to the Rev. Provost of Qu. Coll. in Oxford, and to the Fellows there, and their successors for ever, the sum of 100?. The profit, rent, and increase I do in the first place give unto a poor scholar of my own name, now at

Kendal school, until he, if capable and living, come to be chosen Fellow of the same house, or be M.A, and one year after; and then it is my mind and will, that the profit, benefit, and increase of the said 100?. shall go and remain for ever to sueh poor scholar to be entered upon the Foundation of the said Coll. as shall come and be sent from the said school of Kendal, to be elected by the Mayor, Aldermen, and Vicar of the Parish Church thereof, and the Master of the Free Grammar School there, or the major part of them for the time being, to continue successively to such for and during ye term of 7 years. And if he die before, then the Prov. & Fell, to dispose of the same to whom they please for & during ye remainder of the said term, and then ye electors to chuse a new one. And I desire the Electors (as formerly I have seen) that they chuse not rich men's sons to enter as poor children, but yt really and truly they may be such whose parents are poor and not able to maintain them at ye University. And when there is no such scholar at ye said school, then the Prov. & Fell, to give it to such poor scholar as they please." TO CAMBRIDGE.

The sum of 250?. was left in 1674 by Thomas Brathwaite, Esq., of Ambleside, formerly Recorder of Kendal, "for and towards the maintenance of two Scholars at St. John's College, at Cambridge, going from the Schools at Kendal, in Westmorland, and Hawkshead, in Lancashire; and for want of such two, any other going out of either of the said Counties until they be Masters of Arts or otherwise preferred." By Mr. Brathwaite's will, the said sum of 250J. is ordered to be paid to the Master and Fellows of the said College, &c.

This Thomas Brathwaite we take to have been a nephew of the author of Drunken Barnaby."

The famous Bernard Gilpin, "the Northern Apostle," most willingly, in "godlie zeale," as he himself says, hore his "parte" in raising this School, as appears by the list of donors and by the following letter, written from Houghtonle-Spring, in 1582, which we gladly insert:

"To his verie lovinge freindes in Christe master Alderman of Kendall and his "brethren geve these "In Kendall "Moste due commendacouns premised I am righte glade to heare that your godlie suite for a grammer schoole is like to come to a good ende and so soone as I shal be certified yt it is well established 1 shall moste willinglie perfourme my promisse wth suche spede aa I may convenientlie. But I am so ovcrcliarged with manye paymentes as this bearer can certifie you that I staundo nede to have a quarters warninge to provide for any payment. And although your schoole shoulde not come to a perfectioun aocordinge to your firsts determinatioun yete for ye godlie zeale you all beare to Learninge and for yo great Charges wch I thinke you have alredye sustayned I will beare a parte wth you as shal be thought convenient. And thus trustinge bothe to heare from you and to write to you againe shortlie at better Leysure I praye god preserve you all and prosper your good and godlie work to his honour. At Houghton this xxviiith of June Ao. 1582. Youres alwaye in Christe to his power "Bebnaed Gilpin." This doubtless refers to the 10?. which is included as Bernard's "payment," in the list of donations previously quoted.
n

The following are the regulations of the school:—

That the sohool shall be *free* to all boya resident in the parish of Kendal, for *elastics alone,* excepting a voluntary payment of a cockpenny as aforetime at Shrovetide, and the payment of 5a. as entrance fee.

That in all cases where a boy shall request to be taught (in addition to classics) English, reading, writing, common arithmetic, the routine bookkeeping, geography, English grammar, and history, which branches of learning are considered to comprise a general commercial education, the master shall be authorized to charge 15. per quarter.

That for mathematics (including mensuration) and all the higher branches of learning, the charge may be *11. Be.* per quarter.

That no boy be admitted into the school under eight years of age.

That it be a regulation of this school, that no boy shall be required to learn the Church Catechism contrary to the declared wish of his parent or guardians.

That there shall be a committee of visitors appointed from time to time, by the Corporation annually, to act in conjunction with the_ master, with powers to make such arrangements in the management of the school as they may deem necessary (always provided that suoh arrangements are in accordance with the regulations previously set forth.)

The School, as originally founded, was to be "strictly classical," and was, doubtless, so conducted, in harmony with the prevailing sentiments of the times, so long as the dead languages were the royal road to learning and preferment. And, down to the present time, classics and mathematics have been the chief features and chief aim of instruction here. But "grammar and other good learning" were introduced, even before the end of the 16th century. Miles Phillipson's grant in 1588, and Jopson's in 1590, both contemplate the rudiments of education, and there was an usher, perhaps appointed at that very time, to take charge of the tyros, who had become so numerous in 1641, that the Corporation, in solemn court assembled, felt called upon to issue a decree, that whereas the usher "being much burdened and surcharged, he should not teach or admit any child not capable to read the Psalter, and should disallow such as learnt in the A, B, C, &c."

The Rev. John Sampson was master of the School for nearly forty years, up to March, 1843. He "turned out" many good scholars, some of whom are now living, and enjoying places of distinction in their respective professions. He was eminent both in classics and mathematics: wrote elegant Latin verses, and abstruse problems, for the periodicals of the day.

Among the list of eminent men, formerly educated here, 6were Ephraim Chambers; Doctor Shaw; Edmund Law, Bishop of Carlisle; Dr. Fothergill, &c. &c.

The present master is the Rev. James Frederick Black, B.A., who was appointed on the 9th December, 1845. The number of pupils now on the books is 27.

The ancient ceremony of *barring out,* in which the boys used to take possession of the school early on the morning of *breaking-up* for the holidays, and defy admittance to the master, crying

"Liberty, liberty, under a pin,
Six weeks' holiday, or *nivvtr* come in." (a custom now almost universally discontinued), has here become quite obsolete. Tradition says it ceased in the time of one Towers, who was master in the beginning of2 the last century. Mr. Towers vigorously opposed his rebellious pupils, and in contending with them had one of his eyes put out. This calamity put an end to the practice.

BLUE COAT SCHOOL AND HOSPITAL.

The Blue Coat School, and Hospital connected with it, are so closely related in paternity, means of support, and management, that they cannot be separated in history. The founder, Thomas Sandes, had the reputation of having gained a "considerable estate" in buying and selling wool and cottons, called "Kendal cottons." He possessed influence which extended beyond the sphere of this locality, and must have been a genuine Reformer in days of close "guilds," and chartered monopolies; for we find him engaged in an action at law, in 1685, resisting the monopoly of the East India Company in their exclusive trading to the East Indies. He was, no doubt, largely engaged in the export trade; and the fact of wrestling, in his own strength, with a powerful body like the East India Company, shows the extent of his engagements and great public spirit. Judgment was given against him; but MCulloch says, "the decision was ascribed to corrupt influence." *Vide* M'cllooh's "Commercial Dictionary," 1840, p. 525.

This Thomas Sandes conveyed, by indenture, dated the 6th September, 1670, to the Mayor, Aldennen, and Burgesses of Kendal, the following property, viz.:— 1. The Hospital premises, in Highgate, containing the master's house, school-house and li-

brary, and dwellings for eight widows, with a croft, and gardens behind the same.
2. A dwelling house and out-buildings, and about thirtyeight acres of land in Skelsmergh, called Eidge Bank, now let for 70?. a year. 3. The premises in Strickland Roger, called Baxton Holme, and a close there, called Kettle Croft, consisting of a dwelling house, and about twenty-four acres of land, let for 40?. a year. 4. The moiety of a tenement, called Wasdale Head, which has not been in the possession of the trustees for a great number of years. The whole of this tenement now belongs to the Earl of Lonsdale, by purchase.

"The trustees are to apply the rents and profits of the said premises, after payment of all necessary expenses, towards the maintenance, sustenance, and relief of eight poor widows, to exercise spinning and carding wool, and weaving raw pieces of cloth for Kendal cottons; and also for the use of a schoolmaster there, to read prayers every morning and evening before the said widows; and also there to teach and instruct poor children in good literature until they should be fitted for the Free School, or elsewhere. The appointment of the schoolmaster is vested in the Mayor, Senior Alderman, Vicar, and Schoolmaster, whereof the Mayor to be one. The appointment of the widows, who are to be fifty-two years of age or upwards, and of good reputation, is vested in the trustees, and they are ordered to be appointed in the following manner, viz. three out of Stricklandgate, three out of Stramongate and Highgate, one out of Strickland Ketel and Strickland Roger, and one out of Skelsmergh and Fatton j but in case the like proportion could not be had out of the If there are no widows eligible for the charity in the country townships, single women, of the age of fifty or upwards, and of good reputation, may be elected.
places aforesaid, then the said number to be chosen out of all the places above mentioned, indifferently, having respect to the proportion as near as might be. The Overseers of the places aforesaid, upon notice given them from the

trustees, of any vacancy, are to nominate double the number to be chosen by the said trustees, who, out of the number so nominated, are to elect so many as to make up the number of eight, and, *in default of such nomination within a month of the death of the widow,* then the vacancy to be filled up by the Mayor, Senior Alderman, Vicar, and Schoolmaster, or the major part of them, whereof the Mayor is to be one."
The said Indenture declared, that the widows should have each assigned to them convenient rooms and places in the Hospital premises for their carding, spinning, &c., and for their habitation, and also each a small plot of garden-ground behind the same; and should each receive one shilling every Saturday morning and eightpence on the Eves of Ascensionday, and Whit-Sunday, so as to make up their several allowances to *four marks* apiece per annum out of the revenues of the above premises; and should each have brought for them in the week before Christmas a good horse-load of wood by the tenants of the premises in Skelsmergh and Strickland Roger. The said Indenture also recites, that "Whereas the donor at the entrance of the Widows into the said house hath bestowed upon every one of them a new gown, which they are to wear upon Sabbath and Holy days by the space of three years; therefore, in the meantime, whilst the same is in wearing, every widow and their successors shall have kept back by the said schoolmaster and his successors every quarter of a year, Sixpence, for and towards the buying of them new gowns again, then what as wants shall be made up by the said schoolmaster and render forth of the overplus of the revenues and rents, &c., and at the time of the death, &c. of any widow, such of their new gowns shall go to their successor. " Nothing is now stopped from the widows towards the finding of gowns. The widows now receive 1 The carding and spinning of wool, by manual labour, having been superseded by machinery, the widows are not now required to follow any kind of profitable employment.
Is. *6d.* each per week, and besides

having annually paid to them eightpence each on the Eves of Ascensionday and Whit-Sunday, they receive Is. *6d.* each at Christmas in lieu of firewood. They also receive, on the 5th days of February, May, August, and November, 29s. each; and on the 21st March, June, September, and December, 14s. *6d.* each, out of the proceeds of subsequent donations and bequests to the Hospital.

The said Indenture further declares, that the Schoolmaster should have a School-house within the Hospital premises, and the use of a chamber for his habitation, and should have the custody and care of the library, and be careful to see all the orders relating to himself and the widows properly observed and kept, and that he and his successors should have all the residue of the said premises after the payment of all the allowances above mentioned.

The Library consists chiefly of the ancient Fathers of the Church and Ecclesiastical Historians, many of them scarce and valuable works. So desirous was the Founder to preserve these books from decay, that he not only ordered that they should be kept in "the great room," but also that "two good horse-loads of wood" should be brought, and the Schoolmaster should bestow Is. a quarter in peats, for their better keeping and preservation. On examining this library, in 1827, some volumes appeared to be wanting, of which no traces could be discovered. The books were also found to have been moved from time to time into rooms not well aired The Mayor and Corporation therefore directed that the library should be restored to "the great room," agreeably to the Will of the Founder; and that a new Catalogue should be made out by the Master, and strict attention be paid to the preservation of the books. Till some time back they used to be fastened to the shelves with chains, just long enough to allow the reader to reach them down to the table.

Thus far may be considered the original Foundation of the Hospital and School. The following gifts, beside several other donations, have since been added, amongst which one may be particularized, viz., the donation of Mr. Edward Burrell, of Liverpool. banker, who received his education at this School.

1. *Dawioria Gift,* consisting of a close of land, called Hound Dale, in Natland, containing la. 3r. 6p. and two front dwelling houses and back premises in Highgate, which were devised by will, dated 8th March, 1722, to the Mayor, two Senior Aldermen, and Vicar of Kendal, and their successors, upon trust, to dispose of the rents towards the advancement of the Charity, and maintenance of the blue-coat boys; and in case that Charity should be discontinued, among twelve housekeepers. The premises in Highgate have been rebuilt, and are now used as Miss Dowker's Hospital, and a rent is regularly paid by that institution to the treasurer of Sandes's HospitaL 2. *Woodburn'a Gift.—* Christopher Woodburn, by will, in 1723, charged certain premises in Highgate, and All-Hallow's Lane—the Fleece Inn, and property adjoining, in Highgate, and a house in All-Hallow's Lane—with the payment of 40s. apiece yearly, towards putting out four poor boys to be apprentices, to be paid to their masters, and 10s. apiece for finding them shirts and cravats at the commencement of their service; to be sons of freemen, and two of them to be educated at the Charity School, and to be elected by the contributors and managers of the School, with the approbation of his trustees; and further, with the payment of 20. annually to the master of the School. These premises were conveyed, at the instance of the Trustees of the School, to the Mayor, Aldermen, and Burgesses of Kendal, in 1812. The sum of 10?. is annually received out of the said premises, but the 20s. for the master has not been received for thirty or forty years. 3. *Archer'i Gift—* John Archer, M.D., of Oxenholme, in 1725, devised to the Mayor, two Senior Aldermen, Vicar, and Schoolmaster of Kendal, and their successors, a moiety of the rents of certain premises called Aikrigg, in Kendal Park, to be applied to the maintenance of this School. 4. *Crosby a Gift.—The* Rev. William Cros-

by, in 1732, gave a rent-charge of 3?. annually, on Sydenham Tenement, in Underbarrow, to the Mayor, Recorder, two Senior Aldermen, and Schoolmaster, in trust, for the use of the Bluecoat Charity; and if that Charity should be discontinued, to the poor householders in Kendal. This is regularly paid to the Master, and accounted for by him to the treasurer. 5. *John Gibsons Gift.—An* estate in Brigsteer, called Barrow House, now let for 16?. a year, was conveyed by John Gibson, by indenture, dated 21st November, 1752, to the Mayor, Senior Aldermen, Vicar, and Schoolmaster, in trust for the use of the charity boys then and thereafter to be educated in this School. 6. *Herbert's Gift.—A* close of land called Martin Croft, in Gilling Grove, was devised by William Herbert, in 1765, to the Mayor, Vicar, and Schoolmaster, for the use and benefit of the charity boys in Kendal. 7. *Thomas Gibsons Gift.—*Thomas Gibson, in 1777, charged certain premises, called Ralphford Hall (now the Mason's Arms), in Stramongate, with the payment of *11. Is.* annually to Sandes's Hospital

In addition to the above, the following donations and bequests have been made, at various times, which are advantageously invested; and the funds of the institution are further augmented by annual subscriptions.

DONATIONS AND BEQUESTS: £ «. d. 1723 Mr. William Collingwood, for Boys' School.. 50 0 0

Rev. Mr. Borwicb do 5 0 0
   Rev. Mr. Lancaster do 2 10 0
   Mr. Richard Leece do 5 0 0
   Mrs. Gibson do 40 0 0
   Mr. Robert Simpson do..... 600
   Mr. Crackenthorp do 16 0 0 1724 Thomas Holme do 20 0 0 1731 Mr. Commissary Stratford do 20 0 0 1734 Mrs. Alice Barrow do 10 0 0 1758 Mr. Jacob Holme do..... 500 1781 Mr. Barrington Gibson do 56 0 0 1782 A Person unknown do..... 20 0 0
——The Company of Shearmen Dyers, do.... 800 1783 Mr. Alderman Strickland do..... 20 0 0
1790 Mrs. Isabella Elleray, 200?. for Widows, and 1

100/. for Boys' School) 1794 Mr. Thomas EUeray, for Boys'School.... 50 0 0 1795 Mrs. Elizabeth Cock do 100 0 0 1799 Mr. Thomas Whitwell do 20 0 0 1803 Joseph Maude, Esq. do 25 0 0 £ i. d. 1808 Mr. Garnett Braithwaite, for Boys' School.. 21 0 0 1811 Mrs. Knott (annually) do 110

John Wakefield, Esq. do 50 0 0 1812 Jane Emerson, for Widows 26 12 0 1814 John Postlethwaite, Esq., for Boys 250 0 0

Mr. William Sleddall do 150 0 0 1815 Miss Lambert do 10 0 0 1816 Mr. Joseph Swain son, for Widows 21 0 0

Mrs. Cock do 21 0 0 1824 James Bateman, Esq., for Boys 50 0 0 1825 Mrs. Jackson Harrison do 890 1 8 1827 Mrs. Dorothy Matson do. 100 0 0 1838 Miss Mary Bobinson do 100 0 0

Edward Burrell, Esq. do 525 0 0 1846 Miss Fisher, Hill Top 20 0 0 1848 Miss Sarah Scott 25 0 0

The Annual Subscriptions amount to 3114 6

Previous to 1838, the number of scholars was limited to forty, but at that period the trustees were enabled, from the bequest of Mr. Edward Burrell, to admit five additional scholars. The system of clothing the boys in blue was only introduced about the year 1714, consequently it seems not to form a part of the Founder's Will. When the quaint style of clothing was introduced, the parents sending children were required to sign a memorandum of obedience to the bye-laws, whereby they "respectfully promised to submit the disposal of their sons, as well *in their apparell,* teaching, learning, apprenticeships, as in all other matters," &c. By which it is to be inferred, that the "blew knee breeches" required arbitrary power to bring them into use, as they require extreme tenacity to old "habits" for their retention.

The instruction at this School does not appear to have been restricted in ancient times to boys; for by a memorandum preserved in the records it is stated that "nine poor girls were taught there in 1714, by Isabel Fisher." In 1789, it was determined to admit thirty girls, to be clothed in blue, out of the proceeds of bequests and donations to the institution subsequent to the Foundation; and the number has, since 1838, been increased to forty. These girls are now selected 225*l.* more, left by Mrs. Harrison, will be due to this charity at the death of Mary Bainbridge.

from the most deserving amongst the girls in the National School, and are instructed in reading, writing, arithmetic, and needlework. They are taught in the Girls' National Schoolroom, and attend the parish church with the other children in that Institution.

The Hospital premises were originally built in the form of a square. They were, however, partially rebuilt and altered in 1852; when the widows' dwellings were reconstructed, and the master's house renovated. The widows' houses now extend in a straight line from east to west, with a forecourt, or garden, in front of each. There is also a good garden on the west side, occupied by the master.

The present master is Mr. James Whitaker. He was appointed on the death of Mr. William Lewthwaite, in the year 1837.

The number of pupils now on the books is 45.

Boys' National School.

The National School for Boys is a commodious, handsome, and stately building, situated in a field called Chapel Close, adjoining All-Hallows' Lane, and, standing on an eminence above most of the other buildings in the town, presents on all sides a striking object of interest. It was founded by subscription in 1817. A liberal subscription was then entered into, by which the committee were enabled to purchase the land on which the building is erected It was endowed with the sum of 2.000*l.* by Matthew Pyper, Esq. of Whitehaven, whose remains are buried in the school. The deed of endowment declares, that the Mayor, Aldermen, and Burgesses of Kendal, shall be trustees of the School. And that the said Matthew Pyper and his heirs, for ever, and Daniel Wilson, Thomas Holme Maude, and John Dowbiggin, Esqrs., and their heirs for ever, shall be perpetual visitors of the said

School. And further, that the Mayor and Aldermen, the Recorder and Deputy Recorder for the time being, the Vicar of Kendal, and the Clergy of the Established Church, officiating within the borough, the Churchwardens of Kendal for the time being, the Superintendent, Treasurer, and Secretary of and for the said School, with twelve subscribers or benefactors (to be elected at the annual meeting), shall be also visitors; and that they, and the other visitors shall form a general committee for the management of the said School, in conformity with the rules and regulations of "the National Society for promoting the education of the poor, in the principles of the Established Church throughout England and Wales."

The endowed sum of 2,000*l.* was invested originally by the trustees in the 5 per cent. Annuities. When the reduction of that stock to 4 per cent, took place, the money was invested in the 3 per Cent. Consols, yielding, at the present time, 64*l.* 15s. 2c*l.* per annum.

The only permanent fund of the School, besides this, is the rent of part of the School premises, let off as garden ground, for about 3*l.* a year, and the interest of 100*l.* left by Miss Robinson, formerly of Highgate.

But there is annually brought to the support of the school, a capitation grant from Government, depending, of course, on the number of children at the time, which, however, averages about 15*l.* per annum; also a subscription throughout the town. These together bring about 50*l* per annum. Lastly, there is the children's pence, 31*l.* 2s. 9c*l.*, which complete the ways and means. The present master is Mr. J. J. Hewitt, appointed in 1855, whose salary is 100*l.* per annum. Number of pupils on the books, 245.

Girls' National School.

The National School for Girls was built with funds raised by voluntary subscriptions, in 1823, and continues to be supported in like manner from year to year.

A bequest was made, of 500*l.*, by Miss Lambert, of Bowerbank, Cartmel, in 1857, for augmenting the salary of

the schoolmistress; but Miss Lambert's Will is at present the subject of dispute in the Court of Chancery, and the sum in question has therefore not yet been appropriated.

The School-house is very spacious and commodious, and is annexed to and forms part of the same building as the National School for Boys: but the approaches to the two schools are quite separate and distinct. A convenient committee-room was added to each of the schools, and a plantation made in front of the buildings.

The management of the School is under a committee of sixteen ladies, who are elected as visitors at the annual meetings; and to whose exertions in so good a cause, the discipline, good order, and decent appearance of the children, bear ample testimony. By their constant exertions the fund for clothing, raised by annual subscriptions, has been so augmented as to enable them annually to distribute to each of the children some useful article of clothing; and at the same time to excite a laudable emulation in the school.

The children are instructed in reading, writing, and the common rules of arithmetic; also in knitting and sewing.

Besides the girls, properly belonging to this school, there are forty " Blue Coat Girls" educated here, as is mentioned in the account of Sandes's Blue Coat Schools, p. 202.

The schoolmistress is Miss Heaton, appointed in 1856; salary, *45l.* per annum. The total number of scholars is 120.

Girls' And Infants' School.

The School-house for Girls and Infants stands near Stock Bridge, at the foot of Castle Street. It is a remarkably neat and suitable building, of hewn limestone, with a small playground for the children. This school was established by voluntary subscriptions from among the Society of Friends, in the early part of the year 1830, and is indebted for its continued support to annual contributions, added to a small weekly payment with each of the children. It is now placed, like the National Schools, under Government inspection, and the number of children, stated below, tells the story of its successful management. Schoolmistress, Miss Prettie; appointed in 1855. Number of scholars on the books, 172.

BRITISH SCHOOL.

This School, situated near St. George's Church, was built in 1835, and enlarged in 1857. The principal school-room, 60 ft. x 30 ft., belongs to the original structure. The classroom and committee-room were added in 1857. The cost of the building originally was 610?., of which sum 125?. was obtained from the Parliamentary grant of moneys applied to building schools on the principles of the British and Foreign School Society. It is managed (subject to Government inspection) by a committee of gentlemen, who also appoint the trustees. The present trustees are, Messrs. W. D. Crewdson, John Jowitt Wilson, and Charles Lloyd Braithwaite.

The School is open to children of all religious denominations, and is conducted on the Lancasterian system. There is no endowment fund, and the expenditure, therefore, has to be met entirely by voluntary subscriptions, and the small payments of the children, 2d. and 3d. per week. The following is the income of last year (1860):—

Master: Mr. Thomas Hill, who was appointed in 1835, and through whose able management the School-has so signally prospered Number of scholars, 312.

This School-house, in the old Vicarage grounds, on a site which was given by the Vicar with consent of the patron, has been built within the present year, 1861. It cost upwards of 1,000?., raised entirely by voluntary subscriptions. It is a neat edifice, in the Tudor style, with open roof, and stained rafters, the windows having stone mullions. The fine porch entrance, or vestibule, gives effect to the building. It consists of a double school-room, capable of being used together or separately, one portion of which is 52ft. x 18ft., the other 39 ft. x 18 ft.; height of the roof, 25 ft. Besides these, are two class-rooms, for evening classes or other purposes. The building was designed by Mr. Miles Thompson, architect, and constructed by Messrs. John Fisher and Samuel Compstone.

KIRKLAND GIRLS' NATIONAL SCHOOL.

The children of this establishment were taught in a schoolroom in Jennings' Yard, Highgate, from 1845 until the present year. In 1858, the School was placed under Government inspection, and reoeived grants for the augmentation of the salary of the mistress, and for two pupil-teachers. The amount of children's pence in last year, 1860, was 31*l.* 8s. *tyd.* Schoolmistress: Miss Seed; appointed in 1858. Number of scholars on the books, 148.

ST. THOMAS'S SCHOOL.

This School, connected with St. Thomas's Church, was established in 1841. It comprehends instruction for both sexes. The payments with children are very moderate—only *ld.* and *2d.* per week; nevertheless they amounted, in the last year, to 3U. 3s. 9d. Present number of scholars, 160. Schoolmistress: Miss Smallwood; appointed in 1854.

ST. GEORGE'S SCHOOL.

This School is connected with St. George's Church. It was established in 1852, and the present school-house was built in that year. The number of scholars now on the books is 149. Amount of children's pence, in the last year, 34?. 14s. *l0d.* Schoolmistress: Miss Lord; appointed in 1861.

FELL SIDE DAY AND SUNDAY SCHOOLS.

The handsome building devoted to these Schools is well placed with regard to the needy population for which it is designed. It was erected at three different times: the first part in 1852, the second in 1853, and the last in 1859, at a cost in the aggregate of 1,170?., altogether raised by voluntary subscriptions. This is the most successful scholastic institution in the town. The Sunday School began in 1833, in one small room of a cottage on the Tell Side, on something like the "City Mission" principle, excepting that it was worked by gratuitous teachers, and instead of being supported by an established society, it was succoured by only two individuals, SLEDDALL'S GREEN COAT SUNDAY SCHOOL. 207 the late William Wilson, Esq., of Kent Terrace, and the late W. D. Crewdson, Esq., of Helme Lodge, to whose memory it now stands, better than a marble monument.

The Day School, commenced in 1841, is divided into two, a Juvenile School, under Miss Jennings; and an Infant School, under Miss Taylor. Number of day scholars, 260. Children's pence in the last year, *521.*

The Sunday School is composed of adults as well as children, and the total under instruction on the Sundays is 790!

SLEDDALL'S GREEN COAT SUNDAY SCHOOL.

William Sleddall, by will, dated 11th August, 1801, gave *5251,* upon trust, that two of the Senior Aldermen and two of the Senior Burgesses of Kendal for the time being, should purchase Four per Cent. Bank Annuities, or lend the same upon real or personal security, and apply the interest or dividends in the establishing and for ever supporting a Sunday School in Kirkby-Kendal, for the instruction of thirty-five boys and twelve girls, the children of the poor people of Kirkby-Kendal, to be nominated by the trustees; and for finding and providing a new green coat for each of the boys every year, and new hats once in two years; and for each of the girls a green gown every year, and green bonnets once in two years. And also, that the trustees should yearly treat themselves out of the dividends, when they settled their accounts, with *a crown bowl of punch;* and if any surplus should remain in each year, the same to be laid out in purchasing green baize, to be made into waistcoats or small clothes for the most necessitous of the poor boys, at the discretion of the trustees. It is ordered by the will that no dissenter from the Church of England shall be one of the trustees.

Mr. Sleddall died in 1813, and this legacy was invested in the purchase of *6251. 18. 7d.* Stock in the Four per Cents, then at 83f, and the dividends arising therefrom amounted at that time to *251 0s. 8d.* yearly; but the interest on the Stock having been reduced, the dividend is only 19?. 6. *4d.* at this time, which is insufficient to meet the expenditure; but the residue is supplied from a contribution out of the "Farleton Tithes," in the management of the Corporation.

The boys are supplied with green coats and green caps, and the girls with green gowns, straw bonnets, and white tippets against Easter Day in each year. But as to the " crown bowl of punch," we are assured that the managing trustees consider that custom "more honoured in the breach than the observance," and they omit the beverage.

The children are instructed in the Schools connected with the parish church.

We will conclude this chapter by presenting summaries of the Public Day Schools, Private Day Schools, and Public Sunday Schools, which show, by their aggregate of scholars, the proportion of the population under daily instruction.

These returns have been most carefully made for this purpose, by Mr. Thomas Hill, master of the British School, and may be relied upon for their accuracy.

PRIVATE SCHOOLS.

There are seventeen Private Schools in the town, and the number of pupils in these establishments is 560.

GENERAL SUMMARY.

No. in Public Day Schools ., Private,,
    Total Day Scholars...
    Or, 1 in 528 of the population.
    Total in Sunday Schools
    Or, 1 in 4 31 of the population.,

It thus appears that the education of children in the town is progressing at the rate of more than one in six of the population in Day Schools, and more than one in five of the population in Sunday Schools. When these results are compared with the general returns given by the Government Commissioners of Education, the comparison shows that tuition is proceeding in Kendal in a ratio higher than that of England and Wales. For England and Wales the number under daily instruction is one in 7 7 of the entire population; therefore, Kendal is upwards of 30 per cent, above the average of England and Wales, in this respect.

CHAPTER VI. CHARITIES.

We now come, with pleasurable emotions, to give a sketch of the numerous endowed charities which are in operation in this town. It has been said, that there is no exercise of the mind of man so congenial, so interesting, or affording such real and unmixed gratification as systematic and intelligent benevolence. With what feelings of just pride, then, must. all persons connected with Kendal be impressed, on reviewing these charities, where so much good is laid up in store for future generations. Happy indeed will it be if these examples should open out new fountains of future charity, and cause the stream of benevolence to flow on, widening and strengthening in its course, from one generation to another. Such bequests and benefactions constitute fertile means of human good, and are among the best uses of the bounties of Providence.

For the information respecting these charities, we are indebted to the Report of the Commissioners of Inquiry into the Abuse of Charities, instituted by Act of Parliament, in 1817; and to the Report of a Committee of the Corporation, appointed to inquire into this subject, in 1847.

Gilpin's Rents.—1561.

It is stated, in the History of Westmorland (page 75), that "William Gilpin, steward to Alan Bellingham, of Levens, Esq., purchased of the said Alan Bellingham, certain Rents The following were the Corporation Committee, yiz.:—John Whitwell, John Hudson, Edward Busher, Edward William Scott, John Fisher, and Cornelius Nicholson.

belonging to the Chapel of St. Anne, of 3?. 7s. 8d. a year, at thirty years' purchase; and by his will, dated 1561, bequeathed the same to two Gilpins, his relations, and to others the nearest of his kindred, successively to distribute the same to the poor in Kendal, of his name and family for ever."

No documentary evidence relating to this charity can now be obtained, but the rents above mentioned were regularly collected and distributed till the year 1804. Charles Rooking, some time since deceased, collected them for forty or fifty years, and his father and grandfather collected them before him. Rooking was first employed to collect these Rents for Samuel Newby, who was connected with the Gilpin family by marriage.

The Rents arise out of the following premises:— 1. Out of the White Hart Inn or Coffee House 2. Out of a House and two Shops in Butcher's)

Row adjoining the White Hart, the property of Mrs. Bradley, occupied by Bailie and Hargreaves, ironmongers, and John

Taylor, Tea Dealer

3. Out of a Shop and Premises, the first House in

Stricklandgate, the property of Mr. Thomas Robinson, Grocer

No Rents had been paid from 1804 to the time when the Charitable Trustees undertook the collection and distribution of them; but they are now regularly received and disposed of. It has not been ascertained whether or not the arrears were recovered.

IANSON'S CHARITY.—1015.

This Charity is vested in twenty-seven Feoffees, who were to be appointed by the Alderman, Vicar, and Schoolmaster; and when sixteen of the said Feoffees are dead, the property is conveyed over by a new deed to such persons, inhabitants There not being "a Mayor" at the time.—(Vide History of the Corporation, page 171).

of Kendal, as the corporate officer named in lieu of the Alderman, Vicar, and Schoolmaster appoint. The Property consists of several Burgage Rents, amounting to *21. 16s. 10d.* annually, viz. —

». a.

T. Gough, Esq. Stricklandgate Property 8 0

Mr. James Thompson 134

Odd-Fellows' Hall 8 0

Bev. M. J. Carter 8 0

E. Wilson, Esq 10

Misses Greenhow (Property in Highgate) 6 0

Isaac Braitbwaite, Esq 3 6

New Inn Property, viz.—Henry Douglas.. 3j. *Id. I*

William Bousfield. 1 10 9 0

Joseph Clarke..37)

£2 16 10 and three closes of land situate in Park and Castle Lands, containing 8a. 3r. 39p., customary measure, let for 44?. 7s. annually. The sum of 3s. *4d.* is ordered to be paid annually to the Chamber of Kendal, and 3s. 4c?. to the Churchwardens for the repair of the church. 10s. to be paid to the Clerk for collecting the Rents. 20s. each to be given to six aged and impotent men, natives of Kendal, of above the age of fifty years, of honest and good behaviour, and "whose endeavours and cares have been painful and commendable;" and in want of duly-qualified natives, the Trustees may elect one or more, if wanted, who have lived twenty years in the said burgh, each of such men to have yearly paid to him 20s. on the 21st of December, at the porch of the parish church. The residue to be bestowed in cloth, linen and woollen, for shirts and coats, on the day and place aforesaid, to such other poor people of the town, and in such manner as the said collector, with the consent of the said Trustees, should think fit. The Trustees have power to let the premises for terms not exceeding ten years. The deeds and papers belonging to this Charity are deposited at the Town Clerk's Office.

ALICE DUCKETT'S CHARITY.—1616.

Alice Duckett, by will, dated 27th November, 1616, gave out of her tenement called Netherhouse, in Skelsmergh, to the poor of Kendal, Strickland, and Skelsmergh, 20s. to each township, to be paid for evermore; and after the death of William Newby, she ordered Richard Duckett and Peter Mowson to sell the said tenement and dispose of it to the use of the poor.

In 1052, by a decree of Commissioners of Charitable Uses, it was ordered that the occupiers of these lands should pay *9l.* yearly to the Overseers of Kendal, Strickland, and Skelsmergh, to the use of the poor there.

In 1653 an information was filed in chancery, for administering this Charity, when certain deeds were exhibited, shewing that the tenements had been sold in 1729 to one William Lickbarrow, by Duckett and Mowson, according to the testatrix's will, for *60l.*; that *20l.* of the purchase money had *men* paid to the Overseers of Strickland Roger for the use of the poor, and a rent-charge of 24s. yearly was reserved, payable to the Overseers of Skelsmergh until the like sum of *20l.* should be paid to them; but no information is given as to the application of the other 20?., nor any mention made of any claim of the Overseers of Kendal in respect of it. It is, however, stated in the answer, that, in 1701, the same tenement was conveyed by persons claiming through the Lickbarrows, and had since been divided into two tenements, and variously dealt with, subject to the payment of *hi.* 10s. yearly to the Chamberlains of Kendal.

This sum has been received yearly by the Corporation since 1664, and is entered in the books as a *rent* due out of Lickbarrow tenement. There is nothing to shew on what account it is paid. It is open to presumption, that a part of it might be in respect of what was payable to the poor of Kendal (though that was payable to the Overseers, not to the Corporation); but it appears that the Corporation incurred costs by being made parties to the proceedings in chancery; and it does not appear that the *5l.* 10s. was ever distributed in charity. This sum is now received in moieties from the occupiers of the two tenements called Oak Bank and Redmayne tenement.

Thwaite's Charity.—1616.

Ann Thwaites bequeathed, 24th April, 1616, *10l.* to be lent to five poor tradesmen in Kendal, by the Alderman and Constables after the rate of 1s. *6d.* in the pound, amounting to 15s. yearly; which she directed should be bestowed in shirts for old people and young children of Kendal not being able to work. This money was laid out in burgage rents, and is therefore available, though it has not been lent for many years.

Fleming's Charity.—1627.

George Fleming, in 1627, devised two closes lying in the Lawnd, near Kendal, containing nine acres, of the yearly feefarm rent of 38s. *6d.* to his wife for life, the remainder to his nephew, Miles Fleming, and his male heirs, and, in default of such issue, to the Alderman of the burgh of Kendal, and his successors for ever, upon trust, out of the rents thereof, to pay to poor scholars going forth from Kendal to Queen's College, in Oxford, 40s. yearly. He also gave 20s. yearly towards augmenting the salary of the master and usher of the free school of Kendal, at the discretion of the Alderman and his brethren for the time being; 40s. to poor people within Kendal, to be distributed by the Churchwardens and Constables, or some of them, with the assistance of the said Alderman and his brethren; and 10s. yearly for letting the lands and collecting the rents, to such person as the Alderman and his brethren should appoint for that purpose. The residue of the said rents to be paid yearly to the Chamber of the said burgh, for the good of the burgh. He further bequeathed *10l.* towards the raising of a stock for a Lecturer in Kendal Church, to be disposed of and preserved by the Alderman and brethren for that purpose.

The 40s. are paid to the Churchwardens for distribution every Good Friday. —(See *Good Friday 8 Dole,* p. 229.)

FARLETON TITHES.

Extract from the will of Henry Wilson, of Underlay, dated 29tk August, 1639.

"I give and bequeath unto the Provost or Master, and to the Fellows of Queen's College, Oxford, and to their successors for ever, for the time being, from time to time for ever, the yearly sum of 35?., to be paid unto them by my heirs-general for ever, out of the tithes of corn, grain, or sheaves, yearly arising and renewing within Farleton, Overthwaite, Overforth, and Aikbank, in the County of Westmorland, and all other tithes within the parish of Beethom, which lately I purchased of Anthony Duckett, Esq., and James Duckett, his son, to be by them, the said Provost and Fellows, employed and disposed as follows: viz: first, to four poor scholars, which shall be sent thither from time to time successively for ever out and from the Free Grammar School of Kirkby Lonsdale aforesaid, and born in that parish; and also to three poor scholars which shall be sent from the Free Grammar School of Kendal aforesaid: and they pay to every one of the seven poor scholars so to be sent from the said two Free Grammar Schools, out of the said 35?., the sum of 5?. apiece yearly for ever, for and towards the better help, relief, and maintenance of their studies at Queen's College aforesaid, equally to be divided and shared forth of the said 35?. so given in trust to the said Provost and Fellows of the said College; all the said scholars so to be sent from the said schools to be of perfect gifts and of ingenious disposition of mind, without any by-respect to be had of kindred or friendship, but upon desert, and according to the ancient statutes of the said College; and the payment of the said yearly sum of 5?. apiece to continue to be paid to every of them during the term of seven years next after every of their admittance into the said College, and no longer. And then, or upon any of their departure, or going away from thence, others to be chosen and sent thither in their places from the said schools, as is aforesaid, from time to time for ever, and to have and enjoy the several stipends of *5l.* apiece forth out of the said tithes for ever, according to my true meaning. And for default of any such scholars at either of the said schools, then the same to be supplied by the other school; and for default of scholars at either of the said schools, then the same to remain to other scholars born in other parts of Westmorland and Cumberland, being at the said College, or to be sent thither. And for default of payment of the said 35?. to the said Provost aud Fellows by my heirs-general, their heirs and assigns, at two feasts in the year, viz. Easter and Michaelmas, or within forty days next after in any year after my death, then I do hereby give and bequeath all the said tithes of corn, grain, and sheaves unto the said Provost and Fellows, and their successors, to the uses, intents, and purposes hereinbefore limited, intended, and declared; intreating the Mayor and Aldermen of Kendal aforesaid, together with the Feoffees of Kirkby Lonsdale School, for the time

being, to receive and take all the issues and profits of the said tithes; and out thereof pay as well the said 35?. to the use aforesaid; as also the yearly rent of 40s. to the said Anthony Duckett, Esq. and his heirs, they retaining the overplus thereof, share and share alike, for their care and pains therein, if my heirs-general shall not well and truly pay the said 35?. and 40s."

The corn-rent in lieu of these tithes is regularly received by the trustees appointed yearly by the Council, and the feoffees of Kirkby Lonsdale School. 35?. are paid over to the College, and 40s. to the Vicar of Beetham annually, and the residue is divided in equal moieties between the trustees and the feoffees. The proportion received by the Corporation Trustees amounts annually to about 20?. This surplus is considered as in strictness the property of the trustees, by whom, however, it is always placed at the disposal of the Council.

BARROW, FISHER, WILSON, FOARD, AND HAY'S GIFTS FOR LECTURE. 1641.

Hugh Barrow, by will, devised out of his lands in Skelsmergh 100?. for procuring a Lecturer in Kendal Church, in the afternoon, on every or every other Sunday; and the lands called Must Hill were charged with the said payment. This was paid to the Mayor, Aldermen, and Chamberlain in 1641.

Edward Fisher bequeathed by will, towards the purpose of retaining a Lecturer at Kendal Church, the sum of 20/ ., the principal to be laid out in land, as soon as might be, by the Mayor and Churchwardens of Kendal, and the yearly profits thereof to be paid to such Lccturor; and so often as there should be no such Lecturer, to be distributed to the poor householders in Kendal, at the discretion of the Mayor and Aldermen.

Henry Wilson, before mentioned, by his will, in 1639, bequeathed unto the Mayor and Aldermen of the Corporation of Kirkby-Kendal and their successors for ever, the sum of 50/., "upon this trust and confidence, that they or some of them do bestow the same upon lands or a yearly rent-charge, and with the benefit and increase thereof, togeth-

er with supply of them and other benefactors, do procure a godly, learned, and sober Divine, to preach unto them, at Kendal Church, the Word of God, and instruct and catechise them also in the principles and fundamental points of Christian religion every Sabbath or Lord's Day for ever."

The following entry occurs in the Chamberlains' Accounts in the year 1670:—" Received of Mr. Guy the legacy of Mr. Foard to a Lecture, 10?." This is the only record of that Gift.

It also appears, by the same accounts, that John Hay left 6. *8d.* yearly out of lands in Kendal Parks towards a Lecturer. This is regularly received from the trustees of Brian Lancaster's Charity, the owners of the lands in question.

For many years back these Lectureships have been paid to the Vicar of Kendal, who receives annually from the Corporation 15?. 12s., besides 6s. *8d.* for Hay's Gift, making together 15/. *18s. 8d.* The amount has been uniform since the receipt of Mr. Foard's Gift in 1671, previous to which it was 15?., the 12s. being presumed to have been added as the interest of Mr. Foard's 10?. The annual payment of 15?. 12«. originated when interest was much above the present rate, and it appears that the Corporation have not thought Corporation Register. Idem.

proper to reduce it according to the depreciation in the value of money. The payment of 15?. 12s. was suspended for four or five years, but the opinion of Counsel being that it remained a charge upon the Corporation property, the amount, with arrears, was paid to the then Vicar in 1842. JOHN Towers' Charity.—1677.

John Towers, in 1677, gave to the Chamber of Kendal *601.,* the yearly interest thereof to be distributed to the poor of Kendal on Good Friday.

This money was secured by land out of part of Mr. Thomas Towers' Estate, in 1690.

Bateman And Duckett's Use-money. 1692.

A sum of 5s. *4d.* is annually paid by the Corporation to the Churchwardens of Kendal, under this head, and applied in aid of the Church Rate.

Joshua Nealson paid to the Chamberlains of Kendal, in 1692, l0?. the gift of Nicholas Bateman: 3s. 4t?., the consideration thereof, to be paid annually to the Church of Kendal, and the rest of the gift to be lent out to persons qualified, according to the Donor's Will, upon good security.

A memorandum in the Corporation Register states that Robert Gilpin paid to the Chamberlains, in 1691, 40s., being part of Alice Duckett's Gift, and the interest of this is supposed to make up the 5s. 4i/.

JOHN Prissoe's Charity. 1695.

John Prissoe, by will, dated in 1695, bequeathed to the Mayor and others, upon trust, 130?., to be invested in the purchase of land, the rents thereof to be distributed every Christmas amongst the aged poor sick persons, and poor lame and impotent persons living within the corporation of Kendal. This money was invested in the purchase of two fields called Barn Close and Park Close, lying in Kirk Fields, near Kendal. The amount in question, 130?., appears to have been put out to interest up to 1735, and 14?. 10s. of interest was then added to the principal, which constituted the purchase-money of the aforesaid two fields. In 1730, the yearly rental of the said fields was 6?. It is now (1861) 15?. 5s. JAMES SIMPSON'S CHARITY.—1687.

James Simpson, in 1C87, left to the Mayor and Aldermen of Kendal, 60?. upon trust, the interest thereof to be laid out in cloth called cotton, for six aged men and six aged women of Kendal, free of the town, to make each of them a coat.

To this is added a note that the yearly interest of 60?. is to be paid out of the Great Aynam, lately purchased by the town, it being part of the purchase money for the said Great Aynam, according to the mind of the donor.

James Simpson also left one half of the residue of his real and personal estate, for the benefit of the poor of Kendal, to be distributed according as the Mayor, Aldermen, Vicar, and Schoolmaster shall think fit; and the other half to the poor of Flookborough. On the

10th July, 1698, the sum of 28/. 18s. Id. was received for this moiety. The interest is included in the sums paid by the Corporation.

Wilson's Charity.—Organist. 1698.

Jennet Wilson, by Deed-poll, dated 22nd February, 1698, appointed that her Trustees therein named should permit the Mayor, Recorder, two Senior Aldermen, Vicar, and Schoolmaster of Kendal, and their successors for ever, for the time being, to hold and enjoy certain closes in Kendal Park, called Haverbrack, on Trust, that they and their successors, or the major part of them, should employ the rents and profits yearly, for and towards a yearly stipend or salary for an Organist (to be by them or the major part of them elected and approved), to play every Sabbath day upon a pair of organs in the Parish Church of Kendal.

This land consists of two closes, situate on the north side of Peat Lane, one of which is retained by the Trustees, and is let at an annual rent of 10?. 18s. 6d.; the other was sold to the Kendal and Windermere Railway Company for 1325?., which money is invested in accordance with the Act of Parliament.

Whitehead's Charity. 1712.

Peter Whitehead, of Kirkland, by will, dated 3rd October, 1712, gave a burgage house in Kendal, and a house in Kirkland on the west side of the street, and a bit of land called Little Hoods, in Kirkland, to his sister for life, with devises over as to the first and second premises, and he gave the house in Kirkland, after her death, to Bryan Lancaster, Elizabeth Walker, Thomas Crosby, and Robert Wharton, and their heirs, in trust to sell the same: and out of the proceeds he gave 45?. to the Poor Inhabitants legally settled in the township of Kirkland, which sum he directed the trustees above named to pay over, after the decease of his said sister, to Piobert Shaw, Robert Wharton, above named, and John Simondson, which last three persons he appointed his first trustees of the Charity, any two of which should have power to choose a third on the death of any one, and so from time to time for ever. And he directed the last

named. Trustees to lay the same out at five per cent, and out of the interest to take 20s. annually and therewith buy cloth or kersey for coats for three poor men, inhabitants of and legally settled in Kirkland, and such as in their judgment should stand most in need, and to distribute the same on the Feast of St. Peter and St. Paul. And to distribute the further sum of 20s. amongst the poor Inhabitants of Kirkland, and especially to the ancient, the lame, and blind, widows and orphans, in sums not less than Is. nor exceeding Is. 6d., and the remaining 5s. to be divided amongst the Trustees, and he directed that the coats should have the letters P. W. in red cloth upon the left arm.

The interest of this money (21. 5s.) is given away annually on St. Peter's day, nothing being reserved for the distributors.

STEPHENSON'S CHARITY.—1716.

The property of this Charity consists of the house and premises called the Horse and Rainbow, in Kendal, occupied by Mr. Lipsett, and the house and shop adjoining, occupied by John Greenwood, general dealer. These premises were given by Robert Stephenson, about the year 1716. Mr. William Ellison is the acting manager of the Charity, as agent for Ralph Riddle, Esq., the trustee. The sum of six guineas, out of the rents, is given to the Catholic Priest of Kendal, to be distributed at his discretion amongst poor Catholics on St. Thomas' day. The remainder is given away, under the direction of Mr. Ellison, to poor persons, not pensioners, in small sums from Is. to 2s. 6d., on St. Thomas' day. A part of these premises were rebuilt out of money reserved from the rents, but the new buildings are now, it appears, clear, and the whole of the proceeds are again available for the purposes intended by the donor.

LANCASTER'S CHARITY.—1719.

Bryan Lancaster, by will, dated 8th day of fourth month, 1719, devised his Estate at Kendal Park to certain trustees, for family purposes, which being fulfilled, he directed that, on the 1st day of the month called January, 9l. should be yearly distributed, namely, 20s. each to six poor men, and 10s. each to six poor women, they being legal inhabitants within the corporation of Kendal. without respect to what society or denomination or profession of religion they should go under, but chiefly with regard to their age and poverty. The rest and residue of the proceeds he gave to such charitable use as his trustees should in their discretion think fit.

The above sum of 9?. has been regularly distributed on New Year's day as far back as can be remembered, to poor men and women, settled inhabitants within the borough, and not members of the Society of Friends. The surplus rents are appropriated partly to the funds for relieving the poor amongst the Society of Friends, and partly to other charitable objects. It would appear that the object of the donor was not at all restricted, as he devolves the appropriation of the trust funds wholly upon the trustees.

The trustees are three in number, and when a vacancy occurs by the death of any one of them, the survivors appoint a new one in his place. The property has a rental of about *280l.* per annum. It consists of the dwelling-house and land connected with the Friends' School, in Stramongate, the rental of which is 30?. per annum; and of sixteen fields situated in Kendal Park, containing 89a. 2r. 35p. , yielding about 175?. per annum, together with five fields in Mint's Feet, 25a. lr. 30p., rent about 75?. Four acres, however, of the last-mentioned land have been left at sundry times by different individuals for purposes connected with the Society of Friends only. In respect of these latter trusts, Lancaster's trustees pay out of their income about 14?. yearly.

There is likewise a field called Shaw's Parrock, which is the exclusive property of the Society of Friends.
Archer's Charity.—1725.

John Archer, by will, dated 14th May, 1725, devised a tenement or parcel of ground, with the appurtenances, called Aikrigg, in Kendal Park, after the death of his sister, to the Mayor, two Senior Aldermen, Vicar, and Schoolmaster of Kendal, and their successors, up-

on trust, that they, or any three of them, should, every New Year's Day, apply one-half of the clear rents towards the maintenance and support of the Charity-school in Kendal, and the other half in buying so much cotton or other cloth as would contribute towards the clothing of six poor and deserving men and six poor and deserving women within the town of Kendal, of whom none should be under the age of fifty years; and he directed that, in case the said Charity-school should at any time be discontinued, the rents should be laid out towards the clothing of ten poor men and ten poor women.

The property consists of a barn and four inclosures, called Aikrigg Fields, situate to the south-east of the Castle, containing together about 10a. 3r. 13p., customary measure, and are let for 58?. 12s. yearly.

The clerk of the parish is paid 10s. annually for collecting the rents; and the distribution of the Charity is properly attended to.

REV. W. CROSBY'S CHARITIES.—1732. The Rev. William Crosby, in 1732, bequeathed to the Mayor, Recorder, two Senior Aldermen, and Schoolmaster of Kendal, for the time being, *6QL,* in trust, to be paid to each new Vicar within three months after his induction, towards the payment of First Fruits, such new Vicar giving security that the sum be paid again, so as to be available, in a similar manner, for his successor. To the. same Trustees, also, he bequeathed his library, for the use of the Vicar and Curate, the new Vicar signing a catalogue within six months after his induction, and giving security for the preservation of the books. He also desired the said Trustees to view the said library every third year. To the same Trustees he also devised the annual payment of *31.,* issuing out of Sydenham Tenement, in Underbarrow, to be paid to the use of the Blue Coat Charity Boys, and if that Charity should be discontinued, to the poor Householders of Kendal. The late Vicar, the Rev. J. W. Barnes, at his induction, received the *601,* and gave a bond to the Trustees for the repayment, as directed.

There are about 500 volumes belonging to the library, and amongst them a few good books. *All* the books contained in the old catalogue are not now to be found. A new catalogue has been made.

The rent-charge of *31.* out of Sydenham Tenement is paid annually to Mr. Whitaker, master of the Blue Coat School, and accounted for by him to the Treasurer.

Banks' And Holme's Gift.—1709—1771.

Mrs. Banks, of Kendal, by Indenture, dated 2nd February, 1709, gave to the Mayor, Vicar, two Senior Aldermen, and Schoolmaster of the Borough of Kendal, for the time being, several small sums, secured on Bonds, amounting altogether to *1131. 11s.,* which sum appears to have been increased to 125?., by the interest due upon the said Bonds, when paid over to the Trustees. A part of this sum was lost by Richard Rowlandson, in 1733, whereby the Fund was reduced to 45?.

In 1771, Thomas Holme, Esq. gave by which benefaction the above Fund was raised to 50?.; and in 1798 this sum was laid out in 82?. Stock Four per Cents., and that amount now forms the whole property of this Charity.

The Dividends at present amount to *21. 17s. id.* annually. They are divided between six poor widows, appointed by the Trustees.

Dr. Stratford'g Charity.—1755.

It appears by an entry in the Corporation books, that, in 1755, a sum of 50?. was received from Dr. Stratford, for which *21.* interest is carried out. There is no copy of his will, nor any account of the trust amongst the Corporation records, but the interest has been always applied along with Parks', Towers', and Simpson's charities.

Sleddall's Prayer-book And Bible Charity.—1801.

William Sleddall, by his will, dated 11th August, 1801, gave to the Eev. H. Kobinson, Vicar of Kendal, the Rev. George Kendall, Master of the Grammar School, and Christopher Fenton, Senior Alderman of Kirkby-Kendal, and to their respective successors for the time being, 300?. upon trust, to invest the same in the purchase of Four per Cent. Bank Annuities, or other proper security, and out of the dividend to retain to themselves 10. *6d.* apiece yearly for executing the trust after-mentioned, and apply the residue in the purchase of Books of Common Prayer of the Church of England, with the Companion to the Altar, and the Singing Psalms in the Old Version, like the Book of Common Prayer, and to distribute and divide the same in the manner following:—» viz., one book to every poor housekeeper, a communicant of the Church of England, who should be resident in Westmorland, or in any of the parishes of Cartmel, Hawkshead, and Warton, in the County of Lancaster, or in the parish of Sedbergh, in the County of York, or to such of the poor housekeepers and communicants as they should think the most proper and suitable objects; and to give, as often as they should think convenient and proper, ten Common Prayer Books to the county gaol at Appleby,—five to the House of Correction at Kendal, for the use of the prisoners, and twelve to the Workhouse in Kendal, for the use of the poor inhabitants there; the books to remain in the said prisons and workhouse; and also, upon further trust, after such Common Prayer Books shall have been twice distributed through the county of Westmorland, and the several other parishes above mentioned, to lay out the interest in the purchase of Bibles, and to distribute such Bibles in the same manner as the Books of Common Prayer; and after the Bibles should have been once distributed through the County of Westmorland and the said several Parishes, upon further trust, to distribute twice afterwards, Books of Common Prayer, and once Bibles, for ever, in the same manner and to the same objects as before ordered.

This legacy was invested July 30th, 1814, in the purchase of 357/. 13s. *6d.* Four per Cents., producing a dividend of 14?. 6s. yearly; and the first distribution of the Charity commenced in 1816. On the reduction of the Four per Cents, the money was invested in Consols, and now realizes about ten guineas annually. The books continue to be distributed at irregular intervals, when deemed necessary.

SOCIETY FOR RELIEVING THE SICK POOR. 1811.

This charity is supported principally by subscriptions, and is altogether under the care and management of the ladies. It is due to those connected with it, to say, that while few institutions in the town are more efficient in usefulness, certainly none is conducted with more energy and discretion. The ladies interested in the management of the charity constitute a committee of directors, and having the town divided into wards or districts, each lady takes a district, and visits all the sick poor therein, who may have been recommended by any of the subscribers. The relief is not given in money, but by a ticket which will procure provisions, and by the loan of a general supply of clothing and furniture, needful for a sick room. Whitewash brushes are also lent out, and the visitors take care that cleanliness is duly observed. Many a lesson of domestic economy is at the same time communicated, and habits of prudence and virtue encouraged. But all the blessings of this institution cannot here be made apparent. The indigent alone can know the effects of substantial sympathy; whilst the best earthly reward and the greatest incentives to benevolence, are together conferred on the benefactors, by "the vision indistinct of untold good." The society owes its origin to the benevolence of Mrs. Thomasin Richardson, whose heart and hand were in constant communication in such work. It appears, from the report, that during the last year, 80?. lis. *0d.* was distributed in provisions and clothing. The amount of subscriptions for last year, is 1167. 0s. *11d.*, which includes the interest on *2671.* 10s. *0d.,* being the invested fund

DOROTHY KNOTT'S GIFT.—1812.

Dorothy Knott, in the year 1810, purchased *991.* 17s. *6d.* in the Navy Five per Cents, in the names of the Mayor, Aldermen, and Burgesses, the proceeds to be applied to the following public charities of Kendal; and in 1812 she purchased another sum of 100?. in the same stock, the interest to be paid half-yearly to the rector of Grasmere and the sidesmen, to be applied for the education of five poor children of Grasmere School. These two sums appear to have been sold out in 1831, and secured upon the Corporation property. The interest, at four per cent., is distributed in the following manner:— £ s. d.

Blue-coat School, Kendal. 110
Sunday Schools, do 110
Dispensary, do 110
Lying-in Charity, do the residue.
To Grasmere School 4 4 0

And she directed that if any of the four first-named charities should be discontinued, the proportion applicable thereto should be divided amongst the others, or given to other public charities of the town; and if any part of her legacy to Grasmere School should not be applied as quarter-pence for the education of five poor children of Grasmere School, so much should be withheld and applied to such public charity in Kendal as should be most in want thereof, preferring those for the education of the poor.

MISS DOWKER'S HOSPITAL.—1831.

Dorothy Dowker, by her will, proved 1st June, 1831, bequeathed 3,000/. to the Mayor, Aldermen, and Burgesses of Kendal, in trust, to place the same out in the Three per Cent. Consols, upon trust, that the Mayor, two Senior Aldermen, and Vicar, for the time being, should nominate six females of good and chaste character, born in the borough of Kendal, having attained fifty years of age, without having been married, and whose situation in life should require some assistance; and should hire or provide a home or building in the said town for their reception, and should pay any annual sum not exceeding 45?. in the hiring such building; and she directed that they should permit the six females to reside there so long as they should conduct themselves to the satisfaction of the trustees, and pay the residue of the dividend (deducting all expenses) equally amongst the said six females; provided that, until such house should be procured, the trustees should pay the dividends yearly amongst them;

and the trustees were empowered to make such rules, orders, and regulations, as they should in their discretion think fit; and if any female should refuse to observe the same, she should be removed, and have no benefit from the said will; and that, upon the decease of any female, the trustees should appoint another.

The legacy above mentioned was invested in the purchase of 3,242?. 12s. 9d. Consols, in the name of the Corporation, producing annual dividends to the amount of 97l. 5s. 6d.

A neat and suitable almshouse was erected in 1833, in the the Elizabethan style, on lands in Highgate, belonging to the Blue-coat School, upon which the trustees of that charity laid out 400?. from their funds. The trustees of Miss Dowker's charity pay an annual rent of 40?. to the trustees of the Blue-coat School, and keep the premises in repair. — Architect, Alderman George Webster.

Miss Maria Wilson, augmented this charity by indenture, made 13th May, 1839, which assigned to the Rev. John Hudson, Vicar of Kendal, Christopher Wilson, gentleman, George Gibson, gentleman, and Thomas Gough, surgeon, the sum of 1,000?. in the Three per Cent. Consols, in trust, that they, the said John Hudson, Christopher Wilson, George Gibson, and Thomas Gough, or other the trustees for the time being, stand possessed of the said 1,000?. Three per Cent. Consols, and should continue the same in the then present security, and should receive the interest arising therefrom; and after paying all expenses incident to the trust, should divide the same, or the residue unto and equally between and amongst the six females for the time being in the Hospital in Kendal founded by Dorothy Dowker. And it is declared that the Vicar for the time being should, ex officio, be a trustee.

It was further declared, that when the number of the said trustees should be reduced to two by death, resignation, or incapacity, then, in such case, it should be lawful for the surviving or continuing trustees to nominate and appoint any other person to be trustee in his place; the costs thereof to be paid out of the then next dividends. And that so often as the said Vicar for the time being should depart this life, and a successor should be appointed, and so often as any new trustees should be appointed as aforesaid, the said 1,0007 should, at the cost of the said trust, be transferred in such manner as that the same should be legally invested in the surviving and continuing trustees.

GOOD FRIDAY S DOLE.

There is a sum annually paid by the Corporation to the churchwardens of the township of Kendal, to be distributed amongst the poor on Good Friday. For many years previous to 1822 this was 6?. 10s.; but at that date it was reduced to 4?. 10s., 40s. being deducted and appropriated to George Fleming's Exhibition, in accordance with a suggestion of the Charity Commissioners. There is no express record of the origin or foundation of this charity. The first trace of it is discovered in the Chamberlain's accounts in 1623, when the Corporation are found to have newly come into possession of certain burgage rents, called "Fleming's Rents," amounting to 5l. 9s. ld. per annum, and the rents are accounted for as bestowed upon the poor on Good Friday, after the deduction of certain charges payable out of them. The amount distributed has since varied in different years; and for some years it was as much as 10?., but the variance is not accounted for. These payments are entered sometimes as "Mrs. Fleming's Gift," and, at others, "Mrs. Fleming, of Rydal, her gift to the poor every Good Friday." Upon the Corporation coming into possession of the rents of the closes lying in the Lound, devised by George Fleming, this payment was increased by 2l, charged upon that land for the poor, and since that time the payments are entered sometimes as "Mr. and Mrs. Fleming's Gifts." From 1699 to 1821 the payment was uniformly 6l. 10s. Nothing certain can be said with regard to the origin of this charity, but the circumstances seem to raise a probability that it consists of the burgage rents called Fleming's

Rents (which, for many years amounted to 4?. 10. 4d. annually), and of George Fleming's 40s. a year; and that the burgage rents in question were given by a Mrs. Fleming, of Eydal, to the Corporation for this purpose.

If this conjecture be correct, it follows that the reduction made in 1826 was erroneous, and that the payment should be restored to 6l. 10s.

The usual mode of distribution of this dole money is for the churchwardens of the township of Kendal to take each a portion of the money and to give it away promiscuously to such necessitous persons as they may select.

THE DISPENSARY.—1782.

The Dispensary was established by voluntary subscription in 1782, and was supported in like manner, together with 80l. per annum as an allowance from the township of Kendal, the interest of a legacy of 100?. left by Mrs. Dorothy Dowker, in 1831, Mrs. Knott's annuity of lit. ls. 0d, and the interest of Mr. James Gandy's donation of 500?. It was closed in 1848; and the wants of the poor in medical relief are now supplied by the medical officers of the Poor Law Union. A portion of the invested Fund is now applied to the public baths and wash-houses.

JAMES GANDY'S CHARITY.—1844.

In 1844, James Gandy, Esq., of Heaves Lodge, near Kendal, conveyed to three Trustees, viz. his brother, John Gandy, Esq., of Oakland, Windermere; W. D. Crewdson, Esq., of Helme Lodge, near Kendal; and Samuel Marshall, Esq. of Kendal, the sum of 500?. in trust; the interest of which was directed to be applied for the benefit of the convalescent poor in Kendal, &c., or such poor persons as are not able themselves to obtain restoratives needful to recruit their strength, when recovering from contagious or infectious disorders, or other complaints; to procure nourishing food, wine, &c, under medical direction, during illness or a state of convalescence; to afford additional means of comfort in lingering illnesses; to pay for the cleansing of the dwellings of the invalid poor, or for washing their bedding, linen, &c, when they are themselves unable to do what is needful for the preservation or restoration of their health; to promote proper ventilation in their houses, or in any other way to promote the convalescence of the sick poor, and add to their comforts under their afflictions. The intention is to watch carefully that the fund should not have the effect of relieving the parochial rates, or interfering with the benevolent objects of other public charities, but to apply it when relief would not be obtained from any of these sources; in fact, to supply *additional comforts* to the poor, and not the necessaries of life.

Mr. Gandy confirmed the above by a deed of settlement, dated July 1st, 1852, and his munificent gift is now invested in the Bonds of the Kendal and Windermere Railway; and the interest arising therefrom is efficiently administered by the Trustees, in strict accordance with the directions of the donor, and, we believe, is very useful in mitigating the sufferings of the deserving poor.

THOMAS STEWARDSON'S CHARITY.—1858-60.

Thomas Stewardson, Esq., the celebrated painter, who was a native of Kendal, and who died in London, on the 28th of August. 1859, aged 78, by his will, dated 27th July, 1858, gave " 2007. to the Vicar or Incumbent for the time being of the Parish Church of Kendal, in the county of Westmorland," with a request that he would "have the goodness to distribute it in bread or money, or otherwise, as he may think best, amongst such of the poor people of Kendal, at Christmas next, after he shall receive the same, as he shall, in his uncontrolled discretion, think fit."

The whole sum of 2007, was distributed by the Vicar last Christmas (1860), in coals and clothing, to a large number of recipients in various parts of the town.

THE POOR, BREAD MONEY. 1650.—Rowland Wilson, Esq., by will, dated 5th February, 1650, left 52s. yearly, to be distributed in bread to the poor of Kendal, charged upon his estate at Grassgarth.— Regularly paid. 1750.—John Robinson, of Lane Foot, in Strickland Ketel, left the same sum, 52s. year-

ly, charged upon his estate, called *Green Riggs,* in Underbarrow, for the same purpose. The date of this bequest is 1750.—Regularly paid. 1811.—Mrs. Catharine Bordley, in 1811, left 100l., the interest thereof to be given in bread to the poor. This money was invested in the purchase of 119?. 2s. *11d.* Stock in the Five per Cent. Annuities, in the names of the Vicar of Kendal and Edward Peddar, and produced at the time a dividend of 5?. *13s. 4id.* yearly, but has since been reduced. 1813—William Sleddall, who died in 1813, by will. dated 11th August, 1801, left 130?. to the Churchwardens of Kendal to be lent out at interest, or invested in the Public Funds, and 2s. weekly, laid out in the purchase of bread, to be every Sunday divided among such of the poor people of Kendah attending divine service at the parish church, as the churchwardens should think fit. This money was laid out in the purchase of 156?. *7s. lOd.* Four per cents, and the interest received therefrom was about 6?. 5s. yearly. The two gifts of Bordley and Sleddall now realize only 9?. 12s. 8. annually. 1846. —Mrs. Elizabeth Rigg, of Manchester, left a moiety of the rents of two dwelling-houses in the Woolpack-yard, averaging about 5?. per annum. 1852. Rev. George Braithwaite, M.A., Kendal, left the interest of 198?. 15s. *2d.* in the Three per Cent. Consols. 1856. —A gentleman (unknown), residing in Birmingham, left the interest of 108?. 5s. *Id.,* in the Three per Cents., "in commemoration of the parish church restoration." (The proceeds of the aforesaid moneys are duly laid out in bread, and distributed by the churchwardens among a certain number of poor every Sunday, one loaf to each person.) POOR STOCK, KIRKLAND.

Anthony Yeates, Esq., held, until his death, the sum of 17?., which was in the hands of his father, John Yeates, but of the particulars of which no account can now be obtained, except that the sum was originally 30?., and in the hands of a person in Kendal who failed, and 17?. was all that could be recovered from the estate. Mr. Yeates gave 17s. as interest of this money to the settled poor of

Kirkland on All Saints Day yearly, in sums of Is. and 2s. each, and the same is continued by Mr. Yeates's trustees.

BURGAGE RENTS, KIRKLAND.

There are two Burgage Rents of 5s. *2d.* and 10s. *4d.,* which, for a hundred years, have been given away to the poor of Kirkland. How these payments arose cannot be clearly ascertained. The first is found charged upon premises on the east side of Kirkland, now belonging to Messrs. Bindloss; and the other, viz. 10s. *4d.,* issues out of a house adjoining the former premises, belonging to the executors of the late John Thompson. These sums are regularly distributed to the poor of Kirkland, annually, by the churchwarden, and are entered by him in a book required by the Poor Law Commissioners to be kept for that purpose.

LORD WHARTON'S BIBLE CHARITY.

The Vicar of Kendal receives thirty Bibles yearly, with about thirty-six small books. An examination takes place. and the books are given to such poor children as pass the best examination.

The following are the Trustees of Charities, in Kendal, nominated (under the provisions of the Charitable Trusts' Act), in the present year, 1861, viz..—

Other Charitable Bequests are included in the account of Public Schools, &c.

CHAPTER VII.

MANUFACTURES.

WOOLLEN MANUFACTURE.

It does not, we believe, admit of controversy, that the woollen manufactures of this kingdom were first established, by act of Parliament, in the town of Kendal. John Kemp, a manufacturer from Flanders, was the person who first received "protection" to establish himself in this country.

The following is a copy of the "Letter of Protection" granted by King Edward III. to John Kemp, as translated from Rymer's "Fcedera," vol. ii. p. 283:—

"A.D. 1331, 5 Edw. III.

"On *behalf of John Kempt, of Flanders, cloth weaver, concerning the exercise of his craft.* "The king to all bailiffs, ice., whom it may concern, greeting. Know ye that whereas John Kempe of Flanders, weaver of woollen cloths, hath come to dwell within our kingdom of England for the purpose of practising his craft therein, and of instructing and informing such as might desire to learn it of him, and hath brought with him certain men and servants, nnd apprentices to the said trade, we have taken the same John, and his aforesaid men, servants, and apprentices, and all his goods and chattels whatsoever, under our protection, &c. *(according to the tenor of similar Utters as far as these words: viz.)* for we promise to cause similar letters of protection to be issued to other men of the same craft, and to dyers and fullers, who wish to come from parts beyond the seas to dwell within the same our kingdom for the aforesaid object. In witness whereof, &c. these letters are to hold good during the King's pleasure. Witness the King at Lincoln, the 28th day of July."

This John Kemp settled in Kendal, and, it is said, his descendants are still remaining in the town or neighbourhood. There was within living memory, a family of the name of Kemp, who dwelt on the Fell Side.-(1st edition.)

He settled here in the time of Edward III. In 1336-7-8, great numbers of weavers came over from Brabant. Some say, that King Edward *solicited* them openly: others assert, that he *secretly invited* them. But the most probable account seems to be, that, having revolted against their Prince, they were banished from their native country, and sought an asylum here. Of another and similar, but later event, Dyer says:— "Our day arose When Alva's tyranny the weaving arts Drove from the fertile valleys of the Scheldt."

Kemp, however, could not be among the number of these insurgents, for the insurrection last mentioned did not take place till 1560. Till the year 1337, most of the wool of this country was exported into the Netherlands. In that year an act was passed to prohibit further exportation, but the practice still continuing, a tax of fifty shillings a pack was imposed upon it, and such was the determined spirit for exportation that the sum of 250,()00?. (amazing sum, at that day) was collected annually by the Customs

from this source. Probably the wool of Westmorland, and the other northern counties, might be of too coarse a staple for exportation, and was therefore worked up at home for the use of the inhabitants, cut off by bad roads, and intersected by mountains, from the rest of the kingdom. The women, and indeed, men also, on wet days, and in the evenings, carded and spun the wool, at their homes, for their own use. For many centuries the biickram or druggets, and bump made here, were the common clothing of the poor in London and most other towns; and (as early as 1390) they had "grown into such esteem," that in 13 Richard II. c. 10, there was a regulation "for the length and breadth of cogware and Kendal clothes. " Again, in the 9th Henry IV. (1408), there was an enactment Vide a " History of the Manufactures in the Netherlands," where may be found much interesting information. In the city of Lonvaine alone, at that time, "there were above 4,000 woollen drapers, and 150,000 weavers! When these men went from their work a great bell was rung to give notice to all the mothers to take children in doors, lest they should be trampled under foot by that crowd of workmen." This insurrection ruined the trade of Louvaiue.

Watson' " History of Halifax."

"touching the sealing of Kendal Cloth." And in the 7th James I. c. 16, "An Act for the encouragement of many poor people in Cumberland, Westmorland, and Lancashire, tq continue a trade of making Cogware, Kendals, Cartmels, and coarse cloths." It must be remarked that the cloths here alluded to were coarse woollens, although generally called Kendal *cottons,*—being, perhaps, a corruption of *coatings,* the use they were applied to,—or derived from *cot,* latinized in old writings to. *cottam,* signifying the worst kinds of wool, of which they were made. *Real* cotton manufactures were not known till the middle of the last century. Dr. Fuller, in his "History of Cambridge," relates the following anecdote concerning the origin of Stourbridge fair—once the largest mart of woollen goods in

Europe. The circumstance occurred about the year 1417. "A clothier of Kendal, a town characterized (by Camden) to be 'lanificii gloria et industria precellens,' casually wetting his cloath in water, in his passage to London, exposed it there to sale, on cheap terms, as worse for wetting, and yet, it seems, saved by the bargain. Next year he returned again, with some other of his townsmen, proffering drier and dearer cloth to be sold. So that within a few years hither came a confluence of buyers, sellers, and lookers-on, which are the three principles of a fair. *In memoria* thereof Kendal men challenge some privilege in that place, annually choosing one of the town to be chief, before whom an antic sword was carried with some mirthful solemnities, disused of late, since *these sad times,* which put men's minds into more serious employments."

When the trade in Kendal cottons became systematic and extensive, country weavers were spread throughout all the neighbouring towns, villages, and hamlets. These small manufacturers attended at Kendal on the market days, and sold their goods to the shearmen-dyers, who dyed and finished them. Upon the river Kent, and indeed upon all the streams in this part of the country, there were walk-mills, for the "steads" of which, though not a vestige of them now exists, mill-rents are paid to this day. As in all manufactures at their origin, the mills were small and of rude construction; and as the milling of cloth was, in the infancy of the manufacture, most probably performed by the feet of men, these mills may have had the name of "walk-mills" from that employment. We find, from Dr. Burn, that "in the 4th and 5th Philip and Mary, there was a grant of two fulling-mills nigh Sprent Bridge, in Skelsmergh." And again, "that there is at Staveley one fulling-mill, and it is worth by the year 10."

The Kendal cottons which were for home consumption, were mostly white, made in pieces 20 yards long. Some of them were spotted by the hand with red, blue, or green, and were hence called "ermines," or "spotted cottons." Of this kind, probably, was the dress of the

Kendal bowmen, at the battle of Flodden Field, mentioned at p. 26. The spots might easily, by poetic fancy, be magnified into " crosses red." Or, the "spots" might be designed as the (rude) armorial bearings of the several Barons, for the sake of distinguishing their respective retainers. There were other cloths of a somewhat finer description, dyed mostly blue with a mixture of green, or altogether green. Of this colour was the clothing of Falstaff s "misbegotten knaves," and "Ragged Robins," in Strutt's romance of "Queenhoo-hall." And as the Kendal green was perhaps the first colour of celebrity in the manufactures of this kingdom, it may not be amiss to give a few particulars of the process by which it was obtained. A plant which is known to have abounded in the neighbourhood of Kendal many years ago, though it be now nearly uprooted, called by Linnaeus *genista tinctoria,* and commonly called "Dyer's Broom," was brought in large quantities to Kendal, from the neighbouring commons and marshes, and sold to the Vide Shakapeare's "Henry IV." and Sir Walter Scott9a conclusion of Strutt's romance, "Queenhoo-hall." A fellow, full of queer stories, is thus described, in the year 1564, in a tract by William Bulleyn:—" Sir, there is one lately come into this hall *in a green Kendal coat,* with yellow hose, a beard of the same colour only on the upper lip; a russet hat, with a great plume of strange feathers, and a great scarf about his neck, in cut buskins. He is playing at the traytrip with our Host's son: he playeth trick upon the gittcrn," &c.—(From C. Knight's "William Shaksfkark.") In Hall's "Chronicle," we are told that Henry VIII., with a party of noblemen, "came sodaiuly in a mornyng into the quene's chambre, all apareled in shorte cotes of Kentish-Kendal—Ky. Kendal (grene?) like outlawes, or Robin Hode'a men." dyers. This plant, after being dried, was boiled for the colouring matter it contained, which was a beautiful yellow. The cloth was first boiled in alum water, for the mordant, and then immersed in the yellow dye. It was then dried, and submerged in a blue liquor

extracted from *wood,* which, combining with the yellow, produced the solid green so much celebrated. About the year 1770, the plant above alluded to, fell into disuse, being superseded by the Saxon green,—considered to be a brighter colour, and obtained with less labour. The art of dyeing was introduced into this country about A.D. 1550. From the establishment of manufactures to this period, all goods made in England were sent into Holland to be dyed, and brought back again for the consumption of this kingdom. One William Cholmley, having mastered the secret of the Flemish dyers, offered his discovery, through the English government (temp. Edwd. VI.) as a free gift to his countrymen; and urging the Council to take advantage of his proposal, he added a remarkable prophecy, that if England would develope its manufactures, and rely upon itself for the completion of them, the trade of Antwerp would droop, and London become the mart of Europe!" The dye woods manufactured in this town have been, and are, at the present day, highly approved in the great manufacturing districts.

The woollen manufactures of Kendal appear to have been in highest repute, above those of other towns, about the time of Camden and Speed, in the beginning of the 17th century. The former writer observes, "this is a place famed for excellent cloathing, and for its remarkable industry. The inhabitants carry forward an extensive trade for woollen goods, known in all parts of England." And Speed says "this towne is of great trade and resort, and for the diligent and industrious practise of making cloath, so excels the rest, This dye, it seems, was not unknown to the early inhabitants of this island for it is observed, in Sydney's History of England, "that the Celtes stained their bodies of a sky-blue colour with the juice of *icoad,* and wore no other covering than the skins of beasts." The binding of this Book is about the shade of colour of the true Kendal green.
Frodde's *"History of England,"* p. 280. that in regard thereof it caryeth a supereminent name above them, and hath

great vent and trafficke for her woollen cloaths, through all the parts of England." As this was the time when Shakspeare lived, the colour "Kendal green" had also achieved its popularity. The goods were formerly earned periodically on pack-horses by the makers themselves, or sent to London to be vended by the warehouse-men, among their customers who visited the metropolis from different parls of the kingdom. After the rise of the British Colonies, North America and the West Indies, the greater part of the Kendal cottons were sold to the merchants trading to those countries, for the clothing of the negroes and poorer planters. As the Colonies increased, and slaves along with them, who were employed in the culture of tobacco in Virginia, the demand for this coarse manufacture continued to increase, till the intervention of the American war caused a total suspension of the export trade. Upon the cessation of hostilities it again revived, but our manufacturers not able to keep pace in the improvements in machinery with those of Yorkshire, the latter interfered, and were gradually gaining advantage of Kendal, till the increase of American duties put a stop to the Before turnpike roads were made and before wagons came in use, the following pack-horses, &c. transported the merchandise of Kendal, viz.:—
One gang of pack-horses to and from London every week, of about 20
One gang from Wigan weekly, about 18
One gang from Whitehaven, about 20
From Cockermouth 15
Two gangs from Barnard-castle 26
Two gangs from Penrith twice a week, about 15 each.. 60
One gang from Settle twice a week, about 15 30
From York weekly, about 10
From Ulverston 5
From Hawkshead twice a week, about 6 12
From Appleby twice a week, about 6 12
From Cartmel 6
From Lancaster, two wagons 64
Carriages three or four times a week,

to and from Miln thorp, computed at 40 horse-load 40

From Sedbergh, Kirkby-Lonsdale, Orton, Dent, and other neighbouring villages, about 20 Total... 354
Besides 24, every six weeks for Glasgow.
exportation. A specimen of the large trade carried on in Kendal "cottons" is ascertained from the custom-house books at Liverpool. In the year 1770, there were exported to America, from that port alone, between 3,000 and 4,000 pieces, viz.:—

To Barbadoes 120 pieces.
Dominique 30
Jamaica 810
St. Kitts 4
Newfoundland 194
New York 80
Virginia and Maryland 2,693
Carolina, 640 yards—about.... 40

In process of time the change of fashion demanded a more elegant fabric of wearing apparel, and the celebrated "Kendal cottons" at length became degraded to the use of horse-checks, floorcloths, dusters, mops, &c. Linseys, which for a number of years were parallel with cottons, after the decline of the latter, became the staple manufacture of the place. This article was sent to Holland and Germany, excepting a finer sort which was made, and continues to be made, in increased quantities, for home consumption.

The manufacture of knit yarn and worsted stockings was also a nourishing trade in Kendal. The hosiers used regularly to attend the markets of all the towns, and at stated times all the villages and hamlets within twenty miles of the circumjacent country, to give out worsted which they carried with them for the purpose, and take in the stockings that had been knit during the interval between each visit. On the mountain side, in the valleys, and on every hand were to be seen

"The spinsters and the knitters in the sun." From the Addenda to Burn's Westmorland.
It is not known by whom, or when, the art of knitting stockings was discovered. Savary asserts that the Scotch were the first people in the world that knit stockings, because St. Fiacre was the chosen patron of the stocking knitters in France, and St. Fiacre was a Scotchman! "That great and *txjlentive* prince, Henry VIII.," says Howell, "wore ordinarily cloth hose, except there came from Spain, by great chance, a pair of silk stockings." See, also Smith's "Wealth of Nations," p. 242, as to Queen Elizabeth being the first person that wore stockings; "which were a present to her from the Spanish Ambassador."

E

It is supposed that the hosiery business was most flourishing about a hundred years ago, but we have been unable to obtain any authentic particulars so far back as that time. In 1801 the average quantity of stockings made for the Kendal market, weekly, was

In Ravenstonedale 1,000 pairs.
Sedbergh and Dent.... 840
Orton 560
Total 2,400 pairs.

At the present time there are few knit stockings made here; other descriptions of knit woollens, however, are still, to some extent, manufactured for this market. These are single and double scarlet caps, Kilmarnock and plaid caps, made principally for exportation to America and the West Indies.

These manufactures, altogether, furnished employment not only for the inhabitants of the town, but also for the working population of the surrounding country. By the introduction of real cottons, in later years, and the extraordinary cheapness at which they are manufactured, the linsey trade has been compelled to take second rank; whilst woven hose have superseded the handiwork of the fair artist. But happily, the skill and enterprise of our manufacturers provided, that either the old staple manufactures should be replaced with new ones, or so modified as still to compete with "the millions of spindles worked by steam." Before the almost general introduction of steam engines, and the combination of machinery, the plentiful supply of water might afford some advantages to the manufacturers of Kendal, over those of many other places; but after that, the local situation of the town,—so far removed from the first essential of modern manufactures—coal; so entirely shut out from the facilities of open navigation; and so remote from the home markets, must be confessed to have been greatly detrimental to its prosperity. To what, then, can we attribute the steady and permanent success of trade which has never failed to provide for the population of Kendal? Surely, to the determined spirit of industry and frugality of its manufacturers—to the wise direction of their labour and capital into profitable channels; and, above all, to their habitual attention to the manufacture of goods of undoubted utility. We have had opportunities of ascertaining the reputation of Kendal manufactures, in various parts of the kingdom, and we find their characteristic that which is intrinsically serviceable.

By the introduction of railway facilities, in 1847, the woollen trade of Kendal got a fresh stimulus, in having the price of coals thereby lowered, in having the cost of carriage reduced, and the markets brought nearer. Sir Robert Peel's Free Trade measures, for the removal of " protective " duties, operated also beneficially for the manufacturer. Thirty years ago the "fell sheep" of Westmorland and Cumberland constituted the main supply of wool for the Kendal trade. The home grower was "protected," as it was called, by an import duty on foreign wools of *6d.* per lb. at first, and afterwards of *Id.,* and at last d. per lb. But the best commentary on the policy of that "protective" system, is given by the confession of the growers themselves, that "English wool is now more remunerative to them than when it was protected." CASTLE MILLS.

These mills were originally Corn Mills, connected with the Castle (see ante, p. 98), afterwards Fulling Mills, and Carding and Spinning Mills, for woollens called, by a solecism,"cottons. " They were rebuilt in 1806, extended, by the erection of commodious sheds, in 1855, and filled with the newest machinery, by Messrs. J. J. and W. Wilson, the most spirited and enterprising firm in the trade. The manufacture consists of railway rugs, coat-linings, tweeds, horse-clothing, &c., and every process is carried on within the premises, including carding, spinning, dying, power-loom weaving, fulling, and finishing. It was here that steam-power had its first application, in the district, to the woollen manufactures, Messrs. Wilson having erected a thirty-horse engine in 1855. Their machinery is now driven by three water wheels, equal to fifty-horse power, and thirty-horse power of steam. The "hands " employed by them are upwards of 300.

MEAL BANK WOOLLEN MILLS.
This is, at the present day, one of the most thriving establishments in the trade, carried on by Messrs. Braithwaite & Co. It is, indeed, more like a colony than a simple manufactory. The mill stands in a beautiful ravine, on a crescent of land formed by a bend of the river Mint, where the geologist may see traces, strongly marked, of the diluvial action of former epochs. Advantage is taken of this situation, and a waterwheel is erected for moving the machinery, estimated at 80-horse power. In 1854, a steam-engine was also put down to compensate for diminished water power, in dry seasons. The manufactures consist of collar checks, linseys, coat-linings, tweeds and fancy trouserings. The last named article, fancy trouserings, was introduced in the year 1838, then new to Kendal. The firm obtained a medal for the best cloths, of their kind, at the Paris Exhibition, in 1855; and a still higher compliment was paid to them on that occasion by the report of the Huddersfield Chamber of Commerce, when it was stated that "the black and white tweeds, and shepherd's plaids from Kendal, (Messrs. Braithwaites') are superior to any exhibited in purity and firmness of colour, and fine, soft, woolly handle. Compared with them the Continental manufactures of this class are of very inferior quality. " About 500 "hands" are employed in the manufactory, who reside in neat, healthy cottages, near to the works; and the condition of the children is cared for by the establishment of a school, where upwards of sixty children have the benefit of a good English education.

WEAVING SHED IN LONG POOL.
Messrs. Simpson & Ireland are now (1861) building a large "shed," or mill, in Long Pool, for weaving by power-looms. Their manufactory, at Staveley, moved by water power, is one of the oldest establishments connected with the staple trade of the town.

There are, besides the afore-mentioned, many different kinds of manufacture, by which the working population of the town is supported. We shall enumerate only a few of the seemingly most important, placing them according to seniority.

CARD MAKING.
The manufacture of wool cards is a business of considerable...... but uncertain antiquity in this town; and it is affirmed, that if it was not originated here, it at least received from the ingenuity of our townsmen, so many improvements and stimulants, as should fairly entitle them to the honour of its invention. The first cardmaker of eminence, that we have been able to find, was Mr. John Waide, who served the office of mayor, in 1743. This gentleman realized a handsome fortune by the old, slow processes of single-tooth making and hand-pricking. In 1751, a pricking-engine was invented and constructed by William Fothergill, cardmaker, and William

Pennington, a millwright, of this town; by means of which

Mr. Fothergill extended his trade very considerably. Another establishment took its rise out of Mr. Fothergill's, by Mr.

Dover Bayliff, an ingenious mechanic. In 1775, Bayliff invented an engine for the facilitating the crooking of wire teeth. This invention produced an epocha in card making, and, with the assurance of its general adoption, Mr. Bayliff commenced a manufactory of the engine. In this new trade he admitted, as partner, a person of the name of Lawrence, a clock-maker, who, after being initiated in the mystery, seceded from the establishment, and departed into Yorkshire, to reap the profits of Bayliff's invention. By that time, however, Mr. Bayliff had extended his business, and besides supplying a great portion of the manufacturers of this kingdom, did a considerable export trade.

The present machinery used in card making not merely bends and cuts the wire, but it likewise punches the leather, and sets the teeth, by a simultaneous and instant operation.

When Mr. Waide, who was one of "the old school," had the first intimation of Bayliff's invention, he exclaimed, "Humph! he mud as weel attempt et pluck't moon en't stars frae't sky." Shortly after this he met Mr. Bayliff in the street, with part of his apparatus, in a wrapper, under his arm, "Well, Bayliff," he enquired, "what's that you've got there?" "Nought less than't moon and 't stars," (replied B.), "thou may look for their shining in a few nights hence; at present tbey are under an eclipse."

There is, indeed, scarcely any machinery, in any branch of trade, so perfect and so beautiful in its operations. The large manufactory of Mr. James Thompson, built in 1860, is replete with the newest machinery, and that gentleman now carries on a business far more extensive than any of the most enterprising of his predecessors.

MARBLE WORKS.
The manufacturing, or chiseling and polishing of marble, together with the public profession of architecture, was introduced into Kendal by the late Francis Webster, father of Messrs. George and Francis Webster, his successors. About the year 1800, till which time every branch of the art was executed by manual labour, Mr. Webster erected machinery at Helsington Laithes, on the Kent, for sawing and polishing marble; and this machinery is now brought to such perfection, that all descriptions of mouldings, whether straight or circular, are wrought by it in the most finished style. Mr. Francis Webster, the present proprietor, has an establishment for the exhibition of his manufacture in Preston; and his works of art, scattered throughout the kingdom, with numerous sepulchral monuments, and specimens

of architectural skill which adorn this town and neighbourhood, in particular, will long bear honourable testimony to his merit. In 1830, another manufactory of marble was established by Mr. Edward Bayliff. These works received an auspicious commencement, Mr. Bayliff being employed by Wyatville, the King's architect, to make two large mantelpieces for Windsor Castle. The larger of these is a most superb and finished specimen. It is constructed of Italian dove marble, in the Gothic order of architecture, and is erected in St. George's Hall. The other is made of Kendal Fell limestone, and though less magnificent, is scarcely less beautiful than the former; and shows, that this limestone is capable of a very high polish, and possesses a vein of pleasing variety. These two mantel-pieces were erected in Windsor The Kendal Fell limestone was first polished as marble by the late Alderman Webater, in 1788.

Castle, in February, 1831. But Mr. BaylifFs establishment, notwithstanding, lasted only a short time.

COMB MANUFACTURES.

The horn comb manufacture is of considerable antiquity in this town, having been in existence more than a century; and is carried on with great spirit, at the present time, by Messrs. John Sisson and Son. This establishment has been in the same family since 1794, Joseph Sisson having founded it in that year. The firm maintains a high reputation for the production of a particular description of combs for horses, outrivalling, perhaps, every other house in the trade throughout the kingdom, in that article. London, Edinburgh, and Glasgow are the chief marts. Most of the combs are for domestic consumption; but some of the wholesale houses, in London, export Messrs. Sisson's produce. The manufacture is stimulated by a steam engine and machinery of modern construction. Formerly, from about the year 1800 to 1845 there was also a considerable manufacture of ivory combs in this town; carried on, first, by Mr. Alderman Berry, and afterwards by Mr. James Conway; but, on the death of this last-named gentleman, the ivory comb trade

ceased.

LEATHER AND SHOE MANUFACTURE.

The manufacture of leather is part of the industrial history of Kendal, and it still adheres to the town, but in a different phase from that which it presented a century and a half ago. In»1683, the inhabitants, petitioning Charles II. for a renewal of the Charter, state that "the trade in leather was grown very considerable;" and such as might then be desired "to take toll thereof." (See, ante, p. 175). In 1724, says Wharton, "the companies of tanners and tawers have, at this day, so great a share of trade as enables them to pay to the crown, by way of duty, between 1,600i and 2,000?. per annum." And, at the last Kendal guild, in 1759, it is recorded that there were sixty tanners in the procession who had the arms of their trade painted in the front of their caps, and were attended by "bold Arthur-a-Bland," properly dressed. The tanners and curriers of those days were occupied in producing the heaviest and strongest descriptions of leather, and the same manufacture is continued at the present day, in limited degree. But, within the past two or three years, a new branch of the trade has sprung up which, in extent and importance, outrivals the old branch of the leather business in Kendal, and has struck a "heavy blow and great discouragement" to shoemaking, by hand, in Northampton and Stafford; towns formerly noted for the production of shoes. This new trade is carried on at Netherfield, by Messrs. Somervell Brothers, who employ, in their establishment, between 250 and 300 "hands," male and female; but the greater number are females, The "hands" are occupied principally in preparing the "work" for the sewing-machine —each sewing-machine rcquh8ing only one operator; and the work consists solely of making what are technically called "uppers;" that is, the upper part of a boot or shoe, ready for the sole. The leather used for the purpose is imported, and is almost all of fine quality. The only operation remaining for the shoemaker is to attach a "sole" to the "uppers" here produced; and we are told that these latter are in

some cases sold for less money than would be paid in wages for making them by hand, apart from the cost of leather.

PAPER MANUFACTURES.

The Burneside Paper Mills were started in the year 1833, by Messrs. Hudson and Nicholson (Kendal), and Mr. Foster (Ky. Lonsdale), for the manufacture of printing papers, by "machine." The same parties converted the works at Cowan Head (formerly carried on by Messrs. Branthwaite), from the old "hand-make" process into the machine-producing system. And both mills were conducted under the firm of Hudson, Nicholson, and Foster, till the year 1845, when they were transferred, by purchase, to Mr. James Cropper, who has considerably enlarged the works, and improved the machinery at both places. There is water-power, at the works combined, equal to 120-horse, besides auxiliary steam-power to the extent of 40-horse, making together ICO-horse-power. There are four paper machines, and nineteen rag-engines, employing usually about 120 workpeople (male and female). The produce of paper is nearly twenty tons per week.

CARPET MANUFACTORY.

The mamifacture of carpets is entirely modern in Kendal. It was introduced in the year 1822, by Messrs. Joseph and John Atkinson. Since which time, it has, by progressive steps, become an extensive and lucrative business. In 1828, Messrs. Atkinson adopted some new machinery for weaving damask carpeting. In consequence of this improvement they were able to compete with the first houses in the trade; but the spirit of rivalry was not long in opposing their progress. An action was instituted in Chancery, at the suit of Messrs. Clark and Sons, of Market Harborough, carpet manufacturers, for the alleged infringement of a patent which that house had taken out. It appeared on the trial, that a loom had been introduced from France about six years before. The one adopted by Messrs. Clark was shown to be a modification of this French loom. Messrs. Atkinson's was proved to be a still more improved modification of the

French apparatus. The court therefore decided for the Kendal firm. We have been thus particular respecting this proceeding, because the success of the carpet trade in Kendal seemed to depend upon it. Various descriptions of carpets are made here: Brussels, Kidderminster, Venetian, and others. Most of these are for home use, and sold chiefly in London. Some are exported, generally from Liverpool, to America, Canada, &c. Since the death of the Messrs. Atkinson, the business has been successfully and still more extensively prosecuted by Messrs. Whitwell and Co., who have, in their time, adapted steam power to the production of carpets, and superadded many mechanical and artistic improvements.

AGRICULTURAL IMPLEMENT MANUFACTORY.

This is a new and flourishing branch of business in Kendal, introduced by Messrs. Williamson Brothers, since the establishment of railways, and a large number of hands are employed in this manufactory.

SNUFF MANUFACTURE.

Kendal has long been celebrated for the production of its snuffs. Two descriptions, called respectively, "Kendal brown," and " Kendal rappee," are peculiar to the place,.and are held in great esteem by snuff-takers throughout the country. The principal manufacturers, at this time, are Mr. Samuel Gawith, Mrs. Allen, Messrs. Noble & Wilson, and Messrs. J. & K Busher.

FAIRS AND MARKETS.

Gilbert Fitz-reinfred, 7th baron of Kendal, procured from King Richard I. (we have been unable to find the precise year) a charter for a weekly market at Kendal, on Saturday. In the 3rd Edward II. (1310), Marmaduke de Thweng, who held the Lumley Fee, obtained a charter for *a market and fair.* And again, a grant of a market and fair was obtained by Christian, wife of Ingelram de Gynes, in the 7th Edward III. (1333), "or rather," says Dr. Burn, "these last were confirmations of the former grant." Confirmations, we feel disposed to add, as to the market, but a new privilege as respects the fair; for we can find no allusion to

the fair in the mention of the grant of Richard L These grants were fully confirmed by the Charters of Incorporation of Elizabeth and Charles I., in which are definitely appointed two fairs yearly, and a weekly market.

Camden describes Kendal as being, about the end of the sixteenth century, "one of the best corn markets in these northern parts." This seems almost irreconcileable with the fact, which some persons still living can testify, that 75 years ago, seldom more than a dozen loads of oats were exposed for sale, and not a grain of wheat was brought into this market. Such has been the improvement in agriculture, however, in the neighbourhood, since the period abovementioned, that the quantity of grain (principally wheat and oats) now, exposed in this market, is very large.

In the year 1730, potatoes were sparingly used here; for the quantity consumed was brought from Kirkby-Lonsdale, where a person of the name of Marsden had introduced the culture of this useful vegetable.

Large quantities of butter are sold in this market, the greatest part of which is bought by dealers, and carried for sale to Manchester and other large manufacturing towns, in Lancashire.

Whilst most kinds of agricultural produce appear to have increased, the fish market; on the contrary, has been on the decline. Dr. Burn has supplied a reason for this decline. After enumerating the different kinds of lake fish, he adds, "the southern part of this county is also pretty well furnished with sea fish, caught near Levens Sands, and other places on the sea coast; which heretofore (1777) were weekly brought to Kendal market, insomuch that upon a market day there have been sometimes five and thirty different sorts of fish. But since the great improvement of the town and port of Lancaster, the market for fish is considerably drawn that way." Fish was formerly so abundant in Kendal—something like two centuries ago—that apprentices had to be protected from the *excessive* use of it by masters in whose bouses they lodged; and a clause was commonly inserted in indentures, lim-

iting the supply of fish to three days a week. A royal commission, which was appointed last year (1860), to inquire into the decay of salmon fisheries, visited Kendal among other places, and took evidence as to the decline of salmon in the river Kent. They reported, generally, that the sensible falling off in the quantity of salmon is caused by the building of high wears across the rivers, and by poaching with " stakenets," and "baulknets." And they suggest, that river conservators should be appointed, with salutary powers, to protect the fish.

i "Manners and Customs of Westmorland," an interesting pamphlet, written by the late John Gough, Esq., under the signature of a "Literary Antiquarian." We have not been able to find one of these indentures, but there is no doubt about the fact. Brockktt mentions Newcastle and Kendal as towns where the apprentices had this saviDg clause in their favour. CHAPTER VIII. CLIMATE, HEALTH, MORTALITY.

Kendal has attained to an unenviable and undeserved notoriety in connection with the rain-fall. When, forty years ago, public records of the annual fall of rain were kept at only a very few places, and Kendal was one of the few, the returns from this place indicated the maximum of rain as for the whole kingdom (Epping, in Essex, presenting the minimum). But now, when the range of observation is extended, and the places where registers are kept are vastly increased in number, the fall of rain at Kendal is seen to be nearer the *mean* than the *maximum* of all England. But it is the chief town of the Lake district, and the Lake hills certainly present the maximum fall of rain, so that Kendal, by topographical relation, still maintains its character of inordinate wetness, and it requires a candid examination of the tables to remove this impression. That the hilly districts, on the north of Kendal, should bo remarkable for moisture, is only in accordance with the known laws of meteorology. Rising, as these hills do, tier above tier, from Whitbarrow Scar, on the shores of Morecambe Bay, to the culminating Pike of Scafell, "the last that parleys with the setting sun," here are so many magnets to attract the rain-clouds, which come sailing up from the western Atlantic and the Irish Channel. These rain-clouds, heated by passing over the gulf-stream, come into collision with fields of air, of much lower temperature, floating around the hills, condensation takes place, and down pours the rain; so that, as the phrase goes, "when it rains, *it rains.*" The average fall of This oceanic current elevates the temperature of the air of this part of Europe to the extent of 10" to 15.—See " Life on the Earth," by Professor JonN Pm Lira, p. 154; and " Physical Geography of the Sea," by Lieutenant Maury, p. 48.

rain at Scafell exceeds 120 inches; but, as may be seen by the tables subjoined, the average rain-fall at Kendal is 45 £ inches. The United Kingdom presents the mean of 32 inches; therefore, Kendal is not now (taking the last decade), very materially in excess of the average of the whole kingdom, and has no right, as before said, to participate with the district of the Lake hills, in pluvial notoriety.

We furnish, herewith, tables of the quantity of rain taken at Kendal for fifty years, by meteorologists of unquestionable accuracy. The rain-guage was kept from the year 1811 to 1821 (inc.), by Thomas Harrison, Esq., and John Gough, Esq. successively; and from 1822 to 1860 (inc.), the long period of thirty-nine years, solely by our friend Samuel Marshall, Esq. We have divided the series into five tables, of ten years in each table; and we have appended to these, a statement of the *mean* fall of rain in each decade of years, which enables the cursory reader to compare the results, without travelling through the whole of the figures:

The *mean* 'fall' (in decades of years) is, for the 1st ten years (from 1811 to 1820).... 50.580 inches.
2nd „ („ 1821 to 1830).... 56.365 „ 3rd „ („ 1831 to 1840).... 55.218 „ 4th „ („ 1841 to 1850).... 61.311 „ 5th „ („ 1851 to 1860).... 45.654 „
It is thus seen that there has been a gradual decline in the fall of rain during the past forty years. How far this corre-

sponds with results in other places, we have not the means of knowing; but it will hardly be doubted, that the cause is to be ascribed to the removal of' tarns,' and the general drainage of lands in the valley of the Kent, within the time stated. There have been no changes in forestry, within the period, to affect the fall of rain either more or less. It is probable that more timber has been planted than felled; whilst numerous 'tarns,' and innumerous swampy meadows, have been drained off, and evaporation has thereby been proportionately diminished.

The largest fall of rain, in any one month within these fifty years, was in January, 1834«: quantity, 14758 inches; and the least fall in any month within the fifty years, was in May, 1836: quantity 0 053 inches.

The wettest month of the year, on an average of the months in the fifty years in question, is December; and the driest month of the year, on an average of the fifty years, is May.

The following tables of the number of rainy days, and of the variations of the Barometer, and the Thermometer, for thirtyeight years successively, are from the sole register of our friend, Samuel Marshall, Esq., whose care and pains cannot be exceeded by any living meteorologist:

Monthly *aa* Annual Means *f nt* Thermometer *n* Kendal *nn* n Yearsoto 099 9 899 9n 8nc888. TABLE No. 8V.

The climate of Kendal is less salubrious than the rural districts of the parish, or of the "Union," but more so than many of the manufacturing towns in England. This is conclusively proved by comparison of the Bills of Mortality. Taking the average of the last seven years, the rate of mortality in Kendal is 1 in 48 of the population; whilst in the districts comprised in the whole Poor Law Union of Kendal, the average mortality is 1 in 61. It must be further observed, however, that this rate of mortality in Kendal is decreasing; for at the time of publication of the first edition of this book (1832), the rate was 1 in 39. It is now 1 in 48, as aforesaid—a considerable amelioration. There were several dis-

eases which took off the population, arising from secondary causes, that have been removed. Agues and scrofulous disorders abounded here half a century ago. Typhoid fevers were also very prevalent, especially in the autumn months. These cases are now comparatively rare. Improved drainage, improved ventilation of houses, more cleanliness among the poor, less intemperance, and, lastly, the substitution of water drawn from the silurian rocks, in place of water impregnated with lime, have unitedly raised the general standard of health. Phthisis pulmonalis prevails still, in degree, but less extensively than in former years. Of the artisan class, the weaver is the most sallow and unhealthy in appearance; but this may be attributed to his sedentary, in-door employment, and not to any local causes.

The sanitary condition of the town was made the subject of official investigation in 1849, by a Government officer, connected with the General Board of Health; and the result of this investigation was given in a carefully-drawn Report, by the Superintending Inspector, on the state of the town. We subjoin a brief abstract of this Report. Since that time, however, many improv?ments have been effected in the houses, "crofts," and back lanes (suggested by this Report), and the description here given is, consequently, not strictly applicable to the present condition of drainage and cleanliness: See establishment of Gas ami Water Works, ante p. 158.

"Report of the Superintending Inspector to the General Board of HeaUh, on a. Preliminary Inquiry into the Sewerage, Drainage, and Supply of Water, and the Sanitary Condition of the Inhabitants of the Borough of Kendal, dated May 9, 1849.

"I have the honour to inform yon that, in accordance with your instructions, I have inspected the Borough of Kendal.

"I found that the Corporation, in conjunction with the Board of Guardians, had formed a Local Health Committee, and had applied the provisions of the Nuisances Removal Act very vigorously as far as these could go.

"The natural drainage of the town has three directions: one from the eastern side of the ridge, direct into the river, a second directly into the valley, and thence northwards into the river, a third also directly into the valley, but falling southwards into the river. The whole of the Fell drainage is also divided between the two portions of this valley. As the river flows from north to south, and the outfall of the northern portion of the valley is above the town, its contents are carried by the current quite past the town, and produce a serious nuisance in their progress.

' The Kent is broad and shallow, rippling over a pebble bed, and held up by three considerable, and very many smaller weirs; of the three, Dockwray Hall weir is quite above the town, the Castle Mill abreast of it, and the Lound weir quite below it. The fall from the tail-race of the Dockwray weir to that of the Lound weir is 15 feet and the distance about 2,200 yards. This is within the limit of the fall of the lowest and most level portion of the town.

"Tributary to the Kent are three streams, one on the right bank above or just within the town, drains the west side of Stricklandgate, and falls into the river 350 yards above the Stramongate Bridge, under the name of the Dyer's Beck. The second' stream rises on the Fell-side, in the limestone, flows across a part of the town as the Blind-beck, and reaches the river about 350 yards above the Nether-bridge, and 500 yards below Miller-bridge. Close below this is a second limestone spring, the Anchorite's Well, which is capable of turning a small mill 50 yards below its source. The third principal stream rises on the Hay Fell, flows across the suburb, and enters the river as the Stock-beck, a little below Stramongate Bridge. This spring takes the waste of the waterworks. Thus much, then, of the general disposition of the surface of and about Kendal.

"Government.—In Kendal township a Board of twelve to twenty is elected, and appoints a sub-surveyor, who attends to the roads and sewers. The ex-

pense of scavenging, however, is borne by the Fell Trustees, who allowed at the time of my inspection 50?. per annum for Kendal, and 10/. for Kirkland township, and contracted with the Board of Surveyors to attend to both. These sums have since been reduced, in consequence of the deficiency of the cleansing rate, to 25/. and 5l. "Under a Local Enclosure Act of 1767, power was given to enclose 158 acres of common lands, called the Kendal Fell. The administration of the lands was placed in the hands of trustees, and the surplus rents were directed to be employed in reduction of the poor-rate. These trustees were also empowered to light and cleanse the township of Kendal, and to levy a rate for such purposes, not exceeding 6d. in the pound annually. Afterwards, by an order of the Town Council, under the Municipal Act, certain other districts, completing the present town, were added. Also the Act confirmed a previous agreement between the owners of the Park and Castle lands, and the rest of the township of Kendal, whereby it W;ib settled that the former should pay one-tenth and no more of the whole joint poor-rates for ever. The effect of this enactmeut has been to encourage building operations within the Park and Castle area, which lies on the eastern side of the river, around the Castle, and thus to cause the poor's-rate to fall with undue weight upon the remainder of the town.

"The tables of mortality tend to show the excessive mortality of Kendal as compared with that of the adjacent country. Nor is there anything in the natural position of the town, or in the density of its population, to account for it. This excess is attributable, in my opinion, to the defective drainage and ill-constructed receptacles for filth which are allowed to remain unemptied for an unjustifiable length of time, throwing out their pestiferous exhalations, and thereby generating fevers of a low typhoid character, chronic affections of the chest and bowels, which are so frequently prevailing epidemically here. During my inspection, I had frequent opportunities of observing that

the localities unhealthy, were those in which local nuisances were most offensive, and the absence of drainage most marked.

"Water Supply.—Kendal affords a very strong example of how little a private company, founded on a good principle, and with a liberal and zealous direction and officers, can do to effect a complete distribution of the water supply.

"Besides the pumps, of which the water is, in a sample taken at random of 50 of hardness, and the Anchorite's Well, of which the water is of 14, Kendal is supplied with water by the Kendal Water Company, incorporated for water and gas, 26th June, 1846.

"The supply is by natural pressure commanding the whole town. On the side of Hay-Fell a reservoir has been formed, into which, by catch-water and natural drains, the water from the hills above is led. This water is of 3 of hardness only, very pure, bright and tasteless. Flood-waters are excluded. The quantity stored is 2,000,000 cubic feet, which, at four cubic feet daily for each person, would supply Kendal for about forty-three days.

"This reservoir has only been open about half a year, and the company have purchased land and are about to provide storage for a sixty day's supply. From the reservoir an 8-inch main descends into the town, and gives off branches which are already laid in the principal streets. The mains are in some instances laid along the sides of the streets, in others down the centre; and in some of the widest parts, down both sides. The width of the main streets varies from eighteen feet to sixty-eight feet, and probably averages forty feet. The company, as a matter of course, lay the service pipes from the main to the margin of the private premises, if the distance does not exceed twenty yards. All beyond that limit is the subject of special agreement. As a general rule, the company lay a distinct branch-pipe to each house, and the average length of such branches is twenty feet. They are of lead or iron, as the consumer pleases. The charge is about 8d. a-foot, exclusive of the cocks, which vary from 3s. to 6s. each.

"The supply is constant, at high pressure, of excellent quality, charged at a rate but a trifle above a penny a-week upon the lowest class of houses, and the company have shown great anxiety to keep down the expense of the service-pipes as low as possible, and yet they supply but a small fraction of the population. The distribution of water, throughout the town, is much more general now than it was when this lieport was published.

"street Paving And Scavenging—The highways and thoroughfares in Kendal are by no means in very good order. The main streets have macadamized carriage ways, and pitched footways. There is but little flagged way in the town. In Kendal township, by very much the principal division of the borough, there are about ten or eleven miles of road-way, kept in repair by the sub-surveyor, at a cost, including scavenging, of about 350?. per annum. Broken stone varies according to its quality from Is. lOd. to Is. id. per ton. The material at the latter price is excellent.

"public Nuisances.—There are ten slaughter-houses in the town, and the greater number of them are in its most crowded parts. They form, perhaps, after the private cess-pools, the most pressing evil in the town. 'They are all,' says the Inspector of Nuisances and Police, 'attached to inns or public houses, closely surrounded with dwellings in the centre of the town, and chiefly in confined and improper places.'

"The brooks or becks, crossing the town, have already been mentioned. These, which ought to adorn and purify the town, rank at present among its public nuisances.

"Common Or Public Lands. The only public lands are those on Kendal Fell and a few detached fields belonging to local charities, but these are all at an elevation of from 200 to 400 feet above the sewage outfalls, and, therefore, beyond the reach of the fluid manure.

"REMEDIES.

"Sewerage.—It is in all cases objectionable to turn sewage matter into a river, more especially within a town; but where the river is shallow, and frequently leaves a large portion of its channel dry, such a practice is quite inadmissible. The first requisite, therefore, in the arrangement of a plan of drainage for Kendal, is to carry all the outfalls below the town, and, if possible, to combine them upon one point. This I find to be practicable. The main sewerage divisions will be four, the Fell-side valley north; the same south; the eastern side of the town between the ridge and the river, including Stramongate; and the suburb beyond the river, as far as the railway station.

"Sewage Distribution.—The proposed drainage arrangements, by concentrating the sewage upon one outfall below the town, will render its distribution as a manure extremely easy. It appears, from a plan and section prepared by Mr. Watson, that a lift of from thirty to forty feet will place within reach of this manure a tract of land, chiefly laid down in grass, of about 600 acres, and at a sufficient distance from the town to prevent any possible annoyance from bad smells. The Corporation have recently received offers, from private parties, to rent the sewage of the town, and there can be no doubt but that it will become a considerable source of revenue.

"General Remarks.—Kendal has suffered severely from its long-continued neglect of attention to the public health or convenience. Its ill-paved, close, and crowded alleys, its deficiency of all proper drainage, and until very recently, the absence of a supply of any but hard water, are causes which have tended powerfully to lower the condition of the working classes; to produce sickness, and an excessive rate of mortality; and, as a direct consequence, to load the town with heavy annual expenditure.

"The *direct* money expense of all these evils falls, no doubt, chiefly upon the rate-paying class; but the evils themselves, and their *indirect* expenses, press far more heavily on the poor. The expenses produced by want of soft water and proper drainage weigh heavily on the poor; their homes are rendered

T comfortless; they are driven to the public-houses; and medical evidence has shown that a state of lassitude is produced, which renders those stricken by it careless of consequences, and leads directly to pauperism.

"The present condition of Kendal is, in my opinion, to be attributed solely to the want of the powers and facilities now afforded by the Public Health Act. The town possesses, in an unusual degree, persons of station and influence, who have long been actively engaged in attempts to amend the condition, and add to the comforts of the labouring poor; and their hands will be materially strengthened by this measure. I advert to these circumstances because they appear to me to augur well for the formation of an efficient Local Board, and, therefore, for a full measure of success in the application of the remedies.

"Summarv.—I have then to report:—

"1. That the mortality of Kendal is absolutely high, being 32J in the 1,000, and high relatively as regards that of the registration district, which is about 24 in the 1,000; and this, notwithstanding that the greater part of the town is on high and open ground, in a climate usually regarded as healthy.

"2. That this mortality, and the sickness which it represents, are greatest in certain close, filthy, undrained, and damp quarters of the town.

"3. That the position of the town admits of the economy of the employment of its sewage under the form of fluid manure, and that a revenue may be confidently expected under this head." *May,* 1849.

Since the date of the above Report the Local Board of Health, as before said, have been very active in removing many of the nuisances, and causes of sickness, deprecated in that Report.

POPULATION.

The following returns of the population, from 1784 to 1861, show the variation in the number of inhabitants from time to time, within that period. We believe the returns, up to and including that for 1821, did not include the district of Nethergraveship, but the inhabitants of that district, at the time, were inconsiderable:

The following is the number of dwelling-houses, within the borough, in the present year, 1861, taken from the Census returns, viz.:— PARLIAMEN-TARY REPRESENTATION. The Act of Parliament, popularly called the "Parliamentary Reform Bill," by which many towns in the United Kingdom, not previously represented in Parliament, had representative powers conferred upon them, passed the Legislature in June, 1832. By the operation of this Act Kendal became entitled to return one Member to the House of Commons. The following list presents the Members successively returned from that period to the present time: 1832. James Brougham. Died, in Dec 1833. 1834. John F. Barham. 1835. „ „ re-elected. 1837. George Wm. Wood. 1841. „ „ re-elected. Died, 1843. 1843. Henry Warburton. 1847. George Carr Glyn. 1852. „ „ re-elected. 1857. „ „ 1859. „

Present number of voters on the register for the Borough, 432.

CHAPTER IX. LITEBABY INSTITUTIONS.

It is conceived that very few, if any, of the provincial towns exceed Kendal, relatively, in literary institutions and literary exercises. Samuel Taylor Coleridge, and Thomas De Quincey, resided within a distance that gave them the opportunity of observing this characteristic of the Kendal people; and it is but fair to put their unquestionable testimony on record in this place. "I can add my attestation (says De Quincey) to that of Mr. Coleridge, that nowhere is there more elasticity and freshness of mind exhibited than in the conversation of reading men in manufacturing towns. *In Kendal, especially,* in Bridgewater, and in Manchester, I have witnessed more interesting conversations, as much information, and more natural eloquence in conveying it, than usually in literary cities, or in places professedly learned."

Several works, in science and literature, have proceeded from Kendal, or from authors connected with it (other than those alluded to in the subsequent

biographical sketches), but as we are unable to make a perfect catalogue, it is thought better to omit them. Our notices, under this head, must therefore be limited to the periodical publications and public societies.

It has been asserted that Kendal was one of the earliest places to issue a provincial weekly newspaper. The first newspaper published here was entitled "The Kendal Courant." It commenced on the 1st of January, 1731, and was printed by Thomas Cotton. In size it was a medium 'Autobiographic Sketches," Vol. II. p. 157. 4to, containing four pages, and bearing a *half-penny stamp.* The second newspaper was called "The Kendal Weekly Mercury." We are in possession of a copy, November 5, 1737, which is marked No. 149. This carries the date of its establishment back to January 4, 1734, and proves that "The Courant" had been but short-lived; for it can hardly be supposed that Kendal could at that time support two newspapers, even at a penny apiece; nor is it probable, indeed, that there were then two printing presses in the town. "The Weekly Mercury" was a post folio, with a halfpenny stamp. It was printed and published by Thomas Ashburner, in the Fish Market, who perhaps succeeded Cotton in business, and continued the newspaper, only changing the title when he took it into his possession. Before 1745 or 6, "The Mercury" seems to have been discontinued, and Mr. Ashburner instituted in its place a small pamphlet-like periodical, 8vo size, entitled "The Agreeable Miscellany, or something to please every man's taste." The series for 1749 of this publication contains a full account of the rebellion of 1745, and the passing of the rebels through Kendal. From that volume we obtained many of the particulars of this occurrence, described at p. 135.

In 1777, a sheet almanack, called the "Kendal Diary," was established by Mr. Ashburner, and was continued until the year 1836. It would perhaps be difficult to find a provincial almanack of greater antiquity than this.

The "Kendal Chronicle," a folio,

weekly newspaper, was established in 1811, the title of which was altered to "The Kendal Mercury" in May 1834. In 1818, another weekly paper was commenced, called "The Westmorland Gazette and Kendal Advertiser." These newspapers are both still continued. The " Lonsdale Magazine," a monthly publication, which had two years before been printed and published atKirkby-Lonsdale, was, in 1822, brought over to Kendal, by its talented editor and publisher, the late Mr. John Briggs, who was engaged to conduct "The Gazette" newspaper. But the patronage bestowed on this magazine was unequal to its merits; and after the short and sickly term of twelve months' existence, in Kendal, it was suffered to die for lack of support.

The oldest book society in the town is the " Kendal Book Club." It was instituted in 1761, and is, therefore, now in the centenary year of its existence. Connected with this society there are two feasts annually; the Venison Feast, which is held in September, and the Epiphany Dinner (which has not been held for two years). On the former occasion many of the influential gentlemen in the county, who are mostly members of this club, assemble, though of late years the interest that attached to it is somewhat abated. The Epiphany Dinner is eligible only to members residing in the town. *Librarian,* Mr. W. Fisher, Bookseller.

The " Kendal Library" was established in 1794, since which time it has gradually increased, till it is now computed to contain upwards of 5,000 volumes. *Librarian,* Miss Fisher.

In 1797, a library was instituted, called the "Economical Library," designed principally for the use and instruction of the working classes. The terms of this society were so extremely moderate, that the library never attained much usefulness. In January, 1825, an arrangement was made between the committee of the Mechanics' Institute and the remaining members of the Economical Library, that whatever books the latter contained, which were deemed eligible by the committee for the Mechanics' Library, should be added to it, and the members of the Economical Library were incorporated with the Mechanics' Institution.

NATURAL HISTORY AND SCIENTIFIC SOCIETY.

This Society was instituted in the year 1835. It originated in the conjoint efforts of Mr. Thomas Gough and Cornelius Nicholson, for the declared purpose of exploring and elucidating the Natural History and Antiquities of the County of Westmorland. There had been, fifteen years previously, an attempt made by a select number of literary men, to establish a Society for the objects above stated; but this was frustrated by the divisions consequent on the outbreak of party politics, in 1818. That circumstance, still fresh in the recollection of the inhabitants, hindered the first efforts of the projectors of this Society, and when they assembled, at the Commercial Inn, at NATURAL HISTORY AND SCIENTIFIC SOCIETY. 279 a preliminary meeting, convened by circular, they found the meeting to be comprised of three persons only—one gentleman besides the two projectors! The fact is here recorded, for the sake of encouraging enterprising persons, who may have natural obstacles to overcome in their incipient projects. A second attempt, after a personal canvass, brought together a few gentlemen, and, by dint of perseverance, the Society was established; Lord Brougham, Wordsworth, the poet, Southey, then poet-laureate, Professor (John) Wilson, Dr. Birkbeck, the originator of Mechanics' Institutes, Dr. Dalton, Professor Sedgwick, and other men eminent in science and literature, being ranked among the honorary members, within the first year of the Society's existence. The scheme comprised the reading of papers and discussions once a month; and the formation of a Museum. The discussion meetings began with spirit, in 1835, and have never flagged from that time to this. The Museum, starting with the nucleus of a few stuffed birds, and one or two relics of antiquity, has grown gradually, in objects of value, every succeeding year. The specimens of fossils, illustrating the palaeontology of the Cambrian, Siluri-

an, and Carboniferous rocks of the district, are most complete, being all carefully arranged in classes, orders, genera, and species, in accordance with modern zoological classification. In this particular, perhaps, the Museum stands above all other local collections. In the birds of the district, the Museum is also nearly complete. The Society's rooms, for meetings and the Museum, were originally in New Street, in a house that had been temporarily occupied as the "Bank of Westmorland;" from thence, outgrowing that accommodation, the Museum was removed to the old Roman Catholic chapel (contiguous to the existing chapel). Still increasing, and requiring more space, it was finally, (in 1854), transferred to the existing premises in Stricklandgate. Mrs. Harriman Walker, a most obliging and efficient keeper of the Museum, has held that appointment for twenty-four years. Professor Sedgwick, the permanent President, has greatly promoted the success of the Society, by occasional lectures and illustrations of the geology of the district, assisted by the labours of John Ruthven, a local geologist, who, like Hugh Miller, proves how a man may overcome the want of education, and render important services to science, by the bent of natural genius.

The Kendal Library (formerly an independent establishment), was united with the Scientific Society in the year 1854, when the Museum was removed to Stricklandgate, and the library is now kept in one of the rooms of this Society. Miss Fishek, as before stated, is the librarian.

THE MECHANICS' INSTITUTE.

The formation of Mechanics' Institutes, in the United Kingdom, originated with George Birkbeck, Esq., M.D., then living at Glasgow. He removed to London, about the year 1821, and the design there took root and germinated under the fostering hand of Henry Brougham, who gave to it life and energy. The Kendal Mechanics' Institute was one of the first, if not the very first, *provincial* Institution in England; and its origin was somewhat singular. A public meeting was called, by anonymous handbill, to

consider the formation of a "Co-operative Society," which was to retail meal and flour, and provide a news-room for the members. Curiosity brought together a considerable number of persons, the meeting being held in one of the upper rooms of the White Lion Inn, where William Hudson, the botanist, was born, of which house we have given an engraving. (See ante, p. 126.) The scheme of the Co-operative Society was propounded with laboured detail by its projector, but it was coldly received by the meeting, and the opportunity was seized, by one present, of proposing instead a Mechanics' Institute, and that proposal was hailed with approval. This was in March, 1824. A committee was then and there named; the most active gentlemen of the town, in favour of educational institutions, Mr. Marshall, Mr. John Thomson, Mr. Edward W. Wakefield, and others, soon joined the promoters, and the Institution has proved itself to be eminently successful, and useful.

Lectures are given on subjects connected with literature and science, which are generally well attended; and classes, of young men, for instruction in various branches of knowledge, are held in the evenings.

The present number of reading members is 150. And the number of volumes in the library is 1,800.

President—James Cropper, Esq. *Secretary*—Mr. Jones Taylor WORKING MEN'S READING ASSOCIATION.

Tins Society was established in 1841; but was remodelled, and placed under its present constitution, in the year 1844. It unites the advantages of a library with that of a newsroom. Its annual income and expenditure is about 80?. At the last general meeting, the number of members was declared to be 357; and the number of books in the library 1,524 volumes. The taste for reading is found to be more in the departments of science, history, and travels, than in works of fiction. The subscription for ordinary members is only *6d.* per quarter, or one halfpenny per week! Long may it flourish. Mr. William Longmire is the present Secretary.

CHRISTIAN AND LITERARY INSTITUTE.

This Institution was founded in 1852. It has some points of resemblance with the Mechanics' Institute and the Working Men's Reading Society, and yet differs from these in a distinctive quality. As its title imports, it is "Christian" as well as "Literary." It seeks to disseminate religious truths, based on the revealed Word of God. The library is selected with consistent reference to this principle; and the lectures delivered before the members, generally by men of position and influence, are characterised by a high moral and religious tone. The committee of management are, for the most part, young men, who themselves minister to, and are benefited by the Institution, which, like mercy, thus blesses "them that give and those who take." Young men, under twenty-one years of age, are admitted to all the privileges of the Institute at *two shillings per annum.* The income of last year was 103?. 16s. 7d. The library contains upwards of 800 volumes.

Honorary Secretaries:—Mr. Charles Ireland and Mr. Robert Webster PEERAGE TITLES.

The title of *Baron of Kendal* was enjoyed by the Barons, in succession, from Ivo de Talebois, in the time of the Conqueror, to William Parr, Marquis of Northampton, in the reign of Henry VIII. There have been four *Earls of Kendal,* a *Duke of Kendal,* and a *Duchess of Kendal.* The title of Earl of Kendal was conferred on John de Lancaster, Duke of Bedford, by King Henry IV. (1414); on John Beaufort, Duke of Somerset, by King Henry VI.; on John de Foix, of France, by Henry VI.; and on George, Prince of Denmark, husband of Queen Anne, who had the Earldom of Kendal, along with other honours, conferred on him in 1689. Charles Stuart, third son of James II., was, in 1664, entitled Duke of Kendal Erengard Melusina Schuylenberg, who came over to England with George I., was created Duchess of Kendal This lady was tall, and lean of stature, and hence was irreverently nicknamed "the Maypole." She was lean, also, in another sense, for at her departure from Germany, she could hardly escape from her own country on account of her debts. But she repaired her fortunes in England; and after her death, at Twickenham, "all her jewels, her plate, her plunder, went over to her relations in Hanover." Finally, the old title of "Baron of Kendal" was given to the Earl of Lonsdale, in May, 1784.

There was to have been another creation of Duke of Kendal in the present generation, but it miscarried. The It is only a few weeks since the world heard of the decease of the last descendant of the *TaUbou,* the ancient barons of Kendal. The last of that old house was a young girl, Emily Tailbois, who, at the age of eighteen, died a casual pauper in the workhouse at Shrewsbury I—*Sic tranrit gloria, dec,* (From " Ups and Downs in the House of Peers j" in the *Comhill Magazine* for May, 1861.)

Prince Regent (George IV.) made a promise to Prince Leopold (afterwards King of Belgium), that, on his (Leopold's) marriage with the Princess Charlotte, he should be Duke of Kendal The wedding was once or twice postponed, by the caprice of the Regent; and though the marriage was eventually celebrated, the dukedom was abandoned. On these occurrences, Peter Pindar wrote a lampoon, of which the following lines are part:

"Though wedding days have twice been named,
Yet how can the poor Prince be blamed?
And tho' our Regent, great, to end all,
Declares he shall be Duke of K L"
Thackeray's " Four Georges." CHAPTER X.

A CHRONOLOGICAL TABLE

Of the Chief Magistrates of the Borough of Kendal, from its first incorporation, in 1575, and of the most remarkable events, chiefly in the town and neighbourhood. attmnni:

A.D.

1575-1576 Henry Wilson, of Blackball, Strieklandgate. nominated first Alderman of Kendal, by the Charter of Incorporation, granted to this Borough by Queen Elizabeth, dated November 28, 1575.

Robert Briggs, Esq., nominated Recorder. 1575; Thomas Braith waite, Esq., of Ambleside, elected Recorder, 1576. The first meeting of the Corporation was held January 8th, 1576.

1576-1577 Henry Fisher. 1577-1578 Myles Fox. 1578-1579 Robert Jopaon. 1579-1580 Christopher Bindloss. A dealer in Kendal cottons, afterwards knighted. 1580-1581 Myles Bracken. 1581-1582 j E Swainson. Died during his Officiate. (Edward Potter, elected for the remainder of the year. 1582-1583 Henry Dixon. A great dearth; oatmeal sold for 21 per Win chester bushel. 1583-1584 William Wilson. The boundaries and privileges of the Corpora tion ascertained by a jury of inquiry. 1581-1585 Thomas Potter. 1585-1586 John Armer. 1586-1587 Anthony Pearson. Oatmeal sold for 16. a bushel. 1537-1588 James Wilson. 1588-1589 Henry Fleming. 1589-1590 Edward Wilkinson. 1590-1591 Roger Dawson. 1591-1592 William Swainson. Hoot Hall built. Free Grammar School built by subscription. Ravlph Tirer, RD., inducted Vicar, in the place of the Rev. Samuel Heron, resigned. First published to the year 1724, by Robert Wharton, and continued to the year 1802, by William Pennington. From thence, to 1823, by Mr. John Taylor. (The whole subsequently revised and corrected.)

A. D.

1592-1593 John Thwaites. 1593-1594 William Wilson (second time). 1594-1595 John Smith. 1595-1596 Edward Potter (second time). 1596-151)7 Henry Dixon (second time). Died during his Officiate i John Armer (second time). Died during his Officiate. 'James Wilson elected for the remainder of the year. The plague began in this town about Whitsuntide, and there died in June, in Kendal, 2,500—in Penrith, 2,260—Carlisle, 1,196—Richmond, 2,200. 1598 1599 Edward Wilkinson (second time). 1599-1600 Roger Dawson (second time). 1600-1601 John Thwaites (second time). July 1st, 1601, Heversham Church

"utterly consumed with fire, and all implements, ornaments, books, monuments, chests, organs, bells, and all other things were perished.... fortuned through negligence of a careless work-

man, being a plumber." 1601-1602 John Smith (second time).
1602-1603 Robert Wilkinson. King James I. began his reign, March 24. 1603-1604 Francis Gibson. Gunpowder Plot, November 5th. 1604-1605 Richard Seile. 1605-1606 Nicholas Rowlandson. 1606-1607 James Dixon. 1607-1608 George Fleming. Hard frost from November 3rd, 1607, to March 6th, 1608.

Michael Rowlandson. Died during his Officiate.
Edward Wilkinson (third time), elected fur the remainder of the year.
1609-1610 Thomas Wilson. William Garnett, Esq., elected Recorder, August 21st, 1610.
1610-1611 Thomas Green. 1611-1612 Edward Fisher. A great drought from May 1st to August 8th, 1612. 1612-1613 John Smith (third time). 1613-1614 Edward Wilkinson (fourth time). Speed2s Topography of Kendal, published. 1614-1615 Thomas Wilson. 1615-1616 James Dixon (second time). August 3rd, 1616, Sir Augustine

Nicolls died at Kendal.
1616-1617 John Robinson. King James L, on his progress from Scotland,

August 3th, lodged in a house in Stricklandgate, called Brownsword House. He had been entertained for three days at Brougham Castle on this journey. 1617-1618 Thomas Sleddall.
1618-1619 Richard Pearson. A dear year, being the first of three. 1619-1620 Stephen Newby. Oatmeal 21a. per Winchester bushel. 1620-1621 Rowland Dawson. Oatmeal 18». per Winchester bushel. 1608-1609 The only animal ever known to *return to Scotland,* from England, was a cow, that broke through the "debatable land," to and fro, in the time of this King James, who, being a wit, observed that "she was a brute, and knew no A. D. 1621-1622 Walter Becke. A Wednesday market begun. 1622-1623 Michael Gibson. 1623-1624 William Banke. 1624-1625 James Cocke. King Charles I. began his reign, March 27, 1625. 1625-1626 James Dixon. 1626-1627 Henry Parke. The Rev. Francis Gardener, B.D. inducted Vicar. 1627-1628 James Rowlandson.

1628-1629 Lawrence Parke. 1629-1630 Robert Crosfeild. 1630-1631 Edward Fisher (second time). 1631-1632 James Bateman. 1632-1633 Richard Forth. 1633-1634 William Guy, of Watercrook. 1634-1635 Thomas Sleddall (second time). October 18th, 1635, the river

Kent rose into the vestry. On the following day, Thomas Miller, boatman, drowned in Windermere, together with forty8 seven men and women, and nine or ten horses, having been at a wedding. 1635-1636 Rowland Dawson (second time). Sir John Lowther, Baronet, no minated Recorder by the new Charter, dated February 4,1635-6. 1636-1637 Thomas Sleddall, nominated by the Charter in these terms: "Our welbeloved Thomas Sleddall gent, to be y first and moderne Maior of y" Borough of KendaL" 1637-1638 Walter Becke. 1638-1639 Edward Fisher. 1639-1640 William Banke. The Rev. Henry Hall, B. D. inducted Vicar. 1640-1641 Rowland Dawson. October 23, 1641, the Irish rebellion. 1641-1642 Lawrence Parke. 1642-1643 Robert Crosfeild. 1643-1644 William Guy. 1644-1645 Gervas Benson. 1645-1646 Richard Prissoe. 1646-1647 Allan Gilpin. 1647-1648 Thomas Sandes. Thomas Braithwaite, Esq., of Ambleside, sworn

Recorder, March 80, 1648.
1648-1649 John Archer. King Charles I. beheaded. Sir M. Longdate marched with Kendal men out of the Miller's Close, to besiege Appleby Castle. 1649-1650 Giles Redman. 1650-1651 Anthony Preston. Test Act passed, by which Dissenters were precluded from municipal appointments. 1651-1652 John Towers. 1652-1653 Edward Turner. 1663-1664 James Cocke, late of Birckhagg. 1654-1555 William Jennings. 1655-1656 Robert Jackson. The Rev. John Strickland inducted Vicar. 1656-1657 Thomas Fisher.

A. D.
1657-1658 John Washington. The Rev. W. Brownsword inducted Vicar. 1658-1659 George Archer. Sandea'a Hospital, School-room and Library built. 1659-1660 William Potter. King Charles II. restored, May 29. 1660-1661

Richard Towers. 1661-1662 Thomas Jackson. Hard frost from Nov. 1st, 1661, to March 8th, 1662, during which time it was common to draw timber upon the ice over Windermere water. A market was kept on the Thames. 1662-1663 William Guy (second time). 1663-1664 John Parke. 1664-1665 Edward Turner. 100,000 persons died of the Plague in London. 1665-1666 John Beeke. May 29th, Mayor and Inhabitants rode the boundaries. 1666-1667 Thomas Turner. 1667-1668 John Towers. 1668-1669 Thomas Jennings. The Mill bridge built with stone pillars, the old wooden one having been carried down by a flood. 1669-1670 Thomas Fisher. Hospital, in Highgate, and School, endowed by
Thomas Sandes.
1670-1671 James Simpson. 1671-1672 William Potter. 1672-1673 Stephen Birkett. The Rev. Michael Stanford inducted Vicar.

Alan Prickett, Ksq., of Natland Hall, elected Recorder. September 11, the river Kent swept over the wall of the churchyard, where it left behind it much fish.
1673-1674 William Collinson. 1674-1675 James Troughton. 1675-1676 John Jefferson. 1676-1677 Robert Kilner. 1677-1678 William Guy (third time). Thomas Lamplugh, Esq., elected Re. corder. 1678-1679 Thomas Jackson. 1679-1680 Christopher Redman. A comet appeared, whioh caused great con sternation. 1680-1681 Thomas Turner (second time). 1681-1682 James Cocke, jun. 1682-1683 James Simpson (second time). The Rev. Thomas Murgatroyd inducted Vicar. 1683-1684 Robert Hutton. 1684-1685 Launcelot Forth. Nominated Mayor by the new Charter, which was ushered into the town with great ceremony, December 26, 1684. Thomas Dalston, Esq., nominated Recorder. King James II. began his reign, February 6, 1685. 1685-1686 Richard Washington. 1686-1687 John Ingeraon. 1687-1688 Thomas Towers. The Prince of Orange landed November 4, and the Revolution was effected on the day following. The *Potae Comitatut* assembled in Miller's Close, in this

town, from whence they marched to Kirkby Lonsdale. Friends' Meeting-house built in Stramongate. After the abdication of James II. in the year 1688, a rumour was spread in the north of England, that the abdicated monarch was laying off the York 1695-1696 A. D.

1688-1689 William Wilson. King William and Queen Mary began their reign, February 13th, 1689. 1689-1690 John Garnett. 1690-1691 Giles Redman. Roger Moore, Esq., elected Recorder. 1691-1692 Joseph Symson. 1692-1693 William Cocke. The boundaries ridden, February 28, 1693. 1693-1694 Edward Fairbank. 1694-1695 William Brownsword. Alan Chambre, Esq., elected Recorder. A late harvest; corn to shear on the 18th of October, i Christopher Redman) The Mayor, two Aldermen, and one bur! Robert Kilner. $ gess having refused to sign the Association, at the Midsummer Sessions, according to a late Act of Parliament, were discharged from their offices, and Robert Kilner was elected Mayor for the remainder of the year. 1696-1697 William Curwen. 1697-1698 Jonathan Thompson. 1698-1699 Richard Lowry. The Rev. William Crosby, M A. inducted Vicar. 1699 1700 i omas Middleton; died during his Mayoralty.

I William Wilson (second time); elected for the remainder of the year. Tan-yards made in the fields adjoining the Vicarage.

John Harrison, Esq., elected Recorder, on the resignation of

Alan Chambre.

1700-1701 Henry Cort.

1701-1702 Joseph Dawson. A new organ ereoted in the church, built by

"Father Smith," and a gallery built expressly for the same nt the west end of the church. Queen Anne began her reign, March 8, 1702.

1702-1703 Thomas Bowes. 1703-1704 Robert Wilson. 1704-1705 John Hadwen. 1705-1706 Thomas Holme. 1706-1707 John Archer, M.D., of Oxenholme. The Union with Scotland. 1707-1708 Robert Kilner (second time.) 1708-1709 Launcelot Forth (second time). 1709-1710 Joseph Symson (sec-

ond time). 1710-1711 William Cocke (second time). The great bell in the church re cast. shire coast, ready to make a descent with a numerous army from France, in hopes of regaining his lost throne. This report gave the Lord Lieutenant of Westmorland an opportunity of showing his own and the people's attachment to the new order of things. He accordingly called out the *Pome Comitatut* comprising all able-bodied men from sixteen to sixty. The order was obeyed with alacrity; and the inhabitants met armed in a field called Miller's Close, near Kendal from whence they marched to Kirkby Lonsdale. This historical fact explains the following popular rhyme, the meaning of which is, at this day, not generally understood:

"Eighty-eight was Kerby feight, When nivver a man was slain;

They yatt their meatt, an' drank their drink,

And sae kom merrily haem again."

A. D.

1711-1712 William Wilson. 1712-1713 Richard Lowry (second time). 1713-1711 Henry Cort (second time). The Blue-coat school commenced by subscription, and the boys clothed in "blew. " King George I began his reign, August 1, 1714. 1714-1715 Joseph Dawson (second time). Alan Chambre, Esq., elected

Recorder second time. About 1600 Scotch rebels lodged one night in this town on their march southward. Boundaries ridden, March 22, 1714-15. 1715-1716 Thomas Rowlandsou. May 9, peace with France proclaimed in Kendal.

1716-1717 Thomas Bowes (second time). 1717-1718 John Strickland. 1718-1719 William Herbert. 1719-1720 Thomas Winter. Unitarian chapel built. 1720-1721 Edward Whitehead. 1721-1722 John Hadwen (second time). 1722-1723 Thomas Holme. In this and the two following years the church was new glazed with large square crown glass, and the best of the old painted glass carefully preserved. 1723-1724 Bryan Philipson. 1724-1725 Thomas Scarisbrick. November 5,1724, Robert

Wharton's sheet list of Aldermen and Mayors, &c, published at Manchester, by Roger Adams; price, upon Royal paper, *6d.,* upon common, *id.* per sheet. 1725-1726 Giles Redman. 1726-1727 John Dodgson. King George II. began his reign, June 11, 1727.

The Corporation made an attempt to obtain an Act of Parliament to have "coles imported duty free at Milthrop." 1727-1728 William Hutton.

1728-1729 Simon Moore. 1729-1730 Thomas Scarisbrick (second time). Till this year potatoes were very sparingly used in Kendal. 1730-1731 William Symson. January 1, 1731, the first newspaper published in Kendal—called "The Kendal Courant." 1731-1732 John Miller. The boundaries ridden. 1732-1733 John Fairbank. 1733-1734 Edmund Foster. The Rev. Richard Cuthbert, M.A., inducted

Vicar. January 4, 1734, "The Kendal Weekly Mercury" commenced by Thomas Ashburner.

1734-1735 Christopher Brown. 1735-1736 James Baxter. 1736 1737 I '' Holme; died in his mayoralty.

I Richard Lowry; elected for the remainder of the year. 1737-1738 William Mackreth. Walter Chambre, Esq., elected Recorder, on the resignation of his father. Common Garden commenced in Kendal, 1738 1739 (Shaw. Died in his mayoralty.

I John Hadwen, elected for the remainder of the year.

1739-1740 James Fisher. A hard frost began in December, and continued for thirteen weeks. The fire-engines purchased. 1740-1741 Joseph Birkett.

U

A. D.

1741-1742 Thomas Holme. 1742-1743 John Waide. The Mill Bridge built all of stone. 1743-1744 John Hadwen, Jun. 1744-1745 Jonathan Wilson. The Rev. Thomas Symonds, M.A, inducted Vicar. 1745-1746 John Shaw. About 6,000 Scotch rebels passed through the town,

November 22d, and three following days.

1746-1747 John Braithwaite. 1747-1748 Francis Drinkell. 1748-1749 Edmund Foster (second time). May 13, 1749, the first number of a small magazine, culled the "Agreeable Miscellany," published in this town, by Thomas Ashburner. 1749-1750 Christopher Redman. 1750-1751 Richard Serjeantson. Engines for pricking the leather of wool cards, invented by W. Pennington (see card-making, p. 245). 1751-1752 Robert Rutson. Richard Crowle, Esq., elected Recorder. The

Acts of Parliament passed for turnpike roads from Kendal to Keighley, and from Heronsyke to Eamont-bridge, being the first to or from this town. 1752-1753 William Gurnal. 1753-1754 James Godmond. The first post-chaise kept for hire in this town. 1754-1755 Thomas Kenady. June 24, 1755, St. George's Chapel consecrated by Bishop Keene. 1755-1756 Thomas Holme (second time). Brewery, in Wildman Street, established. 1756-1757 Wilson John Robinson. Roger Wilson, Esq., elected Recorder.

The first stage-wagons from London, in the place of pack-horses. A new oak pulpit and reading desk erected in the Parish Church, in the Roman Doric style. 1757-1758 John Hadwen (second time). 1758-1759 John Shaw (second time). The Town-hall rebuilt. March 26, 1759, the boundaries ridden. Kendal Guild, June 4, and two following days; exceeding any former one in splendour. Abbot Hall built. A snow shower fell in this town, June 4, 1759. 1759-1760 Francis Drinkell (second time). 1760-1761 Christopher Redman. King George III. began his reign, October 25,1760. 1761-1762 Christopher Redman re-elected. The Book-club established. 1762-1763 Richard Fell. The first stage-ooach from London to this town, drawn by six homes, called the " Flying Machine." 1763-1764 Thomas Wilson. Act of Parliament obtained for the Court of Requests, and the first meeting of the Commissioners held, May 3, 1764. 1764-1765 Thomas Strickland. 1765-1766 William Gurnal (second time). Thomas Fenwick, Esq., elected Recorder.
1766-1767 James Godmond (second

time). Act of Parliament obtained for enclosing Kendal-fell Lands, Sec, and the Trustees elected July 1, 1767. The greatest snow-storm ever known; no carriers arrived in the town for a fortnight or three weeks. 1767-1768 Thomas Kenady (second time). Kendal first lighted with oil lamps,
Norman Newby, Robert Tailford, and William Stidman were the
A. D.
first lamp-lighters. The new Workhouse built on the "Waste, near the House of Correction." Mr. Kichard Tedder, the architect, received two guineas for his plans and model. 176S-1769 Christopher Fenton. Oatmeal first sold by the stone in Kendal market. Gunpowder works erected at Sedgwick, by John Wakefield, Esq. 1769-1770 John Hadwen (third time). 1770-1771 William Baxter. 1771-1772 Thomas Scarisbrick. Nether-bridge enlarged. 1772-1773 William Rutsou. The Society of Builders instituted March 1, 1773. being the first benefit society in Kendal. 1773-1771 Thomas Strickland (second time). The bells of the parish church recast, from a peal of six to eight. 1774-1775 Christopher Fenton (second time). 1775-1776 Francis Drinkell (third time). An additional wing to the work house built. 1776-1777 Thomas Miller. Myles Harrison, Esq.,elected Recorder. "The
Kendal Diary," a sheet almanack, first published by James Ashburner. Theatre built in Woolpack yard: the previous theatre was on the north side of the market place. The Friends' schoolhouse built.
1777-1778 Jackson Harrison. 1778-1779 William Baxter. The News-room opened. 1779-1780 Thomas Scarisbrick (second time). 1780-1781 Thomas Miller (second time). 1781-1782 Christopher Fenton (third time). The Dispensary established by subscription. The river the highest ever known, June 15, 1782. Lowther-street built. The May-pole, which stood in Kirkland, removed about this time. 1782-1783 William Petty. Corn to reap at Martinmas. 1783-1784 Robert Harrison. The Wesleyan Methodists first introduced into

Kendal.
1784-1785 Thomas Gaudy. Church Sunday-schools established in Kendal.

Umbrellas first seen in the town about this time; they were made of oil-cloth, and had long sticks to walk withal.
1785-1786 David Jackson. The House of Correction built. The first mail coach from London. Shock of an earthquake felt in Kendal in August, 1786. 1786-1787 William Pennington. John Todd's Plan of Kendal, from actual survey, published. The boundaries ridden, April 10, 1787. 1787-1788 Jonathan Dawson. The Obelisk, in memory of the Revolution in 1688, built on Castlehow-hill. Kendal fell stone first polished as marble, and made into chimney-pieces. The two Banks opened. Destructive fire on the west side of Stricklandgate, caused by an explosion of gunpowder, July 11, 1788. 1788-1789 Joseph Swainson. The Rev. Henry Robinson, M.A., inducted

Vicar. The Blue-coat girls' school begun. Independents' Sunday-school commenced in Kendal.
1789-1790 Batty Hodgson. Kendal fell lands planted this year. 1790-1791 Thomas Dobson. Bull-baiting suppressed in Kendal by the
Corporation.
A. D.
1791-1792 Richard Braithwaite. The Act of Parliament obtained for making the Lancaster canal. (William Petty (second time) died in his mayoralty.
Christopher Fenton (fourth time) elected for the remainder of the year.
1793-1794 John Suart. Stramongate bridge enlarged and greatly improved. 1794-1795 William Baxter. The Lying-in charity begun. The Kendal Library established November. 1795-1796 William Berry. October, 1796, The Museum opened at the corner of the Fish Market, by Mr. William Todhunter, and continued till 1832. 1796-1797 Jackson Harrison (second time). Richard Howard, Esq., elected
Recorder. The Lancaster canal opened from Tewitfield to
Preston. Richard Howard, Esq. elected Recorder.
1797-1798 Robert Harrison (second

time). Thirty persons were interred this year in Kendal church, whose united ages amounted to 2,520 years, averaging 84 each; the frost penetrated so far into the ground as to render it impracticable to dig graves in the churchyard.
1798-1799 Christopher Wilson. The Schools of Industry established. No vegetation in the fields, nor blossoms upon the fruit trees, on the 7th of May, 1799. The skins of upwards of 10,000 lambs, which perished in the spring, were sold in this town. The weather was cold and wet all through the year. August 24, 1799, Kendal Agricultural Society instituted. 1799-1800 Thomas Holme Maude. The last of the Free Companies of

Kendal (the Cordwainers) broken up. Oatmeal sold for 8j. a stone of sixteen pounds. From 1800 to 1806 the main timbers of the Parish Church underwent thorough repair, and Divine service was suspended several weeks. July 10, a faculty was granted to the Mayor, Recorder, &c, for erecting galleries in Kendal Church, the expense of which was 193?. 6«. 3rf.
1800-1801 William Briggs, M.D. Provisions continued at extremely high prices till after the harvest, which was most abundant. At Michaelmas, oatmeal fell to It. Zd. a stone. Union with Ireland, January 1, 1801. 1801-1802 William Briggs, M.D., re-elected. The boundaries ridden on the 12th April, and again on the 20th July, 1802, by William Briggs, Esq., Mayor. (The reason of the boundaries being ridden twice this year was in consequence of a mistake having been made on the first occasion.) 1802-1803 Thomas Hurd. The New Biggin sold by auction, in lots, on May 30, 1803, and taken down immediately afterwards. A corps of volunteers raised. 1803-1804 William Pennington (second time). The Butchers' Shambles opened in the market-place. The Society of "Glassites" introduced into Kendal; now (1861) extinct. 1804-1805 Joseph Swainson (second time). The organ in the Parish Church repaired and enlarged. 1805-1806 Thomas Harrison. Castle Mills built for the manufacture of woollens, by William Braithwaite and

Son, and Isaac and William Wilson. Low-mills built by John and Thomas Ireland. The Rev. Matthew Murfitt, M.A., inducted Vicar.
1806-1807 Smith Wilson.
1807-1808 John Suart (second time). The Methodist Chapel finished, October 1, 1808, and opened in the same month.
1808-1809 Jonathan Hodgson. Thunderstorm, 26th July, 1809, which continued from 10 a.m. till 6 p.m., accompanied with torrents of rain and awful darkness. October 25, grand national jubilee; his majesty George III. having this day entered on the fiftieth year of his reign. 1809-1810 John Pearson. January 15, 1810, Kendal Auxiliary Bible Society instituted. Workhouse established in Kirkland.
1810-1811 Henry Bradshaw. Riot in the streets between the country and townspeople, and a portion of the 55th Regiment of Foot, on WhitMonday, June 3d, 1811. The "Westmorland Advertiser and Kendal Chronicle" first published on Saturday, June 29. 1811-1812 Thomas Dobson (second time). Gibson's-place in Stramongate, built by Mr. Edward Gibson (builder). April, 1812, "Mint's feet" surveyed, and divided amongst the several proprietors, by virtue of a late Act of Parliament. 1812-1813 William Berry (second time). The Green-coat Sunday school en dowed by Mr. William Sleddall, whodied July 25,1813, at the age of 92. The manufacture of carpets introduced into this town by Mr. Rowland Cookson. The Church Missionary Society established in Kendal. 1813-1814. Thomas Holme Maude (second time). Society for Promoting Christianity among the Jews established. A hard frost from Christmas Day, 1813, till the beginning of March, 1814, which penetrated upwards of eighteen inches into the churchyard, and caused great mortality amongst old people. May 17, 1814, a grand festival, consisting of a procession of the Corporation and Trades, and a general illumination, concluding with a ball on the following evening, in celebration of Peace. The potatomarket removed from the Market-place into Stramongate, to make

room for the oat-market, which was brought from the front of the Globe Inn into the Market-place. The Markethouse was appropriated for wheat.
1814-1815 Thomas Atkinson. The Rev. John Hudson, M.A., inducted Vicar.
1815-1816 Thomas Harrison (second time). October 17,18, 19, and 20, 1815, grand musical festival held in the parish church. January 1, 1816, Bank for Savings established. January 15, Mark Thornton whipped through the town for begging and using abusive language. The Friends' Meeting House rebuilt on the site of the former Meeting House. Society for Promoting Christian Knowledge established in Kendal. Wesleyan Methodist Sundayschool established.
1816-1817 Smith Wilson (second time). Four chests of new coinage arrived in Kendal for the use of the town and neighbourhood, January 29th, 1817. Dockray-hall Mills built by James Gandy 'and Sons, for the woollen and drysalting businesses; F. Webster, architect. September 3, 1817, an association of tradesmen formed to patrol the streets. October 22, a destructive fire on the west side of Highgate, at the shop occupied by Mr. Dent (draper), the property of Mr. Alderman Berry: damages estimated at 2,000J. Sunday morning, November 9, the shock of an earthquake felt in Kendal, this being the fifth or sixth shock here since June, 1668. December 16, foundation stone of the Boys' National School laid by Rev. John Hudson (Vicar). 1817-1818 Jonathan Hodgson (second time). February 11, 1818, serious riot in Highgate on the arrival of Lord and Colonel Lowther to canvass for the forthcoming county election, in opposition to Henry (now Lord) Brougham. May 20, foundation stone of the Mill Bridge laid by the Mayor; Alderman F. Webster was the architect of this bridge, which cost 888?., two former ones had each stood seventy-five years. May 23, "The Westmorland Gazette and Kendal Advertiser" first published. Kentlane widened by subscription. August 27, the bridge over the Castle Mills dam finished. December 7, 1818, Fletcher Raincook, Esq., of Liverpool, elected Recorder. 1818-1819

John Pearson (second time). February 22, 1819, Kendal Union

Building Society established. The canal warehouse, basin, and wharfs, built by the Corporation. Juno 18, the canal opened from Towitfield to Kendal, by one of the most splendid aquatic processions ever witnessed in the north of England; two sailing packets for passengers, drawn by horses, were subsequently placed upon the canal, which went at the rate of four miles an hour. August 11, National School for boys opened. October 21, County Meeting held in Stricklandgate, at which it was estimated 4,000 persons were present, occasioned by the "Peterloo massacre. " 1819-1820 Joseph Braithwaite. February 17, King George IV. proclaimed in Kendal with a procession, on which occasion the poor inhabitants of the age of 70 and upwards, had half-a-crown each given them by the Corporation; 118 men and 198 women (four of whom were 90 and upwards) received the half-crown. September 12, 13, and 14, Kendal Races revived, in a field near Burneside, after a lapse of thirty years, having previously been held on the "heights" of Kendal-fell. November 20 and 21, illuminations in Kendal in honour of Queen Caroline (wife of George IV.) November 21, Tradesmen's News Room in the market-place opened. Caroline-street, Union-street, Cross-street, and Strickland-place built. Sooiety of Odd Fellows established in Kendal. Shaw's Brow built, by Mr. Thomas Shaw, Senior.
1820-1821 John Harrison. April 3, boundaries ridden, and the boundaries marked by mere stones (placed August 24, 1821) on the new enclosures on Hay-fell. April 24, severe thunderstorm, which in 2extent and duration surpassed the memorable one of July 26,1809. July 19, the coronation of King George IV. celebrated. New race-course on Fisher's Plain opened, August 7. A regiment of Yeomanry Cavalry raised in this county, Kendal supplying one troop. Provisions reasonable, oatmeal 2s. and flour 3. per etone. 1821-1822 I i' Hunter; died in his mayoralty. i Robert Harrison (third time); elected for the remainder of

the year. A most abundant year; wheat 39s. and oats 16». per quarter—oatmeal Is. I0d,, and flour 2«. per stone of 161b. —beef 34?., and mutton 3d. per lb.— potatoes Id. per stone of 141bs. The churchyard inclosed with iron palisades by subscription. Ladies' Bible Association established. 1822-1823 William Pennington. October, 1822, Edward Tatham, Esq., ap pointed Deputy Recorder, vacant by the death of John Barrow, Esq. November 4, 1822, Kendal Samaritan Society (Wesleyan) established. The Primitive Methodists, or Ranters, introduced into Kendal, preaching in the open air for about twelve months. Ordination in Kendal Church, by the Bishop of the Diocese, of 11 Priests and 8 Deacons. Blindbeck bridge rebuilt. Twelve stage-coaches leave the town daily; the first commenced in 1763. Primitive Methodists' chapel in Castle-street built and optned. 1823-1824 Francis Webster. November, 1823, the Theatre in Wool-pack yard converted into a place of worship. April 12,1824, the Wesleyan Missionary Society organised. April 14, Dockray-hall Mills, belonging to Messrs. James Qandy and Sons, destroyed by fire; the most destructive that ever occurred in this neighbourhood; nearly 700 packs of wool were destroyed, besides the whole of the valuable machinery, which had but recently been erected; the total loss was estimated at from 15,0001. to 20,000/. The mill was rebuilt, fireproof, and the works were again in full operation by the end of the 6year. April 19, Kendal Mechanics' and Apprentices' Library and Institute formally established at a meeting in the Moot-hall, Edward Tatham, Esq. (Deputy Recorder), in the chair; Samuel Marshall, Esq., appointed President. June 21, Church Missionary Society organized. September 13, Girls' National School opened. New chapel for the "Glasaites" built in the Windmill-yard. This society was dissolved a few years ago (1861), and the chapel sold. The first steam-engine erected in Kendal by Mr. Alderman Berry, for cutting ivory combs. Rydal Chapel opened. 1824-1825 Michael Branthwaite. October 24,

1824, the organ in the parish church underwent thorough repair and enlargement by Bewsher and Fleetwood, of Liverpool. From January to March, 1825, a great mortality in this town, 54 males and 77 females (chiefly children) having been buried in the churchyard within three months. April 1, Sprint Mill (near Burneside), belonging to Messrs. James Gandy and Sons, destroyed by fire. July 1, the foundation-stone of the White-hall Buildings laid by the Mayor on the site of " Leaden-hall," (Leather-hall, originally, no doubt) at the head of Lowther-street. One of each of the Kendal newspapere, a fac simile of the corporation seal, printed on satin, with a memorandum of the date of this celebration, and the name of the architect (Francis Webster, alderman), were inclosed in glass and deposited beneath the stone. Helm Lodge, the residence of William Dillworth Crewdson, Esq., erected, F. Webster, architect. July 18 and 19, extreme heat; on the former day the thermometer rose to 836 Fahr. in the shade, and on the latter to 85; haymakers were obliged to retreat from the burning sun; one old man died in a field from a coup de aoleil, and three horses in one of the coaches died in the road between Kendal and Lancaster. Gas-works built, and the town of Kendal first lighted with gas, July 25; the event was celebrated by a public procession and spirited acts of rejoicing. Natland chapel rebuilt. August 9, the Right Hon. George Canning passed through Kendal on his way to Storrs-hall, the seat of John Bolton, Esq. , on which occasion the distinguished statesman was met at the King's Arms by the Mayor and Corporation, and partook with them of a hospitable entertainment. August 16, Messrs. G. and W. Green ascended in their balloon from an enclosed area contiguous to the Gasworks, amidst a vast concourse of spectators. August 30, Mr. George Green made another ascent from the same place, accompanied by Miss Dawson, and descended at the foot of Murtonpikc, twenty-nine miles from Kendal. Cattle-market removed from Highgate to the New-road. Scotch Seceders' Sundayschools established. Low-mills re-built. 1825-1826 George Forrest. November, 1825, the Independent chapel in Lowther-street lighted with gas. November 14, Kendal new Union Building Society established (dissolved November 19, 1827). December, a great run on the metropolitan and provincial Banks, many of which were obliged to suspend payment. It was called the "pa-per panic," and caused great distress in the manufacturing districts. The banks at Kendal stood the issue of the pressure amidst unshaken confidence. March 15, 1826, a meeting held in the Town-hall to devise means for the relief of those out of employment in the township of Kendal, when 141?. was collected, and the amount distributed in meal and pota-toes. The Rev. J. Hudson, vicar, re-moved the tanyards near the vicarage, built a neat lodge, and adorned the grounds. July 29, wheat and oats sold in the market (Saturday), proof of an early harvest. August 6 (Sunday), the new chapel at Burneside, built by sub-scription, opened. A drought prevailed in the months of June and July this year, which had no parallel since 1762.

1826-1827 John Moffett. October 5, 1826, Mail coach between Kendal and Whitehaven, *via* Ambleside and Keswick. November, 1826, Lowther-street and Stricklandgate first macadamized. January 14, 1827, Joseph Garnett, clerk of the parish church, died, aged 78, having fulfilled the duties of that office for the lengthened period of forty-five years. A most abundant year for fruit; apples *2d.* per pannier of six-teen quarts.

1827-1828 Joseph Snainson. October 4, 1827, died Robert Harrison, Esq., senior Alderman and Magistrate, at the ad-vanced age of eightyeight. He had served as a member of the Corporation fifty-two years, and as a magistrate twenty-two years. December 31, 1827, the Whitehall assembly-room opened with a splendid ball. February 14, 1828, severe snowstorm in Kendal, lasting from about 6 A. M. to 5 p. M. j the streets, the next day, were banked up on each side by snow, having the ap-

pearance of breastworks, as if to defend the houses from the attack of an invad-ing army. August 1, Hodgson2s Map of Westmorland published. August 8, se-vere thunderstorm from 2 to 10, P.m.; three coach-horses killed. The Indepen-dent chapel, in New-street, fronted with hammered limestone, and otherwise im-proved. 1828-1829 Thomas Harrison (third time). January 18, 1829, New Hutton chapel opened. February 22, 1829, Divine service suspended in Ken-dal church, in consequence of the im-provements going on there. June 22, 1829, the new theatre, in the "Shaks-peare" yard (built by Thomas Simpson, Esq., of Wath Field), opened, John Richardson architect. (The theatre con-tinued till 1834, when it was converted into stables for the use of the Inn.) 1829-1830 George Webster. October 14, 1829, the river Kent the highest known for twenty or thirty years. Infants' School established, and built by volun-tary subscriptions, chiefly from amongst the Society of Friends; John Richardson, architect. April 5, 1830, the mail coach between Kendal and White-haven discontinued. July 9, Proclama-tion of King William IV. at Kendal: the proclamation was read, in different parts of the town, by Edward Tatham, Esq., deputy recorder, on horseback. There was a large procession, consisting of the Mayor and other members of the Corporation dressed in their, robes, and carrying the insignia of office, together with a numerous train of gentlemen, and the different trades and societies, ac-companied by music and flags: in the evening, an entertainment took place at the King's Anns. July 30, awful thun-derstorm, Christopher Fletcher, garden-er, aged 53, killed by the lightning. The summer of 1830 was remarkably cold and wet in Kendal. October 11, 1830, opening of the beer trade; upwards of a score of beer-houses opened in Ken-dal, at each of which there was more or less feasting and drinking The price of ale fell from 8rf. to 6rf. per quart, on the premises, and from *7d.* to *5d.* off the premises. 1830-1831 Jonathan Hodgson (third time). February 9, 1831, a great flood of the river Kent; it inundated all

the lower part of Stramongate to a-great depth, reaching up as far as the Nag's Head yard. In the Vicarage Library the water was a foot deep; and on Colonel-walk it was nearly seven feet deep. The arches of Nether bridge were full to within a few inches of the keystones, and the ground-floors of the cottages at Castle-mills were filled nearly to the ceilings: the water passed between the 78th and 79th palisades, from the south, at the bottom of Newstreet. September 8, coronation of their Majesties, King William IV., and Queen Adelaide. This event was celebrated in Kendal with every possible demonstration of loyalty, and the spirited rejoicings here sur-passed, it was said, those of any provin-cial town in the kingdom. Several arch-es of different orders tastefully decorat-ed with flowers, evergreens, and flags, and bearing appropriate mottoes and de-vices, were thrown across the streets, in various parts of the town: these were mostly transparent, and in the evening were brilliantly illuminated with gas. The day was observed as a complete holiday. 1831-1832 Isaac Wilson. Oc-tober 26, a ladies' bazaar held in the Whitehall Assembly Room, in aid of the Sunday-schools, and for procuring warm cloth-ing for the aged poor in Kendal and Kirkland. January 6, 1832, a police force, consisting of one superintendent and three police8constables, established in Kendal. February 1, Temperance So-ciety established. (E. W. Wakefield, Esq., chairman.) April: Thomas Harri-son, Esq., surgeon, appointed one of the Senior Aldermen (and Magistrate), *vice* William Berry, Esq., resigned. May: "The Annals of Kendal," first edition, published; price 7s. *6d.* July, the cholera made its first appearance in Kendal. Mr. Green ascended in his balloon from the Gas works, and alighted on Helsfell. August 25, Thomas Harrison, Esq., so-licitor, elected Town Clerk, *vice* Wil-liam Berry, jun., resigned. September 6, a splendid procession this day to cele-brate the passing of the "Parliamentary Reform Bill," and to welcome to Ken-dal, James Brougham, Esq., the desig-nate Borough member. Dinner at the

King's Arms; Jacob Wakefield, Esq., in the chair. "Birklands," the seat of E. W. Wakefield, Esq., built; G. Webster, Esq., architect. Town View, built by Mr. William Wilson; John Richardson, architect.

1832-1833 Richard Riwes. November 22, 1832, Temperance Coffee and

Reading Room opened. December 11, James Brougham, Esq. (brother of the Lord Chancellor Brougham), elected, without opposition, the First representative in Parliament for Kendal. He was chaired through the streets, and afterwards dined with 200 of the electors at the King's Arms. The number of registered electors at this time, 310. December 18 and 19, Westmorland Election. Polling places for the FIRST time at Kendal, Kirkby Lonsdale, Kirkby Stephen, Ambleside, and Shap, in addition to the county town of Appleby. Serious rioting at Kendal, on the first day of Election, when many persons were wounded, and many lives were put in jeopardy. December 27, a fire in the Town Hall, which originated in the justices' room; an oaken book-case, full of valuable law books, in great part destroyed. February 19, 1833, foundation stone laid of the Odd-fellows' Hall, in Highgate. March 15, Bank of Westmorland (Joint Stock Company) established, capital £250,000. July 9, a Swift sailing packet8boat (called "The Water-witch") commenced on the Canal, at about eight miles an hour. The manufacture of paper by machinery commenced in 1833, at Burneside Mills, by Messrs. Hudson, Nicholson, and Foster.

1833-1834 George Forrest (second time). December 22, 1833, died, James Brougham, Esq., M.P. for Kendal, aged 54. He was buried at Brougham Church. Old Maids', or Dowker's Hospital, in Highgate, built.

18348 1835 Joseph Swainson (second time). Served up to 31st December, 1835, when the new (Reformed) Corporation came in. May 7 to 12, 1835, Richard Wilson, Esq., solicitor, elected Coroner for the Kendal and Lonsdale wards, after a hard contest at Appleby A. D. with Thomas Wardle, Esq., of five days' duration and much excite-

ment, there were polled:
For Mr. R. Wilson.... 762
„ Mr. Wardle 569
    Majority.... 193

July 4, died, Thomas Harrison, surgeon, Senior Alderman of the borough, aged sixty. He had been three times Mayor; was a man of varied acquirements, and highly esteemed. August 4, foundation stone laid of St. Thomas's Church. August 20, the shock of an earthquake felt in Kendal and neighbourhood; bells in the houses were set ringing, and fence-walls were thrown down in great lengths. August 20, Natural History and Scientific Society established. The "stocks" removed from the Market-place. August: Alderman John Harrison, of Hundhow, appointed one of the Senior Aldermen (and Magistrate) of the Borough, in place of Alderman Thomas Harrison, surgeon, deceased. September 9, Corporation Reform Act passed (5 at 6 William IV. cap. 76). October, 1835. British School opened; built chiefly by subscription. 1836 January 1, to November 9, 1836. John Richards (afterwards Yeates). First Mayor after the passing of the Municipal Corporations Reform Act. Mr. John Mann appointed Borough Treasurer. May 15, 1836, a visible annular eclipse, the greatest solar eclipse since 1794; at Kendal the sun presented a luminous segment equal only to three-quarters of the annulus; the thermometer fell to the temperature of January. July 15, 1836, first election of Guardians of the Kendal Union; first meeting of the same on the 16th. Regular police force with office and new lock-ups, established in Finkle-street. The old "black hole" under St. George's Chapel, added to the front shop under the same. September 29, deep fall of snow on the Kentmere hills. The severest winter since 1816; potatoes *Id.* and *Sd.* a stone throughout the winter. 1836-1837 John Wakefield. April 3, 1837, repeated snow showers. A year of mercantile disasters, together with numerous bank rg failures. July 3, proclamation of her Majesty Queen Victoria 5 (aged 18). There was a splendid procession in Kendal, comJa posed of the Mayor and Corporation, and the

various clubs;,§ § proclamation was made from the " cauld stean," and other places. §,§ A banquet was given at the King's Arms Hotel, by the Mayor, o who presided on the occasion. July 5, St. Thomas's Church, in Stricklandgate, consecrated by the Right Rev. J. B. Sumner, D.D., Bishop of Chester (Kendal being still in the diocese of Chester). June 25, George William Wood, Esq., Whig, elected M.P. for Kendal, vacancy by Dissolution of Parliament, on the demise of the crown: Edward Wilson, Esq., of Abbot Hall, Tory, was an opposing candidate, but was withdrawn before the time of polling. September 13, new Roman Catholic Church, on New-road, opened for Divine Service, by the Right Rev. Dr. Briggs, the *toi-di-tant* Bishop of the northern diocese.

1837-1838 William Gelderd. January 21, 1838, first interments at St.

Thomas's Church. February 16, fire in the belfry of St. George's Chapel. June 28, coronation of her Majesty Queen Victoria, celebrated at Kendal with great rejoicings; there were five triumphal arches, of tasteful design, thrown across the streets in various parts of the town; there was also a splendid procession, consisting of the Mayor and Corporation, the Vicar and Clergy, the Yeomanry Cavalry, the several benefit societies, and Sunday-schools; a sermon was preached for the occasion by the Rev. J. Hudson, the Vicar, the church being " choke full" even to standing room. Superintendent Registrar's Office and Fire-engine Station8house in Finkle-street, built by the Corporation, 1838. Service finally discontinued in St. George's Chapel. Foundation stone of the Roman Catholic Church laid, by Mr. Strickland, of Sizergh.

1838-1839 Thompson Bindloss. January 6 and 7, 1839, the greatest storm of wind ever remembered; chimney8stacks fell and houses rocked to their foundation; the destruction of timber was everywhere great, but especially in Lowther Park. January 22, 23, the north warehouse at the Canal head totally destroyed by fire, and the south warehouse injured; at the time the fire broke out there were in the warehouse 100 quarter8 barrels of gunpowder, which were providentially removed in time, by four courageous men, whilst the warehouse was still in flames. April 8, foundation stone of St. George's Church laid, without formalities. August, names of the streets painted and fixed up. November 2, extensive fire at the warehouse of Messrs. Isaac and William Wilson, in Stramongate; damages between 2.000/. and 3,000/. 1839-1840 Richard Wilson. January 1,1840, the two Kendal Banks amalga mated. January 10, penny postage commenced. February 10, marriage of Queen Victoria. April 11, slight shock of an earthquake felt in Kendal. August, the dials of the Town Clock made to project forward from the tower. August 17, Fletcher Raincock, Esq., F. S.A, last Recorder of Kendal, died at Liverpool, aged 71. 1840-1841 James Machell. June 17, 1841, St. George's Church consecrated by the Lord Bishop of Chester. St. Thomas's School, Stricklandgate, built. 1841-1842 John Wakefield (second time). September 4, 1842, Firbank

Chapel (rebuilt) opened this day. September 11, Crosscrake Chapel re8opened. A year of great depression in trade, and suffering amongst the labouring classes; this town felt its effects severely.

1842-1843 Richard Wilson (second time). March 17, 1843, the shock of an earthquake felt iu Kendal, accompanied with a rumbling noise. May 16, first interment in the new cemetery, head of Castle street. October 3, George William Wood, Esq., M.P. for Kendal, died at Manchester, aged 62. October 31, the Rev. John Hudson, A.M., Vicar of Kendal, died at Haverbrack, aged 70. November 8, first *contested* election for Kendal, Henry Warburton, Esq., A. D. Whig, being returned by a majority of 63, over George Bentinok, Esq., a Tory.

1843-1844 Samuel W'hinerey. Working-men's News-room in the Market-place opened. March 19, Earl of Lonsdale died, aged 86. April 14, the Rev. Joseph Watkins Barnes, M.A., inducted Vicar. July 27, Dr. Dalton died, aged

77. September: first sod of the Lancaster and Carlisle Railway cut. October 16, Zion Chapel, in New Inn-yard, opened this day. Inghamite chapel, at the head of Beast-banks, re-built.

1844-1845 Thompson Bindloss (second time). June 30, 1845, Kendal and

Windermere Railway Act received the royal assent. July 21, Kendal Reservoir Bill received the royal assent July 23, "Lady of the Lake" steamer launched on Windermere, being the first steam-boat on that lake, or in the lake district: grand banquet given in the saloon to Professor Wilson, and other distinguished guests.

1845-1846 Cornelius Nicholson. April 13, 1846, Steam-power first applied in Kendal for cutting timber into boards with vertical saws by Mr. John Fisher. June 26, Kendal Union Gas and Water Company's Act received the royal assent. July 7, Grand Festival in Kendal to celebrate the passing of the Corn Law Repeal Bill; Mr. Warburton, M.P. for Kendal, the Mayor and Corporation, and all the Societies joined in a procession, which was a mile in length: the Mayoress, assisted by several ladies, distributed in front of the Mayor's house in Stricklandgate more than 3,000 loaves of bread, to the Sunday-school children, and to the aged poor, on the presentation of tickets. September 21, the Lancaster and Carlisle Railway opened from Lancaster to Kendal, and celebrated by a banquet in the Whitehall Buildings, the Mayor in the chair. Passenger packets ceased plying on the canal, the same day.

1846-1847 John Аvakefield (third time). December 15, 1846, the Lancaster and Carlisle Railway opened from Kendal to Carlisle. January 31, 1847, the organ of the parish church removed from the gallery to the floor, having been considerably augmented and improved, was reopened this day. April 20, Kendal and Windermere Railway opened. May 6, first "County Court" held in the Town Hall. September 14, first fortnightly fair for the sale of fat cattle and general stock, held on the New-road; removed to near the railway station in November. September: Wes-

leyan Day and Sunday-schools built. 1847-1848 James Machell (second time). February 5, 1848, the town clock first illuminated with gas. May 27, Fire at Town View, the property of Mrs. Wilson. June: Kendal reservoirs and waterworks completed. August 31, Health of Towns' Act passed. 1848-1849 Samuel Whinerey (second time). The Serpentine Walks thrown open to the public by the Trustees of Kendal fell, at Easter, 1849. August 6, Procession of the Mayor and Corporation and other gentlemen on horseback, Sic. to meet G. E. Wilson, Esq., of Heversham, the newly appointed High Sheriff of the county; the high-shrievalty having been till now hereditary in the Earls of Thanet, for upwards of 600 years. September 4, first meeting of the Council as a local Board of Health. Hartley Coleridge died, at Rydal, aged 53. 1849-1850 George Braithwaite Crewdson. April 23, 1850, William Wordsworth died, at Rydal Mount, aged 80. May 3, Colours of the 55th Regiment of Foot deposited in the parish church. July 2, Sir Robert Peel died, aged 62. July 17, Storm of thunder and lightning, with heavy rain; house set on fire in Kirkland by the electric fluid. September 1, service suspended in the parish church till June 3, 1852, during the restoration. Working-men's public baths, &c. in Market-place opened. 1850-1851 Jacob Giles James Ireland. December 2, 1850, Tagrant Wards brought into use for vagrants this day. January 13, 1851, county meeting held in"the White-Hall, the High Sheriff (G. E. Wilson, Esq.) chairman. June 9, Low Mills, near Kendal, destroyed by fire, the property of Messrs. John Ireland and Co. June 17, widening of Branthwaite-brow commenced. July 1, foundation stone laid of Fellside schools. 1851-1852 Jacob Giles James Ireland re-elected (second time). February 2, 1852, very high flood of the Kent, second only to that of February 9, 1831. February 22, Kendal new Horse Fair established. April 13, Fellside Schools opened. June 3, the Parish Church re-opened by the Lord Bishop of Chester, after its restoration. September 1, Electric Telegraph brought to the town along the Kendal and Windermere Railway. September 14, died the Duke of Wellington, aged 83. October 13, the Queen, Prince Albert, and suite, halted a short time at Oxenholme, on their journey from Balmoral southward. 1852-1853 John Hudson. November 18, 1852, the Duke of Wellington buried in St. Paul's, London. November 28, Preston Patrick Church (rebuilt, by subscription, at a cost of about 1,400?.) opened this day. December 25, violent storm of wind from the S.W., nearly equal to that of January 7, 1839; a lady killed in Highgate, by the falling of a chimney. December 27, again a great storm of wind from the same quarter, accompanied by heavy rain; serious and extensive damage caused by the flood at Foulshaw. January 13,1853, first marriage at St. Thomas's Church. February 21, Procession of the Mayor and Corporation, and a large number of the inhabitants in carriages, ftc, to escort the High Sheriff (John Wakefield, Esq.) through the town, on his way to the Assizes at Appleby. April 6, two Receiving Houses for letters opened at Kendal, viz., one in Stricklandgate, and one in Stramongate. June, the Magnetic Electric Telegraph laid through Kenr'al. June, the river Kent considerably widened south of Mill Bridge. August 9, first Wool and Cheese Fair in Kendal (held in the Market-place). October 10, penny receipt stamps came into use. October 14, Her Majesty the Queen, Prince Consort, Prince of Wales, and suite, sojourned at Oxenholme, on their return from Balmoral; the Mayor, Corporation, clergy, and a large number of the inhabitants, went to pay homage. St. George's Schools built, 1853. Lithographic plan of Kendal by H. Hoggarth, published. The "High front" in Kirkland, reduced to the level of the street. The Widows' Houses, at Sandes's Hospital, rebuilt. 1853-1854 John Jowitt Wilson. February 27, 1854, Burial Board established for the united townships of Kendal, Kirkland, and Nethergraveship. March 10, Alderman Thompson, M.P. for Westmorland, died, aged 61. May 25, St. George's Sundayschool opened. June 14, Ambleside Church opened by

the Lord Bishop of Chester. Wcsleyan burial-ground closed. 1854, the windows on the north side of Kendal Church re-glazed with diamond quarries, instead of the old "square crown." Kendal Natural History and Scientific Society, removed to Stricklandgate House, and a new Lecture Room built. 1854-1855 John Whitwell. November 28,1854, Corner stone of the Cemetery Chapel laid, by Mr. John Hudson. 1855, from February 20, Windermere Lake frozen completely over for several days, and bearable its whole length; again on March 8 and 9, and frozen over also on March 26. July 21, foundation stone of the Covered Market Hall laid, by the Mayor. August 23, the New Cemetery Chapel and burial-ground consecrated by the Bight Rev. John Graham, D.D., Lord Bishop of Chester. September 14, first interment in the New Cemetery. A second reservoir, at Bird's Park, in course of formation. The new sheds and drying stoves at Castle Mills built by Messrs. J. J. and W. Wilson. 1855-1856 William Longmire. March 29, 1856, Kendal new Butter-market first occupied; the first pound of butter sold for 1«. 3 jrf. May 29, on this day the Mayor entertained at dinner the Corporation, Magistrates, and Clergy, and the day was observed as a holiday in commemoration of the return of Peace. July 1, severe frost this morning. The potato tops all killed on the low lands in the neighbourhood of Kendal. Again, frost on the morning of July 10. August 1 to 8, Heat unequalled for thirty years. Thermometer stood at 84 in the shade on the 4th. August 8, Birthwaite (Windermere) Church, dedicated to St. Mary, and Bowness Cemetery, both consecrated by the Lord Bishop of Carlisle. 1856 1857 John Whitwell (second time). January 12, 1857, new painted window placed in the Baptistry of the parish church; the bequest of the late Mr. Joseph Robinson. February 9, the Kendal Chamber of Commerce formed. April, new clock placed in the Tower of Kendal Church, the gift of Mr. Christopher Gardner. May 11, the Prince of Wales and suite visited the Lake District. June 25, the thermometer high-

er by 6i than it was ever registered in Kendal. It stood at 90$ in the shade, and at 1231'' the sun. July, Wooden Bridge over the Kent, at the north end of Colonel-walk, built, at the cost of E. W. Wakefield, Esq., and prolonged across the Mill Race shortly afterwards, by subscription. October 4, Chapel in Sand Area for the Christian Brethren, opened.
A. D.
1857-1858 John Jowitt Wilson (second time). November 10, 1857, Inauguration of the premises in Highgate (late Odd-fellows' Hall) for the Mechanics' Institution, by the Right Honourable Lord Brougham, who was afterwards entertained at the King's Arms by the exMayor (Mr. J. Whitwell), and had an address presented to him by the Mayor and Corporation. Dec. 14, Pillar Letter Boxes erected in Stricklandgate, Stramongate, and Kirkland; the receiving houses being discontinued. January 25,1858, Marriage of the Princess Royal celebrated at Kendal, with considerable rejoicing; the Mayor presented about 1,300 scholars with a currant bun each, in front of his own house on Kent Terrace. April 29, a public drinking fountain erected in Crock-lane, near the Fish-market, by subscription; the fountain bears date 1857. May 3, Amalgamation of the Lancaster and Carlisle and Kendal and Windermere Railway Companies. May 15, the Rev. Joseph Watkins Barnes, M.A., Vicar of Kendal, died at the Vicarage, aged 51. August 15, the Rev. John Cooper, M.A., inducted Vicar. September 1, the Local Government Act came into operation in Kendal, having received the royal assent August 2. October 29, extensive conflagration at Castle Mills, the property of Messrs. J. J. and W. Wilson; damages from 1,200?. to 1,500?. Pale Ale Stores built, in Mints Feet, for Messrs. William Whitwell, and Co., brewers. 1858-1859 John Wakefield (fourth time). December 5, 1858, Helsington

Chapel re-opened by the Rev. G. W. H. Taylor. December 14, a boulevard of trees planted, by Rev. J. Gibson, along the Newroad. December 14, Exhibition of paintings, articles of virtu, &c, opened in the large hall of the Mechanics' Institution, in Highgate, and continued open till January 22, 1859. March 5, foundation stone of the new Vicarage laid, by the Vicar. April 8, the Quarter Sessions held for the first time in the new Town Hall. April 12, the old Town Hall sold by auction, to Mr. Job Bintley. July 16, first steamer on Ullswater. August 24, Association for the protection of ancient footpaths, established. September 22, Dinner given by the Mayor, to the Corporation, Magistrates, lie, in the new Town Hall, to celebrate the inauguration thereof.

1859-1860. John Wakefield re-elected (fifth time). December 8, 1859,

Volunteer Rifle-Corps formed, at a meeting held in the Town Hall. August 23, 1860, ornamental pillar and lamps erected in the Market-place. September 28, the first steamer on the canal, arrived at Kendal. Card-making Steam Mill built, in Potter's Close, by Mr. James Thompson.

1860-1861 William Henry Wakefield. December 21, 1860, destructive fire of the warehouses of Messrs. John Ireland and Co., in " Rosemary-lane," Stramongate; the building was completely destroyed, together with a large quantity of manufactured goods, damages, 3,000/. to *4,000l*. December 24, 25, the thermometer during this night fell to li below zero, as indicated by a self-registering thermometer, placed a few feet from the ground. February 11,1861, Mr. C. G. Thomson,solicitor, Kendal, elected Coroner for the Kendal and Lonsdale Wards, vacant by the resignation of Richard Wilson, Esq. March 28, Burneside Chapel re-opened by the Lord Bishop of Carlisle. April 21, Troutbeck Chapel re8opened by the Rev. Mr. Graves, of " Dove's Nest." May 17, the Kendal Fell Trust (Amendment) Act received the Royal assent. May 26, Ordination held in the parish church by the Lord Bishop of Carlisle (Waldegrave), when five priests and six deacons were ordained; it is forty years since the last Ordination at this place. Kendal new Railway Station built this year, S. B. Worthington, Esq., of Lancaster, archi-

tect. June 11, Tacht capsized in a squall on Windermere, when two but of the three gentlemen sailing in her were drowned, viz. Captain Parke, of the 56th (Westmorland) Regiment, and Captain Forde, of the 2d Lancashire Militia; G. R. Rawlinson, of Graythwaite, the third party, swam ashore, and thus saved himself. CHAPTER XI. NATURAL HISTORY OF THE LOCALITY.

It seems compatible with the history of the town, to put on record a catalogue of the various productions in the several departments of Natural History found in this locality. We, therefore, herewith present a selected list of Quadrupeds, Birds, Reptiles, Amphibious Animals, Land and Fresh-water Shells, Fossils, and Plants, which belong to a circuit within six or seven miles of Kendal. If this were done in all topographical works, the naturalist might be materially aided in forming sound conclusions as to the geographical distribution of plants and animals. But, probably, few towns are so fortunate as Kendal at this time, in having a naturalist competent to present a synopsis of the Flora and Fauna of the district, extinct and existent. Mr. Thomas Gough, who has furnished these catalogues, is eminently conversant with the various branches of Natural History: Kingdom— AN IM ALI A.— *ANIMALS (recen t)*.

Svn Kingdom—VERTEBJIATA (Vertebrated animals).

Class—MAMMALIA (Mammals).

Order I.—*Cheiroptera (Bats)*.

Long-eared Bat *(Pleeotut auritus)*, not uncommon.

Notch8eared Bat *(Vccpertilio emarginatus)*, rare; Garnett-bridge Mill.

Common Bat *(Scotophilia mtirinim)*, common.

Order II.—Inseotivora *(Insect iroroiu quadrupeds)*.

Hedgehog *(Erinaceus europium)*, common.

Common Shrew *(Sorex rusticus)*, common.

Water Shrew *(Sorex fodiens)*, not unfrequcnt; ditch banks.

Oared Shrew *(Sorex remifer)*, rare; ditch banks.

Mole *(Talpa cwopira)*, common.

Order III. —Carnivora *Carnivorous quadrupeds)*.

Badger *(Melts taxus)*, rare; formerly iu Hawes Wood.

Polecat *(Mustela Pulorius)*, not unfrequent.

Ermine *(Mustela erminea)* not uncommon; brown in summer, white in winter.

Weasel *(Mustela vulgaris)*, common.

Marten *(Marie s foina)*, rare; rocky woods.

Otter *(Luira vulgaris)*, occasionally on the banks of the river Keut.

Fox *(Vulpes vulgaris)*, not unfrequent.

Order IV.—Rodentla *(Gnawing quadrupeds)*.

Squirrel *(Sciurus vulgaris)*, not uncommon.

Dormouse *(Myoxus avellanarius)*, not unfrequent.

Black Rat *(Mm rattus)*, rare; formerly common.

Brown Rat *(Mus decumanus)*, common.

Domestic Mouse *(Mus musculus)*, common.

Wood Mouse *(Mus sylvaticus)*, not uncommon.

Water Vole *(Arvicola amphibius)* not uncommon; black and brown varieties.

Field Vole *(A rvicola agrestis)* not uncommon; occasionally in houses in winter.

Common Hare *(Lepus timidus)*, common.

Rabbit *(Lepus cuniculus)*, common.

Class—AVES (Birds).

The following abbreviations are used: S.M., Summer Migrator from south; W.M., Winter Migrator from north; O.V., Occasional Visitor.

Order I.—Raptores *(Birds of Prey)*.

White-tailed Eagle *(Aquila albicilla)*. This bird formerly bred in the Lake hills, but has disappeared within the last forty years. The latest nuthen ticated instance of its being seen was by Cornelius Nicholson, Esq., above Low Wood, in 1822.

Sparrow Hawk *(Accipiter Pringillarius)*, common.

Peregrine Falcon *(Palco Peregrinus)*, rare; Whitbarrow.

Kestrel *(Palco Tinnunculus)*, common.

Merlin *(Palco jEsalon),* not uncommon; breeds on Hay Fell.

Common Buzzard *(Bulto vulgaris),* not frequent; Benson Knot, Rowland Edge.

Marsh Harrier *(Circus rufus),* rare; Hay Fell.

Short-eared Owl *(Otis Brachyotos),* O.V., rare; on moors.

White Owl *(Strix fiammea),* common.

Tawny Owl *(Ulula stridula),* common in woods.

Order II.—*Insessores (Perching Birds).*
The Great Grey Shrike *(Lanius excubitor)* must be looked upon as a rare visitor in this part of the north, one specimen only having been met with, which was killed in Middleton, a few miles beyond the limits of our area.

Pitld Vole.—We have occasionally observed a small reddish variety of Vole on swampy ground. This may probably turn out to be the Meadow Vole *(A. pralensis),* a species first discovered in England by Mr. Yarrell, and subsequently found as well in Scotland and Ireland.

Red-backed Shrike *(Lanius collurio),* S. M., not frequent, hedges near the Castle.

Spotted Flycatcher *(Muscicapa grisola),* S.M., common, arrives May 11.

Pied Flycatcher *(Muscicapa atrieapilla),* S.M., rare; arrives May 8.

Common Dipper *(Cinclus aquaticus),* common on the rocky parts of Kent, Mint, and Sprint.

Missel Thrush *(Turdus viscivorus),* common.

Fieldfare *(Turdus pilaris),* W.M., common, arrives October 30 to November 13.

Song Thrush *(Turdut musicus),* common.

Redwing *(Turdus iliacus),* W.M., common, arrives September 30.

Blackbird *(Meruia vulgaris),* common.

Ring Ouzel *(Meruia torquata),* S.M., on the " Fells;" arrives March 24 to 30.

Hedge Accentor *(Accentor modularis),* common.

Redbreast *(Erythaca rubecula),* common.

Redstart *(Phosnicura ruticilla),* common, arrives April 18.

Stonechat *(Saxicola rubicola),* not common j on Helm, Reston Scar.

Whinchat *(Saxicola rubetra),* S.M., arrives April 24.

Wheatear *(Saxicola amanthe),* S.M., arrives March 29 to April 3.

Sedge Warbler *(Salicaria phragmitis),* S.M., arrives May 5 to 9.

Blackcap Warbler *(Cnrruca atrieapilla),* S.M., arrives April 19.

Garden Warbler *(Curruca hortensis),* 8. M., arrives May 5 to 18.

Common Whitethroat *(Curruca cintrea),* S.M., arrives May 3 to 12.

Lesser Whitethroat *(Curruca garulu),* S. M., not common; Kent Terrace, arrives May 11.

Wood Warbler *(Sylvia sibilatrif),* S. M., common; Spital Wood, arrives April 26 to May 12.

Willow Warbler *(Sylvia trochilus),* S. M., common; arrives April 16.

Golden-crested Regulus *(Rcgulus aurieapillus),* common.

Great Tit *(Parus major),* common.

Blue Tit *(Parus caruhus),* common.

Cole Tit *(Pants atcr),* common.

Marsh Tit *(Parus palustris),* common.

Long-tailed Tit *(Parus caudatm),* common.

Bohemian Wax wing *(Bombycilla garrula),* O.V. in winter; killed at Lowgroves and Gilling-grove.

Pied Wagtail *(Motacilla Yarrellif),* common.

Grey ᴀVagtail *(Motacilla boarula),* common.

Ray's Wagtail *(Motacilla jlava),* S. M., common; arrives April 16.

Tree Pipit *(Anthus arboreu/i),* S.M., common; arrives April 19.

Meadow Pipit *(Anthus pratensis),* common.

Skylark *(Alauda arvensis),* common.

Woodlark *(Alauda arborea),* formerly not uncommon, now rare.

Snow Bunting *(Plectrophanti nivalis)* O.V., in winter, on Kendal Fell.

Common Bunting *(Emberiza miliaria),* common.

Black-headed Bunting *(Emberiza tchaniclus),* common.

Yellow Bunting *(Emberiza citrinella),* common.

Chaffinch *(Fringilla coelebs),* common.

Mountain Finch *(Fringilla montifringilla),* O.V. in winter.

House Sparrow *(Passer domesticus),* common.

Greenfinch *Coccolhraustes ch!oris),* common.

Goldfinch *(Carduelis elegans),* common.

Siskin *(Carduelis tpmus),* O.V. in winter.

Common Linnet *(Linaria cannabina),* common.

Lesser Redpole *(Linaria minor),* S. M., not uncommon.

Mountain Linnet *(Linaria montana),* common.

Bullfinch *(Pyrrhula vulgaris),* common.

Common Crossbill *(Loxia curvirostris),* O.V., Cowan-head and Crosthwaito.

Common Starling *(Sturnus vulgaris),* common in summer, rare in winter.

Raven *(Corvus corax),* not uncommon.

Carrion Crow *(Corcus corone),* common.

Hooded Crow *(Conns comix),* O.V. in winter; killed at Forest Hall.

Rook *(Corvus frugilegus),* common.

Jackdaw *(tortus monedula),* common.

Magpie *(Pica caudata),* common.

Jay *(Garrulus glandarius),* common.

Wryneck *(Yuiuc Torquiila),* S.M., not common; Crosthwaite.

Creeper *(Certhia familiaris),* not uncommon.

Wren *(Troglodytes europaus).* common.

Hoopoe *(Upupa cpops),* O.V., rare; killed May 1, 1859, at Selside.

Cuckoo *(Cuculus canorus),* 8.M., common; arrives April 14 to May 3.

Kingfisher *(Alccdo ispida),* not uncommon.

Swallow *(Hirundo rustica),* S.M., common; arrives April 18.

Martin *(Hirundo urbica),* S.M., common; arrives April 24.

Sand Martin *(Hirundo riparia),* S.M., common; arrives April 13.

Common Swift *(Cypsclus apus),* S.M., common; arrives April 30 to May 12.

Nightjar *(Caprimulgus europwus),* S.M. , not uncommon; arrives May 30.

Order III.—Rasobes *(Gallinaceous*

Birds).

Ring Dove *(Columba palumbus),* common.

Turtle Dove *(Columba turtur),* O.V. in summer, rare.

Common I'heasaut *(Phasianus Colchicus),* common; ring-necked variety also.

Black Grouse *(Tetrao tetrix),* not uncommon; occasionally on Kendal Fell.

Red Grouse *(Tetrao Scoticus),* common.

Common Partridge *(Perdix cinerea),* common.

Common Quail *(Perdix coturnix),* O. V., rare; formerly a regular summer visitor.

Order IV.— Grallatokks *(Wading Birds).*

Golden Plover *(Charadrius pluvialis),* not uncommon on its way to the hills.

LapwiDg (*Vanellus cristatus),* common in summer.

Common Heron *(Ardca cinerea),* common.

Common Bittern *(Botaurus stellaris),* O.V. in winter; several on Brigsteer Moss in 1829.

Common Curlew *(Numenius arquata),* common iu summer.

Green Sandpiper *(Totanus ochropm),* O. V. in autumn; rare, on the Kent.

Common Sandpiper *(Totanus hypoleucos),* S.M., common; arrives April 16 to 22.

Ruff *(Machetes piijnax),* O.V. in autumn on Lj th Moss.

Woodcock *(Scolopax rusticola),* W. M., common.

Great Snipe *(Scolopax major),* O.V. in autumn; rare.

Common Snipe *(Scolopax gallinago),* common; breeds on the bogs.

Jack Suipe *(Scolopax gal/inula),* W. M., common.

Landrail *(Crcx pratensis),* S.M., common; arrives May 9 to 22.

Spotted Crake *(Crcx porzawi),* O.V. in autumn; one taken June ii.

Water Rail *(Rallus aquaticus),* W.M. ; not uncommon.

Moor Hen *(Gallinula chloropus),* common.

Common Coot *(Pulica atra),* common in summer.

Order V.—Natatores *Swimming Birds).*

Grey-legged Goose *Anser palustris),* O.V. in winter.

Bean Goose *(Anser ferui),* O.V. in winter.

Whistling Swan *(Cygnus ferns),* O.V. in winter.

Common Shelldrake *(Tadorna vulpanser),* O.V. in winter.

Shoveler *(Spathulcca clypeata),* O.V. in winter on Brigsteer Moss.

Wild Duck *(Anas boschas),* common.

Teal *(Querquedela crecca),* not uncommon; formerly bred in Dubb's Moss, Lambrigg.

Wigeon *(IHareca Penelope),* winter visitor.

Common Scoter *(Oidemia nigra),* O. V. in spring on the Kent.

Pochard *(Puligvla ferina),* winter visitor.

Scaup Duck *(Puligula marila),* O.V. in winter.

Tufted Duck *(Puligula cristata),* winter visitor.

Golden Eye *(Clangula vulgaris),* winter visitor.

Smew *(Mergus albellus),* O.V. in winter on Lyth Moss.

Red-breasted Merganser *(Mergut serrator),* O.V. in winter; rare; near Milnthorpe.

Goosander *(Mergus merganser),* winter visitor; adult male killed in March, 1S59.

Great-crested Grebe *(Podiceps cristatus),* O.V. in winter, on Tarns.

IJared Grebe *(Podiceps auritue),* O.V. in winter; rare; killed on Whinfell Tarn.

Little Grebe *(Podiceps minor),* not uncommon on the Kent and Tarns.

Great Northern Diver *(Colymbus glacudis),* O.V. in winter; killed on Whinfell Tarn.

Black-throated Diver *(Colymbus arcticus),* O.V. in winter; rare.

Red-throated Diver *(Colymbus septenlrionalu),* O.V. in winter.

Common Guillemot *(Uvia troile),* O.V.; rare; on Lyth Moss.

Little Auk *(Mergulus melanoleucos),* O. V.; rare; Helsington and Crosthwaitc.

Gannet *(Sula bassana),* O.V.; rare; taken alive on Hutton Common.

Common Tern *(Sterna hirundo),* O.V. in winter.

Masked Gull *(Larus capistratus),* O.V.; rare; taken near the town.

Black-headed Gull *(Larus ridibundus),* winter and spring visitor.

Kittiwake Gull *(Larus rissa),* ditto.

Common Gull *(Larus canus),* ditto.

Herring Gull *(Larus argentatus),* ditto.

Lesser black-backed Gull *(Larus fuscus),* ditto.

Great black-backed Gull *(Larus marinus),* ditto.

Richardson's Skua *(Lestris Richardsonit),* O.V. in winter; very rare.

Fork-tailed Petrel *(Thalassidroma BaUoclii),* O.V. in winter; taken alive in the town.

Storm Petrel *(Thalassidroma pelagica),* O.V. in winter; taken alive in the town.

Class—REPTILIA (Reptiles).

Ordei—Squamata (Scaled).

Viviparous or Common Lizard *(Zootoca vivipara),* heaths and mossy walls.

Blind-worm *(Anguis fragilis),* meadows and copses.

Ringed Snake *(Natrix torquata),* peat bogs; not common.

Common Viper *(Pelias Berus),* woods and heaths; common.

Var. (8. Red Viper, ditto.

Class—AMPHIBIA (Amphibious animals).

Order—Anouha Tailless).

Common Frog *(Rana temporaria),* common.

Common Toad *(Bufo vulgaris),* common.

Natter Jack Toad *(Bufo calamita),* in quarries at the limekilns on Kendal-fell.

Order—Urodkla (Tailed).

Common Warty Newt *(Triton cristatw),* in ditches.

Common Smooth Newt *(LUsotriton punttatus),* in ditches.

Class—PISCES (Fishes).

Order—Aoanthofterygii (Some of the fin-rays spinous, others flexible).

Perch *(Percafluviatilis),* in most of the tarns.

(t) *With hard cheeks.*

River Bull-head *(Coitus gobio),* in the Kent and Mint.

Smooth-tailed Stickleback *(Uasteros-*

teus leiurus), in brooks.

Order—Abdominal Malacopteryqii *(soft-finned).*

Gudgeon *(Qobio fiuviatilit),* in the canal.

Tench *(Tinea vulgaris),2m* Whinfell Tarn.

Roach *(Leueiscus rutilus),* in Skelsmergh and Grayrigg tarns.

Rudd *(Leueiscus erythroptlialmus),* in Whinfell Tarn.

Minnow *(Leuciscus phoxinus),* in the rivers and brooks.

Loach *(Cobitis barbatula),* in stony parts of the Mint.

Pike *(Esox lucius),* in some of the tarns; rare in the Kent.

Salmon *(Salmo salar)* in the Kent at Levens.

Sea Trout *(Salmo trulta)* ditto.

Common Trout *(Salmo fario),* in the rivers and brooks.

Ordei—Apodal Malacoptbryqii *(no ventral fins).*

Sharp-nosed Eel *(Anguilla acutirostris),* in tarns; Whinfell Tarn.

Broad-nosed Eel *(Anguilla latirostris),* in brooks and tarns; Hood Tarn.

Sub-kingdom—*MOLLVSCA* (Molluscous animals).

Land And Fresh-water Shells.

Class—GASTEROPODA (Foot on the gastric surface).

The Elegant Circle Shell *(Cyclostoma elegans)* occurs on Arnside Knot; and in the wood near Blawith Cottage, Grange. Bithiniada *(Bithinia Family).*

Tentacled Bithinia *(Bithinia tentaeulata),* canal: Brigstcor Moss. Valvatidjs *(Valve-shell Family).*

Stream Valve-shell *(Valvata piscinalis),* Brigsteer Moss; large in Castle Mills Race.

Crested Valve-shell *(Valvata cristata),* Brigsteer Moss.

Arionidx *(Land-sole Family).* Black Arion *(Arion ater),* abundant.

Helioid *(Snail Family).* Spotted Slug *(Limax maximus), in* gardens and outhouses. Milky Slug *(Limax agrestis),* in gardens.

Transparent Glass Bubble *(Vitrina pellucida),* not uncommon under stones. Garlic Snails *(Zonites alliarius),* Serpentine Walks.

Cellar Snail *(Zonitet cellarini).* Serpentine Walks; and in many other places. Dull Snail *(Zonites nitidulus),* Serpentine Walks.

Crystalline Snail *(Zonites crystallinus),* Serpentine Walks; Hyning Wood.

Top shaped Snail *(Zonites fulvus),* Serpentine Walks.

Common Snail *(Helix aspersa),* in gardens.

Garden Snail *(Helix hortensis),* in gardens and hedges.

Girdled Snail *(Helix nemoralis),* in gardens; large on Kendal-fell.

Shrub Snail *(Helix arbustorum),* Canal bauks, and about the Castle.

White Snail *(Helix pulchella),* on old walls.

Var. with raised cross bands *(costata),* among moist moss near Sizerghfell-side.

Black-tipped Snail *(Helix fasciolata),* on Kendal-fell, rare: abundant above Sunny Brow, Staveley. Heath Snail *(Helix ericelorum),* common on Kendal-fell. Rufous Snail *(Helix rufescenn),* common: large in Serpentine Walks. Neat Snail *(Helix concinna),* under stones on Kendal-fell. Prickly Snail *(Helix aculeata),* near Beckmills: Low Groves: Oxenholme. Radiated Snail *(Helix rotundata),* common under stones; large on Kendal-fell. Open Snail *(Helix umbilicata),* abundant on Kendal-fell, beneath stones, and on walls

Common Amber Snail *(Succinea pvtris),* in the Canal.

Dusky Twist Shell *(Bulimus obscurus),* on Kendal-fell; and at Sizergh-fellside.

Common Varnished Shell *(Zua lubrica),* common under stones.

Glassy Trident Shell *(Azeca tridens),* on Kendal-fell; rare.

Umbilicated Chrysalis Shell *(Pupa cylindracea),* common on Kendal-fell.

Margined Chrysalis Shell *(Pupa mmcorum),* Kendal-fell.

Juniper Chrysalis Shell *(Pupa secale),* abundant on Kendal-fell.

Toothless Whorl Shell *(Vertigo edentula),* scarce; on Kendal-fell.

Pygmy Whorl Shell *(Vertigo pygmaa),* common on Keudal-fell, and old walla.

Alpine Whorl Shell (*Vertigo alpestris),* Kendal-fell; not common.

Six-toothed Whorl Shell *(Vertigo substriata),* scarce; in Serpentine Walks.

Wry-necked Whorl Shell *(Vertigo pusilla),* Hawes Bridge; Serpentine Walks, and Mint Cottage; not common. Fragile Moss Shell *(Balea perversa),* on a wall near Fowl lug. Laminated Close Shell *(Clausilia bideux),* Kendal-fell, Helsfell Wood, and

Madgcgill.

Dark Close Shell *(Clausilia nigricans),* on the Castle walls, Serpentine Walks; common.

Auriculidj; *(Ear-shell Family).*

Minute Sedge Shell *(Carychium minimum),* Hyning, CuU3wick, and Helsfell Woods.

LlMNADiE *(Pond-snail Family).* Wide-mouthed Mud Shell *(Limnans auricularius),* scarce; in the Canal. Puddle Mud Shell *(Limnauspereger),* common in the Canal, Kent, and brooks.

Var. 1, subovate —*ovatus,* and var. 3, spire very short

— *luteiw,* in ditches.

Marsh Mud Shell *(Limnauipaluatris),* Brigsteer Moss, and near Water Crook. Ditch Mud Shell *(Limnant truncatulus),* Brigsteer Moss, Lime Kilns, and Mint Cottage.

Eight-Whorled Mud Shell *(Limnaut glaber),* rare; EUer-flat Tarn, near Docker Garths.

Common River Limpet *(Ancylus fluviatilis),* common in streams; large in the Canal.

Oblong Lake Limpet (*Veletia lacuttris),* in pools on Benson Knot; scarce. Stream Bubble Shell *(Phyia fontinalis),* Canal, and Brigsteer Moss. White Coil Shell *(PlanorbU albus),* Canal, Brigsteer Moss, and Mill-dam at Cowan Head.

Nautilus Coil Shell *(Planorbi s nautileus),* Brigsteer Moss; formerly in Coppy

Tarn, Tenter Fell. 'urinated Coil Shell *(Planorbia carinatua),* Brigsteer Moss. Margined Coil Shell *(Planorbia complanatua),* Brigsteer Moss. Whorl Coil Shell *(Planorbis vortex),* Brigsteer

Moss. Rolled Coil Shell *(Planorbis spirorbis)*, Brigsteer Mosb and Aikrigg Tarn. Twisted Coil Shell *(Planorbis contortus)*, Brigsteer Moss and many other places.

Class—CONCHIFERA BIVALVES or LAMELLIBRANCHIATA (Respiratory apparatus of two pairs of gills).

CYCLAD.E *(Cycle Family)*.

Horny Cycle *(Cyclaa cornea)*, Brigsteer Moss; in a ditch near Helm Lodgo.

Pisidiad-e *(Pera Family)*.

Minute Pera *(Pitidiumpusillum)*, Brigsteer Moss and Kent.

UNiONtn *(Fresh water Maude Family)*.

Swan Fresh-water Muscle *(Anodon cygneus)*, shell large and thin; Canal. Var. *Shell small*; var. *anatina.* Brigsteer Moss.

Pearly Alasmodon *(Alatmodon margaritiferue)*, in the Mint, Kent, and Gowan.

FOSSILS OF THE UPPER PALAEOZOIC SYSTEM. CARBONIFEROUS SERIES.

Mountain Limestone.

Kinudom— AN IM ALI A.—A N1MA LS *(extinct)*.

Hva-Kinauou—VERTFBJIATA (Vertebrated animals).

Clabs—PISCES (Fishes).

Cladodufl striatus, Brigsteer. Helodua planus, Kendal-fell.

Cochiliodus maguus, Kendal-fell. Pristicladodus Goughi, Kettlewell.

Sub-kinqdom—*MOLLVSCA* (Molluscous animals).

Class-CEPHALAPODA (Feet around the head).

Orthoceras inauquiseptum, Kendalfell.

cornu-vaccinum, ditto.

laterale, ditto.

gigantcum, ditto.

Orthoceras Uesneri, Kendal-fell.

cinctum, ditto. Aganides vinctus, ditto. Nautilus Trochlea, ditto. sulcatus, ditto.

Class—PALLIOBRANCHIATA (Respiratory apparatus on the surface of the mantle).

Order—Bbachiopoda (A long arm8like foot on each side of the mouth).

Producta pustulosa, Kendal-fell. punctata, ditto, meaoloba, ditto. Martini, *var.* concinna, Kendal-fell.

Producta margaritacea, Kendal8fell.

lirata, ditto, bemispherica, ditto, oval is, Brigsteer Scar, gigantea, ditto.

Producta fimbriata, Kendnl-fell.

Fleming!, ror. pugilia, do.

var. sulcata, do. *var.* lobata, do. elegans, ditto. corrugata, ditto. ChoDetes papilionacea, ditto. Leptagonia analoga, vor. multirugata, Kendal-fell. Strophomena senilis, ditto.

Sharpii.BrigsteerScar. crenistria, Kendal-fell. Camerophoria sulcirostr2is, Kettlewell.

Orthis gibbera, Kendal-fell.

Pentamerus carbonari us, Kettlewell. Athyris gregaria, far. paradoxa, Kendal-fell.

vor. trapezoidalis,

Kendal-fell.

expansa, ditto.

Spirifera symmetrica, ditto.

glabristria, Brigsteer Scar,

similis, Kendal-fell.

imbricata, ditto,

cuspidata, Kettlewell.

duplicate, Kendal-fell.

virgoides, ditto.

filiaria, Brigsteer Scar,

rhomboidea, Kendal-fell.

Sub-kinqdom—*ARTWVLATA* (Articulated animals). Class—CRUSTACEA. (Crustaceans). Phillipsia seminifera, Kendal-fell. Phillipsia gemmulifera, Kendal-fell. Sub-kingdom—*RADIATA* (Radiated animals). Class—ZOOPHYTA (Zoophytes).

Cyathaxonia cornu, Kendal-fell. Lithostrotion sexdecimale, ditto. nffine, Cunswick.

junceum, Kendal-fell. fasciculatum, ditto. aggregatum, Kettlewell.

Stylastrsea basaltiformis, Kendalfell.

Louadaleia stylastnciformis, ditto. Nematophyllum arachnoideum, Helsington Barrows,

minus, Kendalfell.

Clyaiophyllum multiplex, ditto.

Cyathopsis fungites, Kendal-fell. cornu-copia;, ditto. Caninia subibicina, ditto. gigantea, ditto. Cyathophyllumpseudo-vermiculare, Kendal-fell. Syringopora geniculuta, ditto. reticulata, ditto. ramulosa, ditto. Stenopora inflate, ditto. tumida, Kettlewell. Chcotetes septosus, Kendal-fell. capillaris, ditto. radians, Helsington Barrows.

Michelinea grandis, Brigsteer Scar.

Note.—In the lower beds of mountain limestone occurs a coarse conglomerate, containing the shells of small Mollusca; and in about the same position are to be found deposits, of a more or less arenaceous character, in which are several foasil plants, consisting of species of *Sigillaria, Ca1amites, Lepidodendron,* and, probably, *Caulopteris.*

OLD RED SANDSTONE, OR DEVONIAN SERIES. No characteristic fossils of this series have been met with in this locality among the *Old Red Conglomerate,* which occurs in the valleys of the Kent, Mint, and Sprint, as already noticed in the general observations on the natural situation of the town, at p. 144. But many of the angular fragments and disjointed pieces of which the rock is here made up do contain fossils from the Upper Ludlow formation.

FOSSILS OF THE LOWER PALAEOZOIC SYSTEM. SILURIAN SERIES.

Upper Ludlow Rocks.

Sob-kingdom—*MOLLl'SCA* (Molluscous animals).

Class—CEPHALAPODA.

Hortolus Ibex, High Thorns, Underbarrow.

Cycloceras trachcale, Benson Knot. subannulatum, Brigsteer. tenuiannulatum, ditto Ibex, Benson Knot.

Orthoccras tenui-cinctum, ditto. dimidiatum, Brigsteer.

Orthoceras sub-undulatum, High Thorn, bullatum, Laverocklane. baculiforme, Brigsteer. angulatum, ditto. Bellerophon trilobatus,Benson Knot, expansus ditto.

Class—GASTEROPODA.

Litorina octavia, High Thorns. corallii, Benson Knot. Holopella obsoleta, ditto. gregaria, Underbarrow common, intermedia, High Thorns, conica, Benson Knot.

Holopella cancellata, Lambrigg-feU. Naticopsis glaucinoides, Benson Knot.

Trochus helicites, ditto. Murchisonia torquata, ditto.

Lloydi, ditto. Pleurotomaria crenulata, Brigsteer.

Class—PTEROPODA (a wing-like foot on each side of the neck).

Conularia subtil is, Benson Knot cancellata ditto. ornata (Fossils of Rhenish provinces, Tab. xxix. fig. 5), Benson Knot; rare, Theca Forbeaii, High Thorns.

Class—LASLELLIBRANCHIATA.

Tellinites affinis, Benson Knot.
Nucula anglicn, Brigsteer.
Cucullella ovata, ditto.
coarctata, ditto. antiqua, Benson Knot.
Area primitiva, ditto.
Eilmondiiformis, ditto. Cardiola in-terrupta, ditto and
High Thorns. Grammysia rotundata, ditto.
extrasulcata, ditto. cingulata, *rar.* o, ditto. *var. f5,* triangulata, ditto. *var. y,* obliqua, High Thorns.
Leptodomus undatus, Benson Knot.
truncatus ditto. *vars.* long aud short, ditto. globulosus, ditto. amygdalinus, ditto.
Sanguinolites deeipiens, ditto. anguliferus, ditto, very rare. Orthonotus semisulcatus, ditto. Anadontopsis securiformis, ditto. angustifrons, ditto. Modiolopsis solenoides, ditto. complanata, ditto. Ptermea tenuistriata, ditto. retroflexa, ditto.
Pterinea pleuroptera, Benson Knot.
Pterinea Sowerbyi, Helm.
lineata, ditto. Avicula Daubyi, Benson Knot. deiuissa, ditto. orbicular *var.* ditto.
Pterinea Boydi, Brigsteer. elongate *var.* ditto.

Class—ANNULATA.

Trachyderma squamosa, Benson Serpulites dispar, Benson Knot and
Knot. Brigsteer.
Zoological position uncertain, probably Echinodermata or Annulata.
Tentaculites teuuis, Benson Knot.
Comulites serpularius, Benson Knot
Undetermined fossil, ditto. and Brigsteer.

Scb-kin-cdom—RA DIA TA.

Class-ECHINODERMATA.

Tetragonis Danbyi, Underbarrow Uraster primamis, High Thorns.
Low Common. Uraster Ruthveni, ditto.
Protaster Sedgwickii, Benson Knot Icthyocrinus pyriformis, ditto.
and Docker Park. Taxocrinus Orbignii, ditto.

Class— ZOOPHYTA.

Cyathaxonia Siluriensis, Cowan-I Stenopora fibrosa, Ratherheath head. Graptolites latus, Reston Scar. PLANTS.
Rannnculacea.—Thalictrum minus, Scout Scar, Cowan Head. Anemone nemoposa, common. Ranunculus hederaceus, watery places. R. Ficaria, common. R. Flammula, peat bogs. R. auricomus, shady lanes and thickets. R bulbosus, meadows. R. sceleratus, Brigsteer Moss. Troll in europ&us, damp pastures. Helleborus viridis, near Scarfoot Mills. Aquilegia vulgaris, Brigsteer and Peat Mosses. *Nymphaacea.*—Nymphsoa alba, tarns. N. lutea, tarns and pools. *Papavtracca.*—Papaver Rhaeas, cornfields. Mecanopsis cambrica, Oxeuholme,
Peat Lane, Sprint Bridge. Chelidonium majus, near Natland. *Fnmariacta.*—Corydalis claviculata, Spital Wood. Fumaria officinalis, common.
Oruciferoc.—Ooronopua Ruellii, Beast-banks. Thlaspi arvense, Crook, Stavelcy. Draba verna, common. Cardamine amara, Laverock and Burneside Lanes, C. hirsute, common. Arabis thaliana, common. A. hirsuta. Scout Scar; wall near Castle Mills. Barbarea vulgaris, common. Nasturtium officinale, common. N. terrestre, Aiirigg Tarn. Sisymbrium officinale, common. Krysimum Alliaria, common. *Resedacea;.*—Reseda Luteola, Lime Kilns. *Ciitacea.*—Helianthemum vulgare, common. H. canum, Scout Scar; Burn Barrow Nab. *Violecece.*—Viola palustris, marshy places. V. odorata, Helsington, Gillinggrove. V. hirta, Barrowfield and Cunswick Woods. V. tricolor, common. *Droieracea.*—Drosera rotundifolia, common. D. intermedia, common. D. anglica, Foulshaw Moss; rare. *Polygalacea.*—Polygala vulgaris, common. *Silenacca.*—Saponaria officinalis, Force Bridge. Silene inflata, common.
Lychnis vespertina, Peat-lane. L. Githago, occasionally in cornfields. *AlMnacea.*—Sagina nodosa, Kendal-fell.
Arenaria serpyllifolia, Kendal-fell,
Thorny Hills. A. verna, Kendal-fell.
A. trinervis, Spital Wood.
Stellaria nemorum, Laverock and Burneside Lanes, common. S. holostea,

common. S. graminea, common. *Linacea.*—Linum usitatissimum, occasionally in cornfields. Radiola mille grana, Foulshaw Mobs. *Afalvacece.*—Malva moschata, in pastures. M. sylvestris, Heversham, Cros thwaite. M. rotundifolia, Underbarrow Scar. *Hypericacea.*—Hypericum Androsocmum, Barrowfield Wood, Brigsteer.
H. perforatum, dry banks. H. dubium, near Heversham. H. quadran gulum, common. H. humifusum, dry banks. H. hirsutum, Cunswick and Scout Woods. H. montanum, Cunswick and Scout Woods. H. Elodes, Underbarrow Common.
A ceracea.—Acer campestre, near the Lound.
Qeraniacea.—Geranium sylvaticum, woods and shady lanes. G. pratense, meadows. G. dissectum, common. G. columbinum, Canal banks, Lime kilns. G. lucidum, rocks and old walls. G. Robertianum var. flora albo, lanes near Jenkin Crag, and the Castle. G. sanguineum, Scout Scar.
Celastracea:—Euonymus europeeus, Cowan Head, Hundhow. *Rliamnacea:.*—Rhamnus catharticus, Scout and Cunswick Woods. R. Frangula, ditto. *Leguminifcra.*—Srartiutn scoparium, common. Genista tinctoria, high pastures and commons. Ononis arvensis, common. Anthyllis vulueraria, common on limestone. Medicago lupulina, Kendal-fell. Melilotus officinalis, Fowlshaw Moss. Trifolium medium, Cunswick Wood. T. arvense, sandy pastures. T. fragiferum, near Low Levens. T. procumbens, Kendal-fell. T. minus, Kendal-fell. Lotus corniculatus, common. Ornithopus perpusillus, Tenterfell, near the Workhouse. Hippocrepis comosa, Scout Scar. Vicia sylvatica, Laverock Bridge, Barrowfield Wood. V. angustifolia, occasionally on sandy pastures. Orobus tuberosus, hedge banks. *Rosacea.*—Prunus insititia, hedges. P. Padus, moist woods and hedges. P. cerasus, woods. Spinca tilipendula, Barrowfield Wood and top of Un lerbarrow Scar. G. urbanum, common. G. intermedium, damp woods. G. rivale, sides of brooks. Agrimonia Eupatoria, Laverock Bridge. Po-

tentilla verna, wood on E. aide of Whitbarrow. P. reptans, roadsides. P. Fragariastrum, common. Fragaria vesca, common. Comarum palustre, Cunawick Tarn. Rubus saxatiiis, Cunswick Wood. R. idiEua, hedges and woods. R. exesius, Cunswick Wood. Rosa spinosissima, Barrowfield Wood. R. villosa, woods. R. tomentosa, woods and hedges. R. arvensis, between Beathwaite Green and Brigsteer. Sanguisorba officinalis, meadows. Poterium sanguisorba, Kendal-fell. Alchemilla arvensis, sandy pastures. Crataegus Oxyacantha, common. Pyrus malus, hedges. P. aria, Scout and Cunswick Woods. P. aucuparia, woods. *Onaffracea.*—Epilobium hirsutum, banks of Mint and Kent. Circaea lutetiana, common. *ffaloragiacea.*—Hippuris vulgaris, Brigsteer Moss. Myriophyllum spicatum, river Kent, Brigsteer Moss. Callitriche verna, common. *Lythracem.*—Lythrum Salicaria, Stock-beck. Peplis Portula, Brigsteer Moss. *Sehranthacea.*—Scleranthus annuus, sandy pastures. *Grotfiilariacea.*—Ribes Grossularia, woods and hedges. R. nigrum, damp hedges. R. alpinum, Docker Brow. *Cramlacea* — Sedum Telephium, common. S. anglicum, Underbarrow, Crook, Staveley.

Saxifragaceie.—Saxifraga granulata, Gilling-grove. banks of the Mint. S. tridactylites, old walls and rocks. Chrysosplenium alternifolium, near Benson Hall gate. *Araliaeete.*—Adoxa moschatellina, common.

Comacta.—Cornus sanguinea, hedges near Levens.

UmhelHftra.—Hydrocotyle vulgaris, common. Sanicula europsea, common. Conium maculatum, waste places. Apium graveolens, Fowlshaw Moss. Helosciadium nodiflorum, Stock-beck. H. inundatum, Brigsteer. Pimpinella Saxifraga, dry banks. Sium latifolium, Stockbeck. GJnanthe fistulosa, Endmoor. 03. Crocata, Stock-beck..lEthusa Cynapium, common. Silaus pratensis, Cunswick Tarn. Meum athamanticum, Docker Garths, The Green, and Lambrigg Fell-gate. Daucus Carota, Kendalfell. Torilis Anthriscus, common. Scandix Pecten-veneris, occasionally in

cornfields. Anthriscus sylvestris, common. Myrrhis odorata, near Spital. *Loranthacea.*—Viscum album, on apple trees in Lyth and Crosthwaite. *Caprifoliacea.*—Sambucus Ebulus, Bradleyfield; lane near Staveley Church. Viburnum opulus, common. *Ruhiaetce.*—Galium cruciatum, common. G. uliginosum, moist places. G. Mollugo, Spital, Skelsmergh. G. sylvestre, Kendalfell. G. Aparine, common. Sherardia arvensis, sandy fields. Aspemla odorata, common. A. cynanchica, Kendal-fell. *Yalerianaccce.*—Valeriana dioica, marshy places. V. officinalis, damp hedges. Fedia olitoria, dry banks. *Iiipmcett.*—Scabiosa columbaria, Kendalfell. Knautia arvensis, common. *Composite.*—Tragopogon minor, meadows near the town. Apargia hispida, common. Hypochseris radicata, common. Lactuca muralis, Scout and Cunswick Scars. Sonchus arvensis, Peat Mosses. Crepis virens, common. C. paludosa, wet meadows. Serratula tinctoria, Barrowfield wood; near Ings. Carduus heterophyllus, Peat Lane. Carlina vulgaris, Kendal-fell. Centaurea nigrescens, common. Centaurea scabiosa, Kendalfell. Bidena cernua, Crosthwaite; near TJnderbarrow Toll-bar. Bidens tripartita, Stock Beck; Burneside Hall. Eupatorium canabinum, Cunawick Tarn; peatmosses. Tanacetum vulgare,JenkinCrag; Toad Pool. Gnaphalium sylvaticum, common. G. uliginosum, peat mosses. Filago minima, Crosthwaite, F. germanica, sandy places. Autennaria dioica, Kendal-fell. Erigeron acris, Foulshaw-moss. Aater trifolium, Fowlshaw moss. Solidago Virgaurea, common. Senecio sylvaticus, Pine Crags. S. saracenicus, Stock Beck; Hay Fell; Mill Bridge. Inula helenium, Fellside Farm, Crosthwaite. I. conyza, Cunswick Scar. Pyrethrum parthenium, the Castle. P. inodorum, waste places. Anthemia nobilis, Brigsteer. *Campanulacea.*—Campanula latifolia, hedges. C. Trachelium, near Park Head and Hyning. Jasione montana, dry banks. *Ericacece.*—Andromeda polifolia, Levens-moss. Vaccinium oxycoccos, bogs. Monotropa hypopitys, Barrowfield-wood. *Genlianacea.*—Gen-

tiana pneumonanthe, Foulshaw-moas. G. Amarella, Kendal-fell. G. campestris, Kendal-fell. Erythrsea centaurium, Brigsteer. *Conrolmlacea.*—Convolvulus arveusis, near Heveraham. C. aepium, hedges. *Solanacea* Hyoscyamus niger, near Levens Church. Solauum niger Dulcamara, damp hedges. *Scrophulariacea.*—Verbacum Thapsus, Brigsteer Scar. Veronica scutellata, Brigsteer-moss. Y. montana, between Greenside and Heversham. V. agrestis, common. Melampyrum sylvaticum, Barrowfieldwood, on east side of Whitbarrow. Digitalis purpurea, common. Linaria minor, railway banks between Staveley and Ings. *Orobanchacece.*—Lathrsoa squamaria, Lavorock-bridge, Cunswickwood, Levens Park. *Lamiacea.*—Lycopus europtcus, sides of tarns. Mentha rotundifolia, near Reston Hall. M. aquatics, common. M. arvensis, cornfields. Origanum vulgare, Cunswickwood. Calamintha officinalis, the Castle. Lamium album, Lound. Galeopsis ladanum, foot of Scout Scar. G. versicolor, near Sprint-bridge. *Boraginacea.*—Myosotis palustris, common. Lithospermum officinale, Barrowfield wood. L. arvense, occasionally in corn-fields. Auchusa sempervirens, near Tolson Hall gate. Cynoglossum officinale, near Levens Church. Echium vulgare, occasionally in corn-fields. *Pinguiculacea.*—Utricularia vulgaris, Brigsteer-moss. U. minor, Brigsteer-moss. *PrimiUacca.*—Primula veris, common. P. farinosa, damp meadows and pastures. Hottonia palustris, Brigsteer-moss. Lysimachia vulgaris, ditches on peat bogs. L. nummularis, near Levens. Anagallie tenella, bogs. Samolus valerandi, Brigsteermoss. *Plantaginaua.*—Plantago media, Kendal-fell. P. maritime, Foulshaw moss. *Polygonacta.*—Polygonum bistorts, meadows. P. Peraicaria, common. P. Hydropiper, common. P. amphibium, canal. P. convolvulus, cultivated ground. *Thymeleacea* —-Daphne laureola, North Spring-wood, Staveley.

Empetracece. Empetrum nigrum, Benson Knot, Beaton Scar.

UrticaceB.—Humulus lupulus, Hawesbridge.

Conifer.—Juniperus communis, Kendal-fell. Taxus baccata, Scout Scar.
Orchidacea.—Neottia nidus-avis, foot of Cunswick Scar. Listera ovata, Y woods. Epipactis latifolia, Cunswick-wood. E. palustris, Cunswick tarn. Cephalauthera ensifolia, Barrowfield wood, rare. Orchis masoula, common. 0. latifolia, damp meadows. Gymnadenia conopsea, Cunswick. G. bifolia, pastures. G. chlorantha, Cunawick-tarn edge. Habenaria viridis, Helsfell Nab. G. albida, Barrowfield wood. Ophrys muscifera, Barrowfield wood, east side of Whitbarrow.
A maryllidacea.—Narcissus pseudonarcissus, woods, Pine Crags. *Liliacece.*—Allium seorodoprasum, near Water Crook. A. achoenoprasum, Rusmittle, Lyth. Gagea lutea, wood near Greenside. Convallaria majali, Hels-fell Nab, Cunswick wood. C. polygonatum/Barrowfield wood, rare. *Trilliacect.*—Paris quadrifolia, woods and hedges. *Tamacea.*—Tamus communis, in hedges. *Melanlhiaceoe.*—Colchicum autumnale, Mint's-feet, Greenside. *Alutmacea.*—Alisma plantago, Kent. A. ranunculoides, Brigsteer-moss. *Fluviales.*—Potamogeton crispus, Kent. *Aracece.*—Sparganium natans, Foulshaw-moss. S. ramosum, Stock Beck. *Cyperacea,*—Cladium mariscus, Cunswick-tarn. Scirpus maritimus, Foulshaw-moss. *Gramina.*—Sesleria coeruiea, Kendal-fell. Melica uniflora, shady banks. Festuca bromoides, Kendal-fell. Brachypodium sylvaticum, Cunswickwood. *Filices.*—Ceterach officinarum, Kendal-fell. Polypodium phegopteris, common. P. Dryopteris, common. P. calcareum, Barrowfield; Helsfell Nab. Allosorus crispus, Peat-lane; Reston Scar. Cistopteris fragilis, Kendalfell. Polystichum aculeatum, Gilling grove; Gillbanks, near Stayeley. Lastraea oreopteris, on the north side of the town. Lastrcea rigida, Kendal fell, scarce. L. spinulosa, near Ings. L. dilntata, common. Asplenium triehomanes, common. A. viride, Kendal-fell. A. adiantum-nigrun., Barrows Green. A. rutamuraria, Kendal-fell. Scolopendrium vulgare, common. Osmunda regalis, damp hedges and woods. Botrychium lunaria,

wood near Singleton; Benson Knot. Ophioglossum vulgatum, near Singleton. *Lycopodiacew.*— Lycopodium clavatum, Benson Knot. L. alpinum, Benson Knot. L. selago, Benson Knot. *Ejuietacea!.*—Equisetum hyemale, banks of the Mint, near Old Field-wood.

CHAPTER XIL

B10GRAPHICAL SKETCHES.

QUEEN KATHERINE PARR.

Of those *natives* who, by their lives and character, have conferred honour upon Kendal, undoubtedly the first place belongs to Katherine Parr, the sixth and last wife of King Henry VIII. Not because she was elevated to royalty, but because she "achieved greatness" by the exercise of noble qualities, and a cultivated understanding. She was born at Kendal Castle, about the year 1513. No question is made of the place of her birth, but the exact date is uncertain. Her parents were Sir Thomas Parr, knight, and Matilda, who rejoiced still more in the name of "Maud" Green, daughter and co-heiress of Sir Thomas Green, of Boughton, in Northamptonshire. Katherine was a precocious child, and gave promise of future distinction, both by her natural aptitude and by the divination of the astrologer, whose vocation then obtained credit. "Shee was told by an astrologer that did calculate her nativitie, that she was borne to sett in the highest of Impiall majestie: which became moste true. Shee had all the eminent starrs and planetts in her house: this did worke such a loftie conceite in her that her mother coulde newer make her serve or doe any small worke, saying her handes were ordayned to touch crownes and scepters, not needles and thymbles." Although she lived only thirty-five years, yet she was married four times, and so fair a prize was she reckoned that an alliance with her was sought by JoaDnes Ball's "Scriptorum Mustrium." the Lord Scroop, of Bolton,' when she could he no more than *eleven* years of age! Her first husband was Edward Burgh, or Borough, the eldest son of Lord Borough, of Gainsborough. He was a widower, with children, older far than the newmade

bride. Edward Borough died in 1529? (as it is said.) If so, Katherine was a widow at sixteen. How long she remained so, we cannot find. Nor can we discover the date of her second marriage, which was with Sir John Neville, Lord Latimer. He also was a staid widower, with children, so that Katherine had maternal cares of no ordinary kind to bear at an early age; and according to all accounts, she performed these duties with exemplary circumspection and conscientiousness. She herself had no children to either of the fore-named husbands. Lord Latimer was a bigoted Roman Catholic, and took part in the rebellion called the "Pilgrimage of Grace," as we mention in the account of St. Leonard's Hospital, p. 82. On the 12th July, 1543, Katherine was married to King Henry VIII. with great pomp and splendour, at Hampton Court. Nash says, she enjoyed but little happiness or quiet with him, yet "as she was ever esteemed a lady of much integrity and worth, and some maturity of years (aged thirty t), so the king so lived apparently well with her for the most part." Katherine narrowly escaped the martyrdom of royalty, which most of the former queens of Henry had suffered. Her mother had bestowed on her a learned education, and taught her from her infancy to inquire into the principles of religion. Her fine parts and great application enabled her to make improvements equal to her opportunities. Her piety, humility, and love of wisdom, rather increased with the increase of dignity, and she became in all respects a pattern to her subjects. She was a stout favourer of the gospel, and the Protestant cause, and could not help arguing with the king,— what he could never bear, especially in matters of religion, in which he thought every See the curious history of this transaction, ante pp. 89—93. Herbert's Life of Henry VIII.

"She was a woman of great beauty, adorned with many excellent virtues, especially humility—the beauty of all others."—*Hay ward's "Life of Edward VI."* one should conform to his ideas. He deemed it the highest presumption that "Kate should turn doctor, and pretend to instruct him!" She had the courage to contravene the memorable six acts, and the proclamation against the reading of forbidden books; and the Romanists of the court and council began to consider her a formidable enemy, and were determined to compass her ruin. By the instigation of Bishop Gardiner, articles were drawn up against her, and signed by the king; and her enemies expected only a warrant for carrying her to the tower, from whence, undoubtedly, she would have been conveyed to the scaffold, if her adroitness had not appeased the wrath of her husband. "Soir. e believe," says Herbert, "it was not so much the king's intention herein to use the rigour of the law, as to deter her from reading forbidden books. Howsoever, if he were not in earnest, it was thought a terrible jest, especially *to* a queen that had the reputation of a virtuous and observant wife."

"With the tyrant king," says Nash, "she lived three years, six months, and five days;" but she never was crowned queen. Lastly, she was married to Lord Seymour, of Sudley, uncle to King Edward VI., and brother to the Lord Protector. Latimer sums up Seymour's character in words which look like sending him to perdition, saying that he "was furthest from the fear of God that ever he knew or heard of in England!" They were first *privately* married, and were alike suspected of deceitful manoeuvres, in order to obtain the consent of the Protector and the Privy Council to an open marriage, which Katherine feigned to object to. The dowager queen lived at that time in Chelsea Palace, and Seymour paid her clandestine visits. "When it shall be your pleasure to repair hither (says the queen), ye must take some pains to come early in the morning, that ye may be gone again by seven o'clock, and so I suppose ye may come without suspect. I pray you let me have knowledge over-night at what hour ye will come, that your porteress may wait at the gate to the fields for you." It has been a displvted question as to how soon after the death of Henry VIII. the queen was married Latimer's Sermons before King Edward, to Seymour.

Froude says within two months; and "the indecorous haste had nearly added a fresh difficulty in the succession to the crown." The queen died within a very few days after the birth of the child (a daughter), on the 5th September, 1548, and in the Act of Attainder of Lord Seymour, it is imputed to him that "he had holpen her to her end." But Froude, arguing by inference of character, considers this allegation unfounded. Seymour, he thinks, had greater interest in the queen's life than in her death, and from this circumstance he concludes that she died a natural death. The child was christened Mary, and there is considerable uncertainty as to her life and destiny. The only thing quite certain is that, if she long survived her royal mother, she lived without state; for an Act of Parliament was passed in 1549 "for *disinheriting* Mary Seymour, daughter and heir of the late Lord Sudley, Admiral of England, and the late Queen." This Act of disinheritance must have been one of the consequeuces of her father's (treasonable?) conduct against the Lord Protector, for which Seymour was beheaded on Tower Hill, March 20th, 1549; and a most vindictive thing on the part of Somerset against an infant yet without speech, who could have done him no despite. Miss Agnes Strickland follows the mention of the act of disinheritance, referred to above, by allusion to an act "for the *restitution* of Mary Seymour, passed in January, 1549." But there must be an error here, either in fact or date; for the " restitution" spoken of is prior to the attainder of Lord Seymour; and moreover, the Marquis of Northampton, uncle of the " destitute" child (who obtained Sudley on Lord Seymour's attainder), is found in the enjoyment of Sudley Castle *long after* this reported act of restitution, making no provision for the orphan child, his niece.

The queen was buried in the interior of the lictle church of Sudley, and the funeral solemnized according to Protestaut rites, or, more strictly speaking, according to a *transition* rite "You married the late queen So soon after the king's death, that if she had conceived

straight after, it should have been accounted a great doubt whether the child born should have been the late king's or yours, whereby a marvellous danger might have ensued to the quiet of the realm."—*A rtisles of Impeachment agaimt Lord Seymour.* between Papal and Protestant; for Bishop Coverdale, who preached the sermon, had to make an apology for the presence of the almsbox and the candles, saying that the "*offering* was not done to benefit the dead, but for the poor only;" and the *lights,* which stood about the corpse, "were for the honour of the person, and none other intent, nor purpose." Lady Jane Grey officiated as chief mourner on the occasion.

Strype has given us an epitaph, written by the Queen's chaplain, Dr. Parkhurst, afterwards Bishop of Norwich, which perhaps was engraved on the monument erected for her at Sudley. It is Englished thus,—

In this new tomb the royal Katharine lies,

Flower of her sex, renowned, great, and wise;

A wife by every nuptial virtue known,

And faithful partner once of Henry's throne.

To Seymour next her plighted hand she yields; (Seymour who Neptune's trident justly wields;)

From him a beauteous daughter bless'd her arms,

An infant copy of her parent's charms.

When now seven days this tender flower had bloom'd,

Heaven in its wrath the mother's soul resum'd.

Great Kathrine's merit in our grief appears,

While fair Britannia dews her cheek with tears,

Our loyal breasts with rising sighs are torn,

With saints she triumphs—we with mortals mourn.

Queen Katherine Parr was not only a patron of learning, but was herself a well-informed author; and wrote many letters, prayers, and pious meditations, both in Latin and English. Dr. Nash quotes one prayer of hers, written during the king's expedition in the French war, which he says, "breathes the true spirit of humanity and Christianity, and seems preferable to the prayer directed by our liturgy to be used in time of war. " It runs thus,—

"0 Almighty Kinge, and Lorde of hostes! which, by thy angells thereunto appointed, doest minister both warre and She published, "The Lamentations of a Sinner." Also, a volume of "Prayers and Meditations," collected, as it is expressed in the title, " out of holy woorks. " Some of those, by the queen, were re-published in a volume entitled " The Lady's Monitor." peace; and which diddest give unto David hoth courage and strength, being but a little one, unarmed, and unexpert in feats of warre, with his slinge to sette uppon and overthrowe the great huge Goliath; our cause being just, and being enforsed to entre into warre and battaile, we most humbly beseche thee, 0 Lord God of hostes, sooe to turn the hearts of our enemyes to the desire of peace that no Christian bloud be spilt; or els graunt, 0 Lorde, that, with small effusion of bloud, and to the little hurt and dommage of innocentes, we may, to thy glory, obtayne victory; and that, the warres being soone ended, we may all with one heart and minde knitte together in concorde and unitie, laude, and prayse thee, which livest and reignest world without end. Amen."

"In the summer of the year 1782, the earth in which Qu. K. Par lay inter'd was removed, and at two feet, or little more, her leaden coffin or chest was found quite whole, and on the lid appeared an inscription, of which the following is a copy:—

'K. P.2 vi' and last wife of King Hen. th VIII"
1548.'

"Mr. John Lucas (who occupied the land of Lord Rivers), had the curiosity to rip up the top of the coffin, expecting to discover within it only the bones of the deced, but to his great surprize found the whole body wrap'd in 6 or 7 seer cloths of Linnen entire and *uncorrupted*, altho' it lain there upwards of 230 years. His unwarrantable curiosity led him also to make an incision through the seer cloths which covered one of the Arms of the Corps, the flesh of which at that time was white and moist. I was very much displeased at the forwardness of Lucas who of his own head *open'd* the coffin."

A stone slab was afterwards placed over the grave to prevent any future improper inspection.

In the "Archaeologia," vol. V., there is a fine engraving of Queen Katherine's *great seal,* representing the armorial From " Notes and Queried," by J. B. Brockett. ensigns of this lady, with supporters. It is encircled with the inscription, "Magnum Sigillu Dne Katharine Regime Aglle, Francle Et Hibernie" It contains quarterings of *Parr, Roos* (of Kendal), *Marmion, Fitzhugh,* and *Green* (Dame Maud's three bucks at gaze, for the last), together with the augmentation granted to Katherine by Henry VIII. With regard to this augmentation, it is observed by J. C. Brooke, Heralds' College, that "the king was exceeding kind in giving *arms* to his wives, though he deprived them of their *heads"*

In summing up the life of Katherine Parr, it may be observed, that she was especially an instrument in the hand of God, suited to the great work first set in motion by her— The Reformation. She had naturally a mind of great capacity, which had been early well grounded, under the direction of a devoted mother. She passed through many vicissitudes of life, and had numerous secret sorrows, even before the time when she came to realize the proverb, "uneasy lies the head that wears a crown." If these trials were sent to chasten, they produced that result. Finding very little of truth and goodness on earth, she turned her thoughts towards Him who judges with his truth, who is the Giver of all good. The light that now beamed in her soul became intensified at the critical time when Henry had been fairly sated with pleasure and power, and when the spectre of death flitted across his vision. Some of the reflected rays of that light fell on the sinking heart of the king, —

that heart of stone which had hitherto resisted all influences, both moral and spiritual. His previous rejection of the Pope's supremacy was an act of temper. His suppression of the religious houses was an act of rapacity. But it is possible, that his latest acts, licensing a translation of the Scriptures, and so forth, influenced by the delicate and discreet counsels of Katherine, were the result of faint suggestions of principle, self-accusation, and secret acknowledgment of errors which he did not care any longer to tolerate. Katherine's enlightened principles, religious convictions, and pious example, would, moreover, impress the court, and all the court's attendants; aud in this way, the cause of the Reformation must have been effectually advanced. She had taken Gardiner in his own foils, and he who had no mercy for others was now in her power, who was truly merciful. She had a party round her impressed, like herself, with sentiments of religious toleration; and that liberty of conscience, she so highly prized, allowed Gardiner and his coconspirators to escape the penalty of their last signal crime. Contemporary records are too scanty to be able to shew to posterity all the particular acts and benefits that Katherine conferred on the cause of true religion, and the dawning principles of the Reformation; and this is the reason, no doubt, why her memory has been so insufficiently esteemed. We agree with part of the concluding words of Miss Agnes Strickland, in her Memoir, that "some grateful respect is due, in the shape of a national monument, to the memory of this illustrious English-born Queen," who may be called the nursing mother of the English Reformation!

WILLIAM   PARR,   MARQUIS   OF NORTHAMPTON.

William Parr, son and heir of Sir Thomas, and brother of Queen Katherine, was born at Kendal Castle, in 1515. His father died, as appears by the proving of his will, when William was four years old. We have been unable to find any particulars of his infancy or youth. He succeeded to the barony and manor of Kendal. In the 30th Henry VIII.

(1539), he was created Lord Parr and Roos, of Kendal; and in 1543, Baron of Hart, in Northamptonshire, "to him and his heirs male." He was three times married. His first wife was Anne, only child and heir of Henry Bourchier, Earl of Essex, in right of whom he was, in 1543, honoured with the title of Earl of Essex. They were married in 1541; and this proved a very unhappy match. The Lady Anne having been found guilty of incontinence, an act was passed (after a lengthy discussion in Parliament), in 1551, for disannuling their marriage, and ratifying his union with Elizabeth, daughter of George Brook, Lord Cobham, and legitimating their issue. On the 17th of February, 1547, he was advanced to the further title of Marquis of Northampton, which caused the fourth part of the barony of Kendal to be called the Marquis fee. In the first year of Philip and Mary, 1554, he was attainted of treason, for espousing Lady Jane Grey's interest, with Dudley, Earl of Northumberland, for which his estates were forfeited. However, in the next year, he was restored in blood by Act of Parliament, but not to his honours, and to only part of his estates. By a charter bearing date Jan. 8th, in the 2d Philip and Mary, the said king and queen grant to William Parr, the whole demesne, manor, castle, and park of Kendal, parcel of the possessions of Thomas Parr, Knight, father of the said William Parr, late Marquis of Northampton. And all those free rents of the free tenants of the fourth part of the barony of Kendal, parcel of the possessions aforesaid. And all those demesne lands without the walls of the said park of Kendal, and the mill and burgages in the vill or burgh aforesaid, parcel of the said manor of Kendal. And all those improvement rents, as well nigh Kendal as in the country, extending to the clear yearly value of 50s. 5d. Also, the tallage, market, fairs, toll, stallage, weights and measures in Kendal, demised to Christopher Sadler. And also, Cargo in Cumberland (with divers other possessions elsewhere), parcel of the possessions aforesaid. To hold to him the said William, late Marquis of Northampton, and the heirs of his body

lawfully begotten, of the king and queen *in capite,* by the service of one knight's fee.

In 1559, Queen Elizabeth, " for favouring the Protestant religion," granted him *all* his honours and former possessions, including the lordships of this town, and he kept court here in 1561. He married to his last wife, Helen or Helena, daughter of Wolfangus Suavendurg, a Swede, who survived him. In consequence of the divorce of his wife Anne—by whom only of his three wives he had children—he died, without legitimate issue, in 1571. Bishop Parkhurst (Bishop of Norwich), writing to Henry Bullinger, speaks of this Swedish lady as "very beautiful," and the Bishop was a friend of the family; for he had by his own testimony been chaplain to Katherine Parr. He says, "The Marquis of Lloyd's State Worthies.

Northampton (brother of Queen Katherine, my most gentle mistress, whom I attended as chaplain twenty-three years since) died about the beginning of August (1571). He does not say *where* he died. When I was in London he married a very beautiful German girl, who remained in the Queen's Court, &c. Our Marquis was sixty years old, and I believe much more." If our dates be correct, the Bishop was rather out in his calculations as to 'our Marquis's' age: he was only fifty-six when he died. He was buried at the upper end of the quire of the collegiate church in Warwick. Sir William Dugdale says, his body was dug up in the reign of King James I. to make room for the burial of an ordinary gentlewoman. It was found perfect, with the skin entire, dried to the bones; with rosemary and bays lying in the coffin, fresh and green. All which were so preserved by the dryness of the ground wherein they lay, it being above the arches of that fair vault which is under the quire, and of a sandy condition mixed with rubbish of lime. He says, all this was related to him by those who were eye-witnesses thereof.

The delight of the Marquis was musick and poetry, and his exercise war; being a happy composure of the hardest

and softest discipline, equally made for court and camp, for delight and honour. But his skill in the field answered not his industry, nor his success his skill. King Edward called him his 'honest uncle,' and king Henry 'his integrity!' Active men were recommended by him to Henry's busy occasions, and virtuous men to Edward's pious inclinations. So much solid worth he had, that he had no use of ambition; so much modesty, that he made little use of his worth. Mean thoughts he entertained of himself; and as mean thoughts did he suggest of himself, by his downcast though grave looks, his sparing though pertinent discourse, and his submissive though regardful carriage. A sober and moderate man may be in fashion once in an age; and so it was with the Marquis of Northampton. He brought up many a courtier, yet had not the face to be one himself; until queen Elizabeth, who balanced her council in point of religion in the beginning of her reign, as she did her court in point of interest Zurich Letters (Parker Society), p. 257. Dugdale Bar. 380.

throughout, called him to the council-hoard first, and then to her cabinet,—where none more secret to keep counsel, none more faithful to give it, and none more modest to submit. A sincere, plain, direct man; not crafty nor involved. BARNABY POTTER

Was born at or near Kendal, in 1578. He was educated in Queen's College, Oxford, where he was afterwards elevated to the dignity of Provost. He held this situation for ten years, when he was chosen chaplain to King James I., and by his interest, his nephew, Christopher Potter, succeeded to the provostship. From the university he resorted to the court, where he at first attended on Prince Charles, and was accounted the penitential preacher there. When Charles ascended the throne (1625), Potter was made Bishop of Carlisle, "notwithstanding there were other suitors for it, and he ne'er sought for it. " He was consecrated at Ely House, in Holborn, London; and being a constant preacher, and a devout man in his family, was commonly called "the puritanical bishop." Fuller remarks, that "it was said of him, in the time of King James I., that organs would blow him out of the church, which I do not believe, the rather because he was loving of, and skilful in, vocal musick, and could bear his part therein. He was of a weak constitution, melancholy, lean, and a hard student." He died in London, January, 1641, and was the last bishop that died a Member of Parliament before the Commonwealth; for, soon after, the rest of the bishops were excluded from the House of Peers. He wrote and published two volumes of Lectures, and one book of Sermons.

RICHARD BRATHWAITE,

Of Burneside, Esquire, was born in 1588. He was of the ancient family of the Brathwaites, of Ambleside, and afterwards of Warcop and Burneside. His ancestors, as given by Dr. Burn, were, 1. Thomas, 2. Robert, both of Ambleside, 3. Thomas, of Burneshead. He (Thomas) married Dorothy, i Lloyd's Worthies, 1670.

daughter of Robert Bindloss, of Borwick, Esq. By her he had issue, two sons and five daughters. Thomas, the elder son, removed to Warcop. Bichard, the subject of this memoir, remained at Bumeshead, and afterwards succeeded to the estate, whether by the death of his elder brother, or by some act of favouritism, we are left uninformed. It has been asserted, in Wood's "Athenae Oxoniensis," that our author was bom at Warcop. If the authority of Burn could be doubted, we have the poet's own testimony in favour of Burneside being the place of his birth, in some lines addressed "To the truely worthy the Alderman of Kendall and his brethren." After lamenting the prevalence of drunkenness, he says—

"How happy should I in my wishes be
If I this vice out of request could see,
Within that native place *where I was borne*
It lies in you, dear townsmen, to reforme."

Again, we have an allusion to this as the place of his nativity, in a poem in his "Strappado for the Divel." Addressing "the Cottonneers of Kendal," he says—

"Let me exhort you in respect I am
Unto you all both friend and country-man
Whose ayre I breathed, oh! I were worthy death
Not to love them who suckt with me one breath," &c.

We have no account of his early education. In 1604, at the age of sixteen, he was, according to Wood, entered a commoner of Oriel College, Oxford, " where he avoided as much as he could the rough paths of logic and philosophy, and traced those smooth ones of poetry and Roman history, in which at length he did excel. Afterwards he removed to Cambridge, and then, receding to the north of England, his father bestowed on him Barnside," miscalled for Burneside. He does not appear, as some of his Editors have asserted, to have been a graduate of either University.

Richard Brathwaite was twice married; first to Frances, daughter of James Lawson, of Nesham, near Darlington, by This Dorothy had a brother, Sir Robert Bindloss, knight, who married to his second wife Alice Dockwray, of Dockwray Hall, Kendal.

whom he had nine children; and secondly, to Mary, daughter of Roger Croft, of Kirtlington, in Yorkshire. By her he had issue Sir Strafford Brathwaite, Knight, who was killed in the ship *Mary,* commanded by Sir Roger Strickland, in an engagement with an Algerine man-of-war.

It was in 1633 that his first wife died, and in veneration of her memory, in the following year, he wrote and published "the Anniversaries upon his Panarete:" from which we quote only two lines to confirm the place of her nativity:—

"Near Darlington was my deare darling borne
Of noble house, which yet beares honour's forme."

On his second marriage, says Wood, he removed to Appleton, near Richmond, in Yorkshire, where he died on the 4th of May, 1673, and was buried in the parish church of Catterick, near that place," leaving behind him the character of a well-bred gentleman and a good neighbour." The following is the epitaph on his tomb:— Juxta sitao sunt Ricardi Brathwait de Burneshead in comitatu Westmorlandias armigeri, et Maria; ejus conjugis reliquiae. Ille quarto die Maii Anno 1673 denatus est: Hteo undecimo Aprilis 1681 supremum diem obiit. Horum Alius uuicus, Strafford Brathwait eques auratus, ad versus Mnuros christian! nominis hostes infestissimos fortiter dimicans, occubuit: Cujus cineres Tingi in Mauritania Tingitana humantur.

Requiescant in pace.

Richard Brathwaite must have possessed great versatility of talent, for we find even at the present day various works of his in verse and prose. The only work, however, which is known to the general reader of the present day is "Barnab/s Journal." This poem, in Latin and English, both evidently proceeding from the same pen, had passed through six editions from the time of its first publication until the year 1818, a lapse of two centuries, and no correct traces had been We have in our own possession, four works by this Author.

discovered of the author. The hypothesis that obtained the greatest share of credit, during this long interval, was that the writer's name was Barnaby Harrington. This supposition was founded and supported solely on the following couplet in the Itinerary:

"Thence to Harrington, be it spoken! For *name-lake* I gave a token," &c.

The Editor of the 7th edition, in an able dissertation, overturns the hypothesis, and contends that the equivoque can be construed to imply nothing more than that the itinerant simply gave the beggar a *harrington*—a local token, about the value of a farthing, at that time in circulation. The Editor of this edition adduces so many proofs in favour of Richard Brathwaite being the author of "Barnaby's Journal," by parallel passages and striking coincidences which occur in the works published under the real name of Brathwaite, and that of the fictitious Barnaby, that we think a doubt can no longer remain on the subject. We have room only to cite one or two of these coincidences:

"*Upon the Errata,* in the Strappado for the Divel. By Richard Brathwaite. Know, judicious disposed gentlemen, that the intricacie of the copie and the absence of the author from many important proofes were occasions of these errors, &c.

"*Upon the Errata,* in Barnaby's Journal. Truth is, gentlemen, you are to impute the errors to the absence of the author," &c.

"*Upon the Errata,"* occurs also in Brathwaite's English Gentlewoman, 1631; and again, in his "Essays upon the Eive Senses," 1635:—

"Once in the year laughs wise Appollo."

Barnaby, p. 169.

"Once in the year Appollo laughes."

Brathwaite's English Gentleman, p. 174.

The " harrington" token was issued by John, created (in 1603) Baron Harrington, under a patent granted by King James I. for that purpose.

Among the poems printed with the "Strappado," is one inscribed to "the Worshipful Recorder of Kendal," where it is said "my journey's at an end;" and, as observes his last Editor, if these words may not be applied to one of the first two parts of the Itinerary, they have scarcely any meaning. The first part concludes at Staveley:

"Where I'll stay and end my journay,
Till brave Barnaby returne-a."

The third Journal terminates at Kendal, with the following verse:

' Thence to Kendall, pure her stato is,
Prudent too her magistrate is;
In whose charter to them granted
Nothing but a Mayor wanted:
Here it likes me to be dwelling,
Bousing, loving, stories telling."

To this allusion of a Mayor being wanted, there is, in the original edition, a couplet appended, by way of note:

"Now Saturn's year has drench'd down care,
And made an Alderman a May'r!"

This proves the time when the Itinerary was written, viz. between the Corporation grant in the 18th of Eliza-

beth and that in the 11th Charles I.

In an early edition of Barnaby's Journal, at Dallam Tower, there is an ancient minute, in the handwriting of one of the Wilsons, of that place, which states that the writer knew the author of that book to be Richard Brathwaite, of Burneshead, commonly called *Dapper Dick.* At Dodding Green there is a portrait of Dapper Dick, supposed to be an original.

The author of 'Drunken Barnaby' is inferior to none in vivacity, in wit, or in erudition; and he is evidently, *sub persond,* a drunkard merely in masquerade.

Besides the books above noticed, Brathwaite wrote the "Lives of the Roman Emperors," and two works in dramatic form, but these were never put on the stage. They were "Mercurius Britannicus, or the English Intelligencer," 1641; and "Regicidum," 1665.

z CHRISTOPHER POTTER, D.D., Nephew of Barnaby Potter, was educated at Queen's College, Oxford, where he became Fellow, and, as we before said, Provost. He was accounted an Arminian, and was in high favour with Archbishop Laud. He was made chaplain to King Charles I. in 1635, and afterwards Dean of Worcester; he was also nominated to a canonry of Windsor, and the deanery of Durham, but never enjoyed them, on account of the dissensions between King and Parliament. He was a very religious and exemplary man, learned in general, and a champion against popery. "He wrote," says Fuller, "an excellent book, entitled 'Charity Mistaken,' containing impregnable truth, so that malice may snarl at but not bite it without breaking its own teeth. Yet a railing Jesuit wrote a pretended confutation of it, to which the doctor made no return, partly because the industrious bee would not meddle with a wasp or hornet, and partly because a great master in school divinity, Mr. Chillingworth, took up the cudgels against him."

Christopher Potter was a devout admirer and partizan of the learned Henry Airay, of Kentmere, in this county; after whose death Potter edited and published two of his works, at that time highly

popular.

He died in Queen's College, March 3d, 1645-6, and was buried in the middle of the inner chapel.

"He was a person esteemed by all that knew him to be learned, religious, exemplary in his behaviour and discourse; courteous in his carriage, and of a sweet and obliging nature and comely presence." SIR GEORGE WHARTON

Was born at or near Kendal, on the 4th of April, 1617. We find the particulars of his life and writings in Wood's "Athenae Oxoniensis." He was descended from a genteel and ancient Westmorland family, richly possessed with lands and inheritance. He spent some time in the condition of a sojourner, in Oxford, 1633, where his natural genius leading him to astronomy and mathematics, he almost entirely neglected logic and philosophy; and retired to his patrimony to pursue his more favourite study. By the fictitious title of George Naworth, an anagram of his name, he published Almanacks. But, being discontented at the then growing rebellion, he turned all his inheritance into money, espoused his majesty's cause and interest, and raised a gallant troop of horse therewith. After several generous hazards of his person in battle, he was at last totally routed by the rebellious party in Gloucestershire, where he received several scars of honour, which he carried to his grave. Afterwards he retired to Oxford, where his majesty (King Charles) was then residing, and in recompense for his losses, had an employment conferred on him as sub-paymaster of the artillery. At leisure hours he still followed his studies, and was entered a student of Queen's College, where he might have had the degree of M.A. conferred on him, but he neglected it. After the surrender of the garrison of Oxford, at which time the King's cause daily declined, our author, Wharton, was put to his shifts, and lived as opportunity served, went to the great city, lived as privately as he could, and wrote several small works, both in prose and verse, for a livelihood. But they giving offence to the Protector and his adherents, then in power, he was several times imprisoned; in which sufferings he found a friend in Lilly, his former antagonist. After the Restoration, he became treasurer and paymaster to the Ordnance, repaid Lilly his courtesy, and was finally, for his signal services during the reigns of Charles I. and II., created a baronet, by patent, dated 31st of December, 1677. Sir George was always esteemed the best astrologer that wrote the Ephemerides of his time; and went beyond Lilly and Booker, the idols of the vulgar. He was a constant and thorough-paced loyalist; a boon companion; a witty, droll, and waggish poet. He wrote, besides his Hemeroscopions, or Almanacks, nineteen different astrological and chronological works.

He died in Middlesex, August 10th, 1681, and was buried in the chapel of the Tower, in London. One of his descendants was dignified by the title of Earl of Wharton, and was made Lord Privy Seal, and of his majesty's Privy Council in the reign of George L Another was created a Duke, whom Pope raised to a" bad eminence" in his *Essay on Man*. EPHRAIM CHAMBERS.

Ephraim Chambers, author of the first Cyclopaedia, was the youngest of three brothers. He was born at Milton, near Heversham, Westmorland His parents occupied a small farm there, and spent a harmless and unambitious life. They were dissenters, but not quakers, as has been affirmed; neither were any of their children educated as quakers. He received a good classical education, partly at Heversham, and afterwards at Kendal grammar school, and laid a suitable foundation for those studies which afterwards distinguished him. For a second son, Oxford University was too much for the means of the father, who, dissenter as he was, had sent his eldest son to study on the banks of Isis. All he could do for Ephraim was to apprentice him to a trade of some little scientific pretensions. Accordingly, he was indentured to "Mr. Senex, the globe maker," who lived and did business at the "Globe against St. Dunstan's Church," Fleet-street, London. There was considerable drudgery connected with Ephraim's duties in this business, which

were very little to his taste; but, fortunately, the master, Senex, had connexions with literature generally, and he found out that his apprentice's scientific habits could be made subservient to his interests, and he accordingly employed him with head and pen. It was behind the counter of Senex's shop, in Fleet-street, that Ephraim Chambers formed the idea of a great Cyclopedia of the Arts and Sciences, an original notion then. Scientific knowledge had accumulated; Boyle and others had written and experimented; Sir Isaac Newton was alive, and honoured, while Chambers stood or sat behind the counter of Mr. Senex, l "If schoolmasters may properly be allowed to participate in the honours of those whom they have educated, the greatest honour of my father's life will be the education of Ephraim Chambers. I have seen, among my father's papers, two school exercises, one in Latin, the other in Greek, signed' Chambers. These circumstances render it probable, that the author of the Dictionary was not, as has been said of him, merely educated to qualify him for trade and commerce."—Bishop Watson's "Anecdotes of his own Life." devoting his leisure hours to the arts, the sciences, and the languages. But, how much valuahle knowledge, Ephraim thought, was scattered through hundreds of volumes which might be brought together in one big book, to the delight of the general reading public. At the beginning of the century something of the kind had been done in a small way, the "Lexicon Technicum" of Dr. John Harris, a scientific man, who "read public lectures on mathematics, at the Marine Coffee-house in Birchin-lane;" for, the diffusion of useful knowledge did not entirely originate with the nineteenth century, in which we have the honour and the happiness to live. Harris's "Lexicon Technicum; or, an Historical English Dictionary of Arts and Sciences," compiled for the booksellers, and published by subscription, in 1704, met with considerable success, though its plan and scope were nothing to those of Chambers's book. Revolving the idea behind the counter of the Fleet-street shop,

Chambers, at last, broached the matter to the publishers (Longmans), who took it up, and on the counter itself were written some of its earlier articles. Ephraim Chambers received encouragement, and something more solid, from the London publishers; to such an extent, indeed, that he could retire from the Globe in Fleet-street to quiet chambers in Gray's-inn-lane, where he wore out the rest of his life over his Dictionary: a work which, for those days, even deserves the designation of " great. " It was published by subscription, in 1728, in two volumes, folio, at four guineas, and with a numerous list of subscribers. And there were liberal publishers, too, before our own age; for tho "undertakers," delighted with the unexpected success of the work, presented Ephraim with a free gift of 500?. Thomas Longman and his partner's property in the Dictionary was not large at first—not more, we believe, than a single sixtyfourth share of the whole— and for it they paid about 50/. But Thomas Longman, during his partner's life and after his partner's death, kept buying up shares (though "sellers were There Ib a copy of the 6th edition of this work, in two vols., in the library of the Kendal Literary and Scientific Society; and also a copy of the 7th edition, in four vols, (including two supplementary vols.), in a small library belonging to the Free Grammar School of Kendal. shy," as the Trade reports say), until, in the year 1740, he figures in the books of the Stationers' Company as the owner of eleven out of the sixty-four; a number larger than that held by any proprietor. Thomas Longman liked the book, and liked its compiler, working away in his Gray's-inn chambers, "very cheerful, but hasty and impetuous," not talking orthodoxy; for if Samuel Johnson formed his style, he did not form his religious creed, on that of the Westmorland dissenter. Chambers kept little company and no table. An intimate friend, who called on him one morning, was asked by him to stay and dine. "And what will you give me, Ephraim?" said the gentleman. "I dare engage you have nothing for dinner." To which Mr.

Chambers calmly replied: "Yes, I have a fritter; and if you'll stay with me, I'll have two." Although he lived (metaphorically) in Grub-street, in his last will he declared that "he owed no debts excepting to his tailor for his roquelaure." He died on the 15th May, 178iO, after a sickness brought on by over work. In the five years alone, between 1728 and 1733, his amanuensis, a Mr. Airey, recorded, that, for his employer, "during that time, he had copied nearly twenty folio volumes, so large as to comprehend materials, if they had been published, for printing thirty volumes of the same size as the Cyclopaedia.

He was buried in the cloisters of Westminster Abbey; and in the epitaph, written by himself and placed there, he says (autobiographically): "Multis pervulgatus, paucis notus; qui vitam, inter lucem et umbram, nec eruditus, nec idiota, Uteris deditus transegit."

To the *Gentleman's Magazine,* for September, 1758, a correspondent "M." contributed some particulars respecting Ephraim Chambers, and in the memoir occurs the following passage:—" It has been hinted that Mr. Chambers was not treated in the most liberal manner by the booksellers with whom he was concerned; but this was far from being the case, as he experienced the most generous treatment from them. Mr. Longman, in particular, used him with the liberality of a prince, and the tenderness of a father; his house was ever open to receive him, and when he was there nothing could exceed his care and anxiety over him; even his natural absence of mind was consulted, and during his illness, jellies and other proper refreshments were industriously left for him at those places where it was least likely he should avoid seeing them." Ephraim had basked in the smiles of royalty, both English and French; but "the liberality of a prince" he experienced only from the bookseller of Paternoster-row. The first edition of this Dictionary "was dedicated to his Majesty," King George II. , "and Mr. Chambers had the *honour* of presenting copies of the work, in very elegant bindings, to the King and

Queen, which produced him the *smile of regal* approbation," but nothing else.

The book passed through five editions in the space of eighteen years; a sufficient proof of its merits and popularity, the first edition, as before mentioned, appearing in 1728. During his last illness, when he was in France, vainly seeking for the recovery of his health, "he received an intimation," we are told, "that if he would publish a new edition there, and dedicate it to Louis XV., he would be liberally rewarded; but these proposals his British heart received with disdain, and he rejected the teazing solicitation of men who were provoking him to a sordid retractation of the compliments he had paid to his lawful sovereign." Chambers owed nothing to kings; what little he did owe (beyond the roquelaure to his tailor), he owed to Thomas Longman, whose interest in him did not cease with his death. JOHN WILSON,

Or, as he was more commonly called, "Black Jack," author of a Synopsis of British Plants, in Ray's method, was a journeyman shoemaker of Kendal. He was the first who attempted a systematic arrangement, in the English language, of the indigenous plants of Great Britain. He may be ranked among those who, without the advantages of a liberal education, have distinguished themselves from the mass of mankind by their scientific and literary accomplishments. He exchanged his first calling for the more lucrative employment of a baker. This business was principally managed by his wife, and thus he had leisure for pursuing his researches as a naturalist.

"Life of Thomas Longman."

The profits of this new business being considerable, afforded his family conveniences of life very superior to what have been represented by the author of British Topography. It was no easy matter to acquire the reputation of an accurate botanist, at a time when Linnaeus' admirable method of discriminating species had not given the science its most essential improvement. But the subject of the present memoir, by a perseverance which, when stimulated by

the love of knowledge, often triumphs over every obstacle, overcame the difficulties inseparable from the enterprise, and justly obtained that character, from the intimate acquaintance which he proved himself to possess with the vegetable productions of the north of England. There is, however, good reason to believe, that he was not entirely self-taught; for, under the article *gentiana,* he (accidentally) mentions his intercourse with Mr. Fitz-Roberts, who resided at the Gill, near Kendal, and who was known to both Pettiver and Ray. The name of Fitz-Roberts occurs in the Synopsis of the latter naturalist." Wilson's Synopsis was published in the year 1744. It comprehends that part of Eay's method which treats of the more perfect herbs, beginning at the fourth *genus,* and ending with the twenty-sixth. He promises, in the preface, to complete the work at a future period, but did not live to fulfil his promise. After lingering in a state of debility, which rendered him unfit for mental or bodily fatigue, for three or four years, he died July loth, 1751. Many anecdotes are told of the singularities of his character and conversatioa His discourse abounded with remarks both pertinent and original. Being once in the county of Durham, he was introduced to a person who piqued himself highly on his cultivation of rare plants, and would show Wilson through his garden, animadverting, in a high tone, on the list of rarities before them, and referring to authors where they were described. Wilson, in his turn, plucked a wild herb growing in a neglected spot, and presented it to his host, who endeavoured to get clear of the difficulty of classing it by pronouncing it a weed; but Wilson immediately replied, " a weed is a term of art, not a production of nature;" adding, "your explanation proves you to be a *gardener,* not a *botanist."*

He was peculiarly remarkable for his eccentricities, which, in a literal sense, attended him to the grave; for his last short walk was to the churchyard, where, addressing the sexton, and pointing to an unseemly puddle, he made this whimsical request: "If I have done but little good during life, I desire to be of use after death; let my body fill up this hole." The petition was strictly observed, and the remains of the celebrated botanist were deposited in the puddle.

He lectured on Natural History at different towns in the north of England.

WILLIAM HUDSON, F.R.S.,

Author of "Flora Anglica," and other works, was born at the White Lion Inn, in Kendal (about the year 1730), then kept by his father. He received his education at the grammar school of his native town, under the tuition of the then master, Mr. Towers, who was reputed an able teacher, and of considerable attainments in classical literature. Hudson was removed to London in early youth, where he served an apprenticeship to an apothecary, and spent the remainder of his life. It appears that he had turned his attention to the science of botany when very young, for, during his apprenticeship he obtained the prize which was annually given at Apothecaries' Hall, to the apprentice who should appear to have attained the greatest proficiency in the knowledge of plants. This prize was a copy of " Ray's Synopsis." The publication of his "Flora Anglica," in 1672, which was received with approbation, is said to have contributed, principally, to the introduction of the Linnaean system of botany into England. He did not, however, confine his attention entirely to botany, but extended his researches to different branches of Natural History, more especially to insects and shells. In the latter order he discovered, in the mountains of Cumberland, a new species, viz., the *Trochus terrestris,* which he communicated to to Mr. Pennant, by whom it was figured in the fourth volume of the " British Zoology. " In 1783, when the house was burnt More recent knowledge of land-shells has cast a doubt upon *ZYochus terresins* being a distinct species. The young shells of *Pupa bulimia* and *Clauiilia* are more or less of a trochiform type. These immature forms were apt to be taken by the older conchologists for *Troeki.* in which he lodged, he had the great misfortune to lose his cabinet of insects,

and the greatest part of his herbarium. He retired from business after this misfortune, and died of a paralytic stroke in May, 1793.

THOMAS SHAW, D.D.,

Was the son of Gabriel Shaw, a shearman-dyer. He was born at Kendal, in 1693, and was educated at the grammar school there. In 1711, he was admitted at Queen's College, Oxford. He received the degree of B.A. in 1716, and of M.A. in 1719. He was afterwards ordained, and appointed chaplain to the English Factory at Algiers. There he remained for several years, and thence travelled into various parts of the East. When he was absent, in 1727, he was chosen a Fellow of his college, and after his return became Doctor of Divinity, in 1734. In that year he was also elected a Fellow of the Royal Society in London. In 1738, he published the first edition of his " Travels in Barbary and the Levant," a work which, not only for its accuracy and fidelity, but on account of the illustrations it contains of natural history, of the classic authors, and especially of the Scriptures, holds a distinguished place amongst the literary productions of this country. The first edition of his Travels was published at Oxford, in folio. They were translated into French, and printed in 4to., in 1743, with several notes and emendations communicated by the Author. The second edition, with two supplements supplied by the Doctor shortly before his death, was published in 1757. Both editions, but especially the latter, sold at a high price, and having become extremely scarce, a third was published in Edinburgh, in 1808. He presented the University with some natural curiosities, ancient coins, and busts, which he had collected during his travels. Three of the last of these are engraved in the "Marmora Oxoniensis." In 1740, Dr. Shaw was nominated, by his college, Principal of Edmund Hall; and was Regius Professor of Greek till 1751, when death put a stop to his labours.

He died in high reputation for knowledge, probity, and Editor of the 3rd edition of *he* Travels.

pleasantry. His countenance was

grotesque, but marked most strongly with jocularity and good humour, so as to diffuse into the company of his friends the full effects of his innocent and instructive mirth.

On his monument, in Bromley church, is an epitaph, written by Dr. Brown, Provost of Queen's College, Oxford, of which the following is a copy:— Peregrinationibus variU

Per Europam, Africam, Asiamque,

Feliciter absolutis,

Et exuviis mortalibus hie loci

Tandem depositis,

Cooleatem in patriam remigravit

THOMAS SHAW, S.T.P. et R.S.S.

Qabrielis Fil. Kendaliensis:

Qui

Consulibus Anglicis apud Algerenses

Primum cr.it a Sacris;

Mox Coll. Reginao inter Socioa ascriptus,

Aulas dein Sancti Edmundi Principalis,

Ac ejusdem munificua Instaurator;

Lingua) demum Grsecse apud Oxonienses

Professor Regius.

De Literis quantum meruit Auctor celebratuH,

Edita uaque testabuntur Opera,

Pyramidibus ipsis, quag penitiua inspexerat,

Perenniora foraan extitura.

Hie, Studiis etai severioribus

Indies occupatus,

Horis tamen aubsecivis emicuit

Eruditus idem et facetus conviva.

Optima quanquam Mentis indole

Et multiplici Scientia instructus;

Literatorum omnium, domi forisque,

Suffragiis comprobatus;

Magnatum Procerumque popularium

Familiari insignitus Notitia;

Neo summis in Ecclesii Dignitatibus impnr;

Fato tamen iniquo evenit,

Ut Bramleyensis obiret Paroecias

Vicariua pane Sexagenarius

XVIII. Cal. Sept. A.D. 1751.

Uxor JOANNA, Ed. Holden Arm.

Conaulis

Algerensis olim Conjux, bis Vidua, M.P.

i There is an anecdote told of him and a brother of his, named Miles, a man of abilities, but not of equal honour with his brother. On one occasion, when ANTHONY ASKEW, M. D.,

Was born in a house in the Marketplace, Kendal, which, together with other property contiguous to it, belonged to his father, Adam Askew, M.D. He was born in 1722; and was educated at Sedbergh school, and afterwards at Emanuel College, Cambridge. He was made B.A. in 1745, then went to Leyden, where he remained a year, and next year visited Constantinople with the English ambassador, whence he returned through Italy, to Paris, in 1749, when he was made a member of the Academy of Belles Lettres. In 1750, he took the degree of M.D. at Cambridge. He proposed an edition of iEschylus, and published a specimen of it, but nothing more; and died February 27, 1774, aged 52, leaving a family of five sons and four daughters.

He acquired great reputation, at home and abroad, on account of his collection of Greek manuscripts, which was more numerous and more valuable than that of any other private gentleman in England. These manuscripts Dr. Askew purchased at a considerable expense in the East, and brought with him to England. His collection also of printed Greek books, when sold, was allowed to consist of a greater number of scarce and valuable editions of the classics than had ever before been exposed to sale in this country, and the sale realized upwards of 1,300?. When abroad, he kept an album, which, among other testimonies to his merit from distinguished foreigners, contains many compliments and epigrams addressed to him by modern Greeks. This Album is now among the manuscripts of Emanuel College, Cambridge.

The Appendix to Scapula, published in 1789, was compiled from one of his manuscripts. GEORGE ROMNET.

The distinguished subject of this memoir, although not a native of Kendal, has given us a sufficient title to rank him the Doctor was preaching in Kendal church, he took for his text—"A good name is better than great riches." "So it may," says Miles, after he had heard the sermon out, " but how must they do that have neither?" "Beauties of England and Wales," vol. xv. p. 235.

among the eminent personages properly connected with the town. It was here that he was placed an apprentice to the art in which he obtained celebrity. It was here that his genius developed itself, and received the earliest encouragement. It was in this town that he made choice of a wife, and was married. And it was in this town that, after having attained the highest eminence in his profession, he sought the pillow of repose in the evening of life, and descended, full of honours, to the grave.

It has been remarked, that, "of all our eminent artists, Romney has perhaps been the most fortunate in his biographers;" and since the publication of the Memoir in which this observation is conveyed, we think no one will doubt the justice of the remark. Cumberland, the dramatist, published a Memoir of Romney, shortly after his death. Another, by Haley, the poet, followed soon after. In 1829, the Rev. John Romney, the painter's son, wrote an account of his father's life. None of these publications, nor all of them, were, however, considered perfectly satisfactory; and it was reserved for Allan Cunningham to winnow away the chaff from them, and to delineate, with a master hand, an exact portraiture of the man and the artist.

George Romney was born at Beckside, near Dalton-inFurness, in Lancashire, on the 15th December, 1734. He was the son of John Romney, of that place, a joiner and cabinet-maker, and a man of considerable ingenuity in practical mechanics and architecture. George was at school till eleven years of age, when, having made little progress in learning, he was taken away to be employed in the trade of his father. His leisure hours, at this time, were principally devoted to carving on wood, constructing violins, and sometimes performing on that instrument. He was also beguiled into the unprofitable and mysterious science of alchemy; but this scheme soon exploded; and his other pursuits were gradually, and at length totally, abandoned, as the character of his mind unfolded itself in a devout passion for the arts. It appears that Romney's father had a business intercourse Allan Cunniugham2s Memoir of Romney, in " British Painters," &c. vol. v. with Alderman Redman, of Kendal, which superinduced a friendly intimacy hetween the families. Mrs. Gardner, a sister of Alderman Redman, and a lady of taste and judgment in the fine arts, being on a visit to the house of Romney, and having perceived in the crude efforts of his son the characteristic marks of genius, encouraged him to persevere, and interceded with his father, to let painting be his sole pursuit and profession. Mrs. Gardner sat to him for her portrait; and the indications of talent became so decisive, that his father was induced to bind him an apprentice to a portrait painter of the name of Steele, at that time resident in Kendal. In this servitude Romney complained that he was treated more like a drudge than a pupil. He confessed, however, that he acquired considerable knowledge in the preparation and mixing of colours, through his own spirit of observation, as well as from his master's instruction.

It was during his apprenticeship, on the 14th of May, 1756, that Romney married Mary Abbot, of Kirkland, who, by the unanimous testimony of his biographers, was, in every respect, worthy of his affections and his fame. For more than two years he practised with Steele, accompanying him to Lancaster, York, and other places, as an itinerant portrait painter. After which, his master determining to leave England, Romney prevailed on him to surrender his indenture; and without further instructions or experience, he commenced, on his own account, when twenty-three years of age,

Kendal was naturally selected as the scene of his first exertions; and he appears to have commenced at a favourable moment. At that time Colonel George Wilson was residing at Abbot Hall, and as he was a gentleman ever disposed to encourage rising merit, the struggling artist was taken under his especial protection. It is wisely and beautifully said, in the biography of

Benjamin West, that "those who befriend genius when it is struggling for distinction, befriend the world: and their names should be held in remembrance." Mr. Wilson was the first public patron of Romney, and as such deserves to be had in remembrancei Mrs. Gardner was the mother of Mr Daniel Gardner, an eminent crayon painter in his day, and a native of Kendal.

both for the individual merit of his patronage, and for the example which it displays to others, who have the power and the opportunity to do likewise. He introduced the artist to the Strickland family, at Sizergh, where Romney had the advantage—the only advantage he had before going to London—of studying and copying a few pictures of other masters. One of his early productions was the representation of a hand holding a letter, which he painted for the postmaster of Kendal. This painting formerly distinguished the window of the Post Office in this town. At Kendal he continued four years, painting portraits principally. He found leisure, also, to make about a score of compositions, which were disposed of in a lottery, composed of eighty tickets, price half a guinea each.

On the 14th of March, 1762, Romney set out for London. His thirst of fame was more powerful than his conjugal affections; and whatever were his secret intentions towards his wife on his departure, all that has been said, or can be said, of his subsequent conduct, will not justify the estrangement which it produced. His visit to London brought him all the riches and all the honours that his fancy, in its brightest dreams, could have anticipated; but his wife was, for thirty years, almost entirely neglected; and not until he waxed infirm, and needed a nurse, was her society again courted

He set up his easel in Dove Court, London. The painting that first elicited public approbation was the Death of Wolfe, which obtained for him a prize of twenty-five guineas from the Society of Aits. Reynolds was at that time at the meridian of his fame; notwithstanding which, Romney soon proved a rival

so powerful that it was said "he divided the empire with Sir Joshua." In 1764, he visited Paris, where he remained six weeks, studying chiefly, in the Luxembourg Gallery, the works of Rubens. In 1773, he resolved to devote two years to study in Rome, believing, as Cunningham says all artists do, "that the way to perfection lies through the Sistine chapel." Whilst there, he devoted himself to intense and sequestered study. Having stored his portfolio with images of Italian beauty, both from dead and living models, he returned to London in 1775. Sitters now nocked to his studio, and for several years Komney " had the ascendancy of Reynolds in the scale of popular opinion." Komney was exceedingly industrious, and the intervals between sittings, and his leisure hours, were filled up with fancy sketches and historical delineations. A list of all the works which he executed in those busy days would occupy many pages; and we will not therefore attempt to enumerate them, or make particular allusion to any. Too much of his time was, however, consumed with making sketches, which were merely indicated on the canvas, and no more touched. His professional progress is exceedingly encouraging and interesting, but we cannot here go along with the details. Jealousy between him and Sir Joshua Reynolds prevented Komney's being admitted, or desiring to be admitted, an Associate of the Koyal Academy; but Cunningham concludes his observations on this subject by saying, "that his name has lost nothing by coming down to posterity untagged with *initials.*"

Komney continued to prosecute his labours in London till 1799, when his mental energies began rapidly to decline; and it was in the summer of that year that he repaired to his affectionate wife at Kendal, "who, surviving his neglect, lived yet to prove the depth of woman's love." In the following year he sunk into helpless imbecility, in which state he lingered till the 15th of November, 1802, when he had nearly completed his sixty-eighth year. He died in the house, in Kirkland, now occupied by Misses Wilkinson; and his remains

were interred at Dalton, the place of his birth.

The character of Komney, with the exception of the blemish it bears from his conduct towards his wife, appears worthy of his genius; and his genius, it is proved, was in every respect worthy of the patronage he obtained. He was kindhearted, generous, and upright; charitable to the poor; and, what is a rare virtue in painters, indulgent and encouraging to young artists. His friendships were disinterested and sincere; and except, perhaps, in the case of Hayley, were all happily chosen. Adam Walker, the natural Cunningham's Memoir.

philosopher, and Cockin, the poet and arithmetician, both connected with this county, were among the number of his friends; the former of his earlier, and the latter of his declining years. It is too much the practice of persons who have enjoyed what is called a "liberal education" to derogate from the merit of others who, despite of this advantage, are rising, or have risen to enviable distinction in the world. Cumberland and Hayley, the two earliest biographers of Romney, both, it seems, belonged to this class of *soi-disant* liberals; and, from a coincidence of feeling, withheld the honours that were due for his extraordinary powers of mind. Cunningham has, however, carefully and cleverly analyzed the mental powers of the artist; and amply recompensed whatever his fame had suffered by the neglect or injustice of his contemporary friends. If it should be wondered at that, with all his successful industry, so few of Romney's paintings rank in the galleries of the present day, a reference to Cunningham's Memoir will explain the reason. If we inquire, says the biographer, concerning the fruit of his labours, we shall be told of abundance of great designs begun, and but few happily ended—of portraits enow of the beautiful, the rich, and the titled,—but next to none of men of genius, by the delineation of whose features and minds alone a portrait painter has much chance, to reach posterity. He adopted or followed the fashion and feeling of his day more than a man who believes he is labouring for immortality ought ever to do. As to his historical and inventive productions, he allowed the first heat of his fancy to cool before he rendered some of his fine sketches and designs worthy of taking rank as works of art. The world has been a sad loser in consequence of the multitudes of noteless, nameless faces, which it sent to the painter's easel,, to the continual interruption of his historic productions. The characteristic merit of his works consists in poetic dignity of conception, wherein Flaxman said he was the first of all English painters, and in the harmony and brilliancy of his colouring.

A A SIR ALAN CHAMBRE, KNIGHT,

Was of an ancient and honourable family, which Dr. Burn has traced up to the time of Henry III. Sir Alan, who is the fifteenth in descent from that time, was the son and heir of Walter Chambre, Esq., Barrister-at-Law, and Mary, daughter of Jacob Morland, of Capplethwaite, Esq.

Sir Alan Chambre was born in 1740, in the house which is now the New Inn, in Highgate, Kendal, where his father lived previously to his residence at Abbot Hall. His father and grandfather were both Recorders of Kendal. He obtained the rudiments of his education at the Free Grammar School, Kendal, under the tuition of Mr. Gilbert Crackenthorpe. From hence he was removed to Sedbergh school, eminent for scholastic honours, at that time conducted by Dr. Bateman. From Sedbergh, Sir Alan went into the office of Forth Wintour, Esq., solicitor, in Pall Mall, London; and afterwards practised as a Barrister-at-Law, in Gray's Inn. In 1796, he was elected Recorder of Lancaster, which office he resigned in 1799. In 1800, he was appointed one of the Judges of the Court of Common Pleas, which he resigned in 1816, and was succeeded by Mr. Justice Park. He died in the eighty-fourth year of his age, at the Crown Inn, Harrowgate; and his remains were brought from thence to be interred in the family vault at Kendal.

Sir Alan was esteemed a wise, discreet, and upright judge, and was in high reputation at the bar, both for his professional talents, the justice of his decisions, and the purity of his principles. In private life he wasexemplary in all moral relations, and in Christian benevolence. His heart was ever ready

"To answer to the tender call
Of God-like charity."

Vide the inscription on his monument, at p. 73.

JOHN GOUGH,

Called, by Dr. Kitto and other writers, "The Blind Philosopher," was born in Kendal, the 17th of January, in the year 1757, and was the oldest child of Nathan Gough, of Kendal, shearman-dyer, and Susannah his wife.

His father was the only child, by a first marriage, of Thomas Gough, skinner and glover, of Wyersdale, in Lancashire: his mother was the oldest daughter of Mr. John Wilson, a respectable yeoman, who had a good estate on the west bank of Windermere Lake.

When a man has been a successful cultivator of any department of science, literature, or art, he becomes an object of public curiosity; and the history of his childhood is examined for incidents which may shed a light upon the origin of his pursuits, and the development of his character. To the subject of this biographical sketch, there happened, at a very early age, an event, which, in his opinion, gave birth to his character. Before the completion of his third year, he was attacked with small-pox, which deprived him of his sight. The whole globe of the left eye was destroyed: the damage done to the other was not so extensive: for, though the greater part of the cornea was rendered opaque, there was a minute pellucid speck to the right of the pupil, which permitted a ray of light to fall upon the verge of the retina, and thus he was enabled to distinguish between day and night: but he had no perception of the form or colour of objects around him; so that, for all useful purposes, vision was completely lost.

During the bright days of childhood, brief as they were, the imagery of the external world had found access, through the infantile eye, to the mind;

and lasting impressions of a Thomas Gough was the «on of James Gough, who was the son of William Goff, a general in the Parliamentary army, and one who signed King Charles' death warrant. At the time of the Restoration, he escaped the axe of the executioner by an early flight. The reader may consult. an interesting article on William Goff, entitled "The Cave of the Regicides, and how three of them fared in New England," in Blackwood's Magazine, Vol. LXI., March, 1847.

few scenes and objects were registered on memory's tablet. To the latest period of his life, Mr. Gough had a distinct recollection of being an eye-witness of the last Kendal Guild, in 1759. But the procession with all its gaudy pageantry, had no charms for him. On the contrary, having been carried into an upper chamber for a view of what was passing below, he was greatly alarmed by the multiplicity of strange sights, and, escaping from his companions, took shelter in a bed and concealed his face in the bedclothes. He had also a lively idea of an appearance, which he conceived to be a body of cavalry in motion; but as a distant troop does not constitute an object of touch, he had 110 means of subsequently testing the truth of this supposition. Another object, which he recollected having seen, was a chimney-piece ornament. But as in this instance it was colour probably, to the exclusion of form, that arrested the eye of a child, he failed afterwards to discover by touch the counterpart of that which he had seen; though his restless fingers were accustomed to run over every object within reach, even over the identical ornament itself; for it was on his father's mantelpiece. Hence he was led to remark, "I remember various appearances, which I cannot refer to any particular class of objects." Another object really seen was an earth-worm, crawling among a collection of dirt on a garden-bed, and by a curious coincidence, which we shall presently mention, he verified, "with the greatest certainty," a fact that probably had a material influence in developing that fine appreciation of form, which he manifested so conspicuously at a more advanced stage. But now was a veil drawn over all the visible beauties of creation, and "wisdom at one entrance, quite shut out" for ever; and though other inlets for knowledge were destined to be more widely opened, the time was not yet come. Long after the malady had done its mischief, the victim of its ravages was a being of commiseration, for that watchful sentinel, the ear, was ignorant of its duties. Ordinary sounds added to his wretchedness; because he knew not whence they were, or what was their nature. Time passed heavily. Neither did night bring any solace to the tedium of the day; for his sleep, instead of being tranquil, was disturbed by dreams and visions; so that his existence, at this period, seemed to mark him out as a child of misfortune.

But this wretchedness was to have a limit. His situation hegan to improve: and by degrees he learned to substitute touch in place of sight, and to derive knowledge, as well as pleasure, from the use of his fingers. The education of his touch was promoted by his father, who encouraged him to investigate every object which could be handled with safety. It was on one of these occasions, that the parental instructor, while angling, gave him a worm to examine, in the first year of his blindness. He at once knew that it was a creature of the same kind that he had seen in the garden. The fact is interesting, and forms a curious instance how the image of an object, which has been once impressed upon the sensorium, through the retina, a nerve of special sense, may be afterwards reproduced and recalled to mind, when conveyed through another channel, a nerve of common sensation.

About the expiration of a year from the time that he became blind a trifling incident happened, which greatly relieved his uneasy apprehensions: a hammer was accidentally placed in his hands as a plaything, which he exercised upon a boarded window-seat; and after a few strokes had been given, by means of his own hand, he made an important discovery—the sound produced was similar to a noise which had dis-turbed him so much in the early days of his misfortune. Hence the result of these strokes with his own hammer, was proved to be identical with the perplexing sounds caused by the hammers of a number of carpenters at work in a neighbouring house. His fingers and his ears were now in active employment. Various bodies, which he learned to discriminate by their forms and other tangible characters, were named for him by his parents and friends; and whenever any such objects came a second time into his hands he had no difficulty in recognising them, and recalling their names. These homely lessons soon taught his inquisitive spirit to appreciate the value of conversation in supplying him with the materials of thought and instruction. He began to understand that numbers of animals existed in the world, in addition to the few which were domesticated. His questions, on this subject, were incessant in the presence of his father, who gave him, in return, popular descriptions of the forms and habits of lions and wolves, and various other quadrupeds, as well as of birds, and strange serpents and fishes. As a proof of his progress, he informs us, that before he was the age of four years and a half, he had a clear conception that the animal kingdom was divided into quadrupeds, birds, fishes, serpents, insects, and crustaceous and testaceous animals— a classification generally adopted at that period.

The art of acquiring knowledge, thus begun and pursued at home, was soon extended to a wider circle. Not only was the field of observation enlarged, but a greater variety of objects also was embraced. The horns and violins of itinerant musicians were listened to with delight; the instruments were examined; and, occasionally, an attempt was made to elicit similar sounds by the application of his own lips and fingers; and, while in his father's arms, he was permitted to handle the bears, monkeys, and camels, which travelled the streets. At a later period, he was introduced, by the same cautious guardian, into a travelling menagerie; and, an arrangement having been made with the keeper, he entered many of the cages, and examined all the harmless animals. But the fulfilment of this part of the agreement did not satisfy the curiosity of the blind boy: he begged to be permitted to handle the rest of the collection; and his entreaties prevailed. The result was, that he ran his fingers over all the carnivorous animals, nothing daunted by their expressions of disapprobation; the hyena's cage being the only one which was not entered, though he was ready to make this venture also, had not the keeper refused to comply with his wish.

Such were the simple rudiments of Zoology imparted to Mr. Gough, in his early youth, by his father. A thirst for more information than could be thus obtained was an earnest of the interest which he took in the study of Nature's products. And, small as were these germs of thought in the spring-time of his mental evolution, yet, by self-help and incessant application, they were cultivated and matured, in length of time, into a full and fruitful harvest of knowledge.

In the summer of 1761, before the completion of his fifth year, a circumstance occurred, which materially contributed to a more refined culture of his sense of hearing. He became acquainted with an old man, and his son, who were both partial to music; the former playing upon the violin, and the latter practising the same instrument, and the German flute also. To their performances the blind youth frequently listened with raptures; and the old man as frequently extolled the delicacy and correctness of his ear. The son took a fancy to give him instructions on the violin; but this musical education, though calculated to administer to his enjoyment, was destined to receive an early check. For his father, who was a member of the Society of Friends, from religious scruples, put a stop to his further progress; though at the same time, he had the good sense to perceive the value of some permanent employment.

But the choice of a settled pursuit required due deliberation, and at length the study of Latin was selected. With this intention therefore, at the age of six, he was placed under the care of Mr. Rebanks, at that time master of the Friends' school, in Kendal. Some one of his class-fellows read over the rules of the Latin grammar and accidence, which he committed to memory without much difficulty; yet the amount of knowledge acquired was trifling, as compared with the time consumed. But, fortunately, when the young student was about twelve years old, Mr. Rebanks retired, in favour of Mr. Bewly, who was a good classic; and under his tuition Mr. Gough made rapid progress in Latin. In addition to his classical knowledge, Mr. Bewly was well-read in the different branches of Natural Philosophy, a circumstance which, at a later period, proved of great advantage to the pupil.

The study of classics, however, did not efface his early impressions. He admired the lives of illustrious men, as portrayed in the original language of Cornelius Nepos: but he loved more dearly living animals and their short histories, as given in the few books to which he had access. Nature was ever the idol of his mind; plants found a place in his early affections. For we learn that, in his eighth year, he was in the habit of visiting an aged couple, who had a few flowering plants, standing at a window. The powerful odour of one of these (a Moldavian balm), attracted his attention: groping his way to the specimen, he examined its stem, leaves, and the whorl in which the flowers were arranged; and as carefully also did he compare these different parts with the corresponding parts of another plant, which stood beside the balm. And this comparison led him to conclude that as much pleasure and instruction might be expected from the vegetable kingdom, as from a study of animals. At this period, his knowledge of plants was of small compass. But the information, so acquired, had its value. His fingers were schooled in a minute perception of form; and every fresh specimen being distinguished by the relation which it had to other vegetable productions, already known to him, presented itself as a new species. The distinctive

characters of each plant, therefore, were his own; for, hitherto, Nature was the only book he consulted. Need we, then, be surprised at his own remarks?—" My progress in Botany proved very slow for a long time. It is true I never desisted from the pursuit; for every plant that fell in my way became an object of careful scrutiny. I treasured up in memory the forms of a multitude of vegetables, so as to afterwards recognise many of them, when I came to read their descriptions."

Hitherto, he had no idea that books were devoted to plants. But this ignorance was presently to be removed. It was in his thirteenth summer that his father carried him and his eldest sister into the fields, and observing his son deeply absorbed in examining a specimen of Henbane, he gathered a handful of wild flowers, telling him, at the same time, that plants had been named and described in books; and that this had been done, in part, by a Kendal man, John Wilson. This intelligence excited his curiosity; and he never rested till he had made himself master of a copy of Wilson's "Synopsis of British Plants." His first task was to study the dictionary of terms; then, to master the classification; and after these preliminary qualifications, he commenced the study of practical botany by referring the plants of his neighbourhood to their class, genus, and species. In these attempts, he met with many difficulties. But finding that Wilson made frequent references to the writings of two ancient botanists, Gerrard and Parkinson, he obtained their works. His next proceeding was, to form a small botanical class among his school-fellows. To these he explained his views, and smoothed the way by giving them elementary lessons on classification, and the use of technical terms. Excursions were then made, far and near, in search of plants. On their return home, Mr. Gough examined each specimen, while one of his fellow-students consulted and read the "Synopsis;" and when he had determined the species, the woodcuts of Gerrard and Parkinson were examined by the class, and compared with the specimen he had named. And the herbarium of his boy-

hood proves the industry and accuracy of his first botanical efforts. At a later period, Hudson's "Flora Anglica," according to the sexual classification of Linnreus, became his favourite work; and still later, he consulted Withering's "Arrangement of Plants," and Smith's " Flora Britannica"

With the former of these botanists he was in frequent correspondence, previous to the publication of the third edition of the "Arrangement;" and as a proof of Dr. Withering's confidence in the correctness of his discrimination, he informed his blind contributor that he would accept his habitats and remarks without reserve, and without any more specimens for verification.

But his method of examining plants must be briefly told. Systems of classification were but little valued, except so far as they aided him in recognising individual form. The plant to be examined was held by the root or base in one hand, while the fingers of the other travelled slowly upwards, over the stem, branches, and leaves, till they reached the flower. If the species had been already met with, this procedure was sufficient for its recognition; if it proved to be a novelty, its class was first determined by the insertion of the elongated tip of his tongue within the flower: thus he discovered the number and arrangement of the stamens and pistils. When the flower was small, he requested his reader to ascertain these points with a lens. The class and order being determined, the genus was next worked out, word by word of the description, so far at least as the state of the specimen would allow. But his perceptive power over form was most conspicuous in the analysis of species. It was truly wonderful to witness the rapidity with which his fingers ran among the leaves, taking cognizance of their divisions, shape, serratures, and of the presence or absence of hairs. The finest down was detected, by a stem or leaf being drawn gently across the border of his lower lip; so fine, indeed, that a young eye often required a lens to verify the truth of the perception. Another peculiarity is worthy of notice. Repeated perusal of descriptions had enabled him to pre-figure in his mind's eye, the form without the presence of specimens; so that, when a species for the first time came within his touch, he at once named it from memory.

New plants, new animals, like all other subjects, indeed, in which he was greatly interested, caused him to betray outwardly the power that was actively at work within—the brightness of his intellect beamed upon his countenance. And it was, probably, on one of these occasions, that Mr. Wordsworth, while describing the little cushion-like plant, with white roots and purple flowers, growing near Grisedale Tarn, caught the first glimpse of that conception which was afterwards expanded into the beautiful picture given of Mr. Gough in the *Excursion*. Mark the Poet's recollections of the man, as he stood before him:

"Methinks I see him—how his eye balls rolled,
Beneath his ample brow, in darkness paired;
But each instinct with spirit; and the frame
Of the whole countenance alive with thought,
Fancy and understanding; while the voice
Discoursed of natural and moral truth
With eloquence, and such authentic power,
That in his presence humbler knowledge stood
Abashed, and tender pity overawed."

But some years before the period to which these remarks refer, the same psychological reading had also met the eye of S. T. Coleridge. In a short Essay on "The Soul and its Organs of Sense," he says: "The every-way amiable and estimable John Gough of Kendal, is not only an excellent mathematician, but an infallible botanist and zoologist. He has frequently, at first feel, corrected the mistakes of the most experienced sportsmen, with regard to the birds or vermin which they had killed, when it chanced to be a variety or rare species, so completely resembling the common one, that it required great steadiness of observation to detect the difference,

even after it had been pointed out. As to plants and flowers, the rapidity of his touch appears fully equal to that of sight, and the accuracy greater. Good heavens! it needs only to look at him! Why, his face sees all over!"

We are prevented, by want of space, from giving more than a rapid outline of Mr. Gough's progress. At fifteen, he read Derham's *Physico-Theology*. From this work he gained enlarged views of the structure of the earth and its inhabitants. He was soon busy as an experimenter; and his father's dyehouse was used as his laboratory. Derham's notes, too, which were chiefly extracts from Latin authors, stimulated him to read more extensively the prose and poetical compositions of the ancient authors. Interested by the beauties of the Greek and Latin poets, he courted also all the English poets, from Shakespeare to Goldsmith. Many poetical passages, both from ancient and modern authors, which took his fancy, were committed to memory; and so tenaciously were they retained, that between forty and fifty years after, he could repeat the greater part of them.

But poetry did not exactly harmonize with the character of his intellect. On closing Goldsmith, therefore, he returned with increasing ardour to the study of nature.

He was now about his eighteenth year; and continued for some time plodding among his birds, and plants, and simple philosophical experiments. To relieve the tedium of a wet day, the *Puzzling Rings* were placed in his hands. After several hours of toil he finally triumphed, extricating the nine rings from their staple. This feat, of itself, is of little moment. But the permutations necessary for disengaging the rings impressed him with an idea of numbers. He was now standing on the threshold of a new storehouse of knowledge, for the successful prosecution of which he was indebted solely to his own ingenuity. On this point he says, "I learned arithmetic at home by a contrivance of my own, which is nearly like that used by Dr. Saunderson." From the interest which Mr. Gough took in this new

study, he prevailed upon his father to enter him as a mathematical pupil, under the tuition of Mr. John Slee, at that time residing at Mungrisedale, a sequestered part of Cumberland; and perhaps a more judicious choice of a tutor for such a pupil could not have been made. But as to his progress, all that we can do in this memoir is to give an abstract of Mr. Slee's account, as detailed in an interesting letter to a friend. He took up his abode under his teacher's roof, in some part of the year 1778; and his first step seems to have been to furnish himself with a more polished *abacus*, and a more extensive series of pins for numerical expressions. "He procured," says Mr. Slee, "a board of rectangular form on which lines were drawn at equal distances, both longitudinally and laterally. At the intersections of these lines the board was pierced with so many small holes, so as to receive the lower points of pegs or pins fitted to sink into them. The upper parts of these pins were of so many different forms as we use digits for numerical calculations; and a considerable number of each kind of these pins were put into so many different compartments, formed in a shallow drawer, made for that purpose. It is not difficult, with this contrivance, to see how it would be practicable for him to perform all the common operations of arithmetic He was now prepared to extend his inquiries to other subjects connected with the mathematics, and of course his first efforts were employed in reading the elements of Euclid. With Geometry he connected the study of Algebra; and here again his mechanical apparatus came in for its share of utility. In Geometry, squares, rectangles, triangles, polygons, &c. were readily exhibited by putting a thread around the pins properly placed; and for the purpose of algebraic operations, a set of pins representing the symbols a, b, c, x, y, z, in common use, were, by their peculiar distinguishing varieties, at hand to supply all the purposes, for which their ordinary substitutes for quantities, known and unknown, can be made available." The time which Mr. Gough spent under

Mr. Slee's teaching was about eighteen months. He became acquainted with the principles and elements of mathematics; and in the prosecution of these studies he manifested much talent, and a peculiar interest in and predilection for the different branches of the science. In addition to the subjects before alluded to, he returned home with a knowledge of conic sections, mechanics, and a few initiatory lessons in fluxions. On his again becoming an inmate of his father's house, this latter branch formed a leading object in his pursuits. To select a competent reader for him was no easy matter. At length, however, the choice fell upon his second sister. For some time his progress was slow, but all hindrances yielded to his perseverance and signal exertion of mental power. Every impediment to the acquisition of knowledge was now fairly overcome; and for many years Mr. Gough enjoyed, with uninterrupted good health, the peaceful pursuit of his various studies. His acquirements in the higher branches of mathematics eminently fitted him as a teacher of that science in after-life; and out of the number of his select pupils, some became senior wranglers at Cambridge. Among the most eminent of these pupils, were Dr. Whewell, now Master of Trinity College, Cambridge, who was second wrangler in his year. Dr. Dawes, present Dean of Hereford, was fourth wrangler. Dr. Joshua King, late Master of Queens' College, Cambridge, (esteemed one of the first mathematicians of his day), was senior wrangler in his year. The Rev. Thomas Gaskin, late tutor of Jesus' College, Cambridge, Mr. Gough's last pupil, was second wrangler in his year. John Dalton, the eminent philosopher, was four or five years under his instruction in mathematics and natural philosophy and has left a grateful tribute to the memory of his blind preceptor.

We can only further add that, towards the close of the year 1823, Mr. Gough's health began to decline. Repeated attacks of epilepsy gradually undermined his bodily powers, and clearly pointed out the approaching termination of his earthly course. He died, at Fowl Ing, July 28th, 1825, in the sixtyninth year of his age; and his remains were interred in the parish churchyard of Kendal.

His resting-place is marked by a simple slab, bearing the following inscription: IN MEMORY OP JOHN GOUGH, WHO DIED JULY 28TM, 1825, AGED 68 YEARS.

He was married at Kendal Church, in 1800, to Mary, daughter of Thomas Harrison, of Crosthwaite, and had issue nine children, four sons and five daughters. Of these, three survive to the present time, namely, Thomas Gough, surgeon, Kendal; Mary Atkinson, widow, and Ann Bell, living at Manchester.

In summing up his life it may be said of Mr. Gough, that, though, not to him returned,

"Day, or the sweet approach of even or morn,
Or sight of vernal bloom, or summer's rose,"

still every stage of life had its enjoyments; every change of season brought a change of employment; every day presented his fingers with novelties from Nature's endless territories, his mind with germs of thought from the vast storehouse of knowledge. Resignation was a prominent feature of his character. The inconveniences attendant on his loss of sight never elicited an expression of murmur. And to *ennui,* early or late in life, he was a stranger. For his mind fed upon thoughts harmonious, that dissipated clouds of difficulties, and changed "ever-during dark" into hours of cheerfulness and mental sunshine. To be always employed, he well knew, was essential to his happiness, and no toil was too much to accomplish an object. Without staying, then, to inquire how far his success may have depended upon the inherent strength of the intellectual powers, we have a striking instance of the necessity of self-reliance and self-culture in breaking down every impediment, however much aided by physical imperfections, which may stand in the way of progress. By others, therefore, be they placed in more or less favoured circumstances, the subject of this memoir, and his achievements, are worthy of remembrance. For knowledge is to be acquired by labour alone. "There is want only where no firm *will* exists, where no adequate efforts are made."

The following is a List of Essays contributed by Mr. Gough to the Manchester Philosophical Society, viz.: 1. (1790.) Reasons for supposing that Lakes have been more numerous than they are at present, with an attempt to assign the causes whereby they have been defaced. 2. The Laws of Motion of a Cylinder, compelled by the repeated strokes of a falling block to penetrate an obstacle, the resistance of which is an invariable force. 3. 4. Experiments and observations on the vegetation of Seeds. 5. (1786.) On the variety of voices. 6. (1801.) An investigation of the method whereby men judge by the ear of the position of sonorous bodies relative to their own persons. 7. The Theory of Compound Sounds. 8. (1803.) A description of a property of Caoutchouc, or India Rubber, with some reflections on the cause of the elasticity of this substance. 9. An Essay on the Theory of Mixed Gases, and the state of Water in the Atmosphere. 10. (1804.) A reply to Mr. Dalton's objections to a late theory of Mixed Gases. 11. Theorems and Problems intended to elucidate the mechanical principle called Vis Viva. 12. (1811.) Observations on the Ebbing and Flowing Well at Giggleswick, in the West Riding of Yorkshire, with a theory of reciprocating fountains. 13. (1812.) Remarks on the Summer Birds of Passage, and on Migration in general. 14. The Laws of Statical Equilibrium analytically investigated.

List of Mr. Gough's communications, published in Nicholson's Journal: 1. On the supposed revival of Insects after long immersion in Wine or other intoxicating Liquor. Vol. iii. 2. A Statical Inquiry into the source of nutrition in succulent vegetables. Ibid. 3. Instances of suspended animation in vegetables. Ibid. 4. On the exhibition of a series of Primes, and the resolution of a compound number into all its Factors. Ibid. 5. Facts and observations to explain the curious phenomenon of Ventriloquism. Ibid. 6. Reply to Dr. Young2s Letter on the theory of Compound Sounds. Vol. iv. 7. On the nature of Grave Harmonics. Ibid. 8. On the nature of Musical Sounds, in reply to Dr. Young. Ibid. 9. The Theory of Compound Sounds. Vol. v. 10. Experiments and observations in support of that theory of Ventriloquism which is founded on the reflection of sound. Vol. vii. 11. Scoteography, or the Art of Writing in the dark. Vol. viii. 12. On the Solution of Water in the Atmosphere; and on the nature of Atmospherical Air. Vol ix. 13. Narrative of some less common effects of Lightning, by the Rev. Jonathan Wilson; with remarks by Mr. Cough. Ibid. 14. Strictures on Mr. Dalton's doctrine of Mixed Cases, and an answer to Mr. Henry's defence of the same. Ibid. 15. Atmospherical Air not a mechanical mixture of the oxygen and azotic gases, demonstrated from the specific gravities of these fluids. Ibid. 16. Experiments proving the necessity of atmospherical oxygen in the process of vegetation. Vol. x. 17. Farther observations on the constitution of Mixed Gases. Ibid. 18. Experiments and remarks on the augmentation of sounds. Ibid. 19. A mathematical theory of the speaking trumpet. Ibid. 20. Theorems respecting the properties of the sides of triangles intersected by right lines drawn from the three angles so as to meet in one point. Vol. XL 21. Investigation of the properties of the lines drawn in a circle, by Mr. Boswell. Vol. xii. 22. On the division of an arch of a circle into two such parts that their sines, or co-sines, or versed-sines shall have a given relation. Vol. xiii. 23. On the cause of Fairy Rings. Ibid. 24. Experiments on the magnetism of slender iron wire. Ibid. 25. Experiments on the temperature of water surrounded by freezing mixtures. Ibid. 26. Observations and experiments to show that the effects ascribed by M. Dispan to the perpendicular descent of Hoar Frost are not so general as to support his theory. Vol. xv. 27. Remarks on torpidity in animals. In two letters. Vol. xix. 28. Description of a correct chamber barometer. Vol. xx. 29. An essay on Polygonal numbers, containing the demonstration of a proposition respecting whole numbers in general. Ibid. 30. A mathematical problem, with the investigation. Vol. xxi. 31. Answer to Mr. Barlow's remarks on the essay on Polygonal numbers. Ihid. 32. An abstract of a meteorological journal for the year 1807, and 1808, kept at Middleshaw, near Kendal. Vol. xxii. 33. Experiments on the expansion of moist air raised to the boiling temperature. Vol. xxiii. 34. An inquiry, geometrical and arithmetical, into certain properties of solids in general; and of the five regular bodies in particular. Vol. xxv. 35. On the place of a sound produced by a musical string. Vol. xxxi. 36. Remarks on the perforations made in paper by electrical batteries. Vol. xxxii. JOHN THOMSON, M.D.

Was born at Kendal; August 16th, 1782. He was the only son of John Thomson, Esq., of Stricklandgate, deceased. The subject of this brief memoir received his early education at the Free Grammar School at Appleby, under the tuition of the Rev. John Coward, and his successor, the Rev. John Waller. In 1798, he became a divinity student at the New College, Manchester, at that time conducted by the Rev. George Walker, F.L.S. and M.R.S. Afterwards turning his thoughts to medicine, he pursued his studies at the University of Edinburgh, where he graduated in 1807. He enjoyed the friendship of Dr. Gregory and Dr. Hamilton, to whom he dedicated his inaugural dissertation. In 1808, he settled at Halifax, where he followed his profession, with eminent success, for nine years. During this time he was ever active in the establishment and promotion of public institutions, and still more in the prosecution of those acts of private benevolence which, silent and unostentatious in their progress, produce often greater blessings than deeds which are long and loudly applauded by the world. The Lancasterian School, and the Savings' Bank, in Halifax owe their origin to his suggestions, and their success mainly to his exertions; the Dispensary, also, was much benefited by his unremitting attention. His political sentiments were decidedly in favour of civil and religious liberty; and though candidly and openly avowed, in a town distinguished for much diversity of opin-

ion, were never known to interrupt the friendships formed with those who differed from him, nor shake the confidence which was reposed in him by the general voice of the public. In 1817, Dr. Thomson, courting a wider field for the exertion of his professional abilities, and active benevolence, removed to Leeds, where he died, May 18th, 1818. His remains were deposited in the burial ground of Blackley John Thomson, Esq. , died on the 21st July, 1831, aged seventy-five. He was a gentleman of enlightened understanding, and extensive erudition: endowments which he combined with that liberal spirit of intelligence which alone makes learning honourable to the possessor and useful to mankind.

R B

Chapel, near Elland, in the parish of Halifax, where a sarcophagus is erected, bearing the following inscription to his memory:—

M.S. Joannis Thomson, M.D., Qui Halifaxia) in Agro Eboracenci. Annos circiter decern Artem Hippocraticam, caste canto, probeque exercuit. Natus est Kendalia XVII. Cal. Septemb. A D. MDCCLXXXII. Mortalis esse desiit Leodei XV. Cal. Junii A.D. MDCCCXVIII.

It may be noted that the above dates and those on the monument in Northgate Chapel (quoted below), are in accord, the above being reckoned by the Roman calends.

The sentiments of esteem which so generally prevailed for the public and private character of Dr. Thomson, and the veneration in which his memory was held, are strikingly illustrated by a sepulchral memorial, erected by public subscription, in Northgate Chapel, Halifax. This is a handsome monument, executed by Chantrey, which cost 300 guineas; and such was the anxiety for contributing to its erection that the committee of directors were obliged to restrict the amount of subscription to 1*l.* The monument is of white marble, and presents a profile bust of Dr. Thomson, in *alto relievo,* resting on iEsculapius' staff, with the serpent coiled round it. The following is a copy of the inscription:

To the memory of John Thomson, M. D., born at Kendal, Aug. 16, 1782. After a residence of nine years in this town, he removed to Leeds, August, 1817, where he died, May 18th, 1818, aged 35 years: and was interred at Blackley Chapel, in this Parish. In testimony of public respect for great talents, improved by extensive learning, and employed in the faithful discharge of duty both to God and man; for unwearied activity in the exercise of an useful and honourable profession, without distinction of rich or poor;

for enlightened zeal to promote the purity of the Christian faith,

and especially the purity of Christian practice;

for animated eloquence, always ready in the support of plans of active

benevolence, of seminaries of useful learning, and of the principles of civil and religious liberty;

this Monument has been erected by the voluntary subscriptions of numerous friends in various parts of the kingdom.

Of Dr. Thomson's literary labours, though they were neither few nor unsuccessful, we are unprepared to say much. He was the author of a pamphlet on Vaccination, published during his residence at Halifax, which had an extensive circulation. It was intended to point out the benefits of vaccination to the lower orders, and was reputed to have had considerable influence in removing many rooted prejudices on the subject. He was a favourite correspondent of the Monthly Repository, and other periodicals of his day; the author of some unpublished poems, which possess the true spirit and power of poetry; and had he not been early taken away, it is probable more of his writings would have been given to the world.

JOHN BELL.

John Bell, better known as "Jocky Bell," or, as he was also sometimes called, in legal circles, "the great Bell of Lincoln's Inn," was a celebrated Chancery barrister, of large and lucrative practice. He was born on the 23d October, 1764, in a house in Finkle-street, Kendal, now occupied by Mr. Walker, shoemaker, opposite the printing-office of the "Ken-

dal Mercury." His father, Matthew Bell, was a respectable grocer in this town. John received his early education, partly at Beetham School, and partly at Kirkby Lonsdale School. As a boy, he had a strong fancy for the sea, and would fain have been a sailor, but he had been afflicted with lameness by a fall from his nurse's arms, and was on this account, and by dissuasion of his friends, turned away from his maritime inclinations. He was subsequently removed to Trinity College, Cambridge, where he was admitted under the tuition of Professor Collier. He took the degree of A.B. in January, 1786, when he was Senior Wrangler of his year. In 1789, he became A.M., having been previously elected Fellow of the College. After some hesitation as to what profession he should adopt, he enrolled himself at Gray's Inn, being "called" in 1792, and he afterwards became a Bencher. He started in the profession with about 5000?. personalty, added to the income of his fellowship 90?. per annum, and on this basis he raised a superstructure of at least 200,000?. Mr. Bell's reputation as a lawyer, certainly stood very high. He had a most retentive memory, which was well stored with cases and decisions.

Although far from being gifted with the powers of orator', and tinctured with a northern accent, yet such was the soundness of his judgment, he was listened to both by bench and bar with the most profound attention. He never sought for official preferment, often saying that he felt more independence in a private station. He had no penuriousness in his household, but kept a hospitable table, frequently honoured with the presence of judges, legislators, and men of eminence and science. He carried his nativity in his tongue, being fond of the Westmorland dialect, which he invariably spoke in all its raciness. He was a governor of the Westmorland Schools' Society, in London, and attended its meetings and dinners as often as his legal engagements permitted. The custom of "supper with black puddings," at the London Tavern,—a custom still maintained annually in this So-

ciety —was duly honoured and relished by John Bell; "no puddings no supper" being his maxim. But he rarely gave himself relaxation, his habit being to remain in his chambers till midnight, or later, and to be there again at nine in the morning. In 1810, Henry Bickersteth (afterwards Lord Langdale), became his pupil; and he had other pupils, besides, who rose to distinction. Lord Eldon, of doubting notoriety, was Lord Chancellor in Mr. Bell's day, and Jock/s adverse politics became, consequently, a barrier to his preferment, else he ought to have been appointed Vice-Chancellor when Sir Launcelot Shadwell was made. His clear and perspicuous judgment was celebrated by the following epigram, popular at the time:

"Mr. Leach, Made a speech,
Impressive, clear, and strong;
Mr. Hart, On the other part.
Was tedious, dull, and long.
Mr. Parker Made that darker
Was dark enough without;
Mr. Bell Spoke so well,
That the Chancellor said, I doubt.'"
From " Law and Lawyers," VoL II., p. 248.

And although the Chancellor withheld legal preferment, he ever acknowledged Mr. Bell's great superiority at the bar. For instance, when George III., at a *levSe,* once inquired of Lord Eldon, who was the best lawyer of the day, at the bar, the Chancellor replied, "the soundest lawyer that your Majesty has, at present, is a man who can neither *write, walk,* nor *talk,* but yet has got a head-piece." With regard to his handwriting, it was said, that he wrote three hands,— one that his clerk could read, and he could not; another, that he could read, and his clerk could not; and a third, that neither he nor his clerk nor Lucifer himself could read! He was a staunch Whig, and like many other men of talent in his profession, at first advocated the cause of the French Revolution, but afterwards used to reprobate the violence of its sanguinary proceedings. He was always attached to his *Alma Mater,* and it may seem extraordinary, that when arrived at some eminence at the bar, he kept in his turn a Divinity Act at Cambridge.

During the summer of 1835, he visited Burton, Kendal, and some other places in the north of England, where he invited his relatives, rich and poor, to dine with him at different Inns, affectionately observing, "this is the *last time* I shall ever meet you in Westmorland." It was, indeed, but too obvious that his dissolution was drawing on apace, for his habits had become very lethargic. The meek honesty of his character was such that, when elevated to distinction in his profession, he never forgot his former friends and connexions, and always stretched out a helping hand to indigent merit. Mr. Bell died at his house in Bedford-square, London, on the 6th February, 1836, and his remains were deposited at Milton, near Canterbury, with great funeral magnificence. There is an inscription to his memory on the family tombstone in Kendal churchyard (facing the porch of the church). His immediate ancestors were buried there, as the other inscriptions on the same tombstone testify. Their obituary registers are on the top stone of the tomb. John Bell's epitaph is on one of the side flags.

Mr. Bell has left one son behind him, now living, we believe, in the county of Kent.

EEV. JOHN HUDSON, A.M.

This gentleman was vicar of Kendal, from the year 1815 until 1843. Being the son of a farmer at Haverbrack, in the parish of Beetham, and presenting, in his career, an example of native talent and great industry, a brief Memoir of him is due in this place. He had the foundation of his scholarly attainments laid at Heversham School, a school which has been famous for the number of eminent men it has sent forth. Mr. Hudson left Heversham for Trinity College, Cambridge, in 1793, and in 1797 he obtained the highest mathematical honours which the University has to bestow, being declared Senior Wrangler and Smith's Prizeman in that year. In the following year (at the age of twenty-five), be obtained a Fellowship in his College. He was distinguished not merely by sound scholarship, but also

by considerable scientific attainments, with clear conceptions, and singular judgment. And accordingly, in 1807, he was appointed tutor of Trinity at thirty-four years of age. In this capacity he was successful in the highest degree, one of his pupils being Blomfield, Bishop of London, who was reputed to be among the best Greek scholars of his day. Blomfield was instituted to the see of Chester, and afterwards translated to London. Kendal, at the time, was within the diocese of Chester; and when Blomfield made his first visitation at Kendal, he was, of course, the Vicar's guest. A select party were seated at dinner on the occasion, at the Vicarage, and the Bishop, recollecting the discipline of his former tutor, observed,—" I remember well, Mr. Hudson, how much I stood in awe of you at College." "Perhaps so," rejoined the Vicar; "but your Lordship has turned the tables upon me now." Mr. Hudson left the University to consummate an attachment which he had formed for Miss Culliford, (the only daughter of an officer in the army) and to settle down for the remainder of his days, in his native county. He was appointed Vicar of Kendal in 1815, and married the lady above named, who sweetened

Bishop Preston, of Ferns; Bishop Watson, and Professor Whewell, were educated here; besides other men distinguished for their learning.

his cup of life, and became an exemplar to all the ladies of the parish. Our readers will, many of them, recollect Mr. Hudson's good qualities. He was essentially " a fit person to serve in the sacred ministry of the Church;" full of gentleness, kindness, conciliation; teaching both by precept and practice, as old Chaucer says:

"To drawen folk to Heven by fairnesse,
And good example, was bis besinesae."

He died, at Haverbrack, on Tuesday, the 31st October, 1843, in the seventy-first year of his age, and was buried in the interior of the parish church, at the south-east end, near Parr's Chapel (now the vestry). Archdeacon Evans (of Heversham) preached the funeral sermon,

on Sunday, the 12th November, from 2d Cor. chap. v. 9 ver. The public monument to his memory (for the inscription on which see ante, p. 63) stands against the south wall of the church, not far from the place of sepulture. That monument proclaims, very truly, the esteem in which Mr. Hudson was held by his friends and parishioners.

APPENDIX. *On t/ie Roman Station " Alauna," at Borough Bridge, Westmorland.*

A Lectcbe Delivered Before The Members Of The Kendal Natural History And Scientific Society, Assembled On The Station.

Two observations, founded upon history, will serve as an introduction to this lecture. The first is based upon a coincidence of natural and social phenomena, namely, that wherever the more violent convulsions in the earth's crust have occurred, in these same localities also have occurred, within later times, the greatest human contests and scenes of warfare. The other observation is, that mountain homes have ever been the sanctuary of liberty. In all ages, the dwellers in mountainous regions have been distinguished as the opposers of aggression, and the stoutest defenders of liberty. Hence the abundant memorials, in this locality, connected with the Roman, Saxon, Danish, and Norman conquests.

We are here standing on a spot of ground, within the province of "Maxima Caesariensis," which, 1800 years ago, was occupied by a band of Roman soldiers. They were men highly disciplined in the arts of war; composed of cavalry and infantry, caparisoned in brass or iron mail, with the spear and battle-axe, which they could dexterously wield; well clothed and well fed. Their victories had everywhere been so unchecked, that the world was lying at their feet; and now, in the particular campaign which claims our attention, these soldiers were led by a General, Agricola, who ranked among the most famous of Roman Captains for his skill in battle and his discretion in dealing with conquered races. It had taken about forty-five years, under nine Proprajtors, previous to Agricola, to bring under subjection the several nations of Britons who dwelt south of the Brigantes, that is to say, south of Chester and Manchester. And, as the greatest achievements are fitly reserved for the highest talents, so the difficult task of conquering the Brigantes, on tho west, was appointed to Agricola, the Propraetor, or Governor-General, of Britain.

What were these people, the Western Brigantes? And what was the condition of this district of country, at the time we are speaking of? Fortunately, we are not left entirely to conjecture, as to either the people or the country. Some knowledge has been communicated relative thereto by Caesar, and Tacitus, and the Saxon chroniclers, and some light has lately been thrown on the subject by modern philologists and archaeologists. It is pretty well agreed, that the southern parts of Britain were peopled by nations belonging to the Celtic tribes of Gaul and Germany, whilst the northern parts of this island were inhabited by races more closely related to the Scandinavian (Danish and Norwegian) stock. The very woof of our Westmorland dialect, which is classical English, and the current names of natural and common objects in this locality, are identified with the Scandinavian dialects.

Tho Brigantes were divided into two tribes or nations, by a natural barrier— the great mountain chain (running from north to south) which cuts Yorkshire in two, and separates Durham and Northumberland from Lancashire, Westmorland and Cumberland, and which is sometimes called "the Back-bone of England," and sometimes the "English Apennines." The Western Brigantes, occupying principally this, the western side of these Apennines, were the most powerful tribe of all the aboriginal Britons—powerful by their numbers, by their habits of war, and by the natural fortresses within which they were entrenched. And, besides their natural fortresses, they also constructed works of fortification. Theso were chiefly ramparts of earth, formed in parallel ridges, along the breasts of the hills. Many of these works may still be

faintly traced in Westmorland. Perhaps the best example, and most accessible, is a British camp, right opposito the windows of Shap Wells Hotel, looking across the *Birheck.* Tho one at *Restane,* in Staveley, I also believe to havo been British, afterwards used by the Romans. Tho Britons were men of large limbs and fair hair. They could despise luxuries; could endure hardships, Pope Gregory was moved to the conversion of the Anglo-Saxons by the f i;ht of the " fair8haired captives " (Hritons) in the slave8market at Rome.— *Roberlson9t Chrietiua Church,* p. 19.

even to standing for a whole day up to their chins in water; they could exist even on the bark of trees.

The face of the country was almost altogether covered with wood and swamps. *Sylva Caledonis* extended, in all probability, with slight intermissions, from the Solway, in Cumberland, to Morecambe Bay,—"a boundless contiguity of shade,"—saving, perhaps, a few bare spots on the highest hills. The sacred Oak, the Ash, the Birch, and the Holly, clothed the slopes of the hills, whilst the valleys were, perhaps, still more thickly bearded with the aforesaid timber, mingled with the Alder, the Willow, the Hazel, and tangled brushwood of Brambles and Whins. Tarns, bogs, and morasses, everywhere abounded. The climate, therefore, must have been foggy, damp, and cold, better suited to the amphibious habits of the natives, than to the taste of Roman legionaries bred beneath the sunny skies of Italy or Gaul. The habitations of the Britons were rude huts or wigwams, made with the branches of trees, covered with mud. In times of peace, they occupied themselves in tending cattle, or shooting (for food and clothing) the wolves, wild boars, and wild oats that roamed through the primeval forests. The only article of manufacture known to belong to them are baskets. Their religious offerings were either to the mystio god Baal (the Sun), or to the Oak with Miseltoe, or, for the most part, to the tutelar deity of the local Rivers; for Gildas says, "Rivers were loaded with divine honours" by the Britons. Doubtless

they assembled themselves together, round the Druid's altars, on Potter's Fell; on Kirkstone; at Carl Lofts, on Shap Fells; around "Long Meg and her Daughters," at Mayburgh; at Penhurrock, on Crosby Fell; and at many other places in the district where—

"The white-haired Druid, Hard sublime,
Muttered his rite in Celtic rhyme."

Their arms consisted of small targets, with swords and spears, ot which many samples are in the British Museum. They had also chariots, armed with iron scythes, a kind of rude bayonet, projecting from the extremities of the axletrees. These chariots they managed with great dexterity, but it is hardly likely that they Hence "Wild-6onr-fell," and "*Catx-Hc-c&m.*" Bal, in old Norse and Saxon, signifies "sacrificial fire." "Hill Bell' and "Cat Bolls " may be derived hence. *Bel-atiircader* was a topical Deity to whom several altars were erected in Westmorland and Cumberland.

could be of much use in this hilly country. Agricola could manoeuvre his cavalry iu many situations which would be inaccessible to the lumberly chariots of the Britons.

Whether the *Beacons,* upon these hills, were employed by the Britons, for giving warning of danger, I am not able to make out. Dr. Whitaker rather inclines to that belief. If so, the Western Brigantes lighted the alarum fires, at the approach of Agricola, upon Warton Crag, on Ingleborough, on Barbon Beacon, on Whinfell Beacon, on Orton Beacon, on Tcnrith Beacon, and, perhaps, on other hills whereof neither name nor trace is left.

Let us inquire into the date or the foundation of the Station at Borough Bridge. It is something to say, that, after a lapse of eighteen hundred yeans, we can fix, with tolerable certainty, the year of its foundation. Tacitus married the daughter of Agricola, and he must have known, as he was proud to record, the movements of his distinguished father-in-law. Agricola was made Proprretor of Briton, by the Emperor *Vespasian,* in the year A.d. 77, and was continued in that high office till the year A.d. 87.

Tacitus says that he conquered the Western Brigantes from Deva (which is Chester) to the Sol way Frith in the year A.d. 79. The 20th legion, which was commanded by Agricola, had its head quarters at Deva, and the Editors of." Magna Britannia" state, that Deva continued head quarters of this legion for 200 years. Chester, therefore, to speak iu modern phraseology, was Agricola's "base of operations," in his campaigns against the Western Brigantes. From thence, he pushed forward, northwards, his "expeditionary" forces—(legions and auxiliaries)—by the line of Roads indicated on the Diagram, throwing up, as he proceeded, fortresses, mounds, and redoubts, and leaving, in his rear, garrisons and sentinels to watch and hold what was won. The auxiliaries of his army—Gallish captives, and native Britons, taken prisoners,—were made to hew down the woods, and construct the roads and earthworks. It is on record, that Galcacus excited the courage of his soldiers, the Britons, before engaging with Agricola, by telling them, that if they suffered themselves to be defeated, "they must expect to have their bodies worn and consumed in clearing woods A legion was composed of ten cohorts, and a cohort of six centuries. Thus, the numbers of a legion were SO multiplied by 6, equal to 480, multiplied by 10, equal to 4,800. But the first cohort (which had the custody of the Eagle), was sometimes *double,* or 960. So that a legion was usually 5,280 soldiers.

and paving bogs, whilst the Romans paid their wages in a thousand stripes. " Some of the works so raised, still remain in this locality. One connected with this Station, (and a beautiful monument it is,) may be seen a little way higher up the valley, near Tebay, viz. , a *mom exploratorium,* called " Castle How," constructed, no doubt, to guard the *trajectus,* or passage of the river, at that spot. This exploratory Mount commands the Station at Borough Bridge, the mountain pass to the north of it, and the two lateral valleys of Brederdale, on one hand, and Langdale on the other. It is made entirely of earth, in shape an

oval, or rather a circle adjoined to an oval, the oval and circle having separate ditches and ramparts. The conjoined mounds are about 320 feet by 200 feet, at the swell. Close to this work is a large Brandreth-stone,—a greenstone boulder,—in a field called *Galloivbar,* ignorantly corrupted into " Galloper-field." When, in the Saxon era, after the departure of the Romans, Castle How became a tribune for dispensing justice, Gallowbar was, doubtless, the place of execution, where the gallows stood. I have elsewhere stated, that those mounds in the Vicar's Fields, at Kendal, were for the same purpose as this at Tebay, to guard the *wath,* or ford, at what is incorrectly called "Watts-field," instead of *Wath-feld.* But let me proceed with the history of this Station. Agricola, advancing by steps, and securing his steps as he advanced, planted a garrison at BremetoNac: (Overborough). Having ascertained, by his scouts, or *Vigilue,* the distance, in some measure, from Overborough to the probable site of the first station to be planted *beyond* the great mountain barrier of the Orton Fells, on the banks of the Eamont or the Eden, Agricola would see the necessity of placing a garrison midway between those points. The countiy was hard to win, and not less hard to hold. A resting-place, aud fortification, before the passage of the fells, became, therefore, a necessity; and hence, it is pretty certain, that this Station was founded in the first year of the campaign, A.d. 79. No better situation could be found for shelter against the weather, or for protection against the enemy. Scouts, placed in advance, could signal the approach of the Brigantes from the north, down the Lune, or from the west, over Grayrigg Hause. A place between Tebay and Shap Wells still bears the name of Scout Green. It might not be till after several campaigns, and several years of occupation, that the paved roads, connecting this chain of Stations, were finished. The exact line of the Roman road, below Borough Bridge, is very obscure. Mr. John Just was inclined to the opinion " that the Roman road corresponds with the modern road over the Hause

and down to the Inn." With a strong wish to endorse so high an opinion, 1 am, however, bound to say, that I can find no evidence to support it. If ever there was a military way, or a vicinal way, "over the Hause," it would be for connecting *Concangium,* at Kendal, with this Station, and in that case it belongs to a later period, and to another chapter of history. The name " Hause" indicates nothing in connection with a road; it is a Danish word, and signifies *a neck,* or sloping down from the shoulders of a mountain,—well applied in this case. We cannot find out the crossing of the Luno, south of Borough Bridge; if we could, the discovery of the line of road would be greatly facilitated, but as Mr. Just failed to discover the crossing, I may well despair of finding it. I may, however, make a suggestion. There is a rivulet one mile below called " Carnigillso called, by reason of the gill washing the banks of a *cairn,* or tumulus; and it is a historical fact that these tumuli stood by the sides of the Roman roads. My conjecture therefore, is, that, coming northwards, the Romans kept to the cast or left bank of the Luue, crossing the Rathay opposite to Sedbergh, till they came to *Cairngill,* then crossing Cairngill where the boundary post of the parish of Orton stands, close by the beautiful Cairn before alluded to. From Overborough, upwards, the road proceeded by Casterton, as that name imports. Auother name, two and a half miles north of Barbon, *Borivens* may bo taken as a foot8print in the way; for something Roman must have been where the name *Borwens* occurs. Beyond this, to Borough Bridge, few and faint traces only exist. But the great fact remains, that Agricola marched " straight as the track of a sunbeam and if you place a straight line, on Hodgson's Map of Westmorland, from Overborough to Tebay, you will find it touch upon Casterton, Barbon, and Borough Bridge. Adopting the statement of Tacitus, that all the country between the Dee and the Solway was conquered in this first campaign, the date of the several Stations on the straight line of communication, on the Diagram, may refer to the same year. But it is hardly likely that the Stations on the west, at Lancaster, Kendal, and Ambleside, were fouuded until a future period. Even AgriCola himself might be content with the line of country which lies in the direct route, for the spoils of one campaign. But, since the Stations at Lancaster and Kendal are both ascribed to Agricoj.a, it may easily be imagined how, with strong detachments and garrisons on the Ribble, the Lune, and the Eamont, he could, in two or three *subsequent* campaigns, reduce the Brigantes, on the shores of Morecambe Bay, and Windermere.

The next subject of inquiry is the name by which this Station was called, and its connection with the other Stations north of it. Mr. Just observed that it is still " without a name;" Horsley and Gale both omit all mention of it, and so does Camden; Dr. Whitaker gives nothing more than a hint that it may be either " Galacum" or " Alone." I will venture upon a theory which may, at least, have some plausibility. The 10th Iter of Antonine consists of nine Stations, lying between Hadrian's Vallum and Mediolanum, in Cheshire. They are set down in the following order from north to south, viz.;— ITER X.

A. Glanoventa Mediolanum.
Galava (or Calava *1)*
Alone.
  Galacum (or Galacum?)
  Bremetouacis.
  Cocoio.
  Mancunio.
  Caudate.
  Mediolano.

This Xth Iter of Antonine has been a puzzle to all antiquarians, especially to the early inquirers. And the Station "Alone," has been the most perplexing part of it, which may, perhaps, be accounted for by the fact, that Borough Bridge has lain out of the route of modern highways, and been, therefore, overlooked. In the new book, " Monumonta, Historica Britannica," published by Government, there is a map which places "Alone" at Ambleside, on the single authority of Reynolds, as far as I can find; all other Antiquarians being

against it. Horsley puts "Alone" at Whitley Castle, on the Maiden Way, supposing the Xth Iter to have run from Hadrian's Vallum, whilst Reynolds and Mannert both place Galacum at Kendal. In all these cases, however, the designations are arbitrary, without the support of etymologies or inscriptions. If the hypothesis, which I am now about to advance, can be admitted, as placing "Alone " at Borough Bridge, then six Stations out of nine (from Mediolanum northwards), are accounted for, and the remaining three may be inquired into at a future opportunity. Mr. Whitaker, Dr. Whitaker, and Rauthmell, have proved the three Stations of Bremctonacae, Coccium, and Mancunium, to be indubitably Overborough, Ribchester, and Manchester. I take no notice here of Antonine's table of distances from one Station to another, because all Antiquaries have, in turn, rejected the obligation of adhering to those tables. Rauthmell, and Dr. Whitaker, with the best evidence that lapidary inscriptions can give about the *locale* of Bremetonacae, Coccium and Mancunium, are yet obliged to take ton miles from one station, and add ten to another, in the distances of Autonine's Iter, referable to two of these stations, before they can make the names and distances agree. Nor is it necessary to regard the stations as set down, with unerring accuracy, in the direct order of succession. I shall take a smaller liberty with Antonine's Itinerary than many have taken, if I presume only to transpose Galacum and Alone, putting the latter next to Brematonacee, and referring Alone to the station at Borough Bridge.

In two separate places, in his "History of Richmondshire," (vol. L p. 149, and vol. ii. p. 214), Dr. Whitaker notices the discovery, by previous antiquaries (Gale and Horeley), of votive altars, with inscriptions dedicated to the nymph *Elauna.* In both cases, he appends commentaries (following the observations of Horeley, p. 306), to indicate his opinion, that the name of the river Lune (originally *Lon* ?), is derived from this goddess. Nevertheless, with all his active imagination, and great

powers of association, it seems never to have occurred to the Doctor, that if the nymph is to furnish the patronymic of the river, or *vice versa,* with equal propriety the river or the goddess has furnished the origiu, also, of the name of this station, Alauna. Similar derivations of the names of Roman stations are not wanting (take *Kirkby Thar,* for an instance). I see no reason why the first syllable of Xow-govicum, and Zo»-oaster, may not also be traced to the same nymph of this same river. The different spelling, *Alone,* by Antoninus, or his compilers, (whoever they were?) tells very little against the theory. If this Alone, be taken in the genitive, with a diphthong, "ae," the only alteration I make in the orthography is the substitution of "au" for "o." But I do not care which spelling be adopted; the etymology and signification are still the same. This property now belongs to the Earl of Lonsdale, whose peerage name may be traced back to the goddess "Alonao," or "Alaunce," which you will. One of the altars above referred to was found near Rokeby, and the inscription is quoted in Gough's "Camden's Britannia" (p. 388), and in Horsley's "Britannica" (p. 192, n. 62):

Dels NYMrujj Elanelb, &c. "I draw no argument from numbers which, upon every hypothesis, are allowed to be corrupt."—*History of Whallcy.* » "The shallow stony Lone."—*Spenser's* "Faery Queen."

C C

"Who is the nymph?" says Dr. Whitaker. "These imaginary beiugs were topical deities. One of the mountain streams which unite with the Tees, still retains the name of Lune. Where is the improbability of supposing that its British-Romanised name was 'Elauna,' and its nymph 'Elauneia?'" The other altar was discovered among the Roman remains at Lancaster, and is inscribed:—"deo Ialono *(conterranco f)* Sanctissimo Julius JanuArius," &c. "In this inscription (says the Doctor), no severity of reason, no coldness of caution, can check the enthusiasm of an Antiquary, who persuades himself that he has discovered the topical deity of Lune, Deo

Ialono. *Verbeicc sacrum* has, from the time of Camden, been allowed as a dedication to the nymph of Wharf, and *Ialono* is not more remote from the word Lune." Sound and sense, therefore, conspire to reconcile Alaunae, the river deity, with "Alone," the station set down in Antonine's Xth Iter. Every supposition appears to mo to be in favour of this name. There is a station named "Alauna," by doubtful authority, in Lancashire. And among the Roman stations of Brittany (France), in Antonine's Itinerary, there is one named "Alauna," and so spelt. But, perhaps, the strongest fact in favour of my argument is, that this river Lune is called "Alauna," and so spelt, in Richard of Cirencester's (Ptolemy's) map of Roman Britain. There cau be very little doubt that the name Lune, before the Roman invasion, applied to the whole length of this river, up to the source of the tributary now called Borough, or still more incorrectly " Borrow," as well as to its other feeders, right and left, from Birkbeck Fells and Orton. The name "Borough," clearly, could not have been applied to the arm of this river above, until the Roman occupation; and after that event, it is in no way surprising that, joining the sister stream so close to this station, it should have taken the name "Borough" as a distinction from Lune, which latter name clung to the other, larger, tributary. Now, with reference to the nymph Elauna), it is to be observed, that she seems to have been a Deity of consideration and reputation. Altars, dedicated to her, are found on both sides of the Penine chain; among the Eastern Brigantes, as well as the Western Brigantes. She is supposed to have given name to a river (or the river its name to her?) on the eastern side of the country, as well as on the west. Her name and fame were, therefore, everywhere spread abroad, at least, throughout the powerful nation of the Brigantes. On the other hand, Agiucola was dis tinguished as muoh for the wisdom he displayed in managing and propitiating the people he conquered, as for his skill in battle. "Having sufficiently alarmed them (says Tacitus), his next course was to al-

lure them with the sweetness of peace, and he publicly assisted tbem to *build temples,* and places of assembling." Hence, it is most natural to suppose, that the founder of the station would seek to satisfy the feelings and veneration—not to say the religious prejudices—of the Britons, by adopting the name of their topical deity, who was held by them in 6uch high repute, and so applying it to the station. He had less motive for consulting the Roman than the British vocabulary. His own legionaries were at his beck and call, willing and obedient, whilst, in all probability, at the time the station was named, the Brigantes were only partially vanquished, and those brought under subjection were ill reconciled to their master. If any one, dissatisfied with this theory and derivation, can suggest any other, consistent with the evidence of facts, or the rules of logic, I will cheerfully yield up Alauna. Till then, it must stand, and the station at Borough Bridge may, I hope, be henceforth regarded as being redeemed from the obloquy of an anonymous ruin.

With respect to the military way north of Borough Bridge, I can now speak with some degree of certainty. Thanks to Thomas Bland, and John Bland, his nephew, two Westmorland " worthies" (born geniuses, is the least I can say of them in their presence), a clue has been discovered which unravels almost all difficulties. Mr. John Just spoke, from tradition, of the road proceeding " over Orton-Low-Moor to Brougham." But if, on the contrary, the military way can be traced from Borough Bridge to Kirkby Thor, then Antonine's Xth Iter goes northwards along it to Kirkby Thor, and thence by the *Maiden Way,* over Crackenthorpe Moor, past Whitley Castle, to Hadrian's Vallum. In this case, the four northernmost stations may thus be read off—" Alauna," at *Borough Bridge; "*Galacum," at *Kirkby TJior; "*Galava," at *Whitley Castle,* and "Glanoventa," on *the Wall.* We shall find "Brocavum" next year, if we live, in the Vth Iter. Now, proceeding from Borough Bridge, the Romans crossed the river Borough by a bridge, of which the grout-work may still be

seen, close to this station; and the road is also clearly seen beyond; they thence went right on to the Lune, and twice crossed that river, first at the foot of Jeffrey's Mouut, north of the modem bridge over the river, where a narrow lane points to the ford; and secondly, close to Castle How, at Tebay, under the protection of that fort. Thence, on the west side of the village of Orton, over a depression in the long range of Orton Fell. The road, forward, descends Crosby Ravensworth Fell, by Wicker Street Thorn, where, for two miles, it is plain as a pike-staff, over ground which still retains the significant name of *Wicker Street* (the gate-way of the pass). It is at this point where John Bland made the grand discovery I before alluded to. The line of road is unquestionable, pointing direct to Kirkby Thor! There is, also, here, a fine memorial, which I take to be the basement works of a British village, lying close to the Roman road. Who can tell what resistance the natives offered to the invaders, in these slopes, leading to the Lyvenet (musical river) at Ravenswath *1* The Roman legionaries had scaled the heights of Orton, and were now met, in this Valley of Jehoshaphat, by hardy Britons, fighting for their homes. I dare not give the reins to my imagination; but I can state, soberly, that here are evident traces, on the ground, of Britons and Romans; and, when the Pagan warriors are past and gone, there is proof, also, in the name of the village below, of the introduction of Christianity, for *Crosby Rafenswath* (Dano-Saxon) means a village by the ford where the Christians used to worship. Skirting Crosby Ravenswath, the road goes about half a mile west of the house where Addison's father was born, up to another Borwens a good Roman name is better than a blind road, passing between the mounds at Borwens and a field called vulgarly "Crenylings," which should be *Caerlenff.* Thence to two places of significant meaning, "Lofterns," and "Castrigg" (Caster-rig), both in the township of King's Meaburn. These places are, successively, in order, going straight towards Kirkby Thor, and I have traversed the road for thirteen out of the seventeen miles between Borough Bridge and Kirkby Thor. Brougham is now so far to the left, or north, that it is out of the line. In the meantime I stand upon the conviction that a Roman road communicates between Borough Bridge and Kirkby Thor.

We have now further to inquire into the extent of the station,— its architectural plan and arrangements, and the number of soldiers it was designed to accommodate. If it be admitted that this station was constructed in Agricola's first campaign against the Brigantes, before those tribes were half conquered; that it preceded, by some years, the stations and lines of military way on the west, at Lancaster, Kendal, and Ambleside; that it certainly, also, preceded the stations and the military way called Watling-street on the east, from Brougham Castle by Kirkby Thor, Brough, and Bowes; we should then expect to find, here, the evidences of a station, where a powerful garrison could be encamped. The situation was, as it were, the key which opened the door of the mountain pass; and Agricola was too experienced, and too discreet a general, to proceed over Orton Fell into the plains of the Pettril and the Eden, without first planting at Alauna, Borough Bridge, some veteran Lieutenant, at the head of a considerable detachment of well-tried soldiers. The Picts and Scots, terrible in fame, were before him,—the Brigantes wore on both his flanks, and no means were at his command for estimating the numbers or positions of his enemies. The singular device of raising a watch-tower into the air, in the shape of a balloon, (successfully practised by the Emperor of the French at the battle of Solferino,) had not then been thought of. Therefore, it was not only necessary to place a strong garrison at Borough Bridge, but it was equally necessary to succour that garrison with defensive works and out-posts. The garrison alone might have to defend itself against unequal numbers; or, the whole invading army, even, might be repulsed, and need a safe citadel. In any event (without reference to these possible casualties) the

military way, or line of communication throughout the Lune valley, and the difficult pass of the mountain chain, had to bo kept open by the band of soldiers planted here; hence, we ought to find traces of a station of no mean magnitude and importance.

It is on record that the Roman armies never halted for a single night without forming a regular entrenchment, termed a *centrum.* So essential was this operation considered, that even when preparing for an immediate engagement, or when aotually assailed by an opposing force, it was never omitted. A portion of the soldiers were employed in constructing the necessary works whilst the remainder were standing to their arms or resisting the enemy. If a camp was designed to be held only temporarily, the field-works were but slight, and such camps took the general name of *castra;* but if circumstances rendered it expedient for a force to occupy the ground for any length of time, the works were significant, and these larger camps were denominated *Castra Stativa.* That this station, Alauna, was designed for permanent occupation, there can be no doubt; nor any doubt, therefore, that it belonged to the class *Castra Stativa,* The soldiers stationed here were a cohort of Dr. Wm. Smith's " Roman Antiquities," p. 244.

Nervians, according to the *Notitia:*— " Tribinus cohortis tertiae Nerviorum Alionae mauebat." The word " manebat" (which occurs only occasionally iu similar places), shows, that this cohort *remained* here, and the commander being a Tribune proves, that these soldiers were legionaries of Rome; for, according to Caesar and Suetonius, "the Praefects were appointed to command the allies in the same maimer as the Tribunes commanded the legionaries. Mr. Noble, formerly of the Inn at Borough Bridge, dug up fragments of *hypocaustt* (of which he said there were numerous traces), and pieces of charcoal, from the flues, which had been drawn in with soot, by the draughts from the fire. These fires and flues were for the double purpose of heating the baths, and for warming the tents, which stood in rows,

like cottage houses in a street or lane. Several pieces of Rornau pottery— some common, and some Samian wares were found by Mr. Noble, and are still on the spot. Four Querns, or hand-grinding mills, were dug up in the works for the railway. I had the honour of presenting two of these to the Kendal Museum, and the other two are here. Pieces of Roman money (leather pieces stamped as coin) were found here, but are now lost. Here is, however, an undoubted Roman coin, of silver, which I conceive to be a coin of Vespasian, who was reigning emperor when Agricola was in Britain. Mr. John Just observed "sacrificial relics" among the remains, which are part of this pottery. These several remains, then, prove conclusively, that this station was occupied both iu winter and summer, that baths were indulged in, that corn was ground and bread baked here, kc. Provision in luxuries, and necessaries, implies the presence of leaders as well as followers. "Sacrificial relics" indicate the presence of priests and augurs, with the performance of idolatrous rites. Priests and augurs may be reckoned as attendant upon the commanding officers and their staff, ready to proclaim good omens or expiate evil ones. Altogether, then, the inference is, that this station was permanently occupied for a considerable number of years, whether for a period extending from the time of Agricola till the final departure of the Romans, A.d. i3i, must remain Adam's " Roman Antiquities," p. 371. "Beauties of England and Wales," p. 208.

» Certain birds and wild beasts crossing the road, before an army, gave presage of bad or ill luck. Our superstition, connected with a solitary magpie, may be a lingering instance of these omens. De Quincey puts this among the Pagan superstitions.

undetermined. So long as the Lune Valley continued to be the great artery of communication between Britain and Caledonia, the station at Borough Bridge would be occupied and upheld. But in process of time, there were at least two, if not threo, other military ways through Westmorland—one from

Concangium, Kendal, by way of Re-ston, over High-street to Brougham Castle, another from *Dictis,* Ambleside, over Woundale, uniting with the last named by "Scot-rake" at High-street, and possibly another from Ambleside over Dunmail Raise. Mr. Wordsworth believed in the Roman road over the Raise,-but it is more a matter of belief than of evidence. But, as regards the two roads converging upon Highstreet, I satisfied myself by actual traces of them, where portions of pavement are still visible. After so many lines of com-munication were opened, the station at Borough Bridge would lose some of its importance as a stratagetical position, and the number of its occupants would be reduced. What these numbers, when so reduced, may have been, we can nev-er tell; but we can tell, approximately, and with tolerable certainty, the total number of soldiers that could be accom-modated here, for the internal arrange-ments and mode of encamping a Roman army were, in almost all cases, identi-cally the same.

"The general form of the inclosure for a camp," says Dr. Smith, "was an ob-long square, so that the length should exceed the breadth by one-third." This station was, therefore, designed on the general plan. It is an oblong square, 420 feet from north to south, by 320 feet from east to west. The dimensions of the station at Old Penrith are 420 feet by 300 feet. That at Ambleside is 480 feet by 300 feet. It will be noted how very much of the same size these three sta-tions are. The one at Brougham is up-wards of 1,000 feet, by about 800 feet. The external defences of this station were a ditch and mound, technically called a *fossa,* and *agger,* or *vallum.* The agger, as it appears, on the west side, was constructed of earth, faced and strengthened by a barrier of stone. It is nearly five-and-twenty years since I first examined this *Rhiwstane,* or *Rey-stane,* signifies "stony road, or paved road, over the hill," from Rhiw, "a brow" (Brit.) and "stane" (Sax.)! The *fivst* syllable of "Ry-dale," and the *last* syllable of "Elleray," are among the variable spelling of this word *Rhiw.*

» "The massy ways, carried across *these lieights,*
By Roman perseverance, are de-stroyed," &c.
Wordsworth, 1S2G.
station. The railway works, since then, hayO done something to change its fea-tures. I myself interceded with the sur-veying engineer, and begged hard that the "fine Roman hand" might not be ef-faced. But for this interference, the line of railway might, perhaps, have gone right over the *Pretorium.* The iron heel, of this iron age, might literally have pressed the neck of a centurion "dead and turned to clay." The Pretorian agger is nipped in between the railway and the turnpike road. What were the height, and thickness, of this *fossa* and *agger,* cannot now be accurately stated. The usual depth of the fossa was three feet, and the usual breadth across, five feet. The vallum of earth and stone together, would not be less than eight feet broad at the top, and six feet high. There were four openings into the area, within the vallum, and each opening, or *porta,* as it was called, was defended by an outwork of earth or stone. When special precau-tions were required, the porta were closed by regular gates, defended by towers. Such appears to have been the case in this instance. Luckily some of the posts, to which the gates had been hung here, have been dug up. One of these was taken away by Mr. Noble, and put into the foundation of a chimney, in one of his farmbuildings. The other, fel-low-stone, I have had removed to about the exact spot where it originally stood, at the Dextra gate. And a third, similar post, which was on a wall in a farm-yard, I have now placed at the same gateway, though this probably belonged to one of the other porta. You can see how the pivot of the gate has worked it-self out of the socket, and enlarged the hole. The four entrances were called re-spectively, *Porta Pretorium, Porta De-cumana, Porta Dextra,* and *Porta Sin-istra.* The first was so called because it faced the Pretorium, where the Proprae-tor had his hall of audience, and where he bivouacked, with his staff, or body-guard. The *Porta Decumana* (at the op-posite extremity of the camp), took its title from the circumstance of the tenth maniples being quartered in its vicinity. The *Porta Dextra* and *Sinistra* explain their own derivation. The *Via Princi-palis* took its name from that street be-ing the promenade of the principal offi-cers; and those tents, which stood above it on each side of the intersecting street, were the officers' tents. The *Porta De-cumana* was the gate through which a supply of water and provisions, general-ly, were carried into the fortress. It was uniformly placed farthest from the ene-my, and, generally, nearest to the river. Four principal streets (as shown on the diagram) intersected the camp, cutting it into four quarters; and these were again subdivided by lateral passages, leaving regular spaces for *papilUmes* (tents), which were set in rows, or *striga,* as they were called; besides these lines, were spaces for stands of arms, for bag-gage, beasts of burden, and cavalry horses. The common soldiers were quartered at the rate of ten men to each *papilion;* but, since sixteen men, or four guards, in each century, were always out of camp, on duty, there were never more than eight men actually in a tent at the same time. According to the admea-surement, which I have already stated, this station occupied an area of about 130,000 square feet. Now, the space re-quired for each cohort of 480 men, is stated to be 21,000 square feet. It fol-lows, therefore, that there was accom-modation at Borough Bridge for *six* le-gionary cohorts of 480 men, or a total of 2,880 soldiers, supposing the garrison to be wholly of infantry, and the camp closely packed with common soldiers. But, since it is certain, that the army of Agricola was composed of horse as well as foot, some space must be allowed for horses, some extra for superior officers, and the number of men must be pro-portionately Hence our word "pavilion. " "Roman Antiquities," p. 254. reduced. Mr. John Just said, with reference to the accommodation of the station, " each of these (four equal angles) would suffice for a century of soldiers, and four cen-turions, with their cohorts, would con-stitute the garrison." If he meant to say,

that there would be *four* cohorts of 480 men (for he could not mean four centuries only), and, since he alluded to infantry alone, there seems to be little difference between my calculation and that of Mr. Just; and an antiquary may be excused, for rejoicing in any data, and any coincidences of reckoning, which enablo him to arrive at an approximation of numbers, re-peopling, as it were, an encampment, or, as Wordsworth finely says, making—

"The men that have been re appear."

In the Museum at Naples, is the skeleton of a sentinel, with the veritable helmet on his head, which the man wore at one of the gates of the city of *Pompeii,* when the lava of Vesuvius transfixed him to the spot. We cannot get any reality, or by aid of the most vivid imagination, anything that gives us such a distinct idea of the Romans "as they stood" at Borough Bridge; but we can put together a few facts, and several analogies, and by such means acquire some notion of the state of things as they existed here, during the Roman occupation.

The last observation suggests, in conclusion, a moral to this story. I find it impossible to leave the subject without drawing one or two obvious reflections from it. One cannot look into the grey twilight of history, through a space of eighteen hundred years, comparing that time with the present, without thinking of the events that have intervened, or the steps of that grand march of social and national improvement, which is seen consummated in a contrast, between the forms of life8 and the phases of society, in the first and those in the nineteenth century. The few sentences at my command will suffice only for a bare mention of the most striking of those events—the most marked period of the country's career; you will, in your own minds, fill up the details of the passing events, and supply all the connecting parts.

It is a coincidence not to be omitted, that the very year (a.d. 79), in which the Roman Propraetor, Agricola, was engaged in passing through these Westmorland defiles, was the same year that witnessed the overthrow of the Roman cities of *Pompeii* and *Herculaneum.* That terrible judgment overtook the " Mistress of the World," as she proudly called herself, at the moment she reached her farthest limit of conquest; and, it may also be said, at the moment of her greatest lust and luxury. The destructive element, pouring down the sides of Vesuvius, almost overtook thousands of people in the amphitheatre, at Pompeii, whilst revelling, with savage delight, in the blood of gladiators—slaves, taken captive in the subjugated provinces of the Empire. After an occupation of 400 years, the Romans withdrew from this island, leaving little behind them—little at least in this part of the country—but their paved roads and half-ruined fortresses. The Saxons succeeded better, and better deserved success. In their time, however, the country, and this district in particular, passed through much strife. The Danes—rival invaders—descended upon the northern coasts, and the frequency of old Danish and Scandinavian names among " these vales and valley streams," tell how long the Northmen must have contended with the Saxons, for permanent possession of the north of England. At length, the Saxon established his footing, gave laws and language to the people, and introduced Christian ordinances—the precursor of all other blessings. It is believed that Pauliuus, the first Christian preacher, passed up the vale of Lune, as I have elsewhere supposed that he visited also the Kent. The poet *Drayton* thus sings of a fact, founded on history:

"For when the Saxons first received the Christian faith,
Paulimia, of old York, the zealous Bishop then,
In Swale's abundant stream christened ten thousand men."

That was the period of the foundation of the Saxon churches, (I do not mean the present structures, but the first Christian tabernacles), on the three rivers, all natives of Westmorland, the *Lune,* the *Eden,* and the *Kent;* that is to say, the churches of Kirkby Lonsdale, Kirkby Thor, Kirkby Stephen, and Kirkby Kendal. But, short were the respites and intervals of peace. Not long after this again, the sword was unsheathed; and the bow again bent:—fresh shouts of war re-awoke the mountain echoes, and much blood was spilt in these districts; at the Norman Conquest, for instance, for the Domesday Surveyors reported, that they could make no schedule of the lands " in these parts," the said lands being so completely wasted and destroyed, and worth nothing I At that time the Roman Empire extended over 90 degrees of longitude and 45 degrees of latitude.

"A. 965.—In this year Thoreth, Gunner's son, ravaged Westmorland. And that same year Oslac obtained an ealdordom."—*The Saxon Chronicle.*

The wars of the Roses,—of the Reformation,—of the Commonwealth,—and the Border wars, which lasted throughout all the others,—kept Westmorland men engaged in hostile occupations, with a continuance. Of one revolution, only, have we bloodless record (1688):

"In eighty-eight, was Kirkby fcight,
When nivver a man was slain,—
They ate their meat and drank their drink,
And then com merrily hame again."

But peace mingled her triumphs with those of war, and ultimately achieved the greater victories. If the blood of martyrs be the seed of the Church, the blood of patriots is the seed of the Nation. As the adversities of life chasten and improve the character of individuals, so the straggles of free citizens chasten and elevate the State. The procession of events, in the train of the peaceful arts, may be made up of the following (summary) catalogue: the consolidation of property,—the "essarting" of woods,—the draining of lands,—the introduction of the plough,—the carving out districts into parishes,—the establishment of schools,—the institution of ecclesiastical dioceses,—the great spread of churches (especially in the 13th century),—the introduction of printing,—turnpike roads, —stage coaches,—railroads,—mining, smelting, forging, weaving, &o. Such are some of the ameliorating agencies, stimulated by the human faculties strengthening with their strength, which have wrought the great change in men and manners, in habits, creeds, and opinions, evidenced in the contrast between the Roman era, in Britain, and the present time. Thus, it may be literally as well as metaphorically said, that the valleys have been exalted, the mountains and hills brought low, the crooked made straight, and the rough places plain. And thus has " freedom widened slowly down to our own times." What remains, then, for us, but to look gratefully back, through the long vista which I have faintly and imperfectly brought before your contemplation, and thank God that our lines have fallen in pleasant places. This is the true lesson of history!

SUBSCRIBEES TO THIS BOOK; *Procured, upon tlie previous issue of a Prospectus, in order to obtain a Register of Persons and Places, for future reference:*

dal.

Bateson, Mr. Thomas, Highgate, Kendal.

Beadle, Mr. John, Painter, Cliff Terrace, Kendal.

Bell, Mr., New Inn, Kendal.

Bell, James, Esq., 4, Dalton Place, Old Trafford, Manchester.

Bell, Mr. Thomas, Chemist and Druggist, Ambleside.

Bellasis, Daniel H. Esq., Bowness.

Bibby, Mr. John, Highgate, Kendal.

Bindloss, Mr. Robert, Ironmonger, Kirkland.

Bintley, Mr. Job, Engineer, Kirkland.

Bird, William, Esq., Crouch Hall, London.

Birkett, Mr. Allan, Ann Street, Kendal.

Birkett, Mr. George, Tailor, Staveley, near Kendal.

Birkett, Mr. G., 14, Regent's Park Road, Primrose Hill, London.

Birkett, Mr. John, House of Correction Hill, Kendal.

Birkett, Miss Dinah, ditto.

Black, Rev. James F., B.A., Grammar School, Kendal.

Blacow, Mr. James, Hatter, Finkle Street, Kendal.

Bland, Mr. Thomas, Reagill, Westmorland.

Blatherwick, Charles, Esq., M.D., Highgate, London.

Blyth, Mr. John, Grocer, Far Cross Bank, Kendal.

Boak, Mr. Thomas, Beast Banks, Kendal.

Boucher, Mr. James, Excise Officer, Ann Street, Kendal.

Bousfield, James, Esq., Broom Close, Kendal.

Bowness, William, Esq., London.

Braithwaite, C. L. Esq., Manufacturer, Kendal.

Braithwaite, Mr. Charles Lloyd, jun., Highgate, Kendal.

Braithwaite, Rev. George, M.A., the Sub-Deanery, Chichester.

Braithwaite, George Foster, Esq., Manufacturer, Highgate, Kendal.

Braithwaite, Isaac, Esq., 68, Old Broad Street, London.

Braithwaite, Mr. J. O, Carpet Manufacturer, Stricklandgate, Kendal.

Braithwaite, Rev. Robert, Keynsham Lodge, Cheltenham.

Braithwaite, Mr. R., 11, Warrington Street, Oakley Square, London.

Braithwaite, Mr. Thomas, Printer, Grandy Nook, Kendal.

Braithwaite, Mr. Thomas, junior, Joiner, Stricklandgate, Kendal.

Branthwaite, Edward, Esq., Lowther Street, Kendal.

Briggs, Mr. Thomas, 36, Hunter Street, Liverpool.

Brisley, C. Esq., Surgeon, Kent Lane, Kendal.

Brockbank, Mr. Henry, Bookseller, Cartmel (2 copies).

Brockelbank, Miss, Highgate, Kendal.

Brooks, Mr. Thomas, Tailor and Draper, Windermere.

Broughton, Frederick, Esq. (Ulster Railway Company), Belfast.

Brown, Mr. Martin, Brown Cow Inn, Kendal.

Brumwell, James T. Esq., Surgeon, Stricklandgate, Kendal.

Brunskill, Stephen, Esq., Sand Area, Kendal.

Burnett, Mr. W. J., Castle Crescent, Kendal.

Burrell, John Stamp, Esq., Merchant, Lancaster.

Burrow, Mr. Davis, Carr Lodge, Leeds.

Burton, Mr. Edward, Rock Ferry, Birkenhead.

Burton, Mr. John, Auctioneer, Avenham Lane, Preston.

Busher, Mr. James, Tobacconist, Gandy Street, Kendal.

Butterwith, Mr. John, Grocer, dsc, Highgate, Kendal.

Butterwith, Mr. Robert, Grocer, &c, Kent Cottage, Kendal.

Caine, Nathaniel, Esq., Iron Merchant, Egremont.

Cannon, Mr. Thomas, Marine Store Dealer, Fell Side, Kendal.

Capstick, Mr. J., Tailor and Draper, Finkle Street, Kendal.

Carlisle, Mr. Thomas, Stramongate, Kendal.

Carradus, Sergeant James, Strickland Place, Kendal.

Carradus, Thomas, Esq., Barwell

Court, near Kingston, Surrey.

Carter, Mr. John, Cliff Terrace, Kendal.

Chaplin, Rev. W., Staveley, near Kendal.

Chorley, Mr. R., 7, Church Terrace, Kentish Town.

Churchill, Henry, Esq., Clapham Road, London.

Clapham, Mr. G., 5, College Place, Camden Town, London.

Clapham, Mr. J., 36, Rochester Road, Camden Road Villas, London.

Clarke, Seymour, Esq., Hatfield. 6

Clay, Miss, Green Bank, Kendal.

Cockshutt, Mr. Edmund, Draper, Market Place, Kendal.

Cookson, Rev. H. W., D.D., St. Peter's College Lodge, Cambridge.

Cookson, Rev. J., Marton, near Blackpool.

Compston, Mr. Samuel, Builder, Highgate, Kendal.

Cooper, Mr. James, 9, College Street, Camden Town.

Cooper, Rev. Canon, M.A., Vicarage, Kendal (2 copies).

Cottam, H. R. Esq., Hornsey, London.

Cowherd, James, Esq., Stony Dale, Cartmel.

Cowherd, Miss, Lowther Street, Kendal.

Cox, Mr. Eli, Architect, Kirkland, Kendal.

Cragg, Mr. Christopher Robinson, 123, Stanley St., Pimlico, London.

Cragg, Mr. Henry, Maltster, Mount Pleasant, Kendal.

Crawley, Mr. Matthew, Marine Store Dealer, Stricklandgate, Kendal. Crewdson, G. B., Esq., J. P., Windermere.

Crewdson, Edward, Esq., Banker, Kendal.

Crewdson, Mr. John, Shoemaker, Allhallows' Lane, Kendal.

Crewdson, William Dilworth, Esq., Helme Lodge, Kendal.

Cropper, James, Esq., Ellergreen, Kendal.

Crosfield, John, Esq., Rothay Bank, Ambleside.

Crossley, H. D.,Esq., 11, Bentinck Street, Manchester Square, London.

Dakin, Alderman Thomas, Hornsey,

London.

Davis, Mr. Benjamin, Plasterer, Highgate, Kendal.

Dawson, James, Esq., M.D., Wray Castle, Windermere.

De Lambert, Robert, Esq., Commonhcad, Staveley, near Kendal.

Dennison, Mr. John, 15, Inkerman Road, Kentish Town.

Dent, Mr. Robert, Gas Works, Kendal.

Derome, Mr. Matthew, Auctioneer and Accountant, Kendal.

Dewhurst, Mr. Thomas, Green Area, Lancaster.

Dinsdale, Mr. Alexander, House of Correction Hill, Kendal.

Dinsdale, Mr. William, Stricklandgate, Kendal.

Dixon, Capt. Thomas, 20th Middlesex Volunteers, Railway Clearing House, London.

Dixon, John, Esq., Solicitor, Whitehaven.

Dixon, Mr. Robert S. S., Post-Master, Kendal.

Douglas, Mr. James, Grocer, Stricklandgate, Kendal.

Duncan, Mr. Henry W., Schoolmaster, Highgate, Kendal.

Dunnage, Thomas, Esq., Muswell Hill, London.

Eady, William, Esq. (for the Hornsey Book Society), Campsbourne, Hornsey.

Farquharson, Mr. James, 2, St. Mary's Place, Edge Hill, Liverpool,

Farrer, Mr. John, Tea Dealer, Stricklandgate, Kendal.

Fawcett, Mr. Christopher, Governor of the House of Correction, Kendal.

Fawcett, Mr. Miles, Wood Bridge, Dent.

Fell, William, Esq., Surgeon, Ambleside.

Fenton, Myles, Esq. (Lancashire and Yorkshire Railway Company), Manchester.

Fenton, Rev. Thomas, M.A., Ings, near Kendal.

Fenwick, E. M. Esq., J. P., Burrow Hall, Lancashire.

Field, Mr. Isaac, South View, Kendal.

Fisher, Miss, Bebington, Cheshire.

Fisher, Mr. John (Aid.), Builder, Stricklandgate, Kendal (2 copies). Fisher, Mr.William, Booksellor,&c.,Stricklandgate, Kendal (Ccopies).

Fleming, Rev. Fletcher, M.A., Rector of Grasmere.

Foster, Mr. William, 4, Seymour Crescent, Euston Square, London.

Gahriel, Rev. E., B.A., St. George's Parsonage, Kendal.

Gandon, Mr. H., 181, Euston Road, Euston Square, London.

Gardner, C. Esq., Barwise Court, English Street, Carlisle.

Gardner, Mr. Christopher, Brazier, Kendal.

Garnett, Mr. John, Draper, Highgate, Kendal.

Garnett, Mr. Anthony, Dyer and Drysalter, Kendal.

Garnett, Mr. James, Collegiate Institution, Liverpool.

Garnett, Mr. Thomas, Entry Lane, Kendal.

Garnett, Mr. William, 8, Albion Place, Leeds.

Garnett, Mr. AV., Crosthwaite, near Kendal.

Garnett, Mrs., Bank House, Barbon, Kirkby Lonsdale.

Gaskell, Mr. George, Coal Dealer, Stricklandgate, Kendal.

Gawith, Mr. J., Clogger, Highgate, Kendal.

Gawith, Mr. Samuel, Tobacco Manufacturer, Lowther Street, Kendiil.

Gelderd, Geo. Atkinson, Esq. Aikrigg End, Kendal.

German, Mr. Henry, Tailor, Highgate, Kendal.

Gibson, George, Esq. Kent Terrace, Kendal.

Gibson, Mr. Christopher, Architect, Kendal.

Gibson, Mr. Matthew, Accountant, Kendal.

Gillbanks, Mr. William, Rope Manufacturer, Allhallows' Lane, Kendal.

Glyn, George Carr, Esq. M.P., Stanmore Park, Middlesex.

Gott, Mr. Thomas A., Castle Street, Kendal.

Gott, Mr. J. 38, College Place, Camden Town.

Gough, Thomas, Esq., Surgeon, Kendal.

Grant, Charles W. Esq., Solicitor, Highgate, Kendal.

Grayson, Mr. Frank, 9, Edward Street, Hampstead Road, Loudon.

Grayson, Mr. John, Dentist, Highgate, Kendal.

Green, Thomas, Esq. M.B., Aynam Lodge, Kendal.

Gudgeon, Mr. Thomas, Shoemaker, Siricklandgate, Kendal.

Had wen, Miss, Highgate, Kendal.

Halhead, Hilton, Esq., Merchant, Liverpool.

Hargreaves, Mr. W. B., Ironmonger, Kendal.

Harker, Mrs., Cartmel, Lancashire.

Harris, Rev. Charles Butler, Luton, Beds, late Incumbent of Heslington.

Harrison, Thomas, Esq., Singleton Park, Kendal (2 copies).

Harrison, Daniel, Esq., Solicitor, Kendal.

Harrison, Edmund, Esq., J. P., Abbot Hall, Kendal.

Harrison, John, Esq., J. P., Summerlands, Kendal.

Harrison, Mr. J. P., Castle Crescent, Kendal.

Harrison, Matthew Benson, Esq. (High Sheriff of Westmorland), Ambleside.

Harrison, Mrs. John, Hundhow, Kendal.

Hartley, Mr. G. W., Baker and Confectioner, Stricklandgate, Kendal.

Hartley, Mr. Isaac, Railway Clearing House, 101, Seymour Street,

Euston Square, London. Hawkes, Rev. Edward, M.A., Parsonage, Market Place, Kendal. Hayes, Mr. Thomas, Market Place, Kendal. Head, Mr. Thomas, Draper, Westmorland House, Kendal. Heaps, Mr. James, Beast Banks, Kendal. Heslop, Mr. James, 15, Oxford Street, Caledonian Road, London. Hewetson, Henry, Esq., Entry Lane, Kendal. Hewitt, Mr., National School, KendaL Hill, Mr. Thomas, British School, Castle Street, Kendal. Hiscock, Mr. William, Relieving Officer, Kendal. Hodgson, Miss, Highgate, Kendal. Hodgson, Mr. Rainforth, Brush Manufacturer, Kendal. Hogg, Mr. James, Painter, Kendal (2 copies). Hogg, Mr. James H., Photographic

Artist, Kendal. Hogg, Mr. John, 7, Torriano Grove, Kentish Town, London. Hoggarth, Mr. Henry, Surveyor, Kendal. Hoggarth, Mr. W., 78, Westminster Bridge Road, London. Holden, Mr. John, Churchyard Cottage, Kendal. Home, Mr. Henry, Cabinet-maker, Highgate, Kendal. Howarth, Mr. Robert, Tailor, Stricklandgate, Kendal. Hubbersty, Philip, Esq. Wirksworth. Hubbersty, Rev. N., Eastwell Hall, near Melton Mowbray. Huck, Mr. Thomas, Highgate, Kendal. Huddleston, Mr. William, Union Bank, Liverpool. Hudson, Thomas, Esq., 3, Highbury Park, London. Hudson, Thomas, Esq., Stockbroker, Kendal. Hudson, Mr. Cunningham, Calcutta, India. Hudson, Mr. T. B. Bookseller, Manchester. Hudson, John, Esq., Larch How, Kendal. Hudson, Mr. John, Allahabad, India. Hudson, Mr. Richard, Chemist, Highgate, Kendal.

Hutchinson, Mr. George A., Fishhook Manufacturer, Stramongate, Kendal.

Hutton, Mr. Robert, 45, Grafton Road, Kentish Town, London.

Inglis, Rev. John, Stricklandgate, Kendal.

Ion, Mr. Thomas, Shoemaker, Lowther Street, Kendal.

Ireland, J. G. J., Esq., Manufacturer, Kendal.

Ireland, Mr. John, junior, Stramongate, Kendal.

Ireland, Mr. Charles, Manufacturer, Stramongate, Kendal.

Ireland, Mrs. G. W., West View, Kendal.

Jackson, Mr. John, Master of Workhouse, Kendal.

Jackson, Mr. George, Painter, Cliff Terrace, Kendal.

Jackson, Mr. John, Academy Place, Warrington.

James, Mr. Richard, 7, Chester Street, Toxteth Park, Liverpool.

Jennings, Mr. Thomas, Tailor, Highgate, Kendal (2 copies).

Johnson, J. Henry, Esq., Solicitor, 47, Lincoln's Inn Fields, London.

Johnson, James G. Esq., Funchal, Madeira.

Johnston, Mr. John Henry, The Lound, Kendal.

Jones, Rev. David, Independent Chapel, Kendal.

Jopson, Mr. William, 17, Mark Lane, London.

Kendal, Alfred, Esq. Heath Bank, Cheadle, Manchester.

Knipe, Mr. Joseph, Collegiate Institution, Liverpool.

Langhorn, Hugh, Esq., Wildman Street, Kendal.

Lee, Rev. George, Finkle Street, Kendal.

Lewthwaite, Mr. Thomas, Far Cross Bank.

Line, Mr. John, 319, Wolverton, Bucks.

Lipsett, Mr. David, Rainbow Inn, Highgate, Kendal.

Livesey, Mr. James, Railway Inn, Wildman Street, Kendal.

Long, Mr. William, Highgate, Kendal.

Longmire, William, Esq., Surgeon, Stramongate, Kendal.

Lyon, Mr. George, Painter, Highgate, Kendal.

Lyon, Mr. Joseph, Pipe Manufacturer, Wildman Street, Kendal.

Mabson, William, Esq., Hyning, Milnthorpe.

Mackereth, Mr. Thomas, Accountant, Stricklandgate, Kendal.

Mallinson, Mr. J., 16, Alma Terrace, Kentish Town, London.

Mann, Mr. John, West View, Kendal. Mann, Mr. William M., Pear-tree Cottage, Kendal.

Marshall, Richard, Esq., The Limes, Muswell Hill, London.

Marshall, Samuel, Esq., Kent Terrace, Kendal (4 copies).

Martindale, II. Esq. County Treasurer, Crosthwaite, near Kendal.

Martindale, Mr. William, Draper, Stricklandgate, Kendal.

Martineau, Miss Harriet, The Knoll, Ambleside.

Mason, Mr. John, Cabinet-maker, Highgate, Kendal.

Msdcalf, Mr. Edward, jun., Manufacturer, Highgate, Kendal.

Meldrum, Mr. James, Seedsman, Market Place, Kendal.

Miles, Joseph, Esq., Muswell Hill, London.

Moffett, Mrs. Highgate, Kendal.

Moore, Mrs. 25, Thomaston Street, Great Horner Street, Liverpool.

Morland, Mrs. 99, Ebury Street, Eaton Square, London.

Morphet, Mr., Bookseller, Kirkby Lonsdale.

Morris, Mr. Thomas, Grocer, Highgate, Kendal.

Moser, Roger, Esq., Solicitor, Kendal.

Musgrove, Mr. William, Draper, Finkle Street, Kendal.

Nelson, Mr. Richard, Carpet Manufacturer, Kent Terrace.

Nicholl, Mr. Thomas, Supervisor, Stramongate, Kendal.

Noble, John, Esq., 39, Cloudesley Terrace, Islington, London.

Noble, Samuel Clarke, Esq., Surgeon, Stricklandgate, Kendal.

O'Connell, Mr. John, 15, Liverton Street, Kentish Town, London.

Paisley, James, Esq., The Wray, Ambleside.

Parke, Mr. Rowland T., Draper, Highgate, Kendal.

Parker, Francis, Esq., Sydenham, London.

Parker, Mr. James, Town View, Kendal.

Parker, Mr. Rowland, Moss End, Preston Patrick.

Pearson, Francis, Esq., Briery, Keswick.

Pearson, Mrs. William, Border Side, Crosthwaite.

Pennington, Mr. James, Grocer, Highgate, Kendal.

Pickthall, Robert, Esq., Coal Agent, Kendal.

Preston, Mr. Thomas, 4, Grafton Road, Kentish Town, London.

Price, James, Esq., Clarence Terrace, Regent's Park, London.

Proudfoot, Mrs. Milnthorpe.

Redhead, Mr. Matthew, Ironmonger, Kendal.

Relph, Miss, Highgate, Kendal.

Relph, Mr. William, (Lancashire and Yorkshire Railway,) Liverpool

Rhodes, Mr. Samuel, Draper, Bank Top, Kendal.

Rhodes, Mr. John, Draper, Bank View, Kendal.

Rhodes, Mr. William, Draper, Castle Park House, Kendal.

Richardson, Mr. W. Gandy Street, Kendal.

Richmond, Mr. Thomas, Grocer, Stricklandgate, Kendal.

Rigg, Mr. George, Joiner and Builder, Castle Street, Kendal.

Rigg, Mr. Richard, Windermere Hotel, Windermere.

Robinson, Mr. Benjamin, Engineer, Houraw, Calcutta, India,

Robinson, Mr. John, Horn Cop, Kendal.

Robinson, Mr. Joseph, Shakspeare Tavern, Highgate, Kendal.

Robinson, Mr. James, Bookseller, Kendal (5 copies).

Robinson, Mr. William, Vale House, Garstang.

Robinson, Mr. Richard L., Highgate, Kendal.

Robson, Rev. William H., St. Helen's, Lancashire.

Rodick, The Misses, Stricklandgate, Kendal.

Rodick, Thomas, Esq., Ashmeadow House, Arnside.

Rogers, Rev. T. W., M.A., Helsington.

Russell, Mr. Thomas, Castle Inn, Castle Street, Kendal.

Ruthven, Mr. George, No. 3, New Broad Street, London.

Ruthven, Mr. John, Kirkland.

Ruthven, Mr. John, Irwell Vale, Edenfield, near Bury, Lancashire.

Scarisbrick, Mr. Thomas, Organist, Kirkland.

Scott, Mr. James Wilson, Far Cross Bank, Kendal.

Scott, Mr. John, Joiner, Stricklandgate, Kendal.

Scott, Mr. William, Grocer, Highgate, Kendal.

Shaw, Mr. Richard Carradus, Architect, Kendal.

Shaw, Mr. Thomas, 4, North Place, Hampstead Road, London.

Shaw, Mr. William, Constantinople.

Shepherd, James C, Esq., Surgeon, Cross Brow, Ambleside.

Simpson, Misses, No. 7, Highgate, Kendal.

Simpson, Thomas, Esq., Manufacturer, Highgate, Kendal.

Sinkinson, Mrs. James, Stramongate, Kendal.

Sisson and Son, Messrs., Comb Manufacturers, Market Place, Kendal.

Sisson, Mr. Edward, 109, Bishopsgate Street Within, London.

Sisson, Mr. Richard, Comb Manufacturer (Firm of John Sisson, and Son), Kendal.

Skelton, Mr. Robert, Market Place, Kendal.

Slater, Mr. William Bell, Coach Builder, Ann Street, Kendal.

Slee, Mr. William, Seven Stars Inn, Kendal.

Sraallwood, Mr. William, Organist, St. George's, Kendal.

Smith, Mr. William, Innkeeper, Stramongate, Kendal.

E E

Smithson, Miles, Esq., Lane Head, Kendal.

Somervell, John, Esq., Merchant, Kent Terrace, Kendal.

Somervell, Robert M., Esq., Merchant, Windermere.

Steele, John, Esq., Ivy Cottage, Burneside.

Stock dale, Mrs., Kendal.

Swainson, Joseph, Esq., Highgate, Kendal.

Tatham, Edmund, Esq., Surgeon, Stramongate, Kendal.

Tatham, Edward, Esq., J. P., Summerfield, Kirkby Lonsdale.

Taylor, Mr. John, Grocer, Highgate, Kendal.

Taylor, Mr. Jones, Stricklandgate, Kendal (2 copies).

Taylor, Mr. Isaac Flatts, Manchester.

Taylor, Mr. James, Union Bank, Liverpool.

Taylor, Mr. John (Lancashire and Yorkshire Railway), Liverpool.

Taylor, Mr. T., 1, New Hampstead Road, Kentish Town, London.

Taylor, Mr. Thomas, Brazennose Street, Manchester (2 copies).

Taylor, Mr. Thomas, No. 3, New Broad Street, London.

Thompson, Miles, Esq., Architect, Lound, Kendal.

Thompson, Mr. John S., Builder, Highgate, Kendal.

Thompson, Mr. Thomas, Valparaiso, South America.

Thompson, Mr. William, Painter, Highgate, Kendal.

Thomson, J. P., 7, Leigh Terrace, Mere Lane, Walton, Liverpool.

Thomson, Mr. William, Kendal Bank, Highgate, Kendal.

Thornton, Joseph, Esq., Beaver Hall, Southgate, London.

Thwaites, Mr. John, White Hart Inn, Kendal.

Thwaites, Mr. Thomas, Dyer, Kendal.

Tomlinson, Miss Elizabeth, Biggins, Kirkby Lonsdale.

Turton, Mr. Benjamin, Staveley, near Kendal.

Udall, Mr. W., Tailor, Low Fell Side, Kendal.

Udall, Mr. Thomas, Woolpack Yard, Stricklandgate, Kendal.

Wadeson, Mr. Joshua, Gandy Street, Kendal.

Wakefield, John, Esq., J. P., Sedgwick House, near Kendal.

Wakefield, William, Esq., Birklands, Kendal.

Walker, Robert, Esq., Surgeon, Highgate, Kendal.

Waller, Mr. John Johnson, Draper, Highgate, Kendal.

Walling, Mr. Christopher, Wine and Spirit Merchant, Kendal.

Washington, Mr. John, Parish Clerk, Kirkland.

Watson, John, Esq., Albion Lodge, Stamford Hill, London.

Webb, Mr. G. H., Claughton, Birkenhead.'

Webster, Francis, Esq,, Marble Works, Kendal.

Webster, Francis, Esq., Solicitor, Kendal.

Webster, George, Esq., Eller How, Newton-in-Cartmel.

Webster, Miss, Beezon Lodge, Kendal.

Webster, Mr. C, Borough Surveyor and Land Agent, Kendal.

Webster, Mr. Robert, Marble Works, Kendal.

Webster, Mr. William, Cross House, Kendal.

Welch, William, Esq., Spring Villa, Lancaster.

Whinerey, Mr. John, Grocer, Stramongate, Kendal.

Whinery, Mr. Samuel, junior, Highgate, Kendal.

Whitaker, Mr. James, Blue Coat School, Kendal.

Whittam, Mr. J., 25, Stevenson Terrace, Caledonian Road, London.

Whitwell, Edward, Esq., Kent Street, Kendal.

Whitwell, John, Esq., Stricklandgate, Kendal.

Whitwell, Mr. Thomas, Stockton-on-Tees.

Whitwell, William, Esq., Tolson Hall, Kendal.

Wilkinson, Charles, Esq., Solicitor, Bank House, Kendal.

Wilkinson, Mr. James, Kendal.

Wilkinson, Mr. R., G, Roxburgh Terrace, Haverstock Hill, London.

Wilkinson, Rev. Robert, Parsonage, Killington.

Willan, Mr. Thomas, Sawrey, Spirit Merchant, Windermere.

Willan, Mr. Simpson, Tailor and Draper, Stricklandgate, Kendal.

Williamson, Mr. William, The Lound, Kendal.

Willison, Mr. William, Pawnbroker, Highgate, Kendal.

Willock, Mr. George, Cabinet-maker, Stramongate, Kendal.

Wilson, Mr. L Whitwell, Manufacturer, Castle Lodge, Kendal.

Wilson, John, Esq., 17, Compton Terrace, Islington, London.

Wilson, John, Esq., Solicitor, Kendal.

Wilson, John Jowitt, Esq., Manufacturer, Kent Terrace, Kendal.

Wilson, Mr. John, Strickland Place, Kendal.

Wilson, Miss E., Stourport, Worcestershire.

Wilson, Mr. Henry, Castle Park Terrace, Kendal.

Wilson, Mr. James B., 4, Grafton Road, Kentish Town, London.

Wilson, Mr. John F., Middlesborough-on-Tees.

Wilson, Mr. Robert, 9, Edward Street, Hampstead Road, London.

Wilson, Mr. Titus, Whitesmith, Market Place, Kendal.

Wilson, Mr. Robert, Organist, Heversham.

Wilson, Rev. John, D.D., Durham House, Chelsea.

Wilson, Rev. W., Southampton, Vicar of Holy Rhood, and Canon of Winchester. Wilson, Robert, Esq., Forth House, Neweastle-on-Tyne. Wilson, Mr. T., Bookseller, Highgate, Kendal (10 copies).

Wilson, William, Esq., J.P., High Park, Kendal.

Wilson, William, Esq., Manufacturer, Castle Meadows, Kendal.

Wilson, Mr. William, 69, Pall Mall, London.

Winder, Mr. Robert, Plumber, Highgate, Kendal.

Wiper, Mr. William, Finkle Street, Kendal.

Woffendale, Mr. Z. B., 6, Mary's Terrace, Camden Town, London.

Working Men's News and Reading Association, Kendal.

Wright, Mr. Henry, Windermere Villa, Windermere.

Yeates, Anthony, G. Esq., Collinson House, Brixton.

R. CLAY, SON, AND TAYLOR, PRINTERS, BREAD STREET HILL

Lightning Source UK Ltd.
Milton Keynes UK
UKOW010721300912

199825UK00006B/158/P